KOYOHARU GOTOUGE

Good work! I'm Gotouge. I get to bring out
volume 7! Thank you very much to everyone
who supports me and everyone who helped me.
Recently, I've been into fried dishes seasoned
with miso. On weekends, I take whatever my
eyes fall upon and fry it with miso. And how
have you been? I suppose you have problems, but
I'd be happy if, while you're reading this series,
you forgot the real world and had an enjoyable
time, if only for a little while.

DEMON SLAYER:
KIMETSU NO YAIBA
VOLUME 7
Shonen Jump Edition

Story and Art by
KOYOHARU GOTOUGE

KIMETSU NO YAIBA
© 2016 by Koyoharu Gotouge
All rights reserved. First published in Japan
in 2016 by SHUEISHA Inc., Tokyo. English
translation rights arranged by SHUEISHA Inc.

TRANSLATION John Werry
ENGLISH ADAPTATION Stan!
TOUCH-UP ART & LETTERING John Hunt
DESIGN Adam Grano
EDITOR Mike Montesa

Printed in the U.S.A.

Published by VIZ Media, LLC
P.O. Box 77010
San Francisco, CA 94107

10 9 8 7 6 5 4 3 2 1
First printing, July 2019

viz.com

shonenjump.com

7

TRADING BLOWS AT CLOSE QUARTERS

DEMON SLAYER

KIMETSU NO YAIBA

KOYOHARU GOTOUGE

CHARACTERS

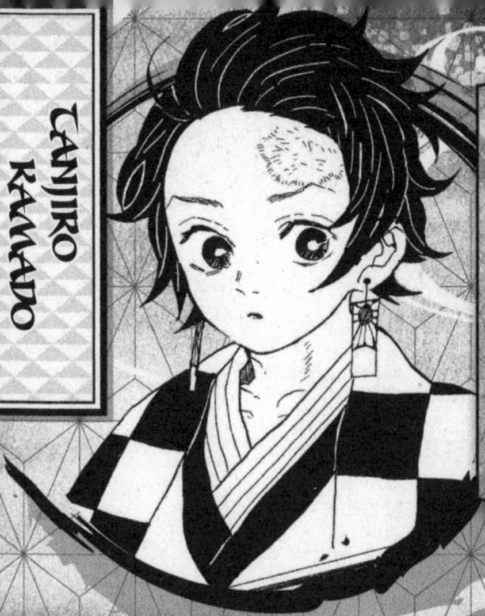

TANJIRO KAMADO

A kind boy who saved his younger sister and now aims to avenge his family. He can smell the scent of demons and an opponent's weakness.

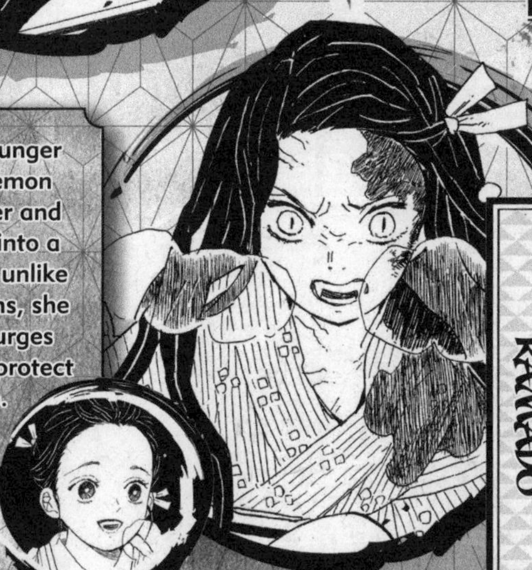

NEZUKO KAMADO

Tanjiro's younger sister. A demon attacked her and turned her into a demon. But unlike other demons, she fights her urges and tries to protect Tanjiro.

STORY

In Taisho-era Japan, young Tanjiro makes a living selling charcoal. One day, demons kill his family and turn his younger sister Nezuko into a demon. Tanjiro and Nezuko set out to find a way to return Nezuko to human form and defeat Kibutsuji, the demon who killed their family!

After joining the Demon Slayer Corps, Tanjiro meets Tamayo and Yushiro—demons who oppose Kibutsuji—who provide a clue to how Nezuko may be turned back into a human. On a new mission, Tanjiro goes to Mount Natagumo with Zenitsu Agatsuma and Inosuke Hashibira. However, after being severely injuried in a fight against spider demons, the three recuperate in Shinobu's mansion and gain new strength.

Meanwhile, Kibutsuji summons demons from the lower ranks of the Twelve Kizuki and, after expressing his displeasure with their failures, orders the surviving one to kill a Hashira and Tanjiro…

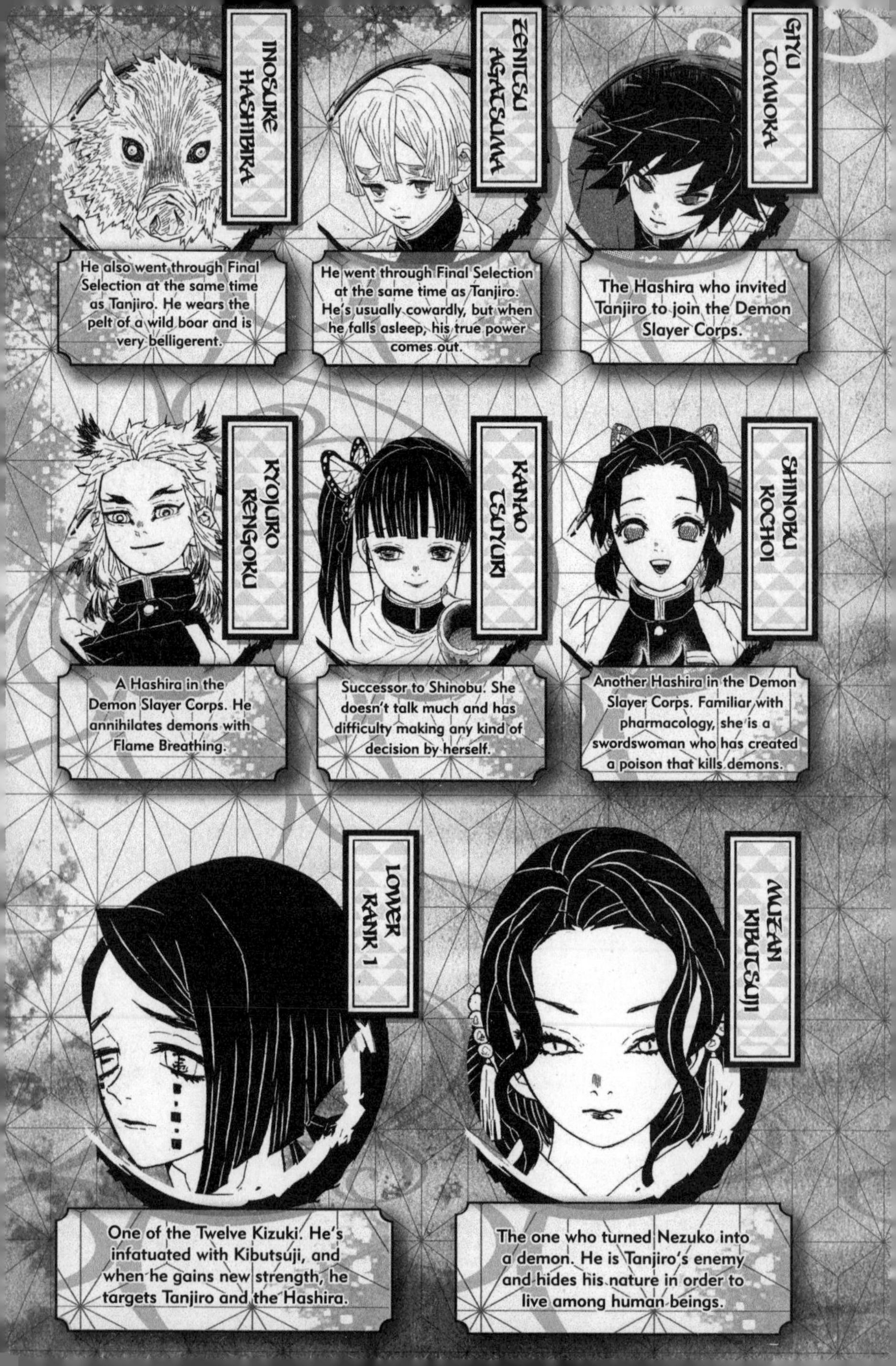
GIYU TOMIOKA
The Hashira who invited Tanjiro to join the Demon Slayer Corps.
ZENITSU AGATSUMA
He went through Final Selection at the same time as Tanjiro. He's usually cowardly, but when he falls asleep, his true power comes out.
INOSUKE HASHIBIRA
He also went through Final Selection at the same time as Tanjiro. He wears the pelt of a wild boar and is very belligerent.
SHINOBU KOCHO
Another Hashira in the Demon Slayer Corps. Familiar with pharmacology, she is a swordswoman who has created a poison that kills demons.
KANAO TSUYURI
Successor to Shinobu. She doesn't talk much and has difficulty making any kind of decision by herself.
KYOJURO RENGOKU
A Hashira in the Demon Slayer Corps. He annihilates demons with Flame Breathing.
MUZAN KIBUTSUJI
The one who turned Nezuko into a demon. He is Tanjiro's enemy and hides his nature in order to live among human beings.
LOWER RANK 1
One of the Twelve Kizuki. He's infatuated with Kibutsuji, and when he gains new strength, he targets Tanjiro and the Hashira.

CONTENTS

DEMON SLAYER
KIMETSU NO YAIBA

7

TRADING BLOWS AT CLOSE QUARTERS

CHAPTER 53: YOU ARE

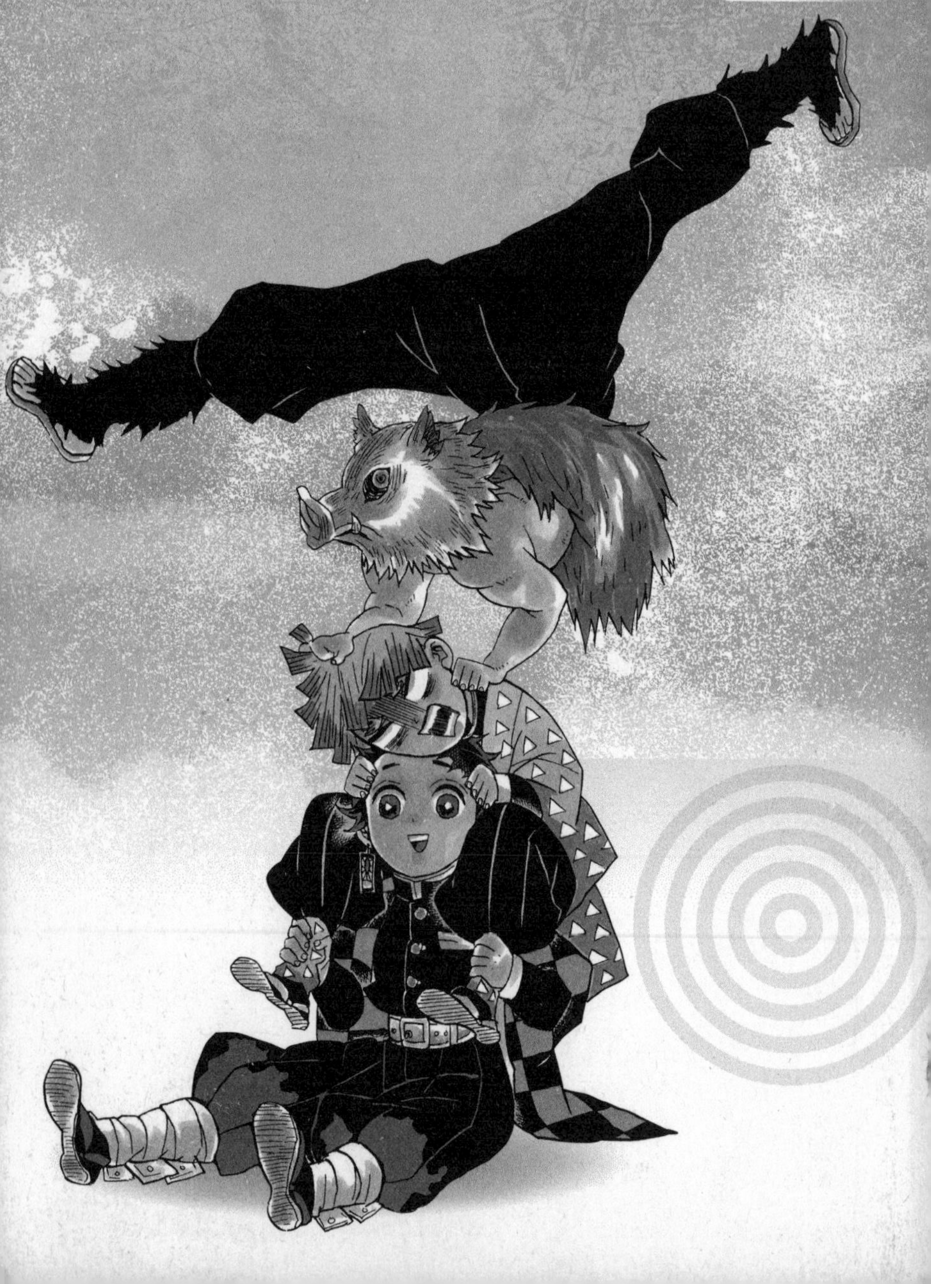

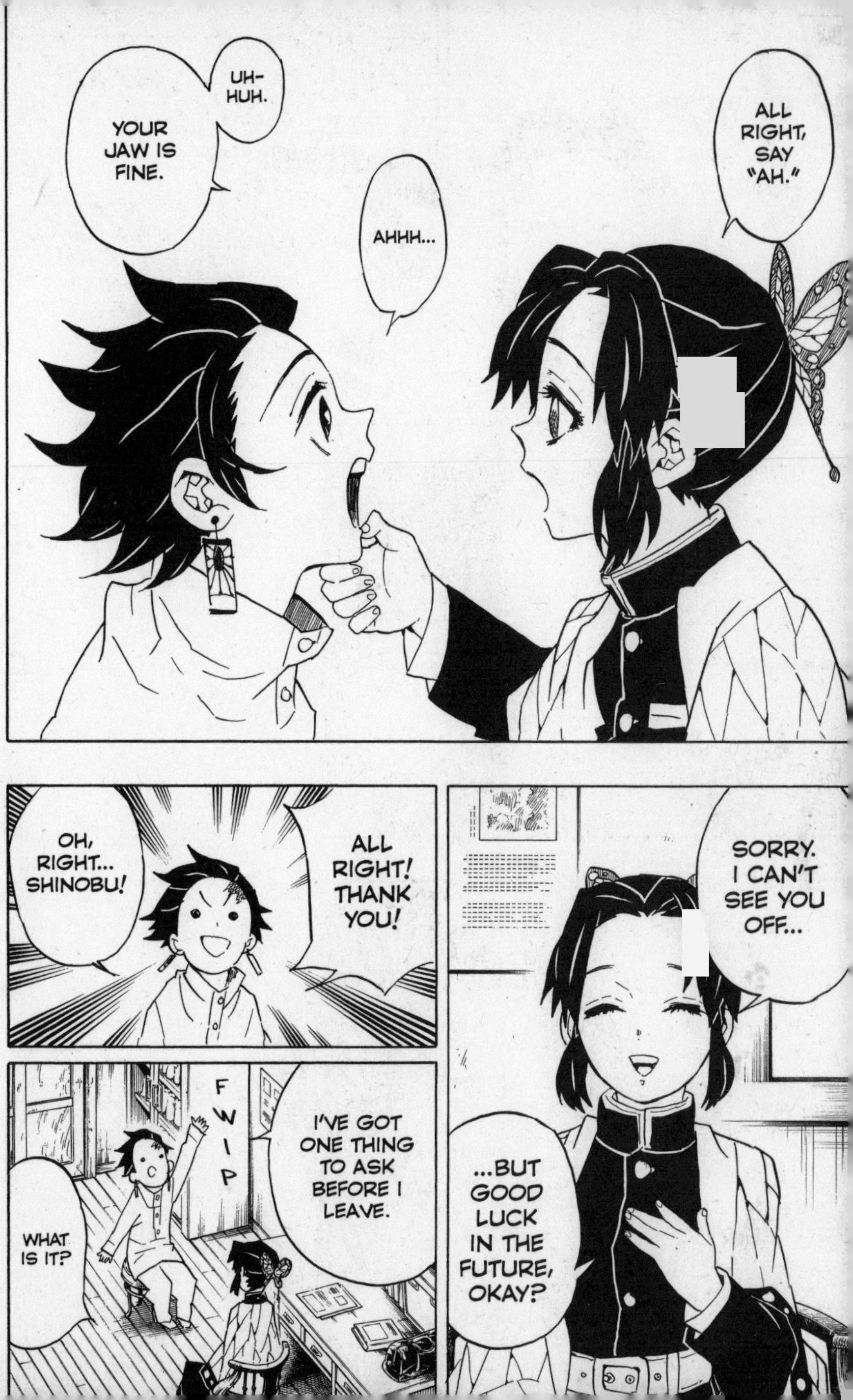
ALL RIGHT, SAY "AH."
AHHH...
UH-HUH.
YOUR JAW IS FINE.
SORRY. I CAN'T SEE YOU OFF...
...BUT GOOD LUCK IN THE FUTURE, OKAY?
ALL RIGHT! THANK YOU!
OH, RIGHT... SHINOBU!
I'VE GOT ONE THING TO ASK BEFORE I LEAVE.
FWIP
WHAT IS IT?

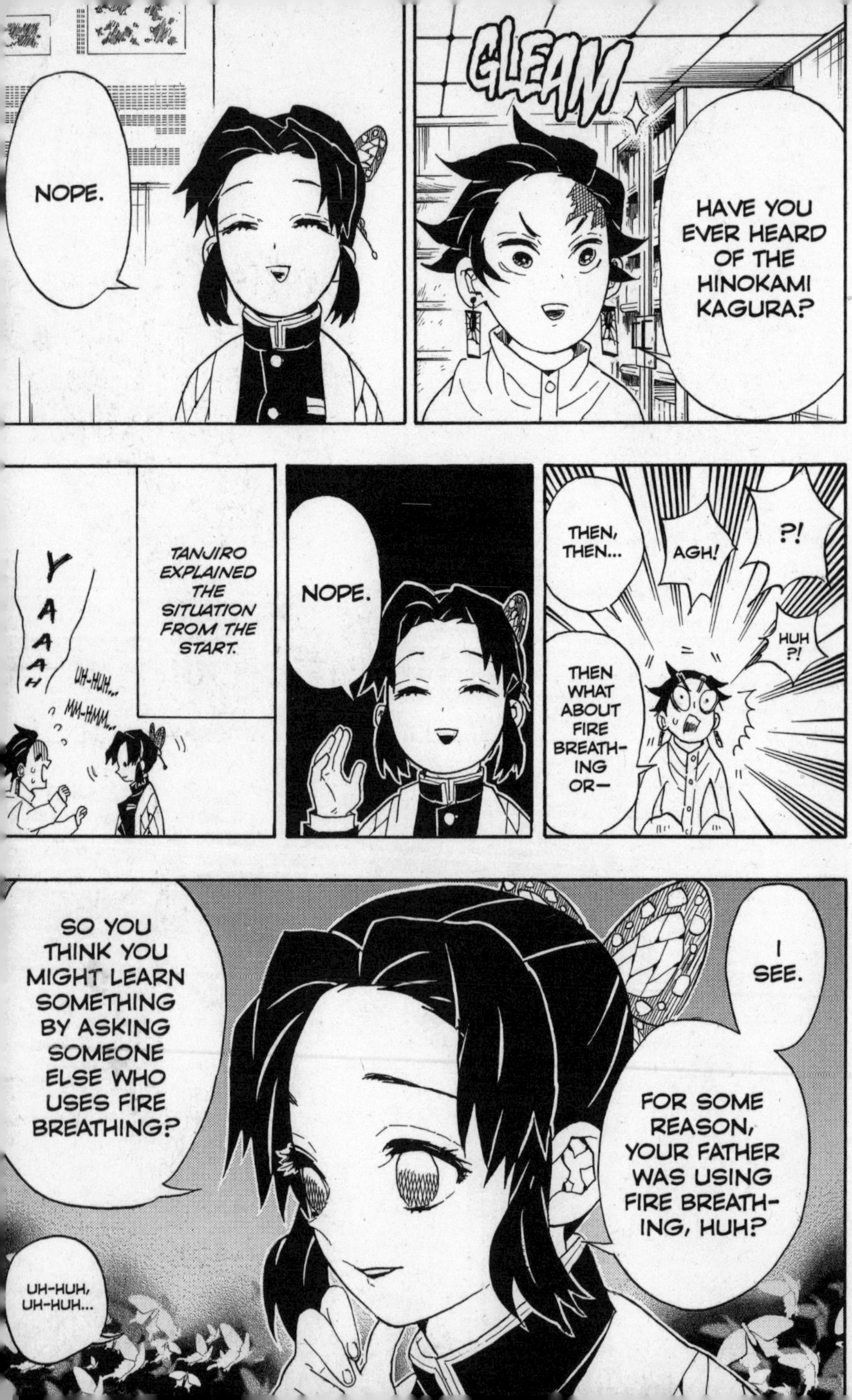

GLEAM
HAVE YOU EVER HEARD OF THE HINOKAMI KAGURA?
NOPE.
THEN, THEN...
THEN WHAT ABOUT FIRE BREATHING OR—
AGH!
?!
HUH ?!
NOPE.
TANJIRO EXPLAINED THE SITUATION FROM THE START.
YAAAAH
UH-HUH...
MM-HMM...
I SEE.
FOR SOME REASON, YOUR FATHER WAS USING FIRE BREATHING, HUH?
SO YOU THINK YOU MIGHT LEARN SOMETHING BY ASKING SOMEONE ELSE WHO USES FIRE BREATHING?
UH-HUH, UH-HUH...

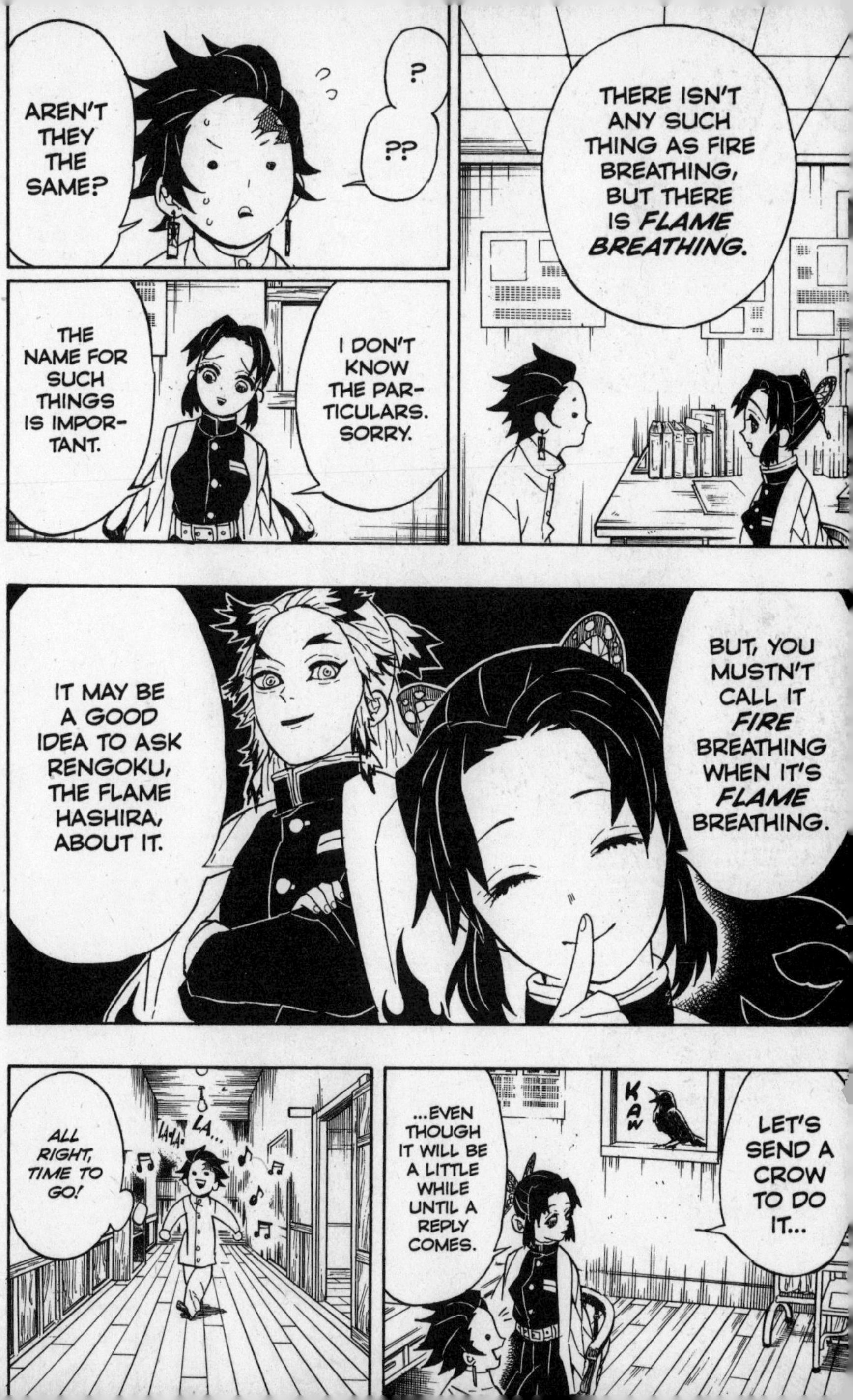
THERE ISN'T ANY SUCH THING AS FIRE BREATHING, BUT THERE IS *FLAME BREATHING*.
?
??
AREN'T THEY THE SAME?
I DON'T KNOW THE PAR-TICULARS. SORRY.
THE NAME FOR SUCH THINGS IS IMPOR-TANT.
BUT, YOU MUSTN'T CALL IT *FIRE* BREATHING WHEN IT'S *FLAME* BREATHING.
IT MAY BE A GOOD IDEA TO ASK RENGOKU, THE FLAME HASHIRA, ABOUT IT.
LET'S SEND A CROW TO DO IT...
KAW
...EVEN THOUGH IT WILL BE A LITTLE WHILE UNTIL A REPLY COMES.
LA...
LA-LA
ALL RIGHT, TIME TO GO!

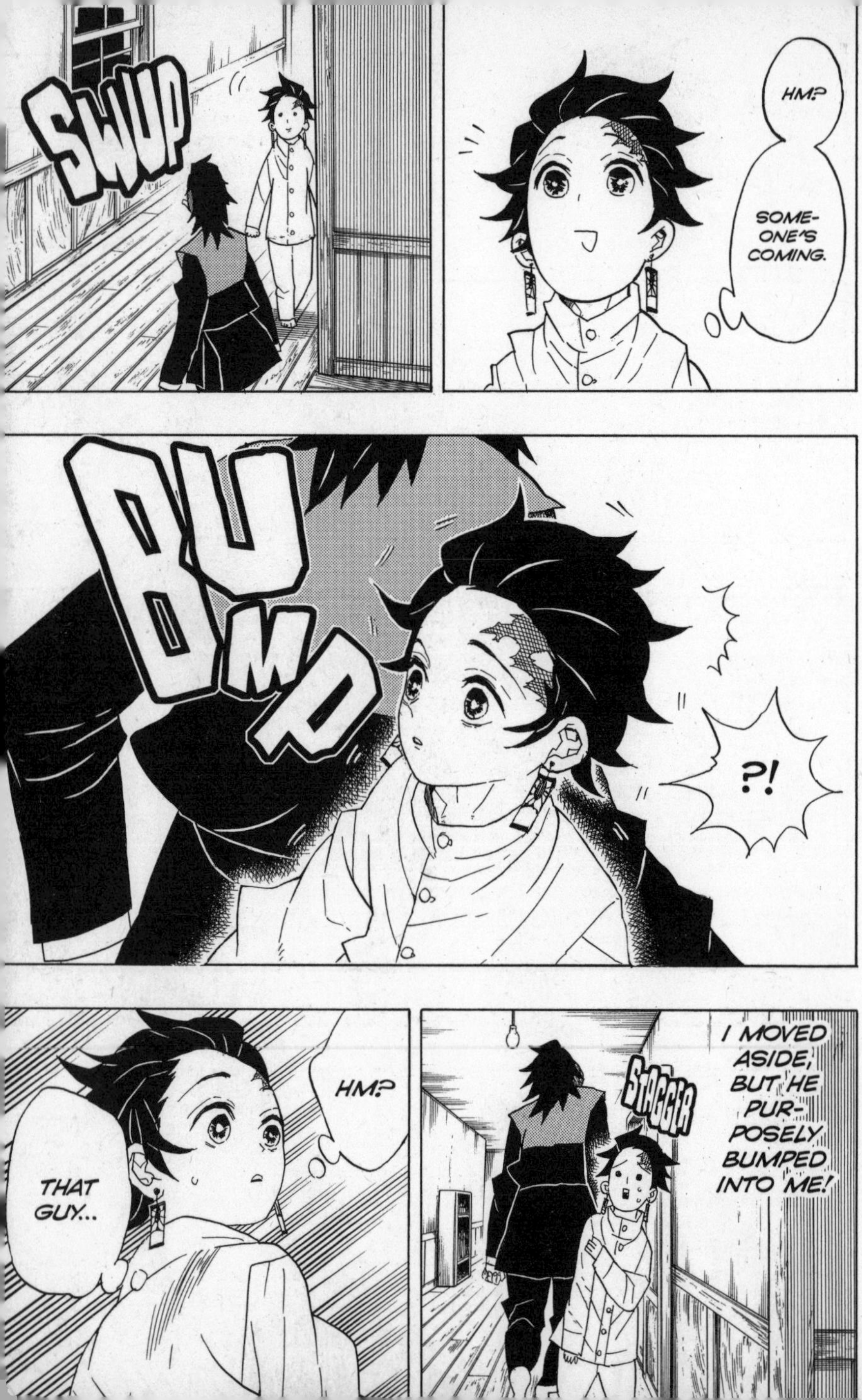
HM?
SOMEONE'S COMING.
SWUP
BUMP
?!
I MOVED ASIDE, BUT HE PURPOSELY BUMPED INTO ME!
STAGGER
HM?
THAT GUY...

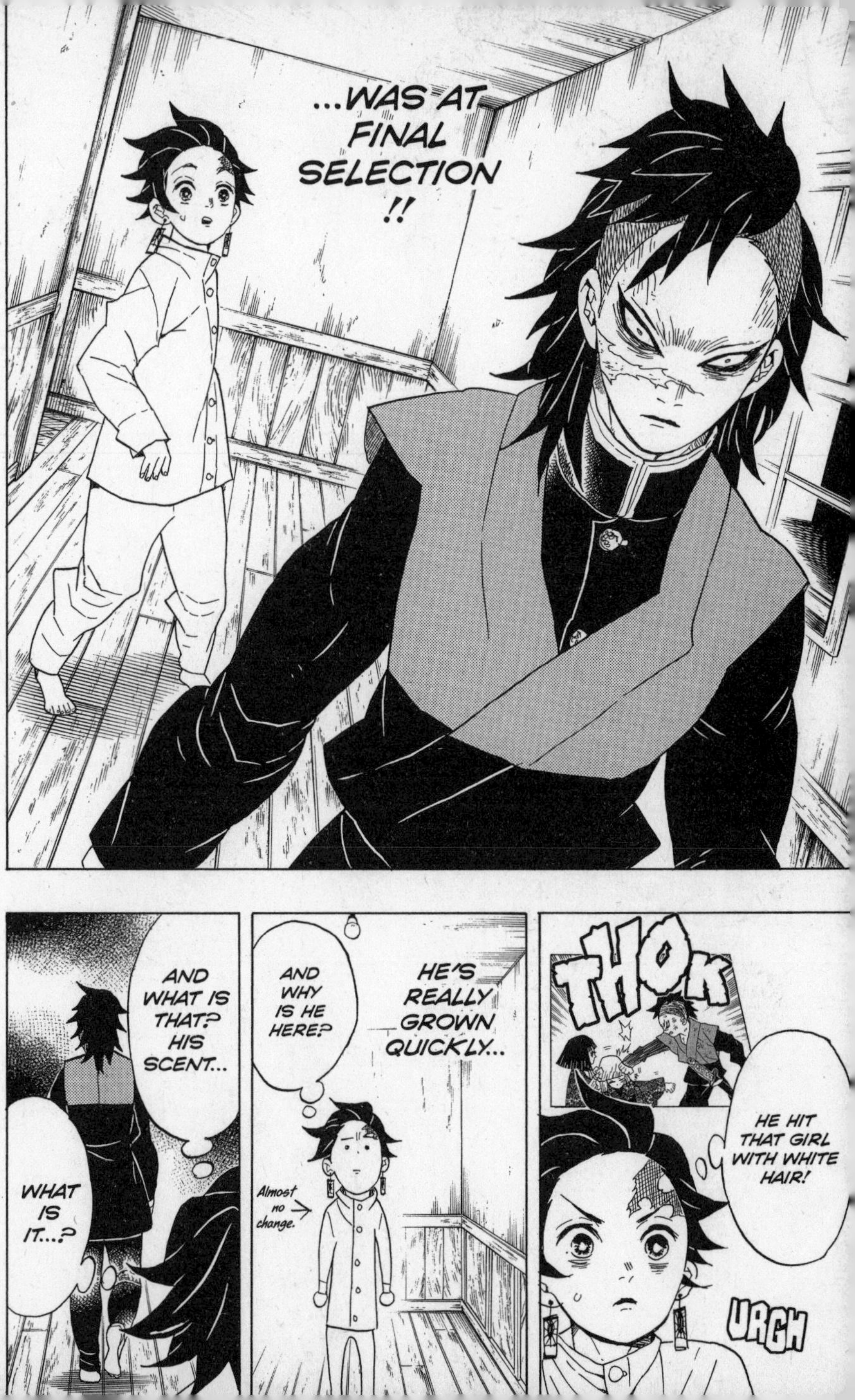
...WAS AT FINAL SELECTION !!
THOK
HE HIT THAT GIRL WITH WHITE HAIR!
URGH
HE'S REALLY GROWN QUICKLY...
AND WHY IS HE HERE?
Almost no change.
AND WHAT IS THAT? HIS SCENT...
WHAT IS IT...?

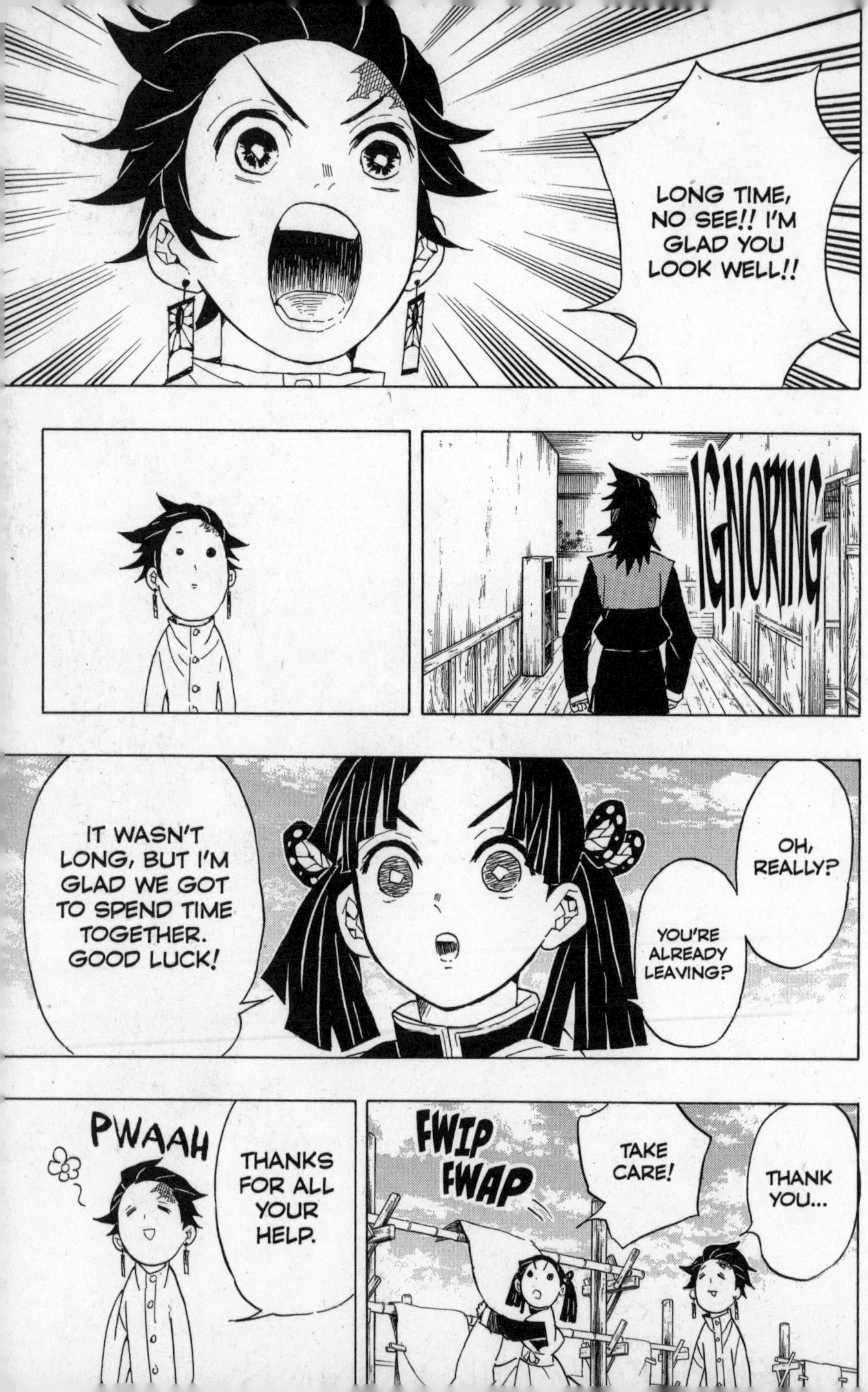
LONG TIME, NO SEE!! I'M GLAD YOU LOOK WELL!!
IGNORING
OH, REALLY?
YOU'RE ALREADY LEAVING?
IT WASN'T LONG, BUT I'M GLAD WE GOT TO SPEND TIME TOGETHER. GOOD LUCK!
THANK YOU...
TAKE CARE!
FWIP FWAP
THANKS FOR ALL YOUR HELP.
PWAAH

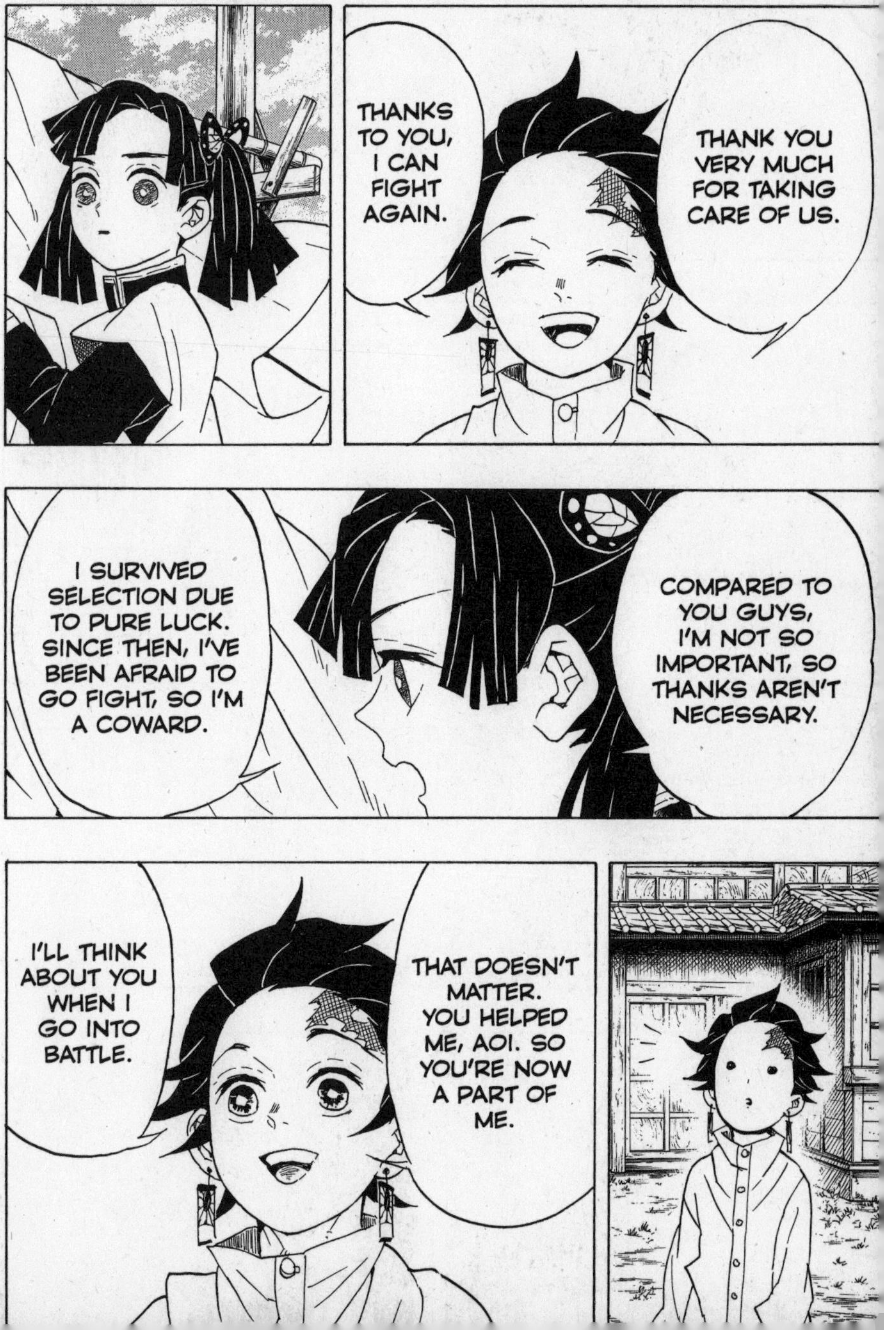
THANK YOU VERY MUCH FOR TAKING CARE OF US.
THANKS TO YOU, I CAN FIGHT AGAIN.
COMPARED TO YOU GUYS, I'M NOT SO IMPORTANT, SO THANKS AREN'T NECESSARY.
I SURVIVED SELECTION DUE TO PURE LUCK. SINCE THEN, I'VE BEEN AFRAID TO GO FIGHT, SO I'M A COWARD.
THAT DOESN'T MATTER. YOU HELPED ME, AOI. SO YOU'RE NOW A PART OF ME.
I'LL THINK ABOUT YOU WHEN I GO INTO BATTLE.

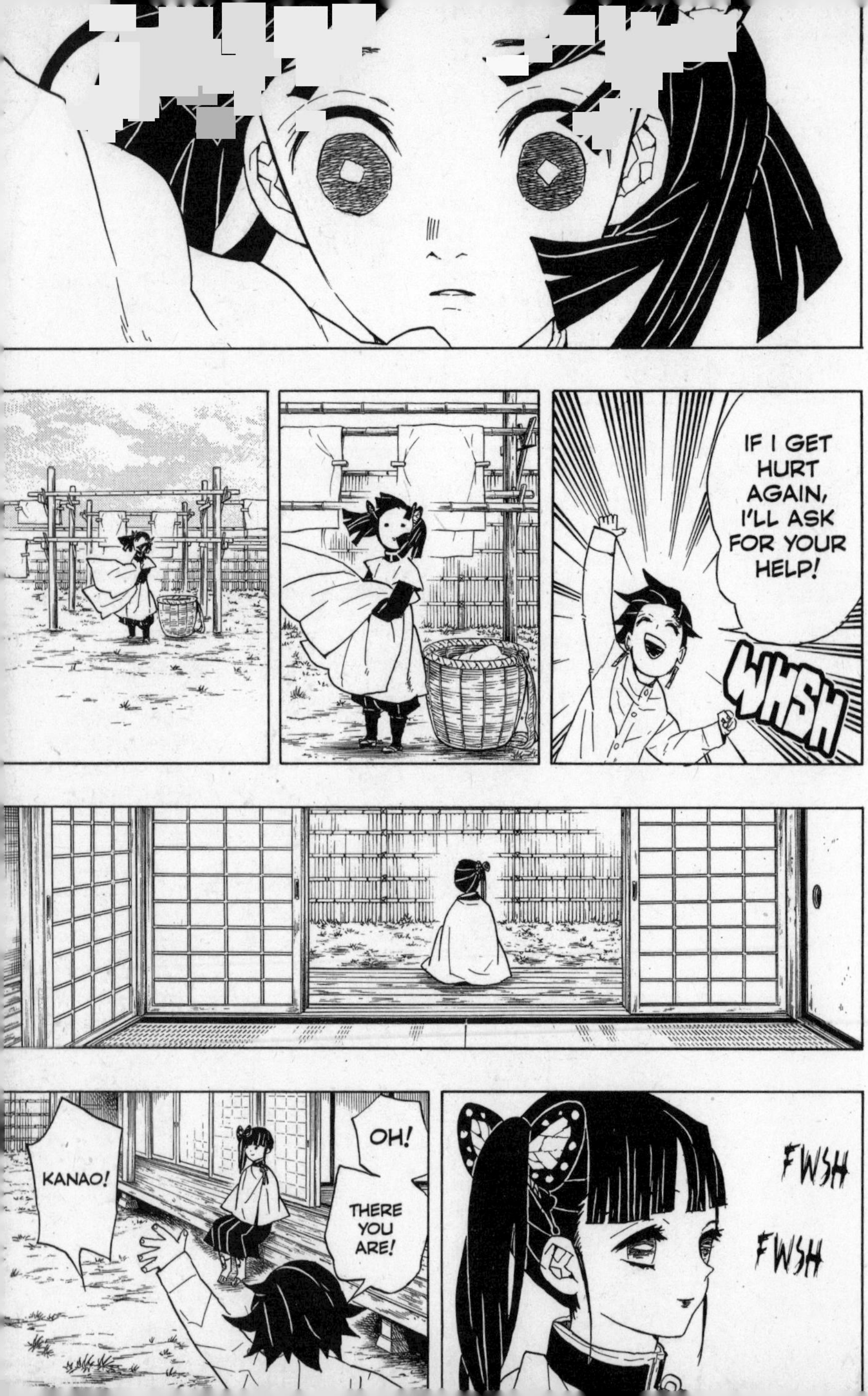
IF I GET HURT AGAIN, I'LL ASK FOR YOUR HELP!
WHSH
FWSH
FWSH
OH!
THERE YOU ARE!
KANAO!

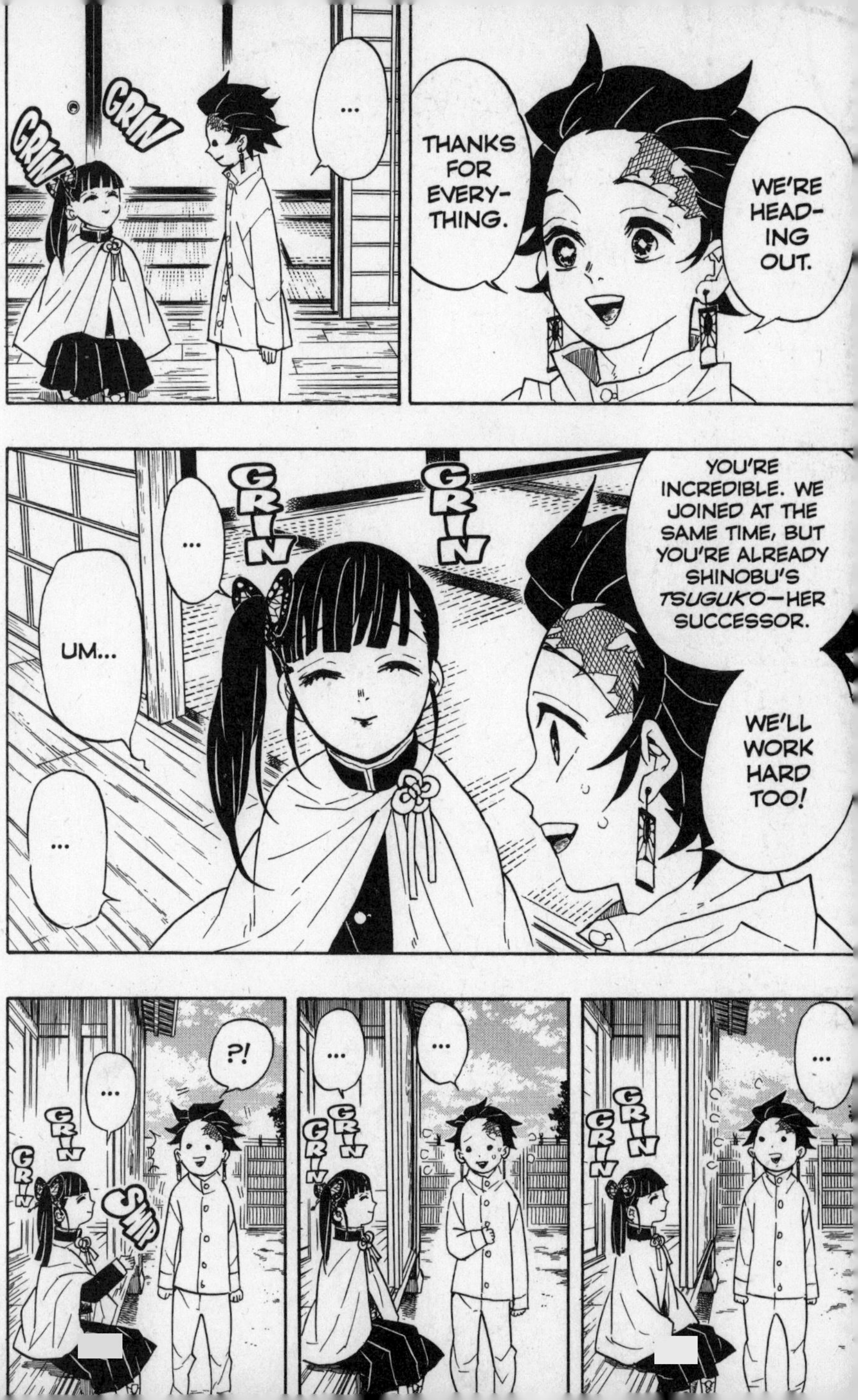
WE'RE HEADING OUT.
THANKS FOR EVERYTHING.
...
GRIN
GRIN
YOU'RE INCREDIBLE. WE JOINED AT THE SAME TIME, BUT YOU'RE ALREADY SHINOBU'S *TSUGUKO*—HER SUCCESSOR.
WE'LL WORK HARD TOO!
GRIN
GRIN
...
UM...
...
...
GRIN
GRIN
...
...
GRIN
GRIN
?!
...
GRIN
GRIN
SMP

*COIN: FRONT (HEADS)

*COIN: BACK (TAILS)

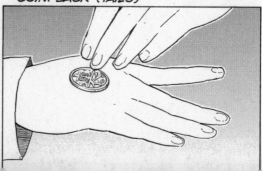

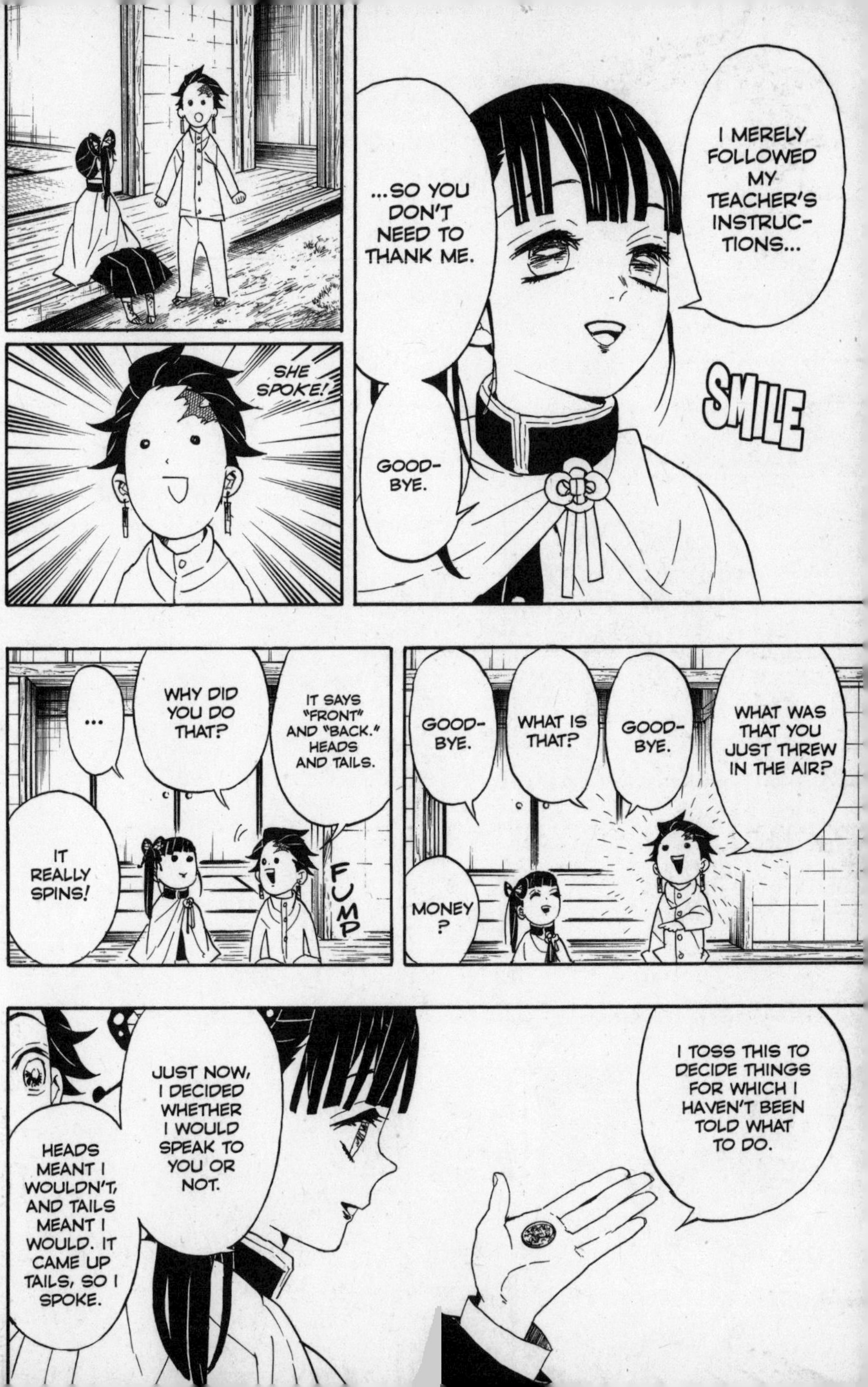
I MERELY FOLLOWED MY TEACHER'S INSTRUCTIONS...
...SO YOU DON'T NEED TO THANK ME.
SMILE
GOOD-BYE.
SHE SPOKE!
WHAT WAS THAT YOU JUST THREW IN THE AIR?
GOOD-BYE.
WHAT IS THAT?
GOOD-BYE.
MONEY?
IT SAYS "FRONT" AND "BACK." HEADS AND TAILS.
WHY DID YOU DO THAT?
...
FUMP
IT REALLY SPINS!
I TOSS THIS TO DECIDE THINGS FOR WHICH I HAVEN'T BEEN TOLD WHAT TO DO.
JUST NOW, I DECIDED WHETHER I WOULD SPEAK TO YOU OR NOT.
HEADS MEANT I WOULDN'T, AND TAILS MEANT I WOULD. IT CAME UP TAILS, SO I SPOKE.

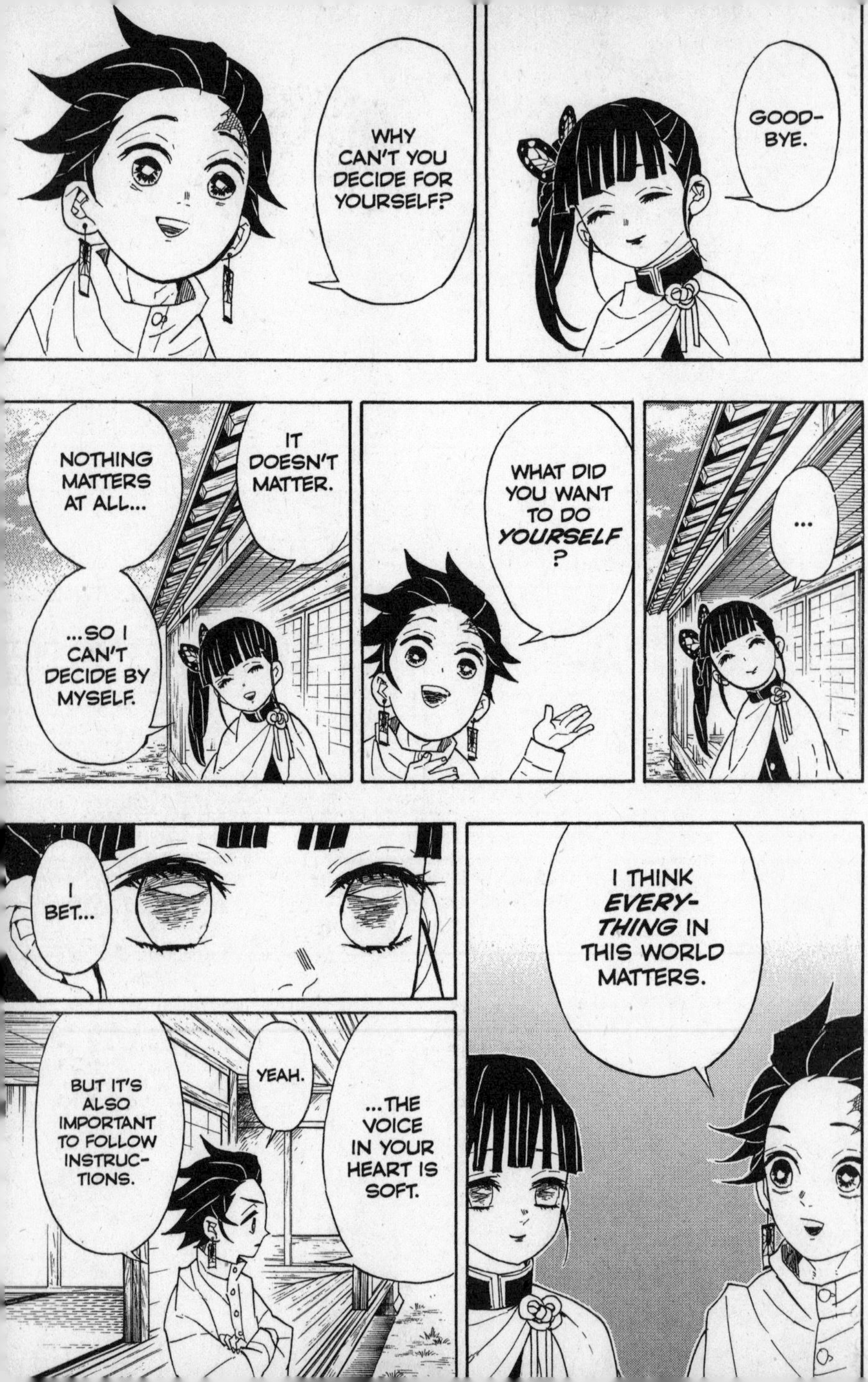
GOOD-BYE.
WHY CAN'T YOU DECIDE FOR YOURSELF?
...
WHAT DID YOU WANT TO DO *YOURSELF*?
IT DOESN'T MATTER.
NOTHING MATTERS AT ALL...
...SO I CAN'T DECIDE BY MYSELF.
I THINK *EVERYTHING* IN THIS WORLD MATTERS.
I BET...
...THE VOICE IN YOUR HEART IS SOFT.
YEAH.
BUT IT'S ALSO IMPORTANT TO FOLLOW INSTRUCTIONS.

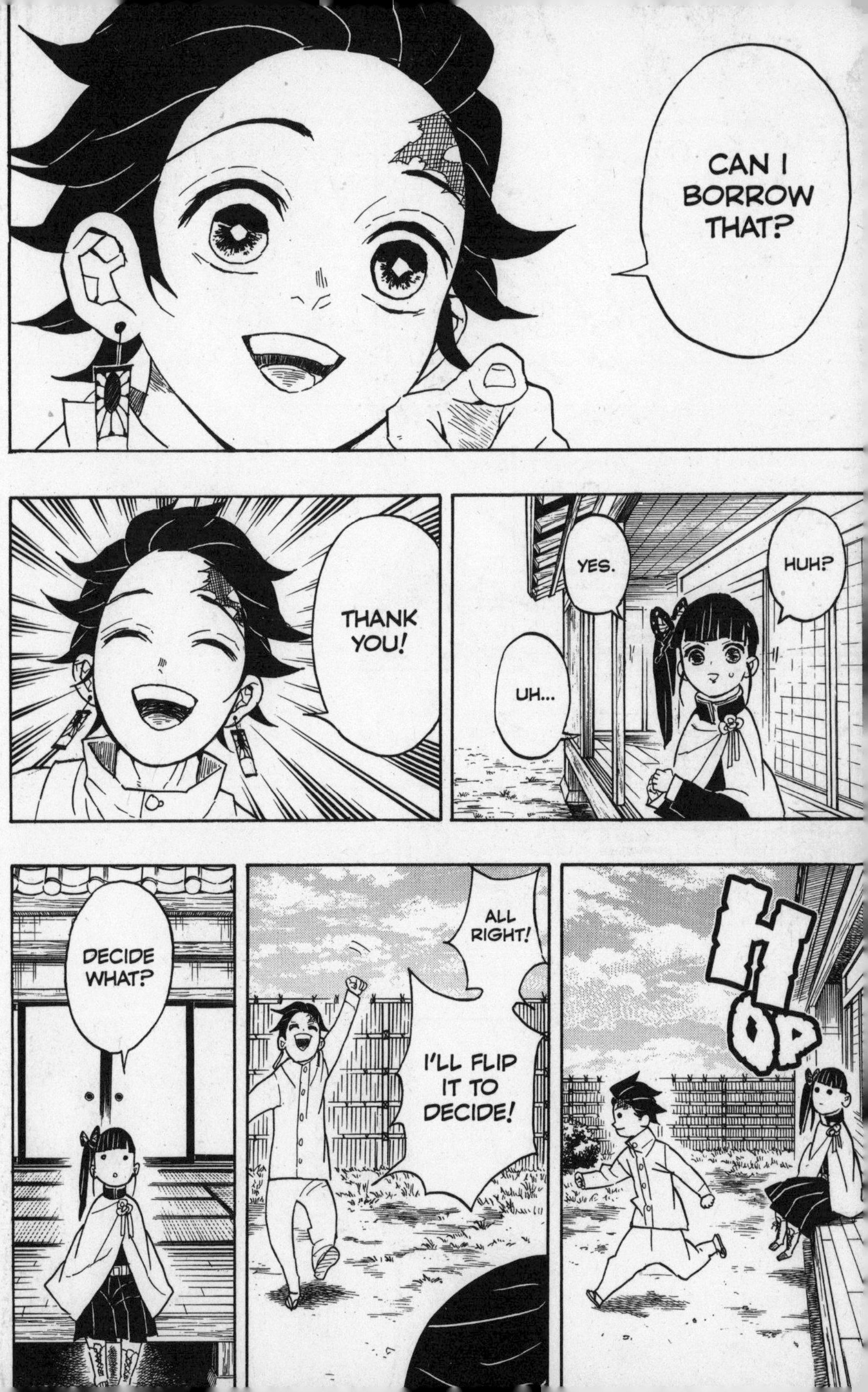

CAN I BORROW THAT?
HUH?
YES.
UH...
THANK YOU!
HOP
ALL RIGHT!
I'LL FLIP IT TO DECIDE!
DECIDE WHAT?

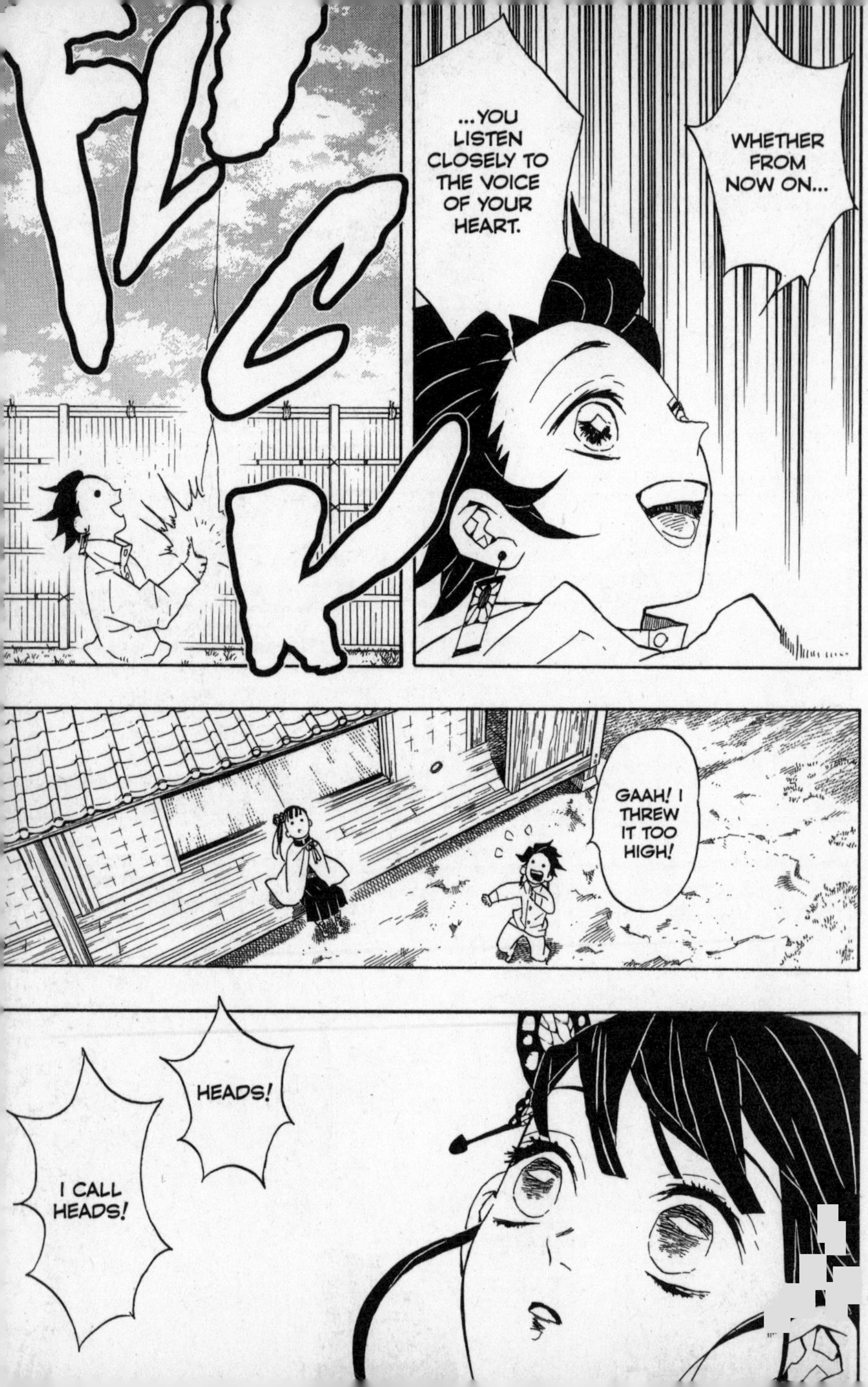
WHETHER FROM NOW ON...
...YOU LISTEN CLOSELY TO THE VOICE OF YOUR HEART.
GAAH! I THREW IT TOO HIGH!
HEADS!
I CALL HEADS!

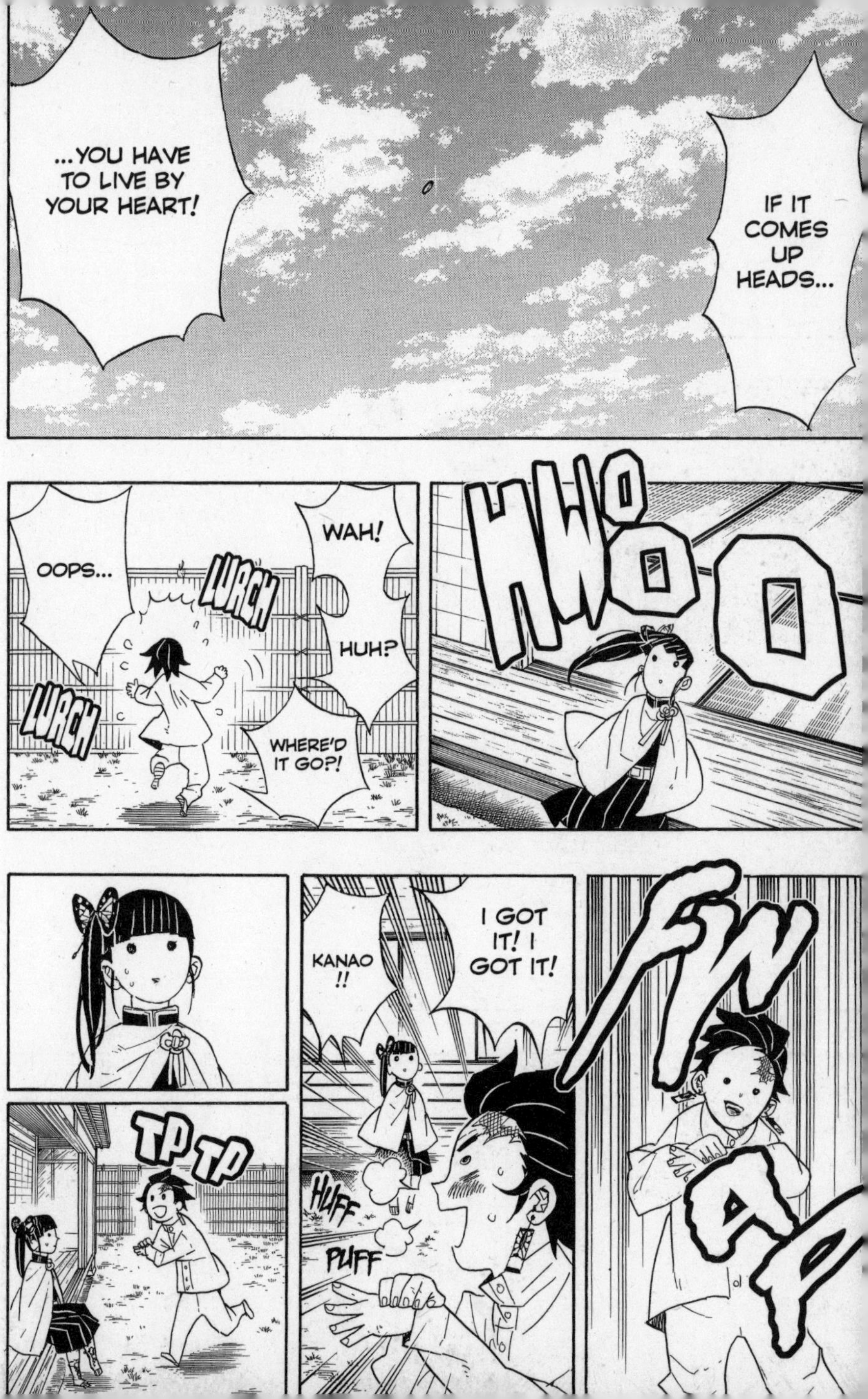
IF IT COMES UP HEADS...
...YOU HAVE TO LIVE BY YOUR HEART!
HWOOO
WAH!
LURCH
HUH?
OOPS...
WHERE'D IT GO?!
LURCH
FWAP
I GOT IT! I GOT IT!
KANAO!!
HUFF
PUFF
TP TP

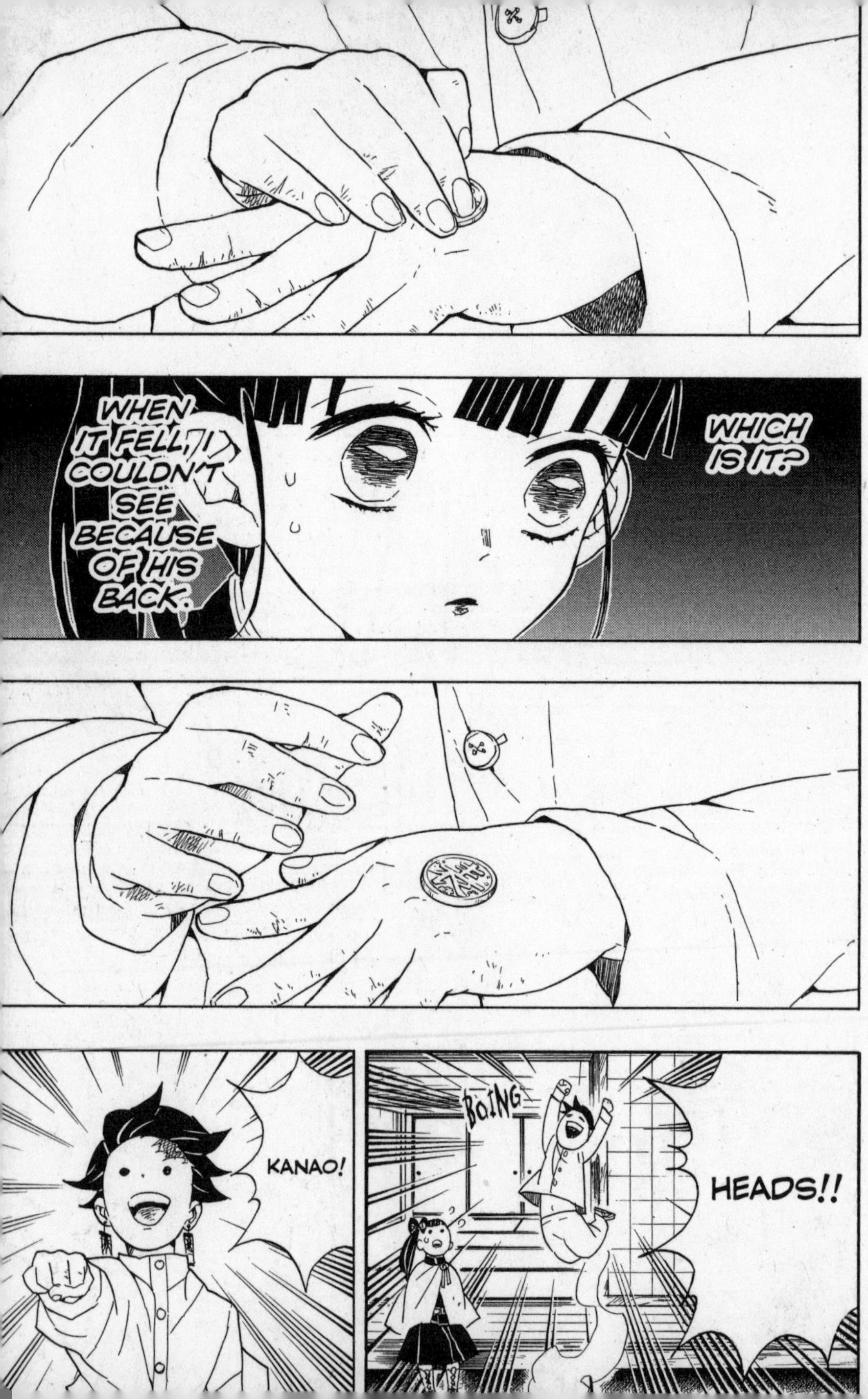
WHICH IS IT?
WHEN IT FELL, I COULDN'T SEE BECAUSE OF HIS BACK.
BOING
HEADS!!
KANAO!

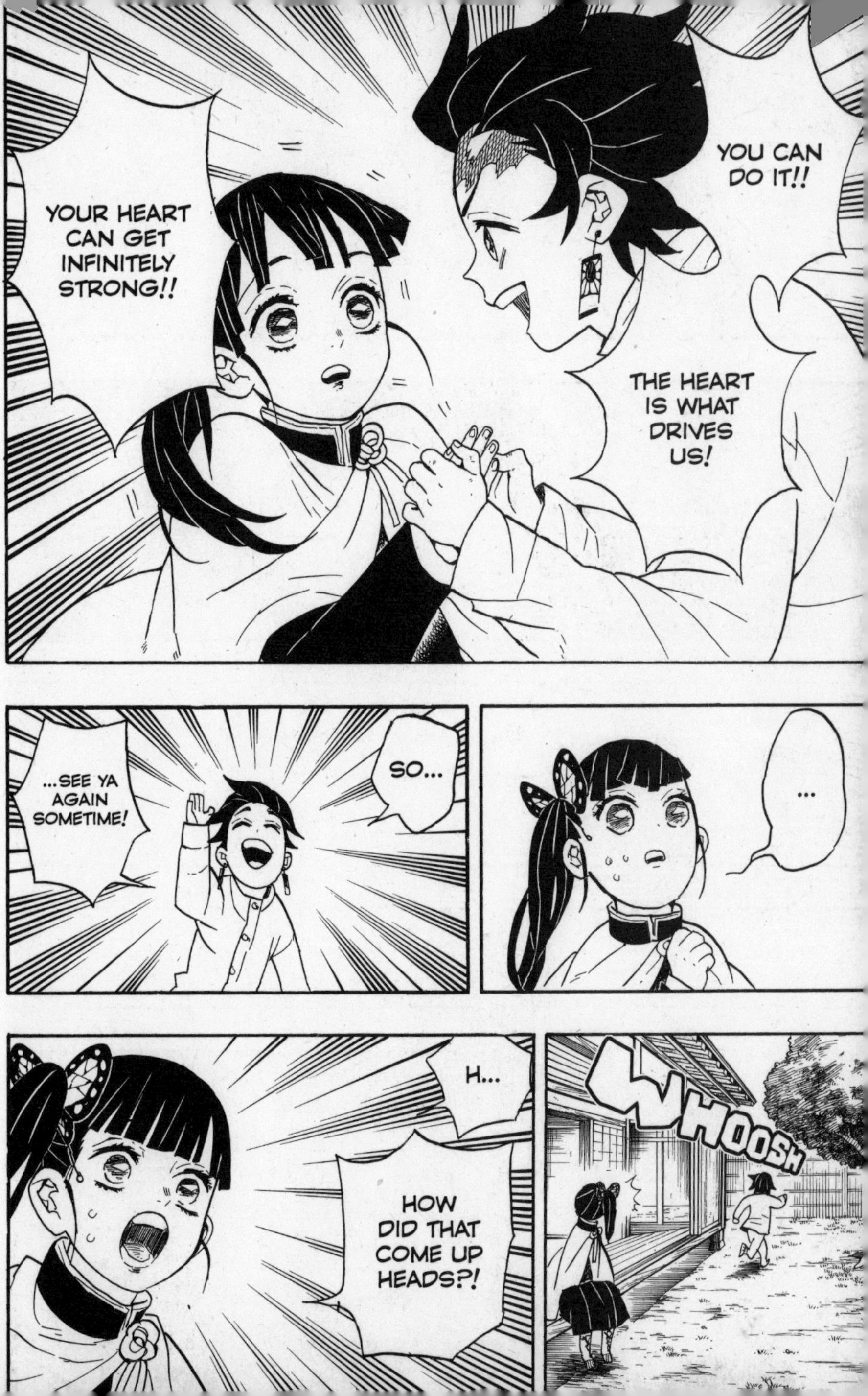
YOU CAN DO IT!!
THE HEART IS WHAT DRIVES US!
YOUR HEART CAN GET INFINITELY STRONG!!
...
SO...
...SEE YA AGAIN SOMETIME!
WHOOSH
H...
HOW DID THAT COME UP HEADS?!

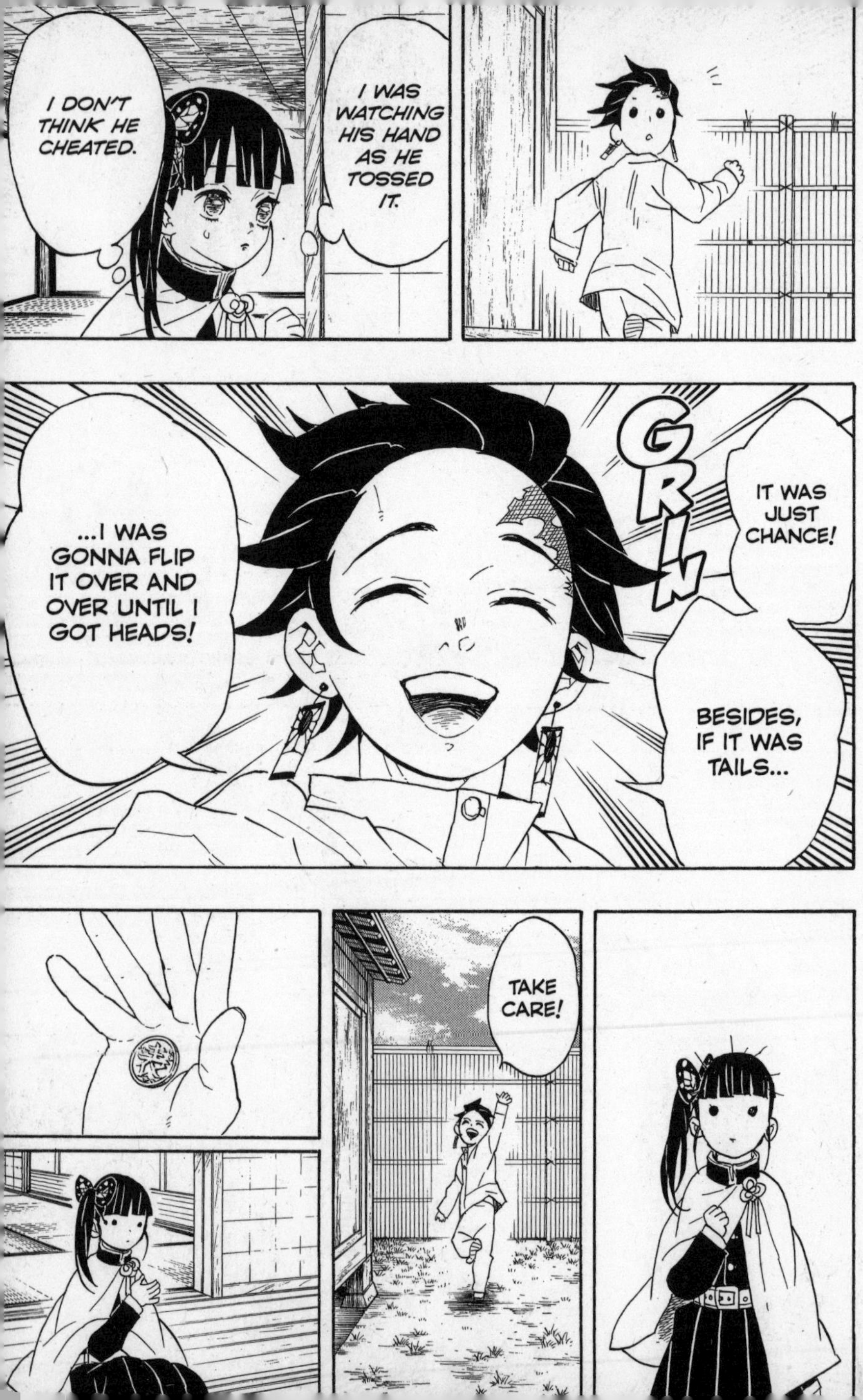
I WAS WATCHING HIS HAND AS HE TOSSED IT.
I DON'T THINK HE CHEATED.
GRIN
IT WAS JUST CHANCE!
BESIDES, IF IT WAS TAILS...
...I WAS GONNA FLIP IT OVER AND OVER UNTIL I GOT HEADS!
TAKE CARE!

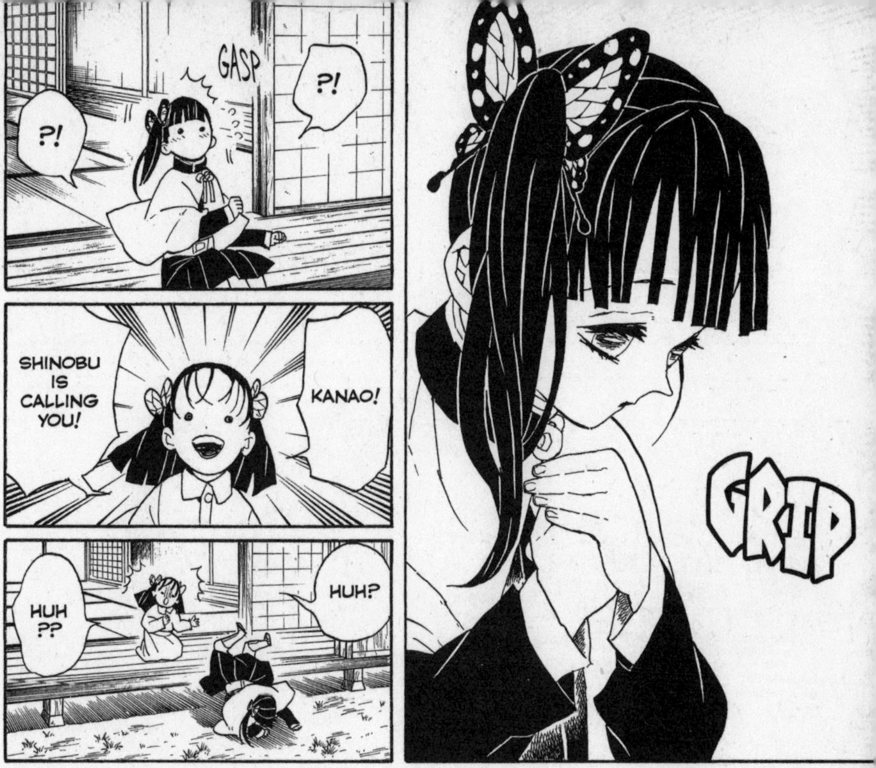
GRIP
?!
?!
GASP
KANAO!
SHINOBU IS CALLING YOU!
HUH?
HUH ??

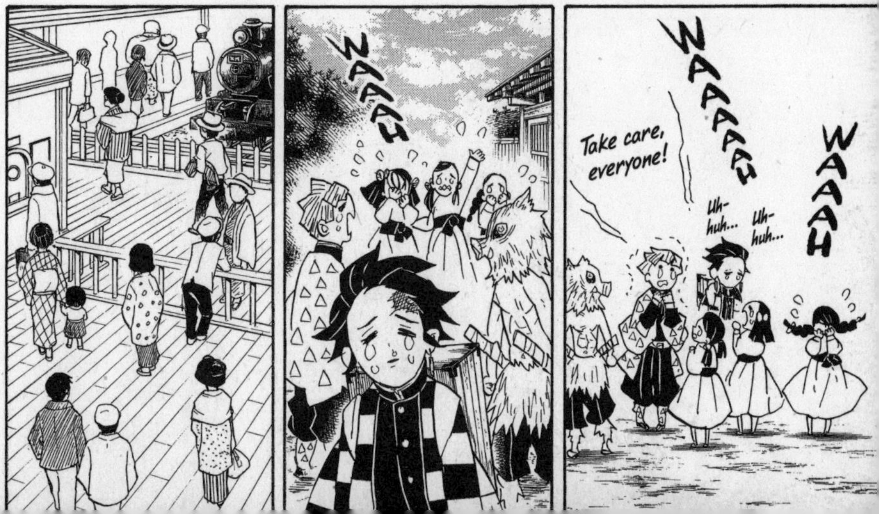
WAAAH
WAAAAH
Take care, everyone!
Uh-huh...
Uh-huh...
WAAAH

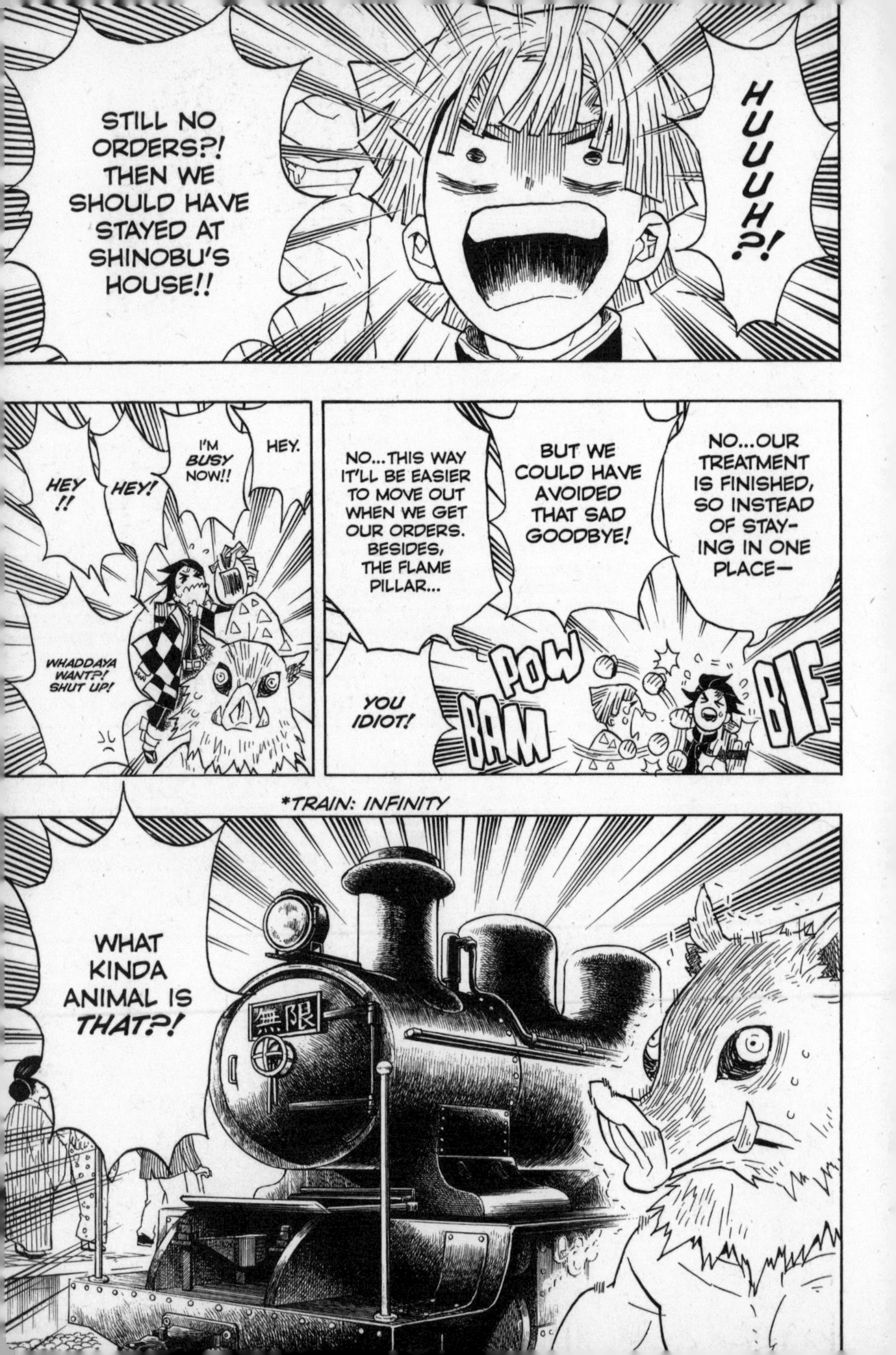
HUUUUH?!
STILL NO ORDERS?! THEN WE SHOULD HAVE STAYED AT SHINOBU'S HOUSE!!
NO...OUR TREATMENT IS FINISHED, SO INSTEAD OF STAY-ING IN ONE PLACE—
BUT WE COULD HAVE AVOIDED THAT SAD GOODBYE!
NO...THIS WAY IT'LL BE EASIER TO MOVE OUT WHEN WE GET OUR ORDERS. BESIDES, THE FLAME PILLAR...
BIF
POW
BAM
YOU IDIOT!
HEY.
I'M BUSY NOW!!
HEY!
HEY!!
WHADDAYA WANT?! SHUT UP!
*TRAIN: INFINITY
無限
WHAT KINDA ANIMAL IS THAT?!

...

Inosuke
immediately before
seeing a steam train
for the first time.
There were too many
people, so he was a
little startled.

CHAPTER 54: GOOD EVENING, RENGOKU

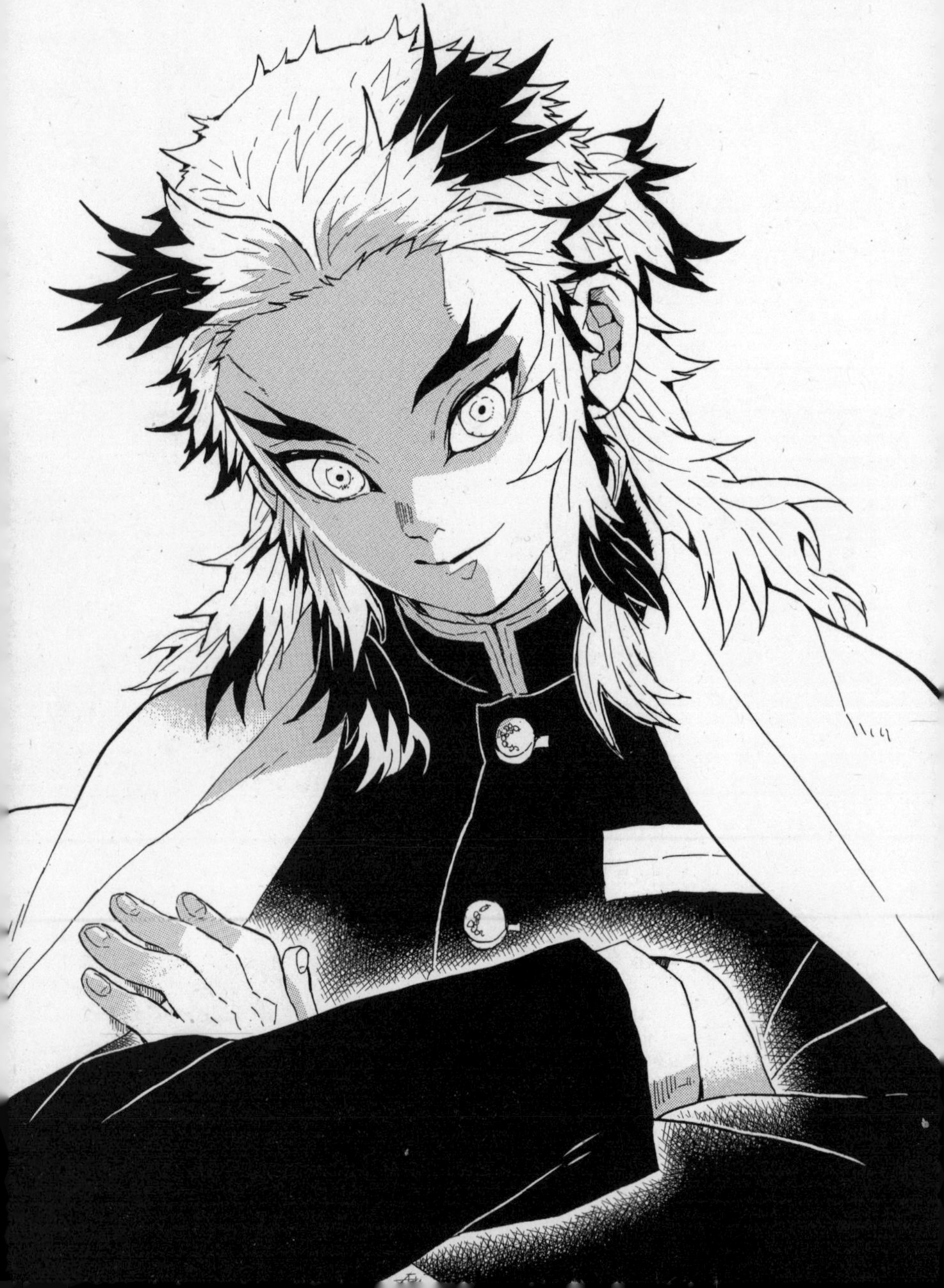

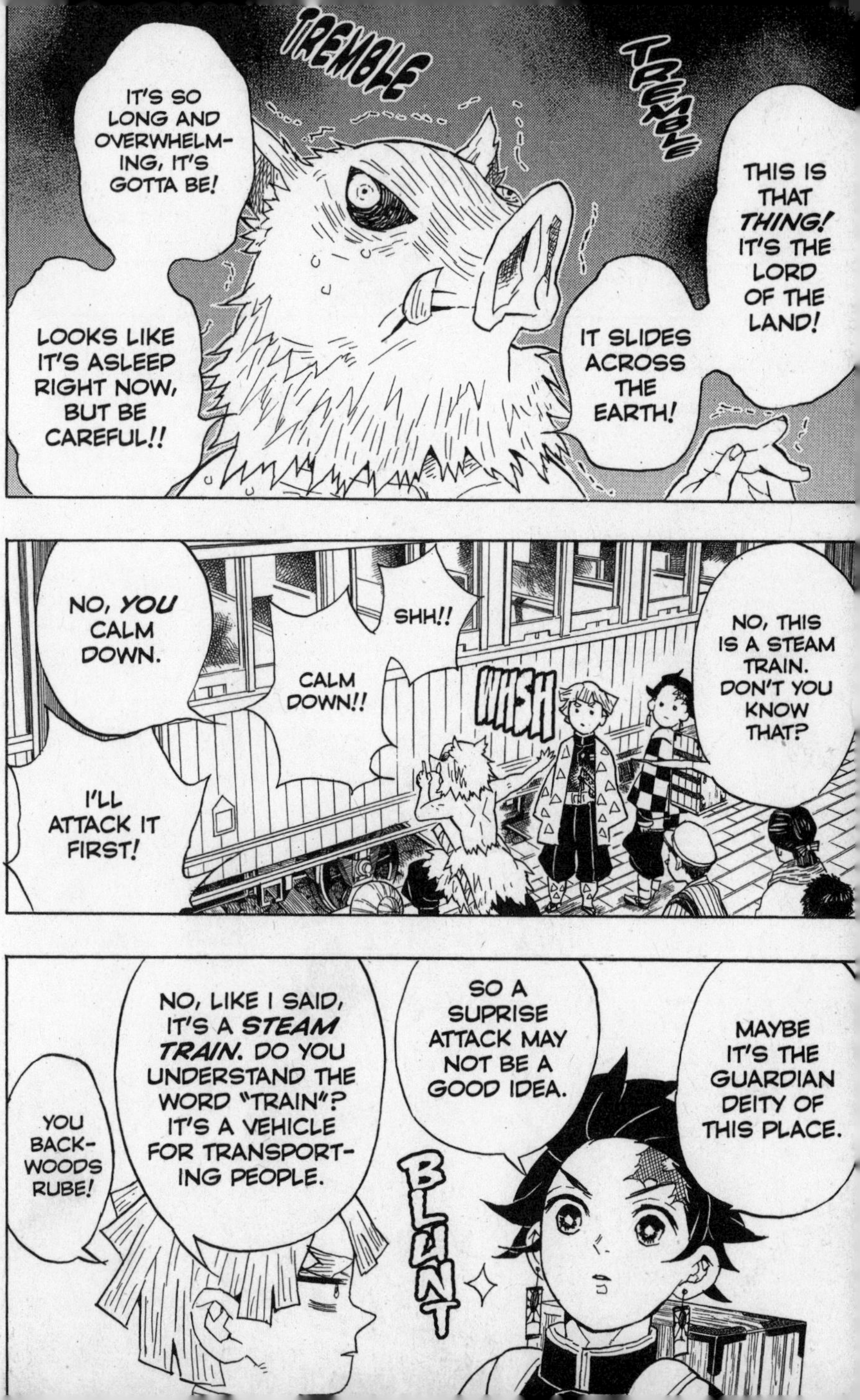
TREMBLE
THIS IS THAT THING! IT'S THE LORD OF THE LAND!
IT SLIDES ACROSS THE EARTH!
TREMBLE
IT'S SO LONG AND OVERWHELM-ING, IT'S GOTTA BE!
LOOKS LIKE IT'S ASLEEP RIGHT NOW, BUT BE CAREFUL!!
NO, THIS IS A STEAM TRAIN. DON'T YOU KNOW THAT?
WHSH
SHH!!
CALM DOWN!!
NO, *YOU* CALM DOWN.
I'LL ATTACK IT FIRST!
MAYBE IT'S THE GUARDIAN DEITY OF THIS PLACE.
SO A SUPRISE ATTACK MAY NOT BE A GOOD IDEA.
BLUNT
NO, LIKE I SAID, IT'S A ***STEAM TRAIN***. DO YOU UNDERSTAND THE WORD "TRAIN"? IT'S A VEHICLE FOR TRANSPORT-ING PEOPLE.
YOU BACK-WOODS RUBE!

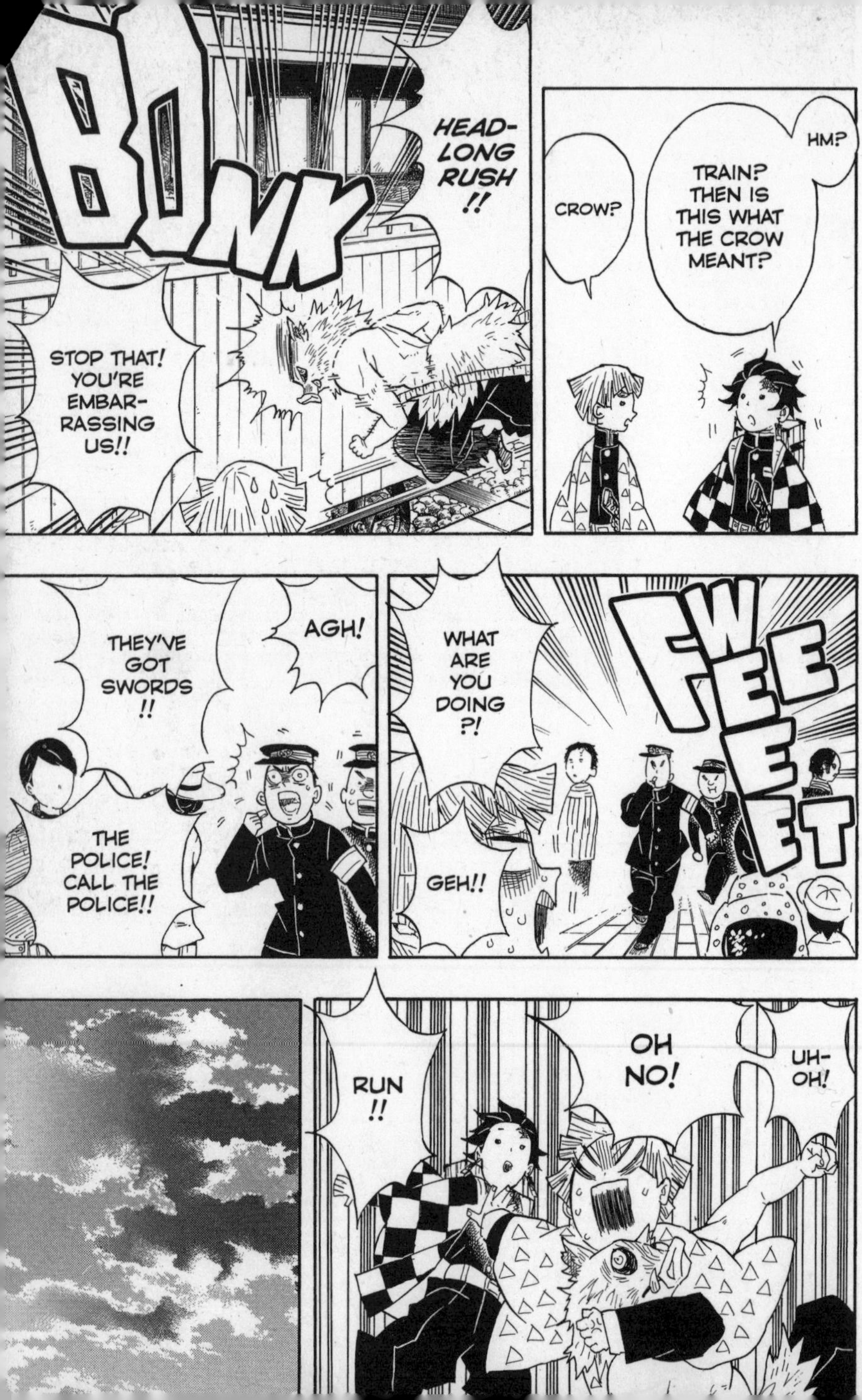
HM?
TRAIN? THEN IS THIS WHAT THE CROW MEANT?
CROW?
BONK
HEAD-LONG RUSH!!
STOP THAT! YOU'RE EMBAR-RASSING US!!
FWEEEET
WHAT ARE YOU DOING?!
GEH!!
AGH!
THEY'VE GOT SWORDS!!
THE POLICE! CALL THE POLICE!!
UH-OH!
OH NO!
RUN!!

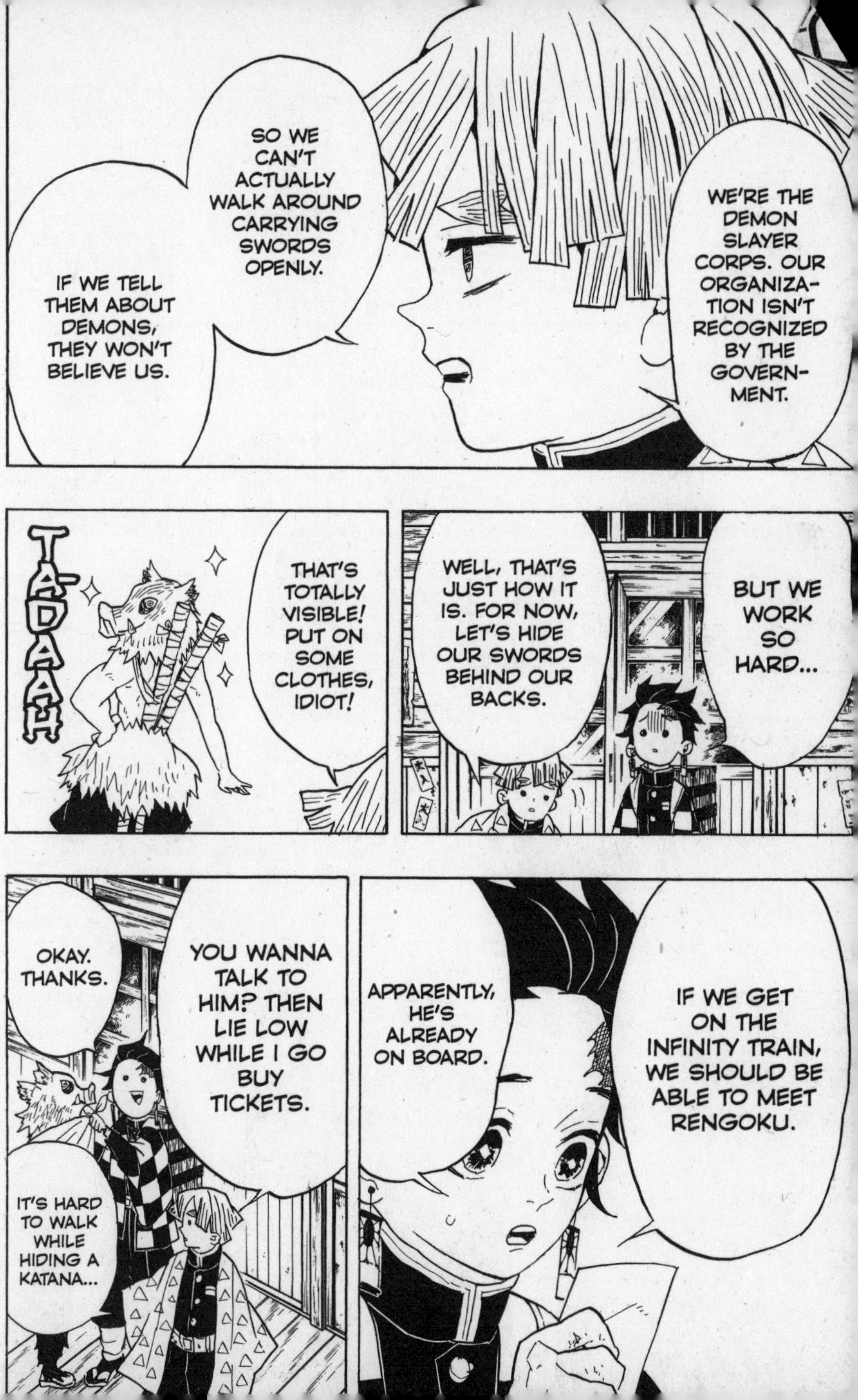

WE'RE THE DEMON SLAYER CORPS. OUR ORGANIZA-TION ISN'T RECOGNIZED BY THE GOVERN-MENT.
SO WE CAN'T ACTUALLY WALK AROUND CARRYING SWORDS OPENLY.
IF WE TELL THEM ABOUT DEMONS, THEY WON'T BELIEVE US.
BUT WE WORK SO HARD...
WELL, THAT'S JUST HOW IT IS. FOR NOW, LET'S HIDE OUR SWORDS BEHIND OUR BACKS.
THAT'S TOTALLY VISIBLE! PUT ON SOME CLOTHES, IDIOT!
TADAAAH
IF WE GET ON THE INFINITY TRAIN, WE SHOULD BE ABLE TO MEET RENGOKU.
APPARENTLY, HE'S ALREADY ON BOARD.
YOU WANNA TALK TO HIM? THEN LIE LOW WHILE I GO BUY TICKETS.
OKAY. THANKS.
IT'S HARD TO WALK WHILE HIDING A KATANA...

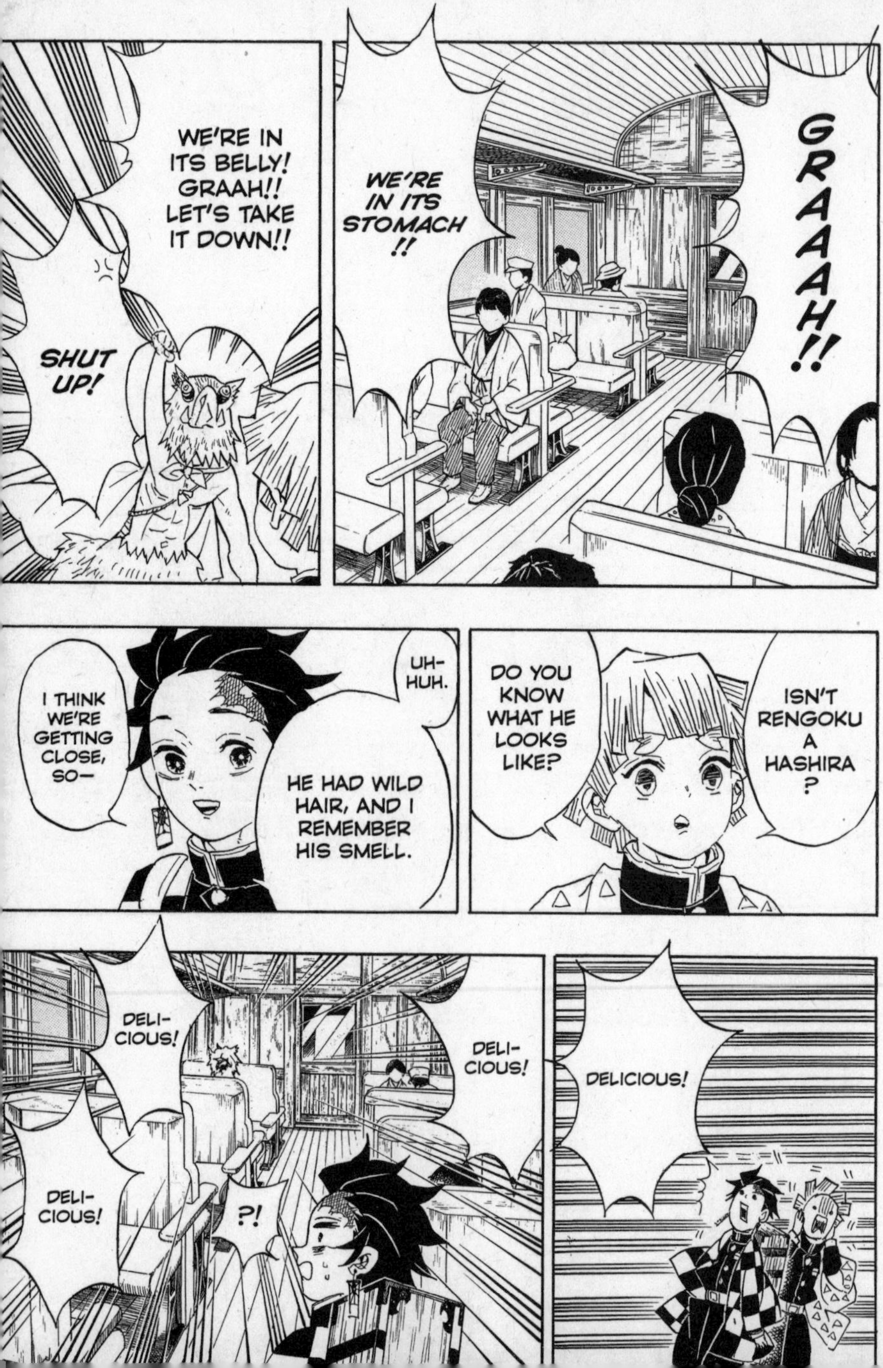
GRAAAAH!!
WE'RE IN ITS STOMACH!!
WE'RE IN ITS BELLY! GRAAH!! LET'S TAKE IT DOWN!!
SHUT UP!
ISN'T RENGOKU A HASHIRA?
DO YOU KNOW WHAT HE LOOKS LIKE?
UH-HUH.
HE HAD WILD HAIR, AND I REMEMBER HIS SMELL.
I THINK WE'RE GETTING CLOSE, SO—
DELICIOUS!
DELI-CIOUS!
DELI-CIOUS!
?!
DELI-CIOUS!

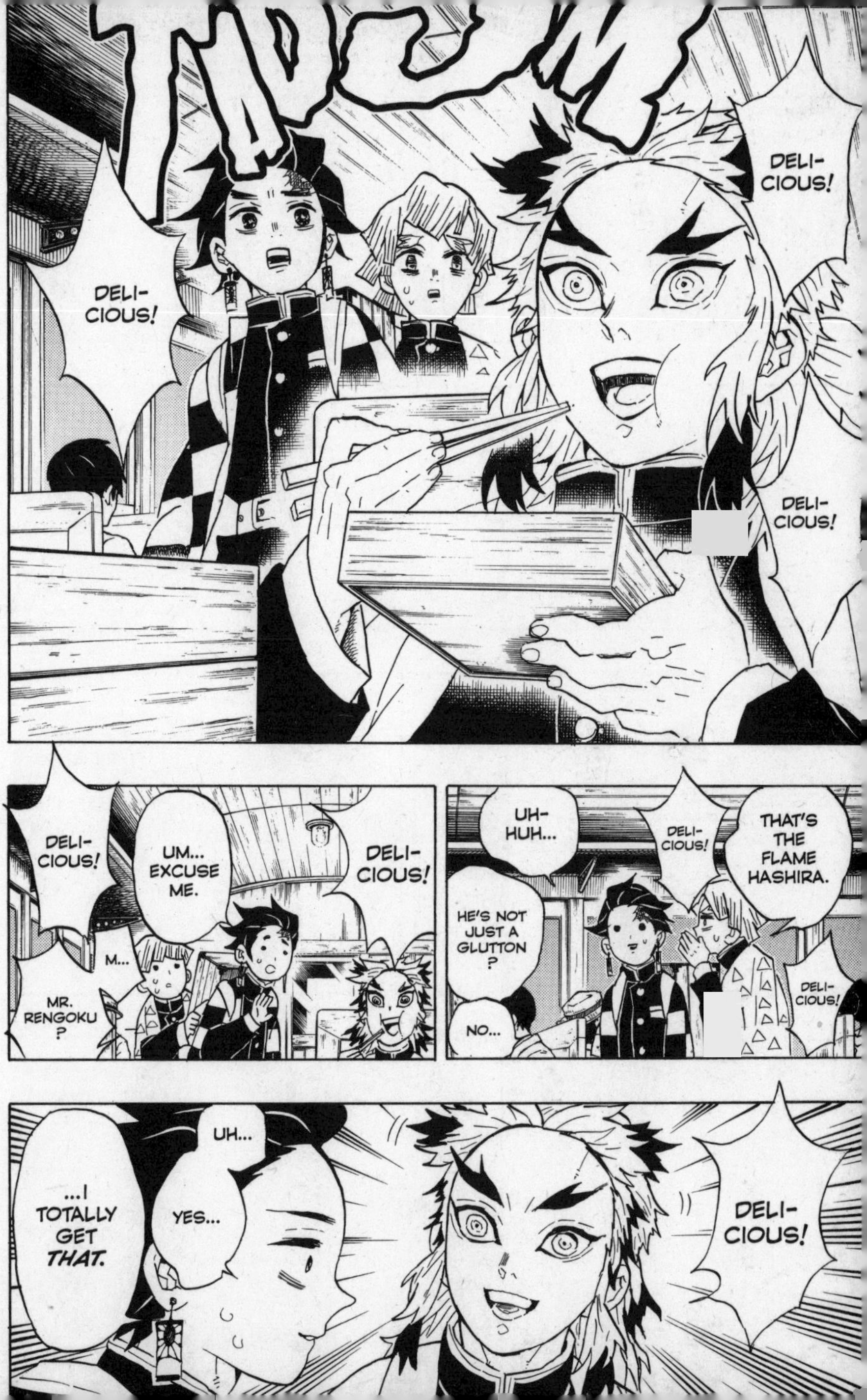
DELI-CIOUS!
DELI-CIOUS!
DELI-CIOUS!
THAT'S THE FLAME HASHIRA.
DELI-CIOUS!
UH-HUH...
HE'S NOT JUST A GLUTTON?
DELI-CIOUS!
NO...
DELI-CIOUS!
UM... EXCUSE ME.
DELI-CIOUS!
M...
MR. RENGOKU?
DELI-CIOUS!
UH...
YES...
...I TOTALLY GET *THAT.*

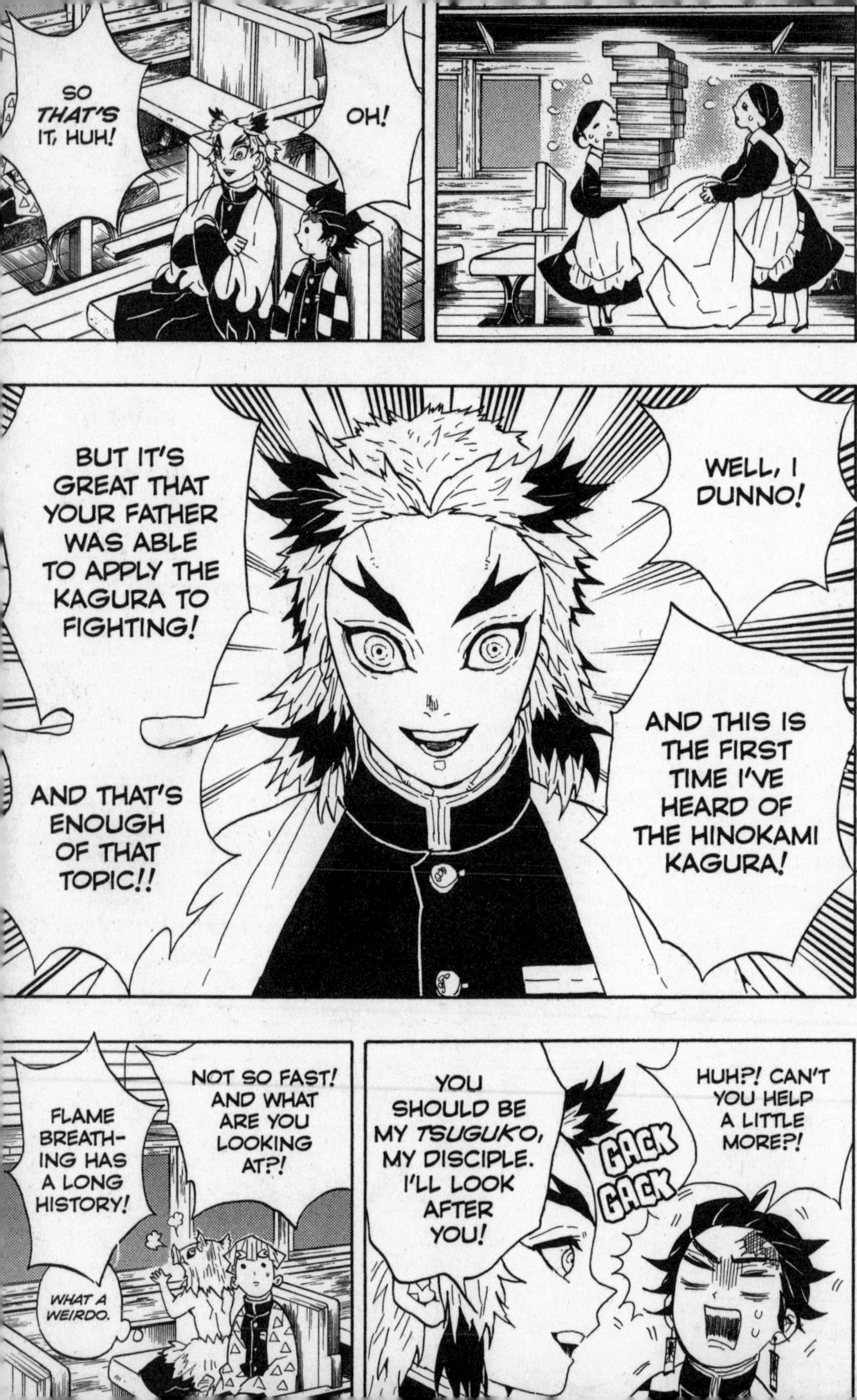
OH!
SO *THAT'S* IT, HUH!
WELL, I DUNNO!
AND THIS IS THE FIRST TIME I'VE HEARD OF THE HINOKAMI KAGURA!
BUT IT'S GREAT THAT YOUR FATHER WAS ABLE TO APPLY THE KAGURA TO FIGHTING!
AND THAT'S ENOUGH OF THAT TOPIC!!
HUH?! CAN'T YOU HELP A LITTLE MORE?!
GACK GACK
YOU SHOULD BE MY *TSUGUKO*, MY DISCIPLE. I'LL LOOK AFTER YOU!
NOT SO FAST! AND WHAT ARE YOU LOOKING AT?!
FLAME BREATHING HAS A LONG HISTORY!
WHAT A WEIRDO.

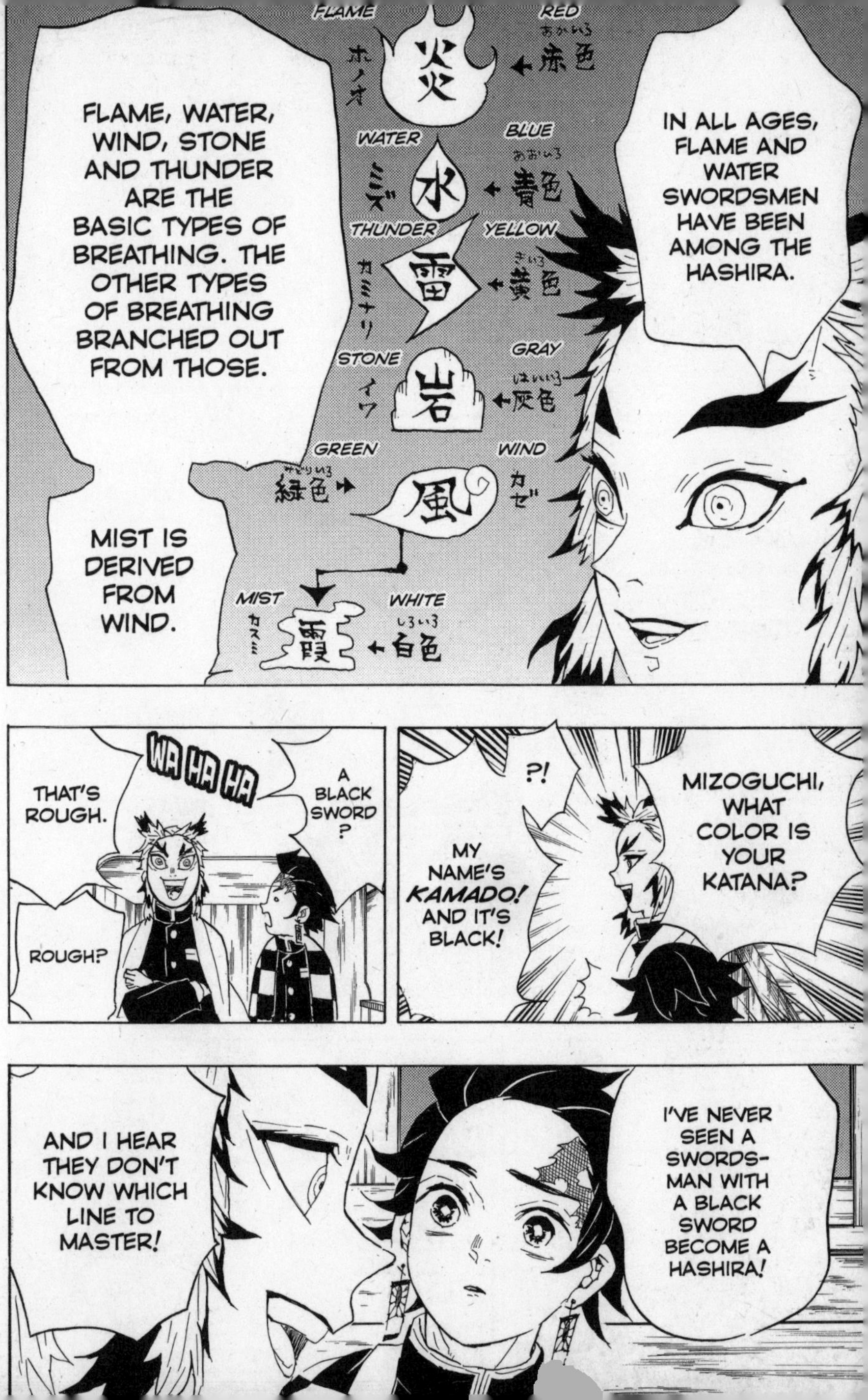
IN ALL AGES, FLAME AND WATER SWORDSMEN HAVE BEEN AMONG THE HASHIRA.
FLAME 炎 ホノオ ← RED 赤色 あかいろ
WATER 水 ミズ ← BLUE 青色 あおいろ
THUNDER 雷 カミナリ ← YELLOW 黄色 きいろ
STONE 岩 イワ ← GRAY 灰色 はいいろ
WIND 風 カゼ ← GREEN 緑色 みどりいろ
MIST 霞 カスミ ← WHITE 白色 しろいろ
FLAME, WATER, WIND, STONE AND THUNDER ARE THE BASIC TYPES OF BREATHING. THE OTHER TYPES OF BREATHING BRANCHED OUT FROM THOSE.
MIST IS DERIVED FROM WIND.
MIZOGUCHI, WHAT COLOR IS YOUR KATANA?
?!
MY NAME'S *KAMADO!* AND IT'S BLACK!
A BLACK SWORD?
WA HA HA
THAT'S ROUGH.
ROUGH?
I'VE NEVER SEEN A SWORDSMAN WITH A BLACK SWORD BECOME A HASHIRA!
AND I HEAR THEY DON'T KNOW WHICH LINE TO MASTER!

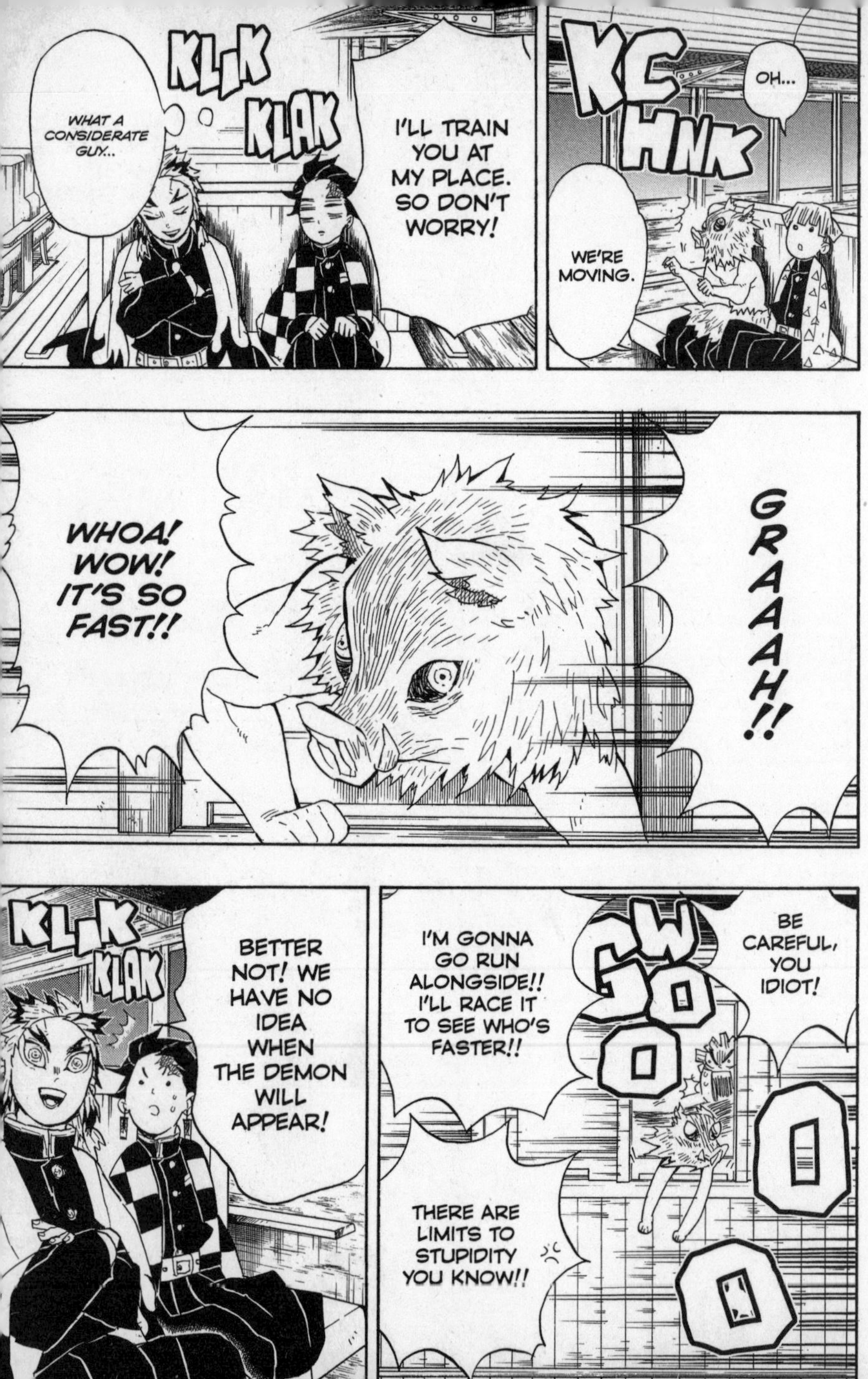
OH...
KC HNK
WE'RE MOVING.
I'LL TRAIN YOU AT MY PLACE. SO DON'T WORRY!
KLIK KLAK
WHAT A CONSIDERATE GUY...
GRAAAAH!!
WHOA! WOW! IT'S SO FAST!!
BE CAREFUL, YOU IDIOT!
GWOOOO
I'M GONNA GO RUN ALONGSIDE!! I'LL RACE IT TO SEE WHO'S FASTER!!
THERE ARE LIMITS TO STUPIDITY YOU KNOW!!
BETTER NOT! WE HAVE NO IDEA WHEN THE DEMON WILL APPEAR!
KLIK KLAK

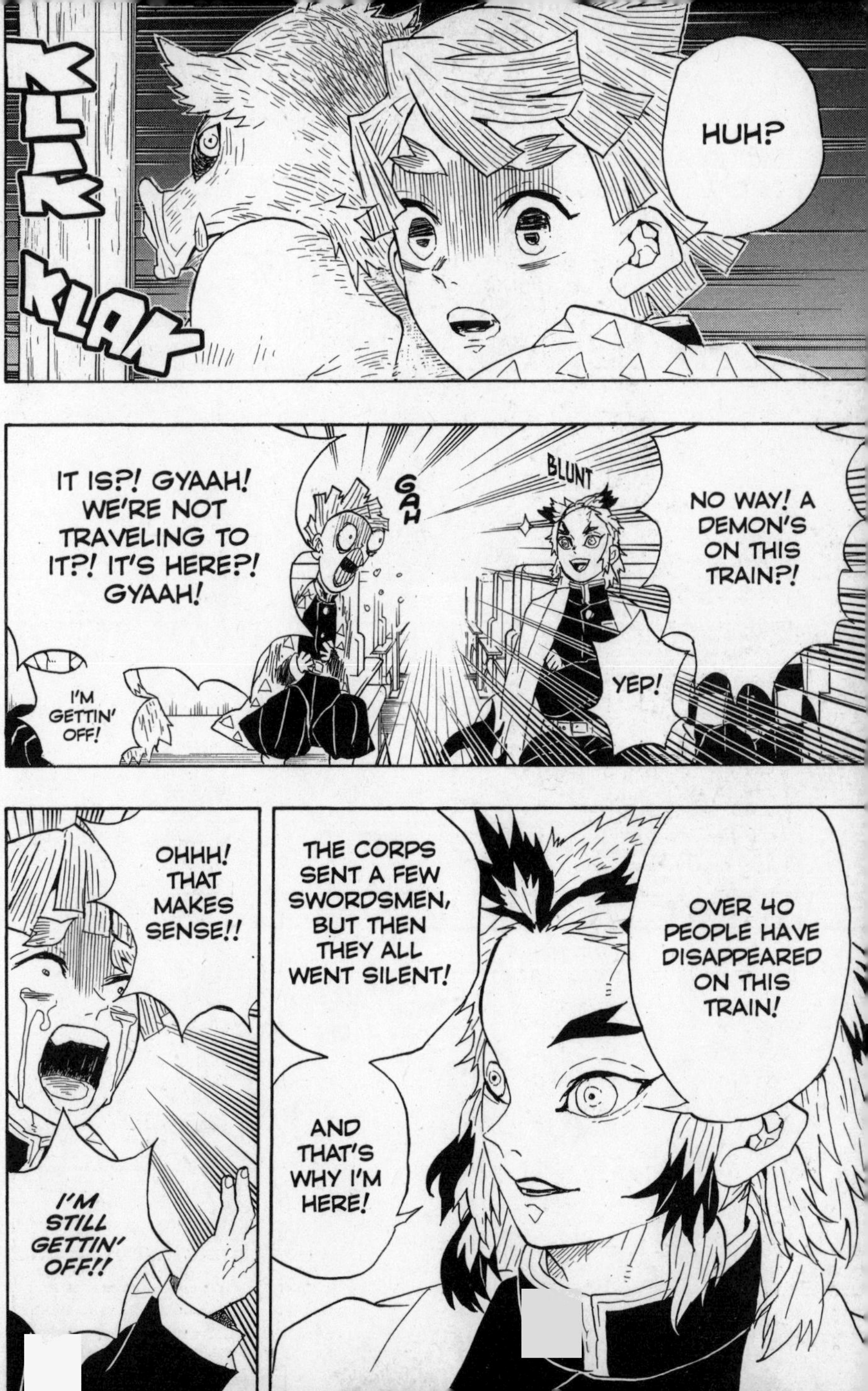
HUH?
KLIK
KLAK
NO WAY! A DEMON'S ON THIS TRAIN?!
YEP!
BLUNT
GAH
IT IS?! GYAAH! WE'RE NOT TRAVELING TO IT?! IT'S HERE?! GYAAH!
I'M GETTIN' OFF!
OVER 40 PEOPLE HAVE DISAPPEARED ON THIS TRAIN!
THE CORPS SENT A FEW SWORDSMEN, BUT THEN THEY ALL WENT SILENT!
AND THAT'S WHY I'M HERE!
OHHH! THAT MAKES SENSE!!
I'M STILL GETTIN' OFF!!

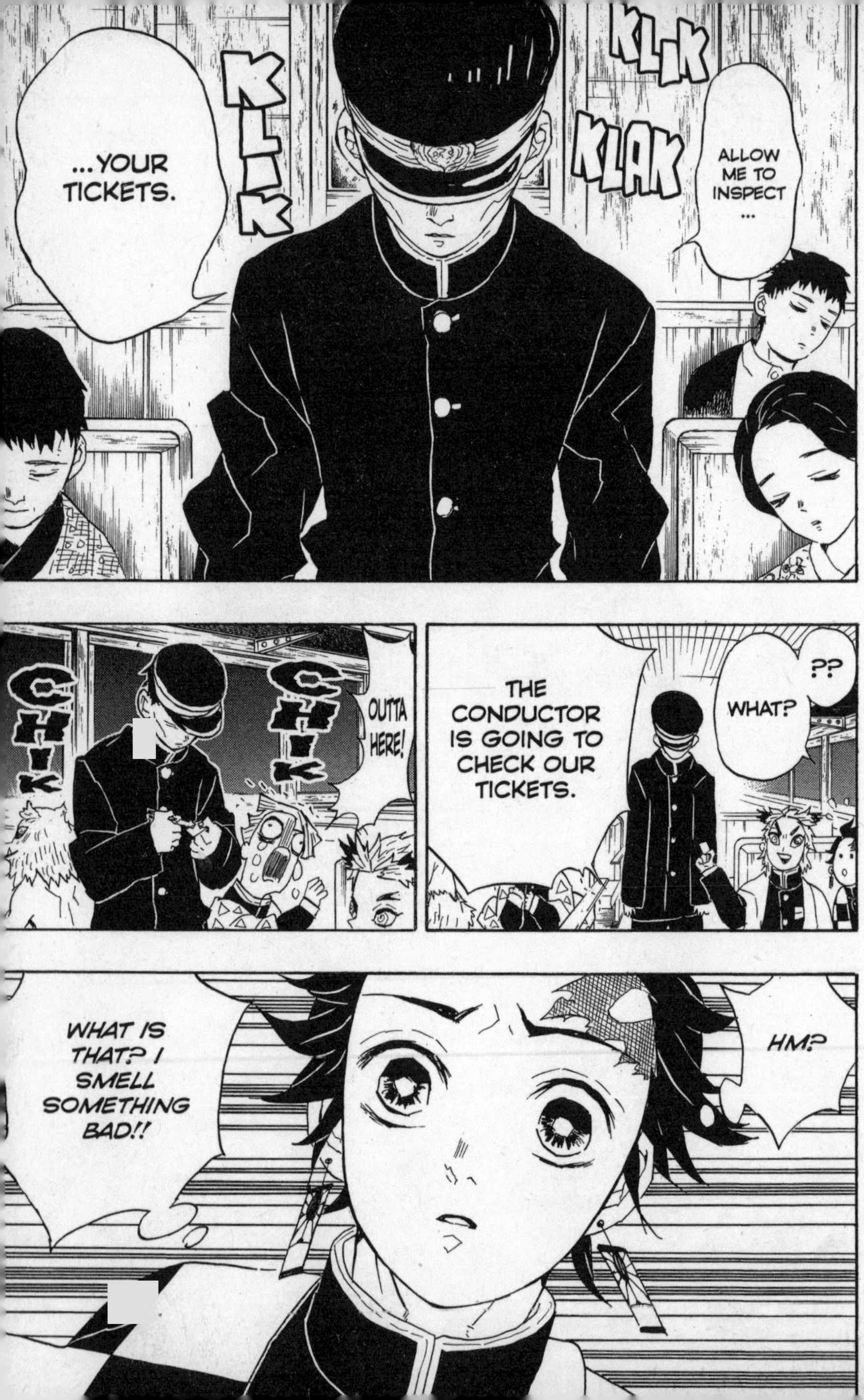
KLIK
ALLOW ME TO INSPECT ...
KLAK
KLIK
...YOUR TICKETS.
??
WHAT?
THE CONDUCTOR IS GOING TO CHECK OUR TICKETS.
OUTTA HERE!
CHIK
CHIK
HM?
WHAT IS THAT? I SMELL SOMETHING BAD!!

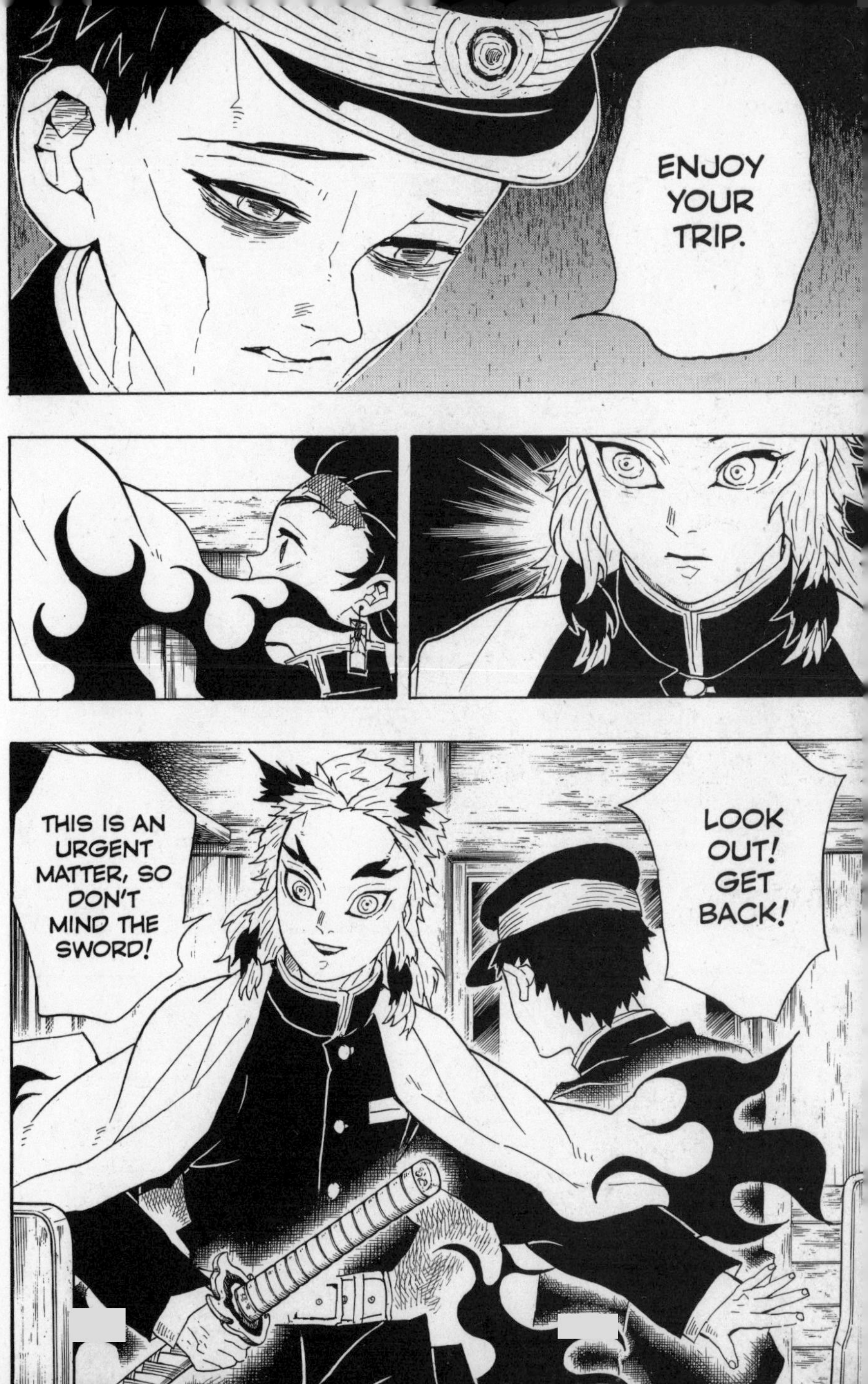
ENJOY YOUR TRIP.
LOOK OUT! GET BACK!
THIS IS AN URGENT MATTER, SO DON'T MIND THE SWORD!

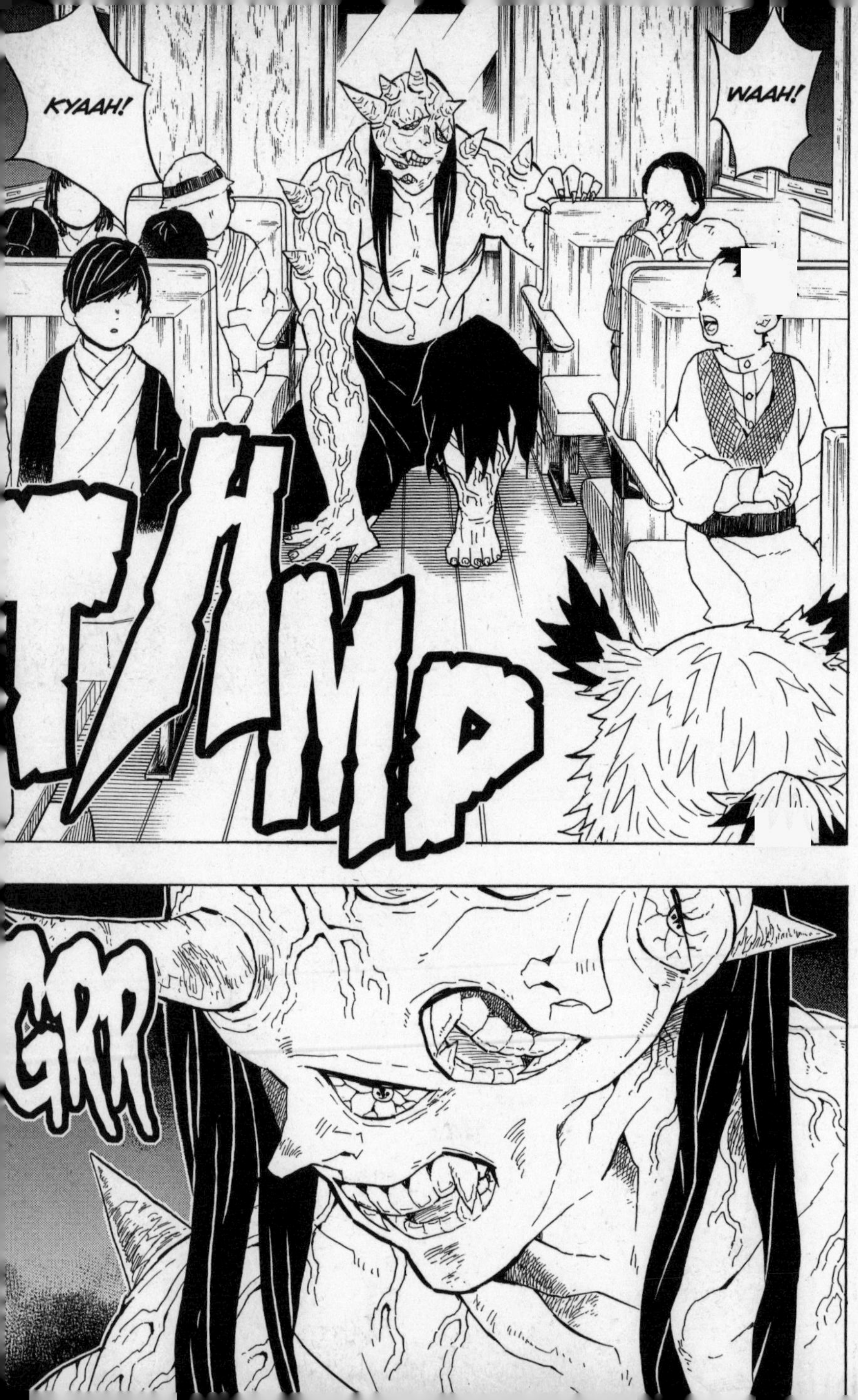
WAAH!
KYAAH!
GRR

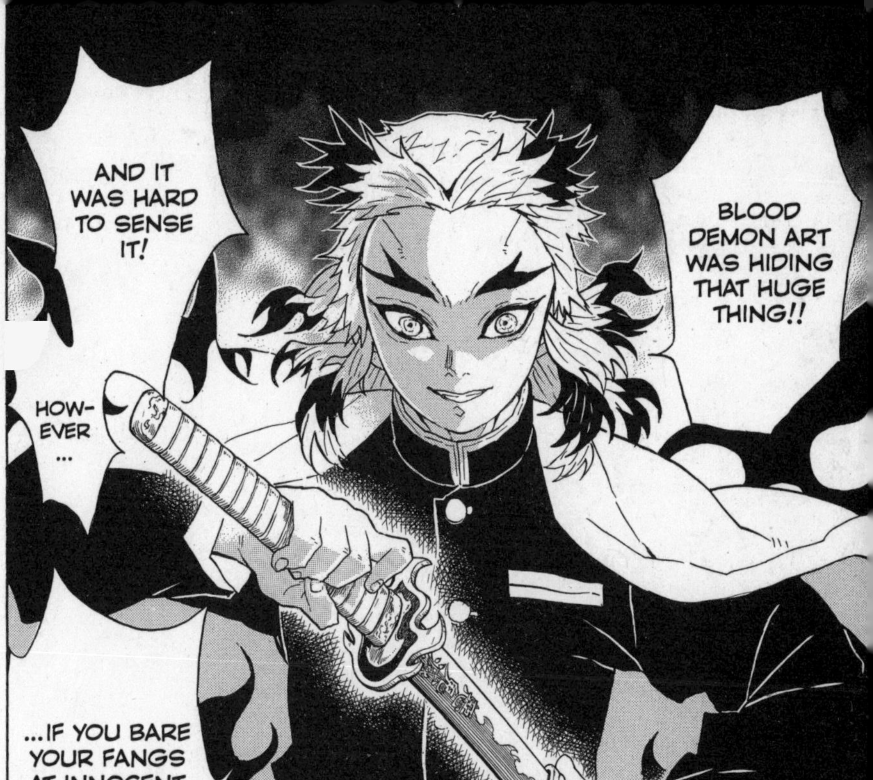
BLOOD DEMON ART WAS HIDING THAT HUGE THING!!
AND IT WAS HARD TO SENSE IT!
HOW-EVER ...
...IF YOU BARE YOUR FANGS AT INNOCENT PEOPLE...
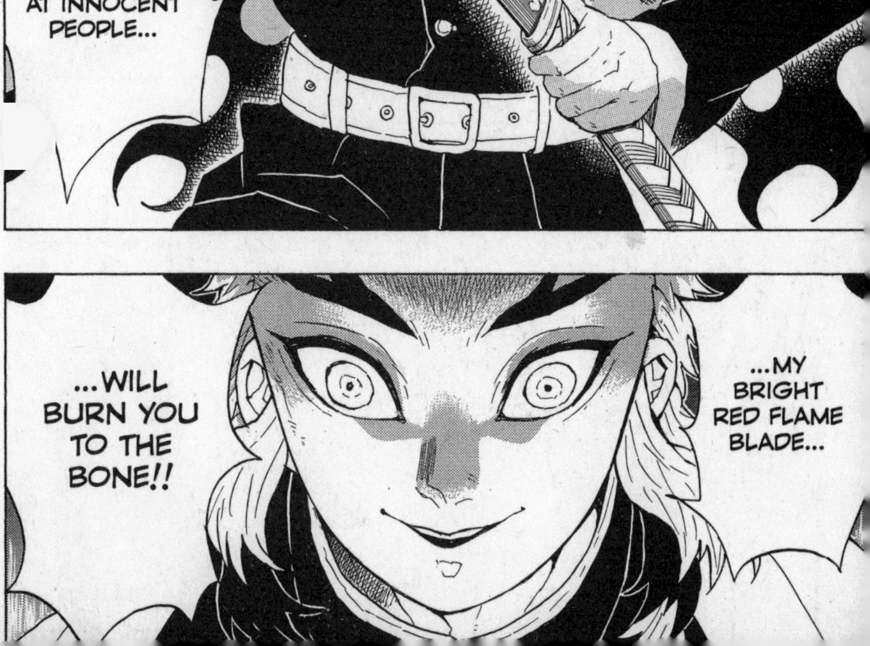
...MY BRIGHT RED FLAME BLADE...
...WILL BURN YOU TO THE BONE!!

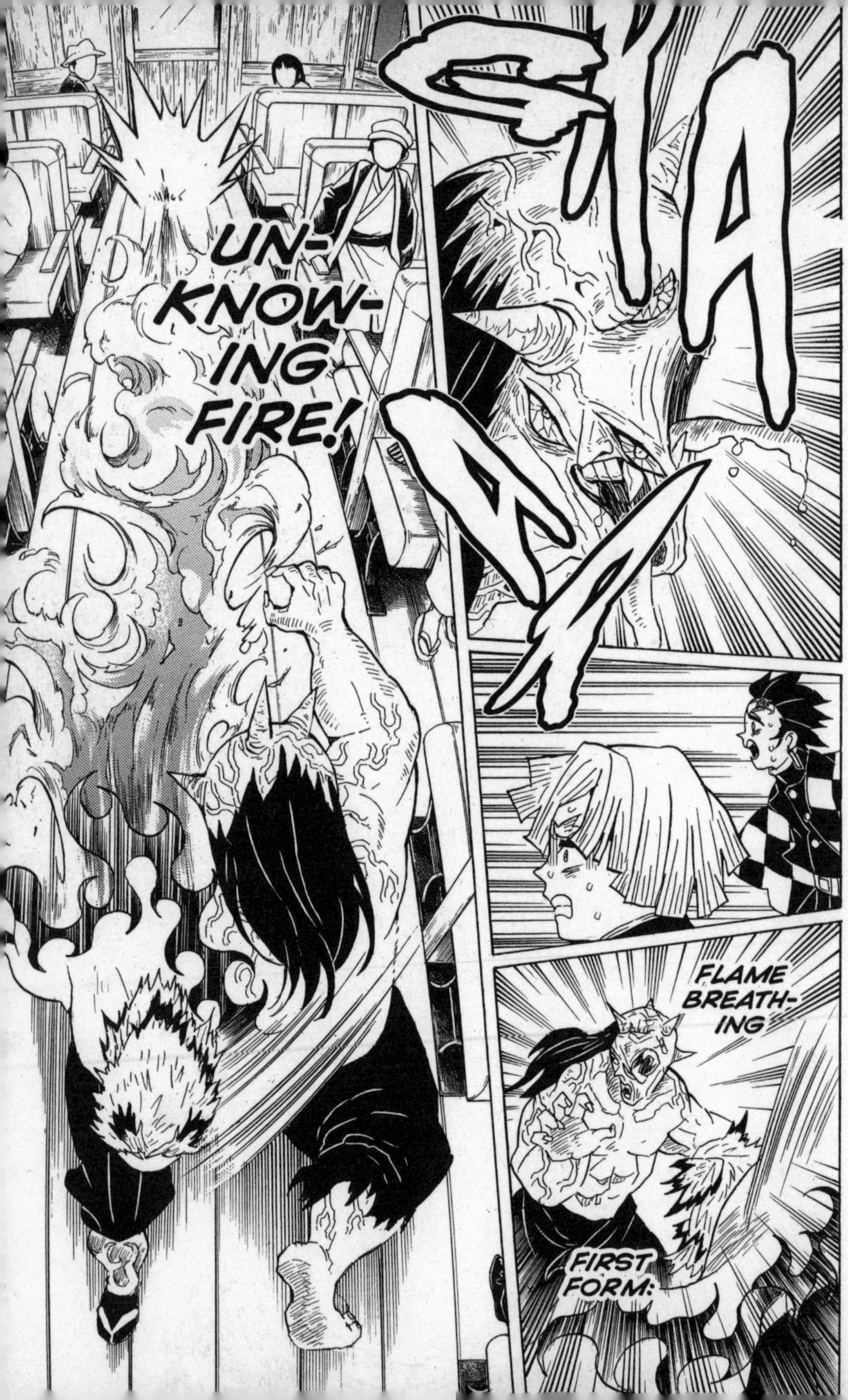
GYAA
FLAME BREATHING
FIRST FORM:
UNKNOWING FIRE!

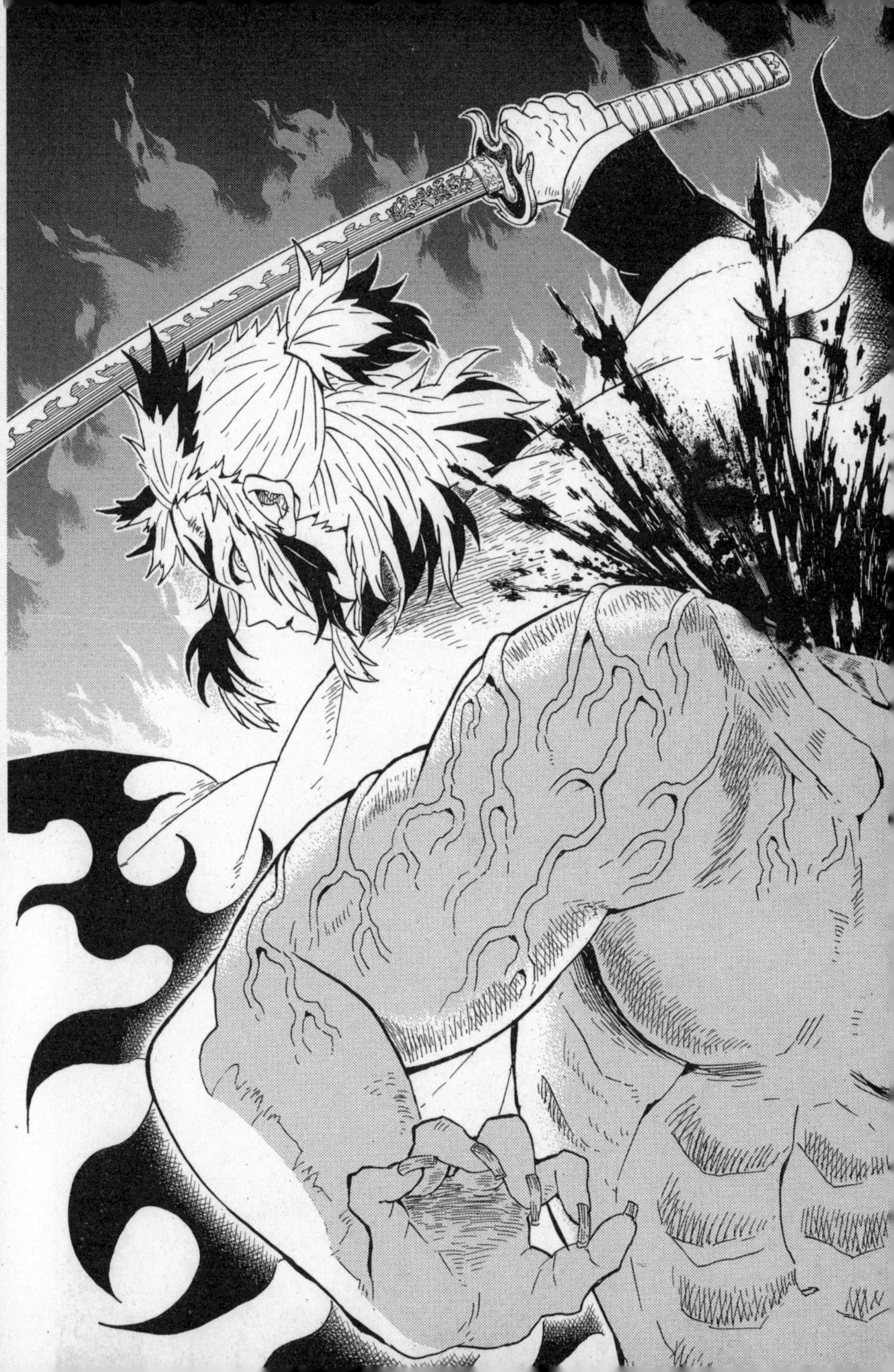

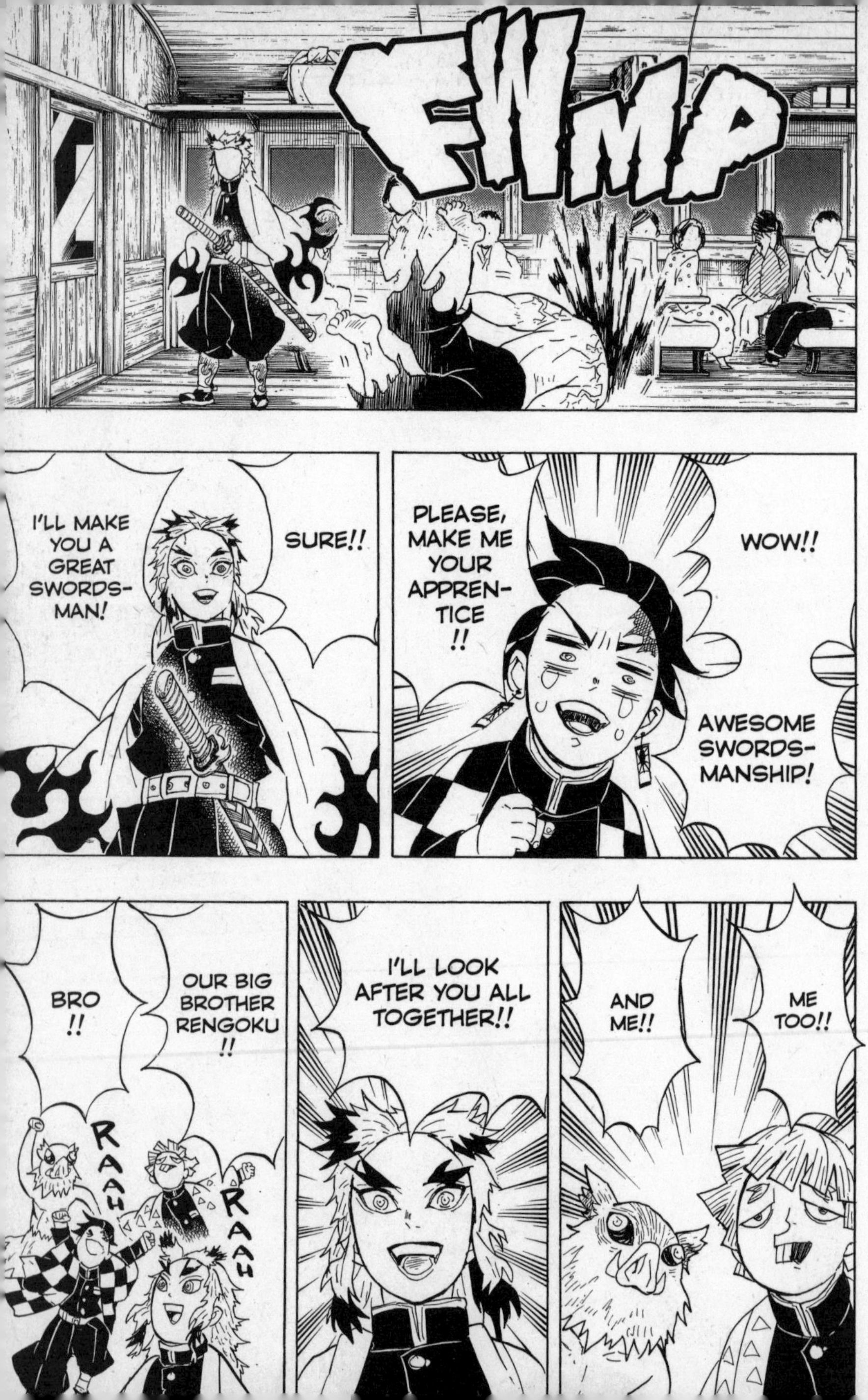
FWMP
WOW!!
AWESOME SWORDSMANSHIP!
PLEASE, MAKE ME YOUR APPRENTICE!!
SURE!!
I'LL MAKE YOU A GREAT SWORDSMAN!
ME TOO!!
AND ME!!
I'LL LOOK AFTER YOU ALL TOGETHER!!
OUR BIG BROTHER RENGOKU!!
BRO!!
RAAH
RAAH

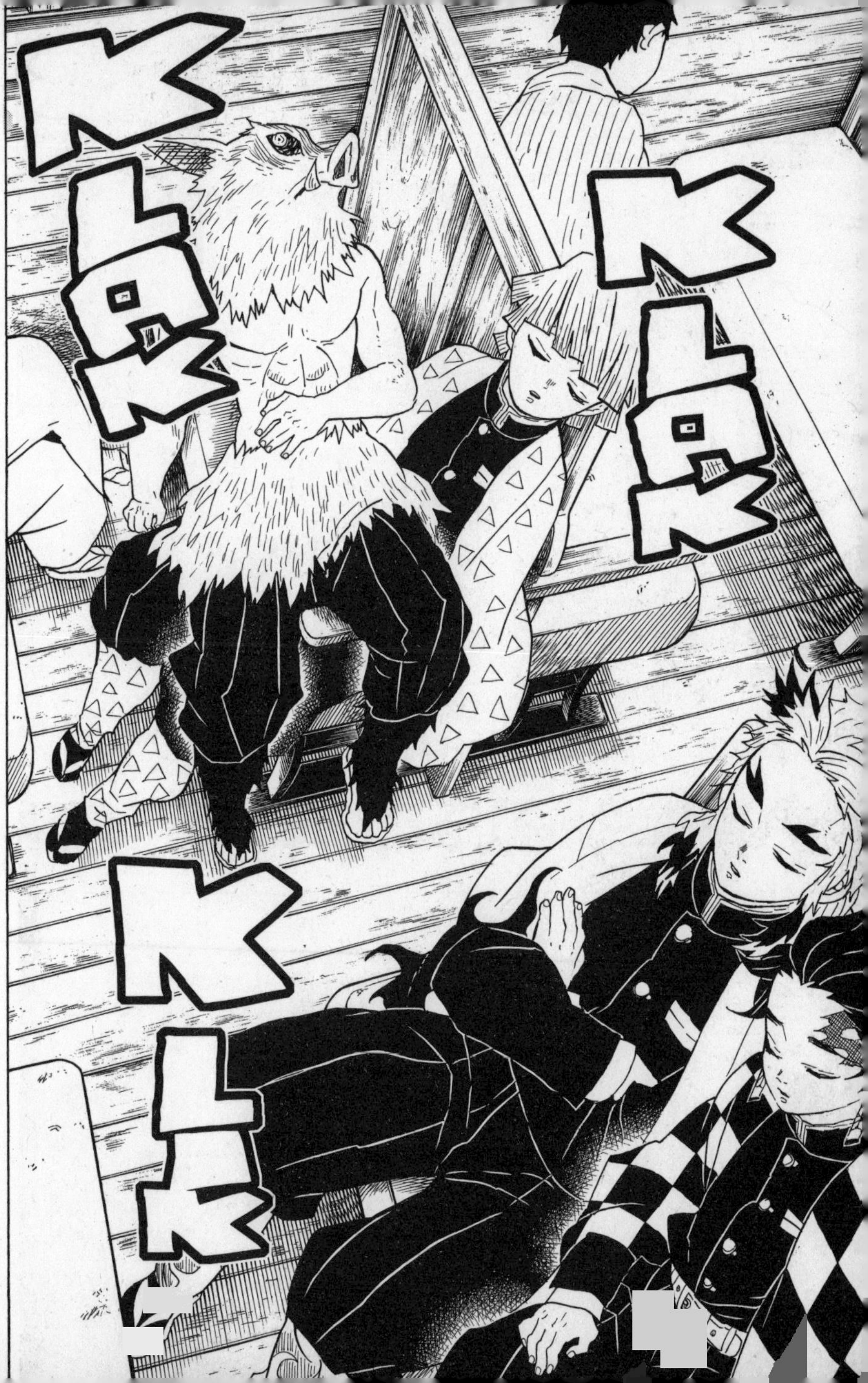
KLAK
KLAK

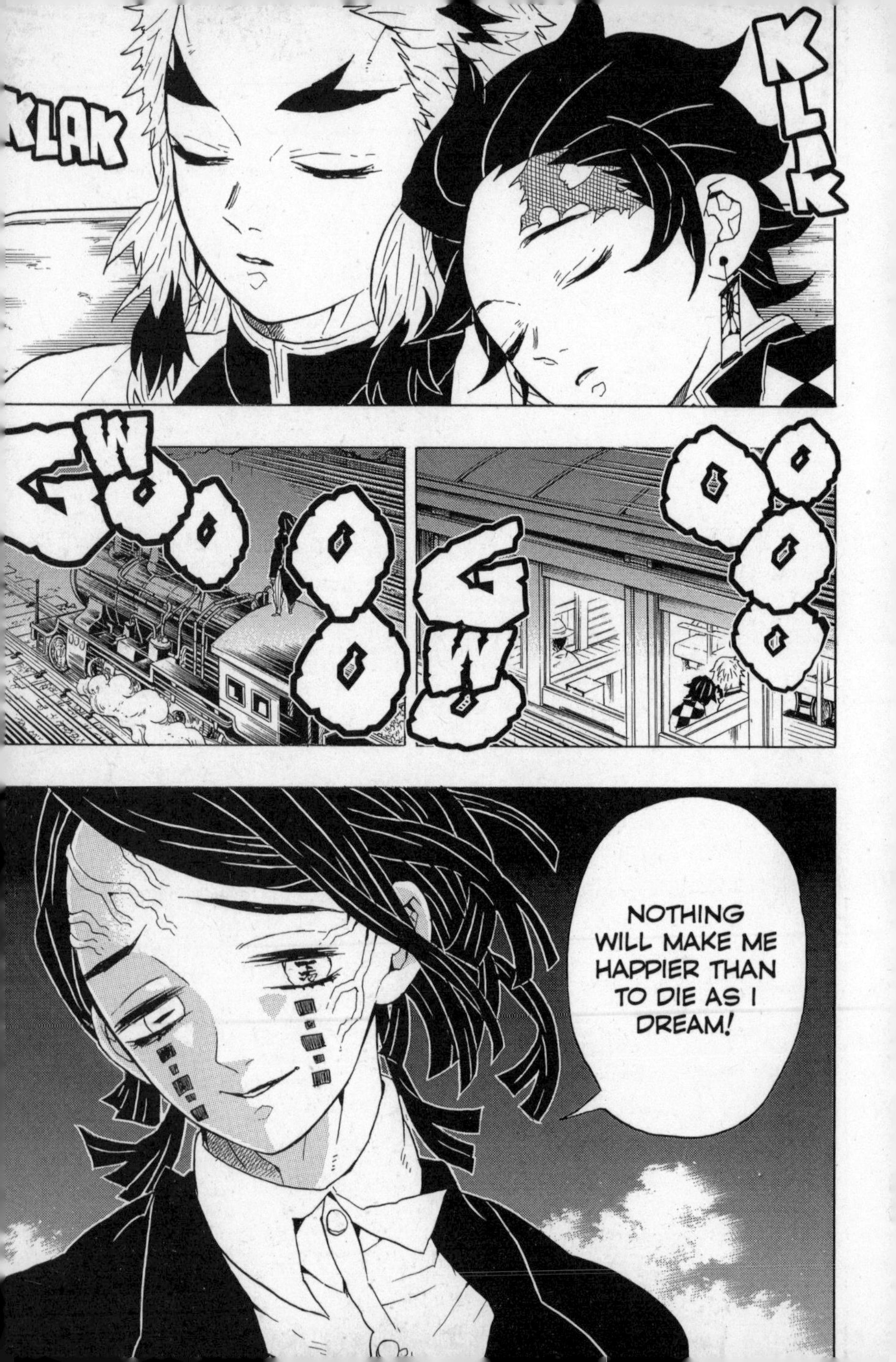
KLIK
KLAK
GWOOOO
GWOOOO
NOTHING WILL MAKE ME HAPPIER THAN TO DIE AS I DREAM!

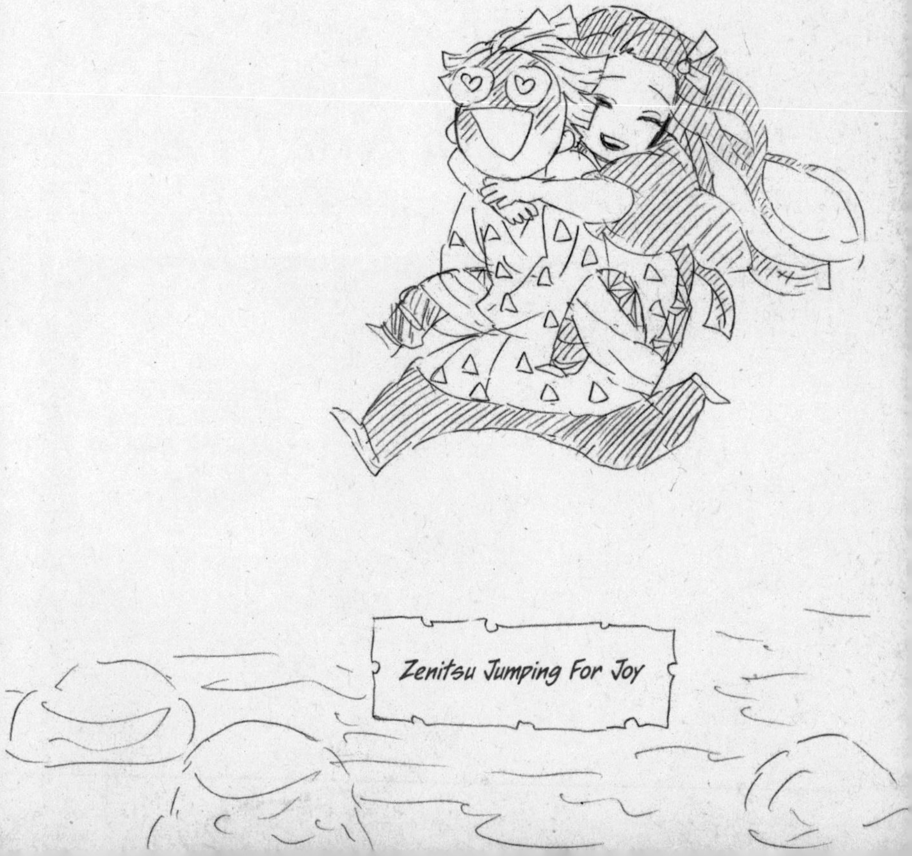

Zenitsu Jumping For Joy

CHAPTER 55: TRAIN OF INFINITE DREAMS

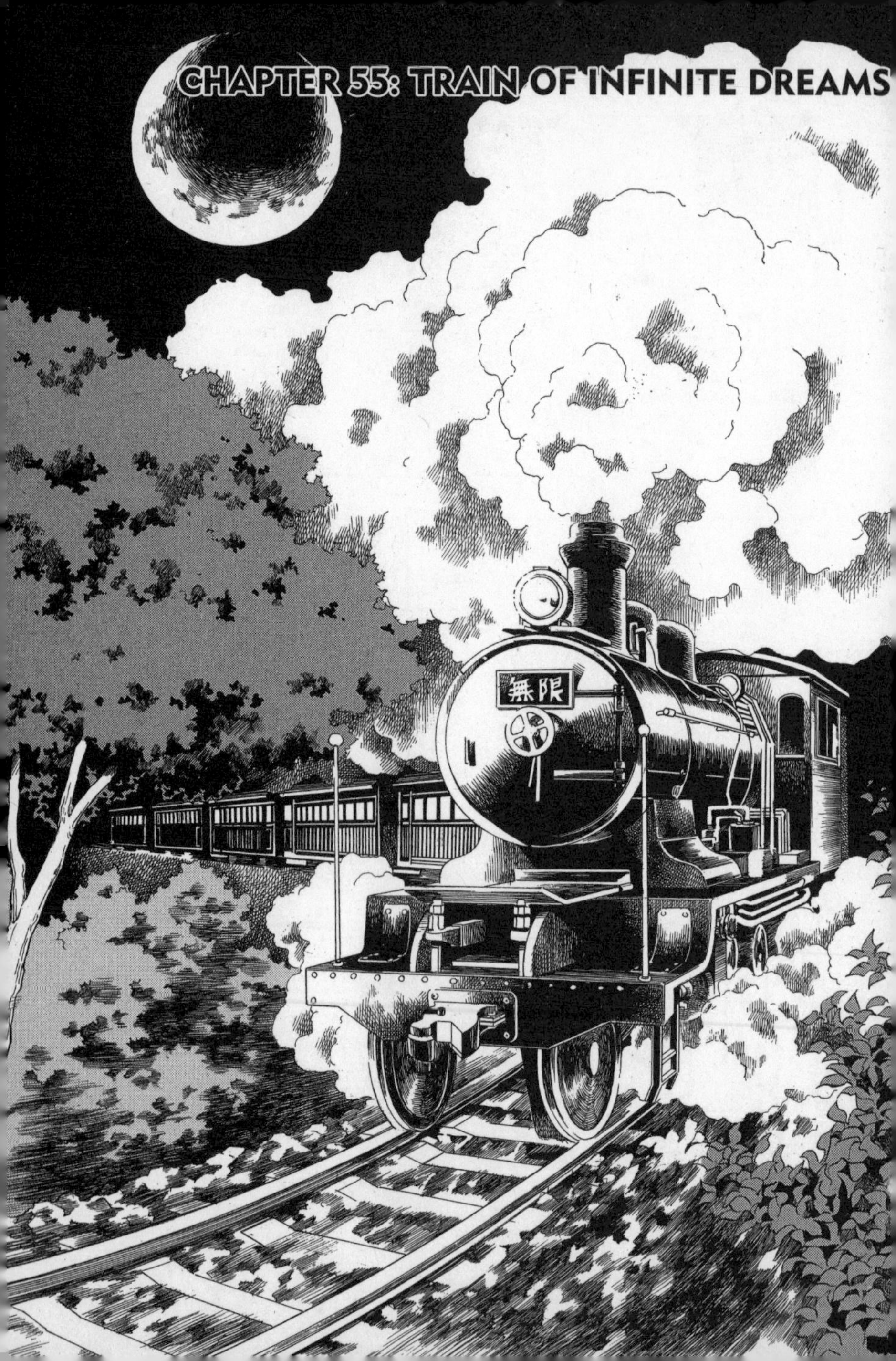
無限

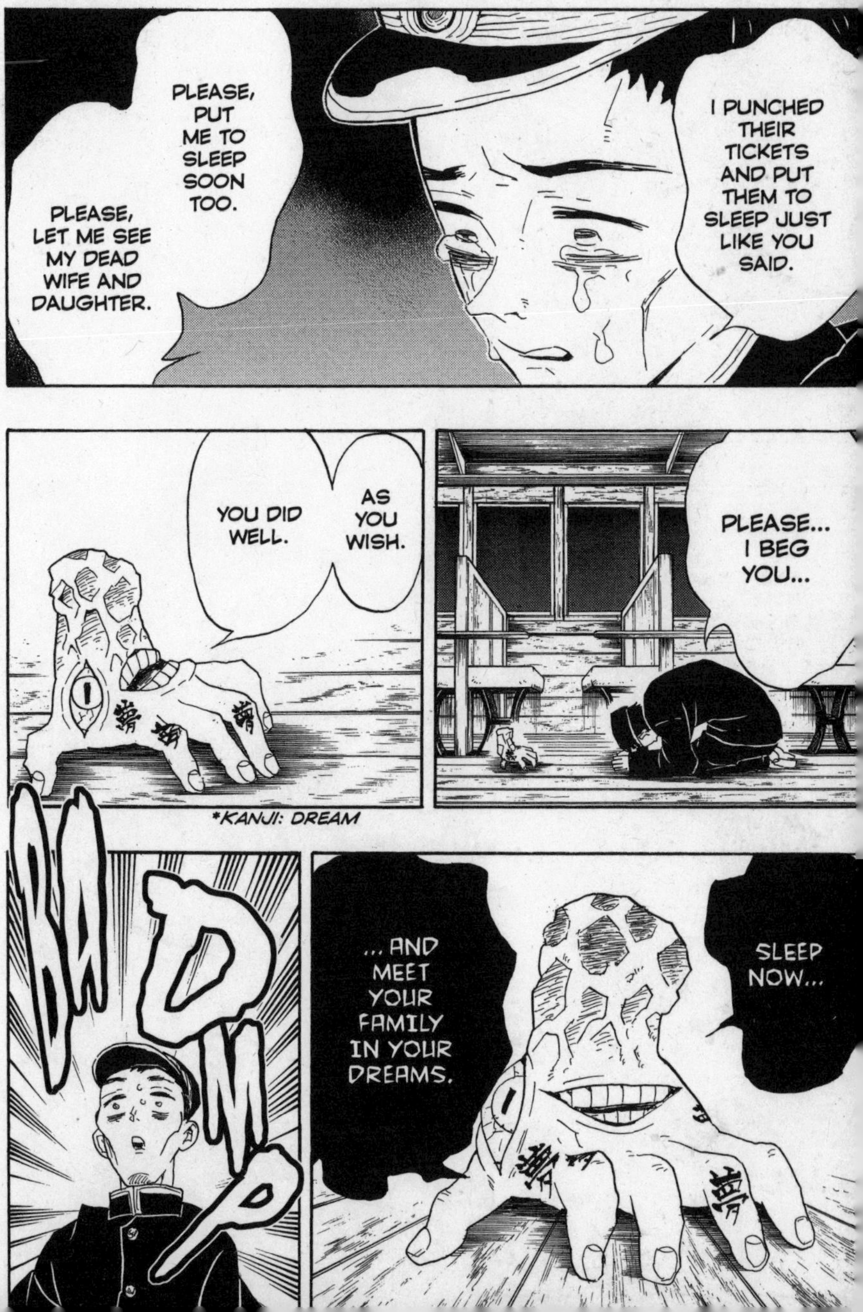
I PUNCHED THEIR TICKETS AND PUT THEM TO SLEEP JUST LIKE YOU SAID.
PLEASE, PUT ME TO SLEEP SOON TOO.
PLEASE, LET ME SEE MY DEAD WIFE AND DAUGHTER.
PLEASE... I BEG YOU...
AS YOU WISH.
YOU DID WELL.
*KANJI: DREAM
SLEEP NOW...
... AND MEET YOUR FAMILY IN YOUR DREAMS.
BA DUMP

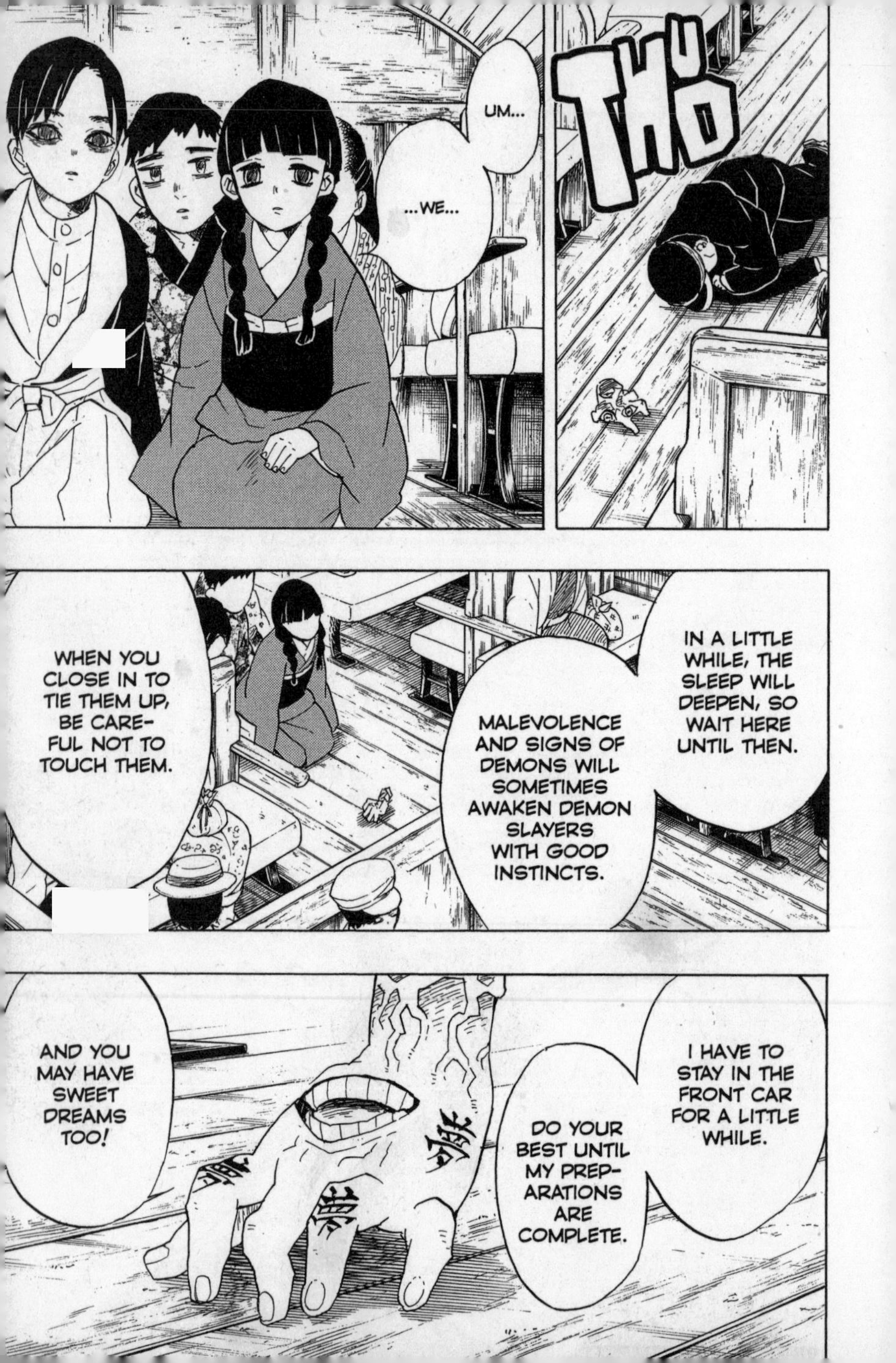
THUD
UM...
...WE...
IN A LITTLE WHILE, THE SLEEP WILL DEEPEN, SO WAIT HERE UNTIL THEN.
MALEVOLENCE AND SIGNS OF DEMONS WILL SOMETIMES AWAKEN DEMON SLAYERS WITH GOOD INSTINCTS.
WHEN YOU CLOSE IN TO TIE THEM UP, BE CARE-FUL NOT TO TOUCH THEM.
I HAVE TO STAY IN THE FRONT CAR FOR A LITTLE WHILE.
DO YOUR BEST UNTIL MY PREP-ARATIONS ARE COMPLETE.
AND YOU MAY HAVE SWEET DREAMS TOO!

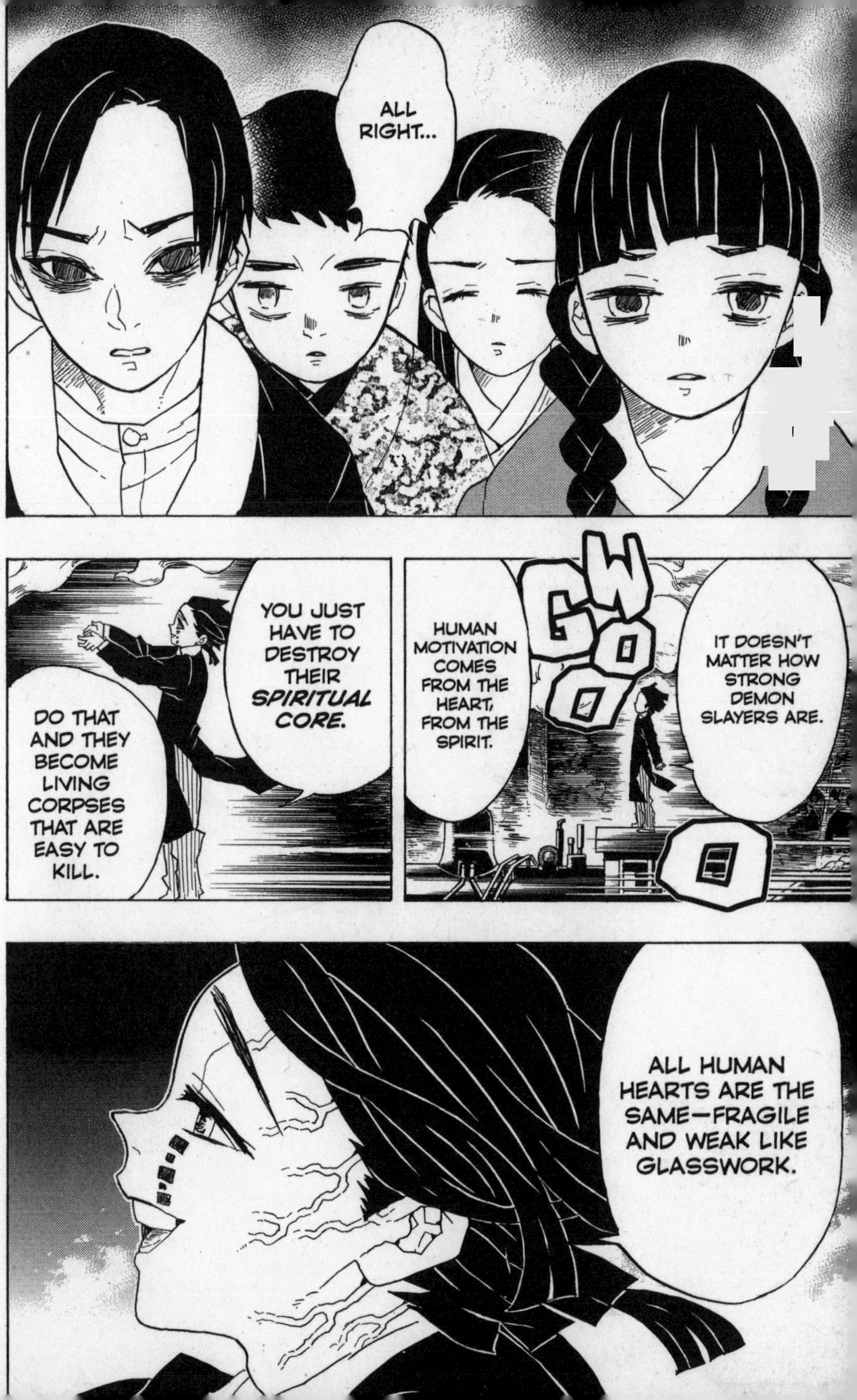
ALL RIGHT...
IT DOESN'T MATTER HOW STRONG DEMON SLAYERS ARE.
GWOOO
HUMAN MOTIVATION COMES FROM THE HEART, FROM THE SPIRIT.
YOU JUST HAVE TO DESTROY THEIR *SPIRITUAL CORE.*
DO THAT AND THEY BECOME LIVING CORPSES THAT ARE EASY TO KILL.
ALL HUMAN HEARTS ARE THE SAME—FRAGILE AND WEAK LIKE GLASSWORK.

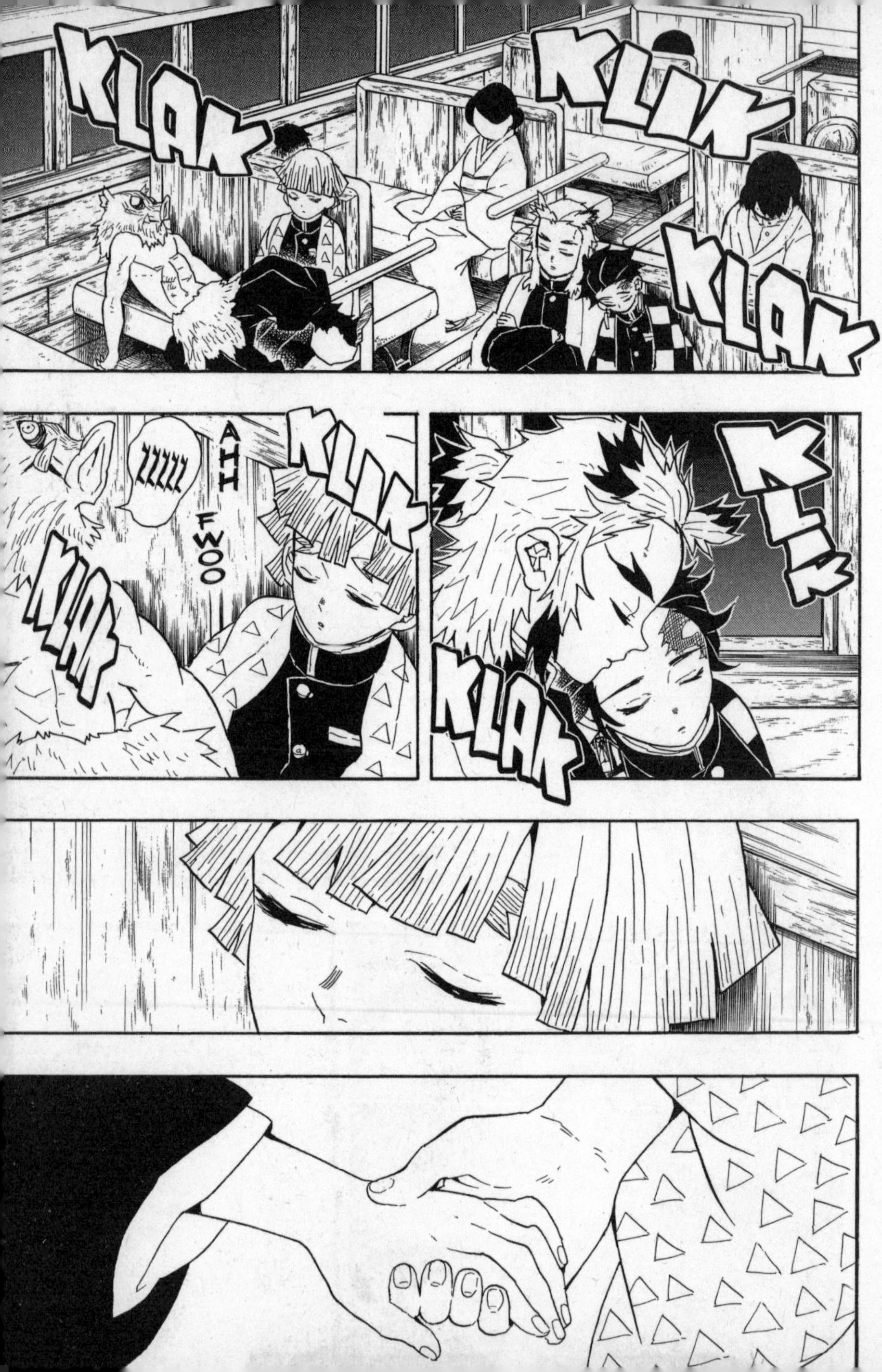
KLIK
KLAK
KLAK
KLIK
KLAK
KLIK
AHH
FWOO
ZZZZZ
KLAK

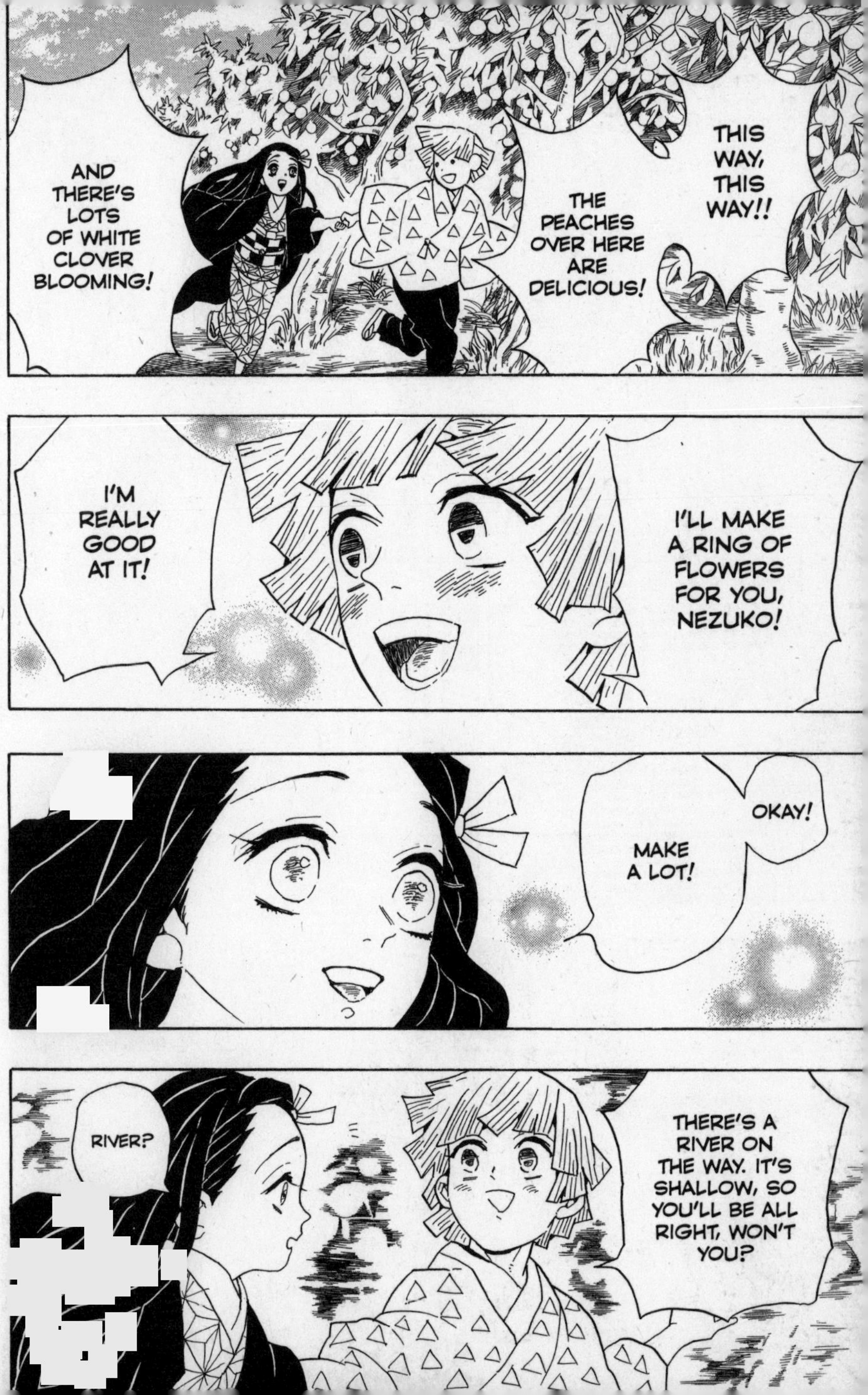
THIS WAY, THIS WAY!!
THE PEACHES OVER HERE ARE DELICIOUS!
AND THERE'S LOTS OF WHITE CLOVER BLOOMING!
I'LL MAKE A RING OF FLOWERS FOR YOU, NEZUKO!
I'M REALLY GOOD AT IT!
OKAY!
MAKE A LOT!
THERE'S A RIVER ON THE WAY. IT'S SHALLOW, SO YOU'LL BE ALL RIGHT, WON'T YOU?
RIVER?

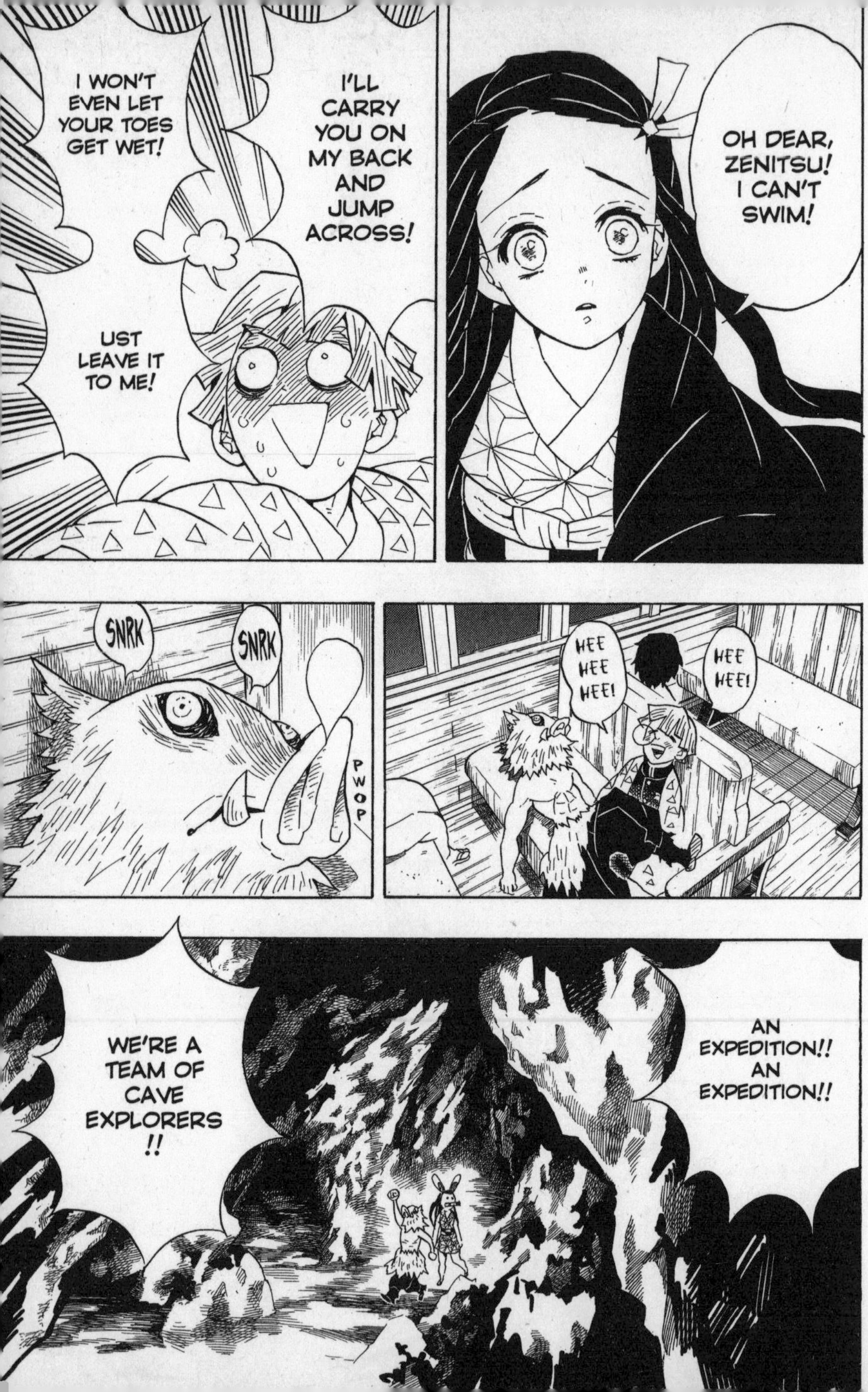
OH DEAR, ZENITSU! I CAN'T SWIM!
I'LL CARRY YOU ON MY BACK AND JUMP ACROSS!
I WON'T EVEN LET YOUR TOES GET WET!
UST LEAVE IT TO ME!
HEE HEE!
HEE HEE HEE!
SNRK
SNRK
PWOP
AN EXPEDITION!! AN EXPEDITION!!
WE'RE A TEAM OF CAVE EXPLORERS!!

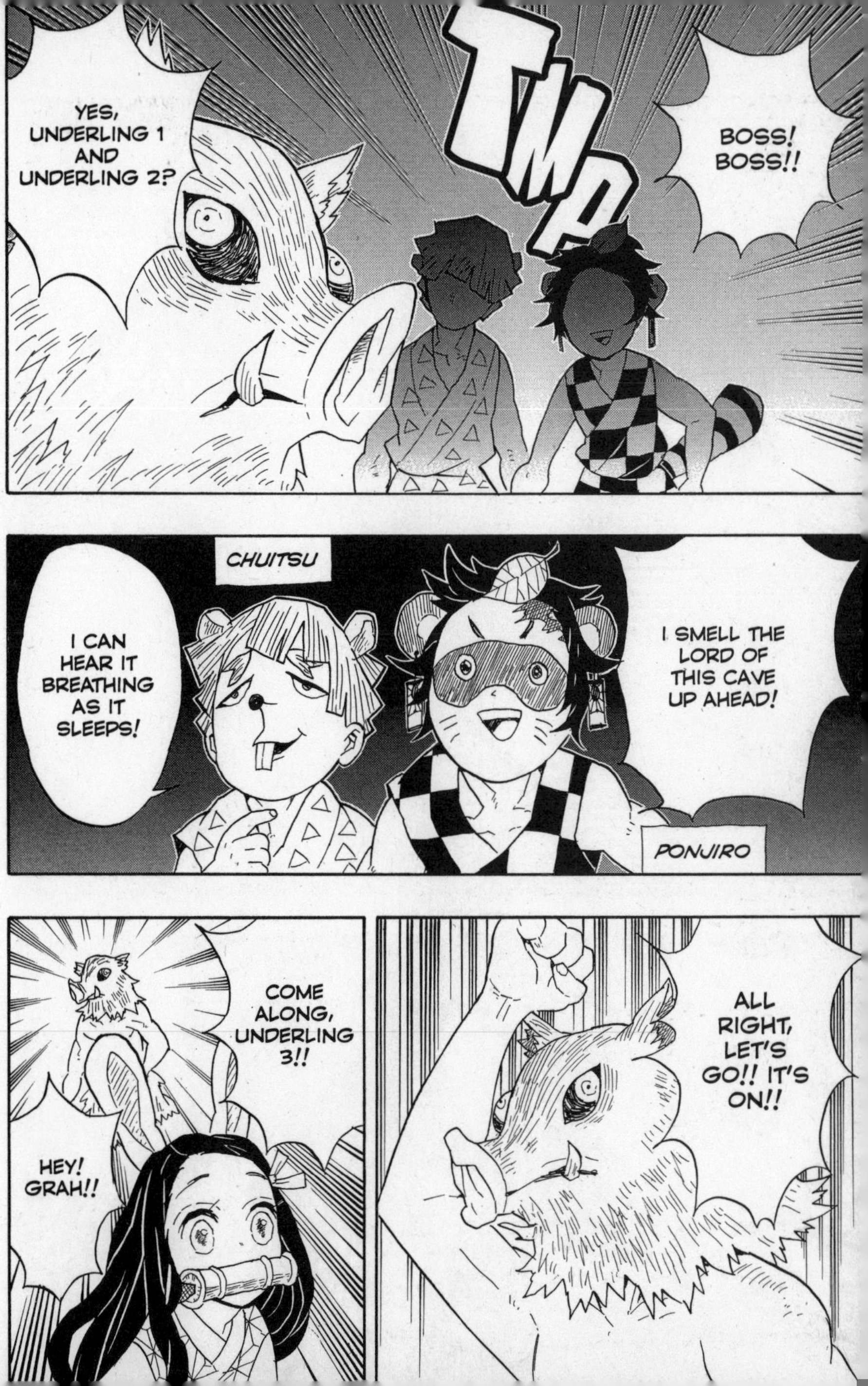
BOSS! BOSS!!
TMP
YES, UNDERLING 1 AND UNDERLING 2?
I SMELL THE LORD OF THIS CAVE UP AHEAD!
PONJIRO
CHUITSU
I CAN HEAR IT BREATHING AS IT SLEEPS!
ALL RIGHT, LET'S GO!! IT'S ON!!
COME ALONG, UNDERLING 3!!
HEY! GRAH!!

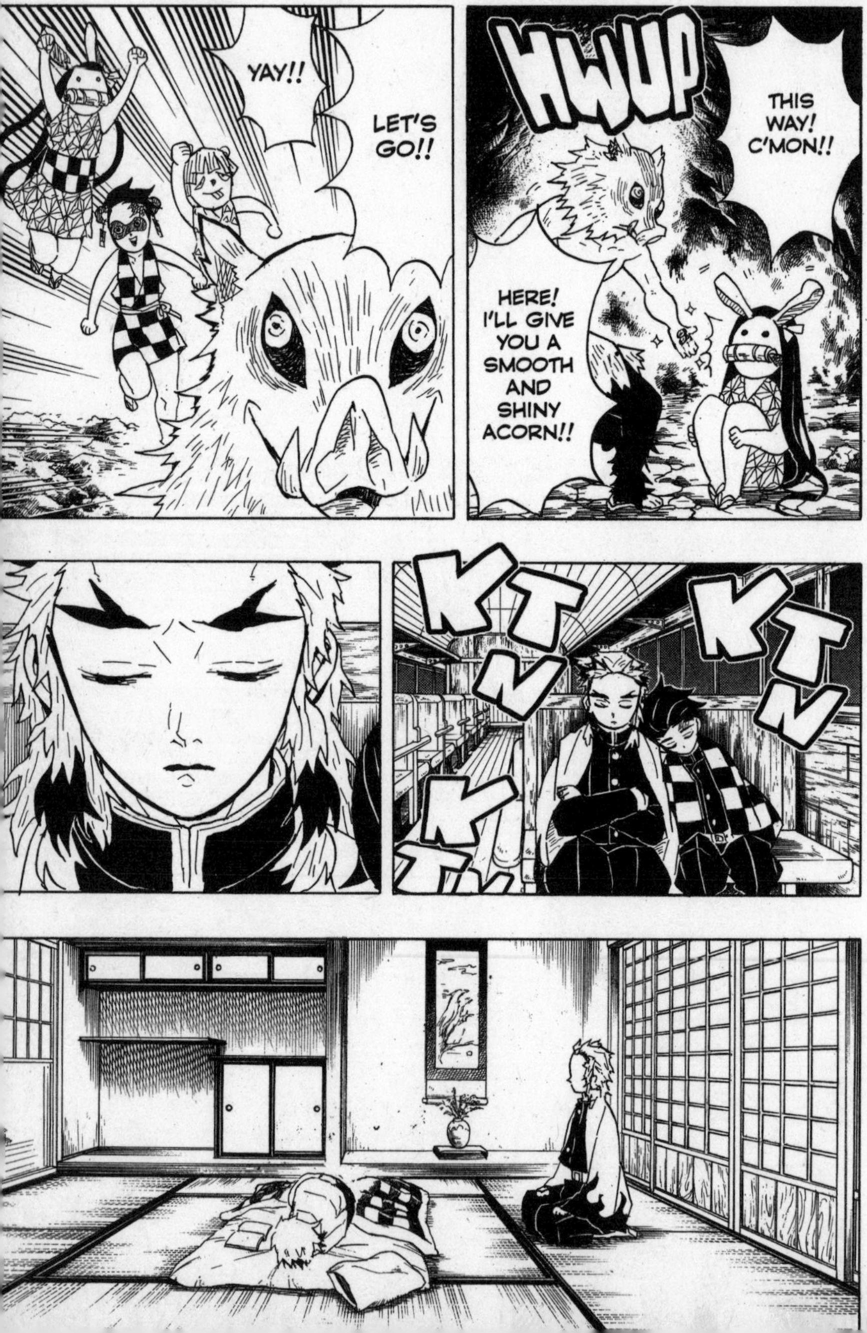
THIS WAY! C'MON!!
HWUP
HERE! I'LL GIVE YOU A SMOOTH AND SHINY ACORN!!
YAY!!
LET'S GO!!
KTN
KTN
KTN

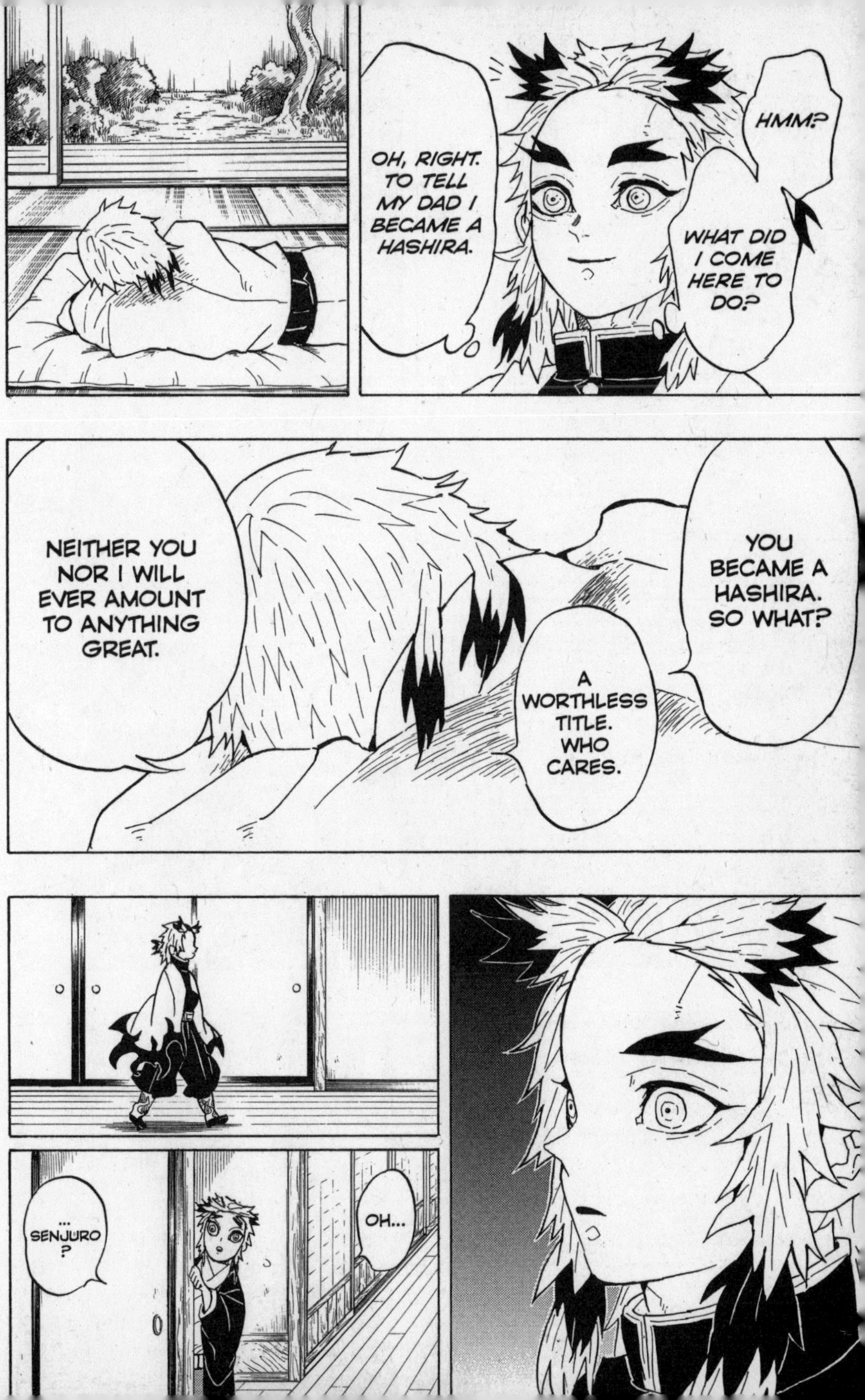
HMM?
WHAT DID I COME HERE TO DO?
OH, RIGHT. TO TELL MY DAD I BECAME A HASHIRA.
YOU BECAME A HASHIRA. SO WHAT?
A WORTHLESS TITLE. WHO CARES.
NEITHER YOU NOR I WILL EVER AMOUNT TO ANYTHING GREAT.
OH...
...SENJURO?

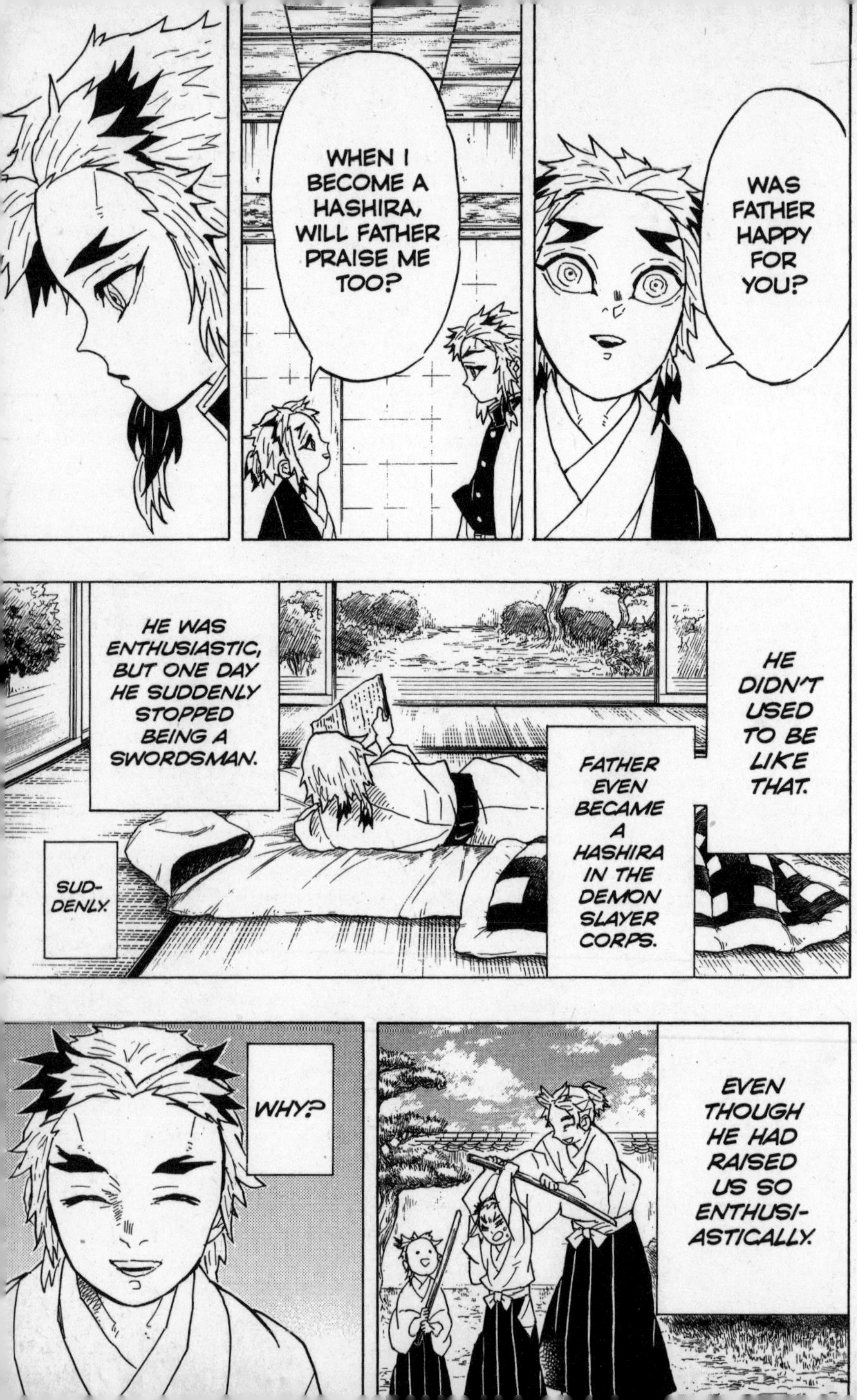
WAS FATHER HAPPY FOR YOU?
WHEN I BECOME A HASHIRA, WILL FATHER PRAISE ME TOO?
HE DIDN'T USED TO BE LIKE THAT.
FATHER EVEN BECAME A HASHIRA IN THE DEMON SLAYER CORPS.
HE WAS ENTHUSIASTIC, BUT ONE DAY HE SUDDENLY STOPPED BEING A SWORDSMAN.
SUD-DENLY.
EVEN THOUGH HE HAD RAISED US SO ENTHUSI-ASTICALLY.
WHY?

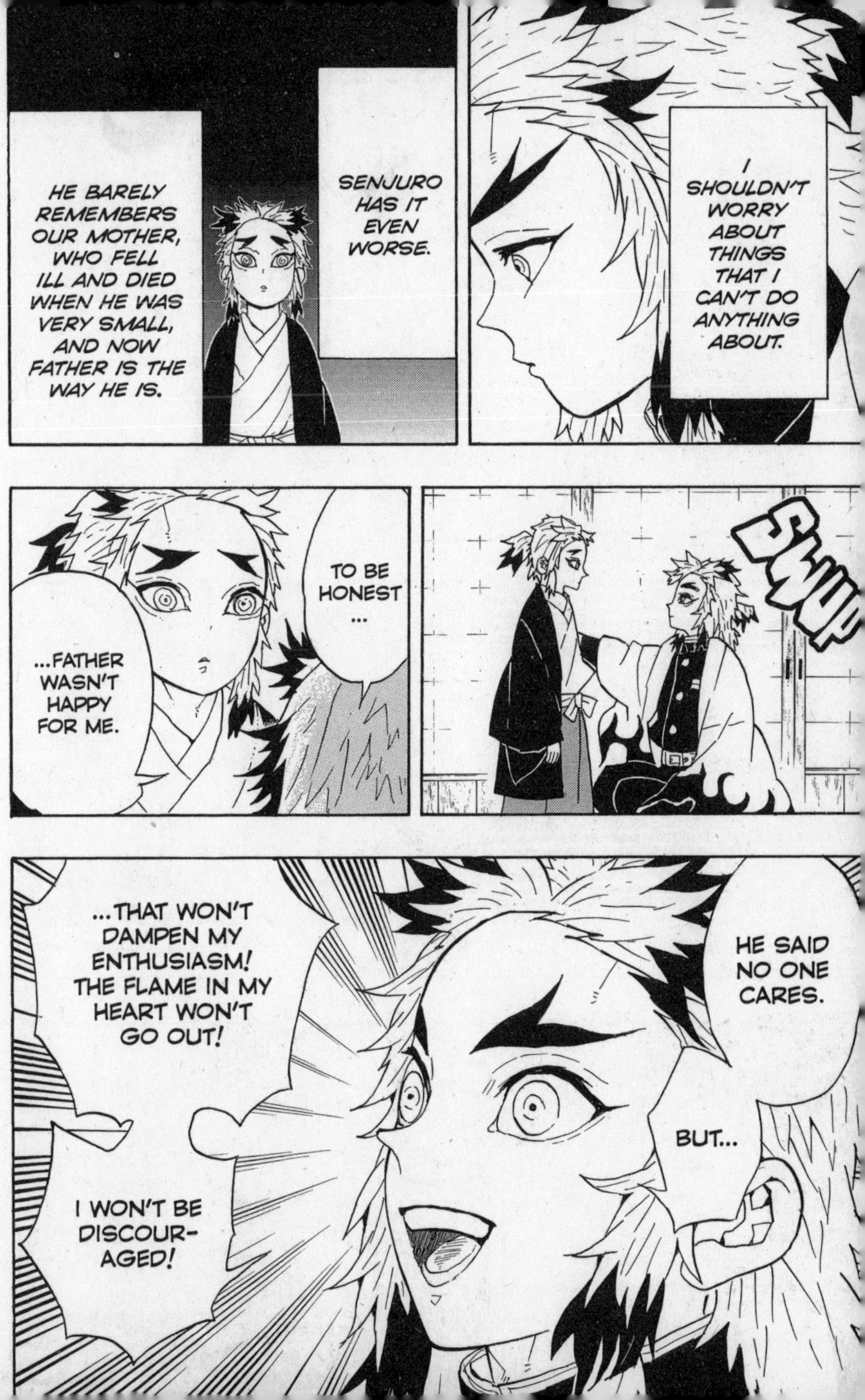
I SHOULDN'T WORRY ABOUT THINGS THAT I CAN'T DO ANYTHING ABOUT.
SENJURO HAS IT EVEN WORSE.
HE BARELY REMEMBERS OUR MOTHER, WHO FELL ILL AND DIED WHEN HE WAS VERY SMALL, AND NOW FATHER IS THE WAY HE IS.
SWUP
TO BE HONEST...
...FATHER WASN'T HAPPY FOR ME.
HE SAID NO ONE CARES.
BUT...
...THAT WON'T DAMPEN MY ENTHUSIASM! THE FLAME IN MY HEART WON'T GO OUT!
I WON'T BE DISCOUR-AGED!

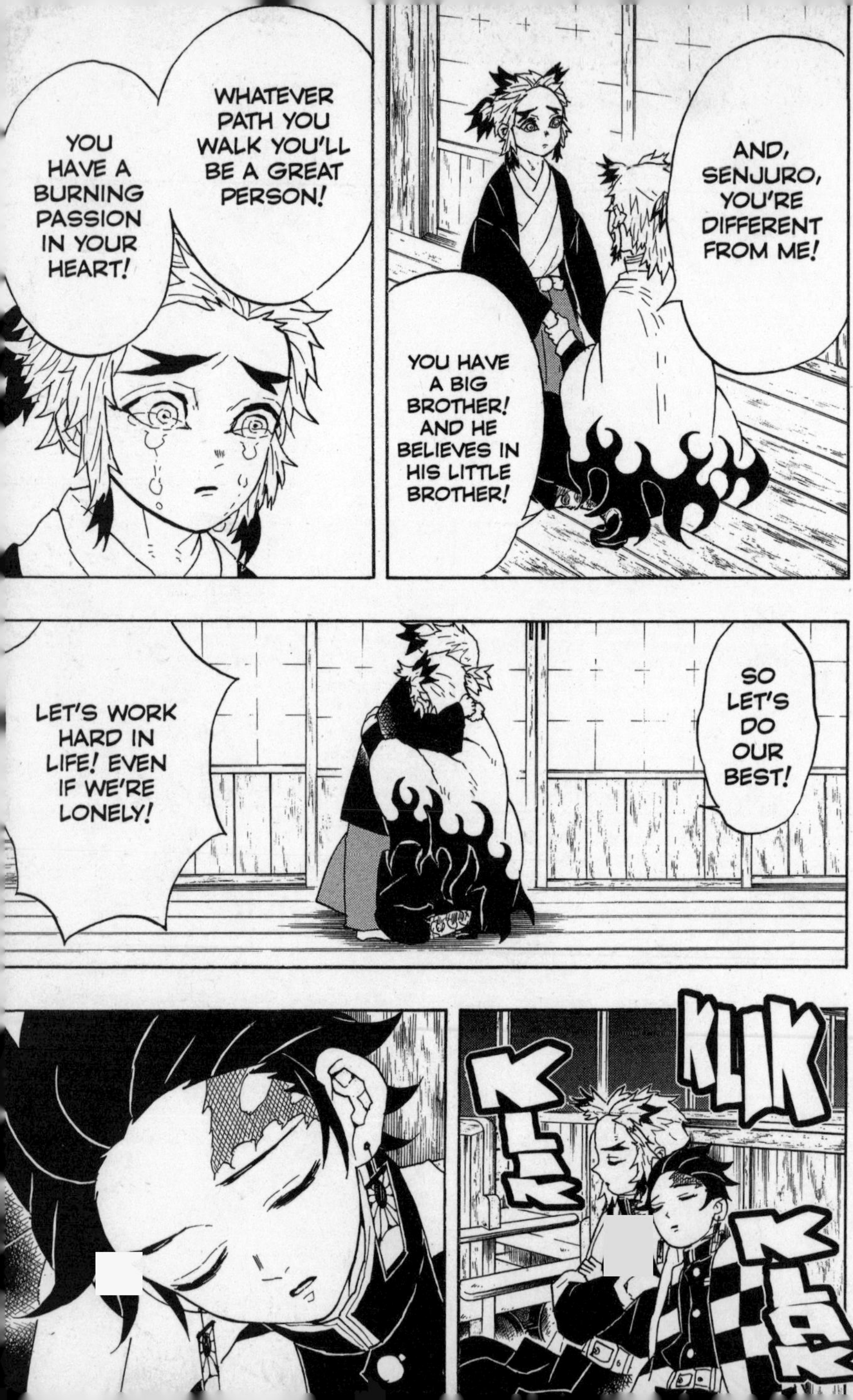
AND, SENJURO, YOU'RE DIFFERENT FROM ME!
YOU HAVE A BIG BROTHER! AND HE BELIEVES IN HIS LITTLE BROTHER!
WHATEVER PATH YOU WALK YOU'LL BE A GREAT PERSON!
YOU HAVE A BURNING PASSION IN YOUR HEART!
SO LET'S DO OUR BEST!
LET'S WORK HARD IN LIFE! EVEN IF WE'RE LONELY!
KLIK

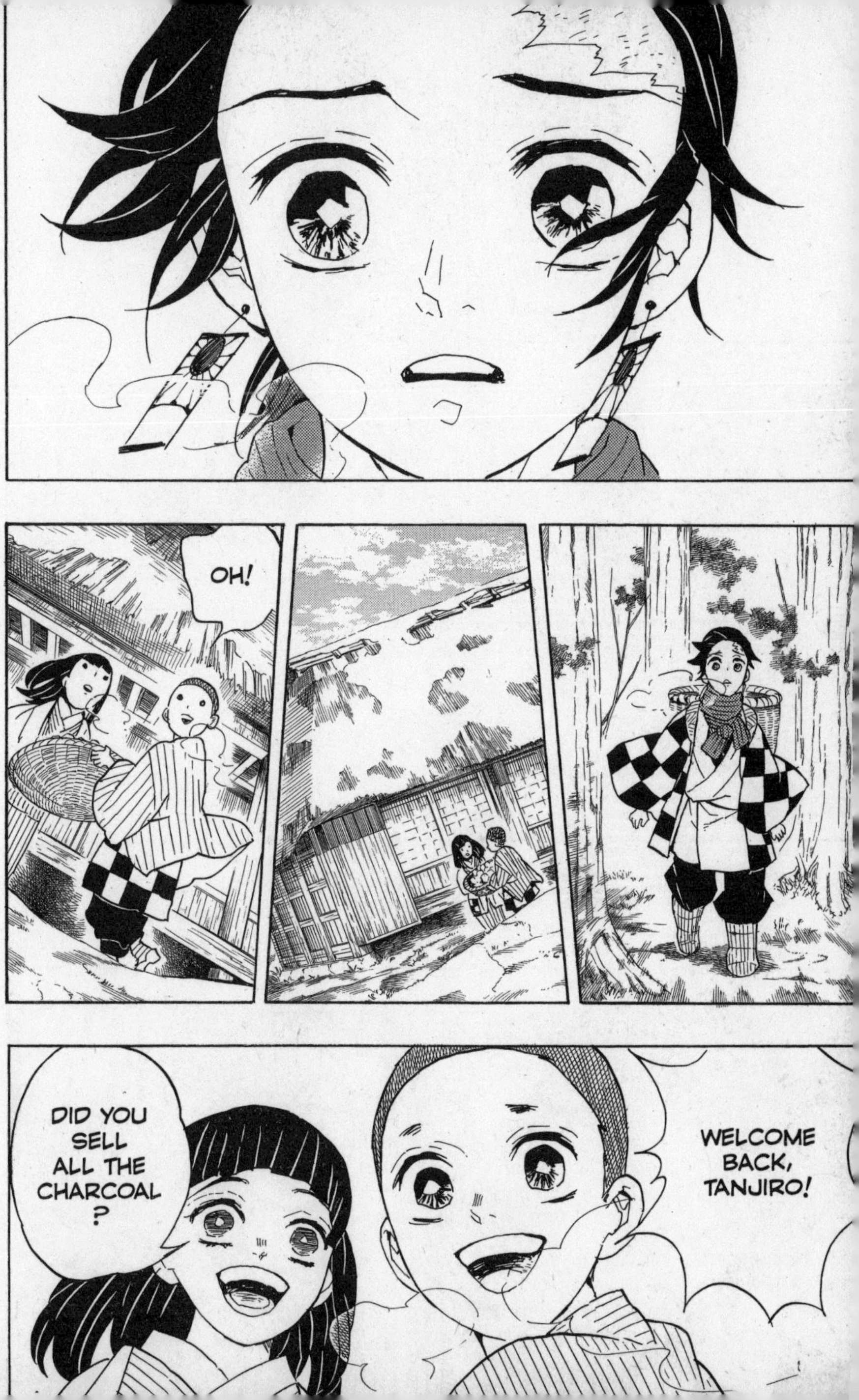
OH!
WELCOME BACK, TANJIRO!
DID YOU SELL ALL THE CHARCOAL?

? ? I'M SORRY!

SORRY!

I'M SO SORRY !!

WAAH!

AAHHH !!

WAAAAAH!

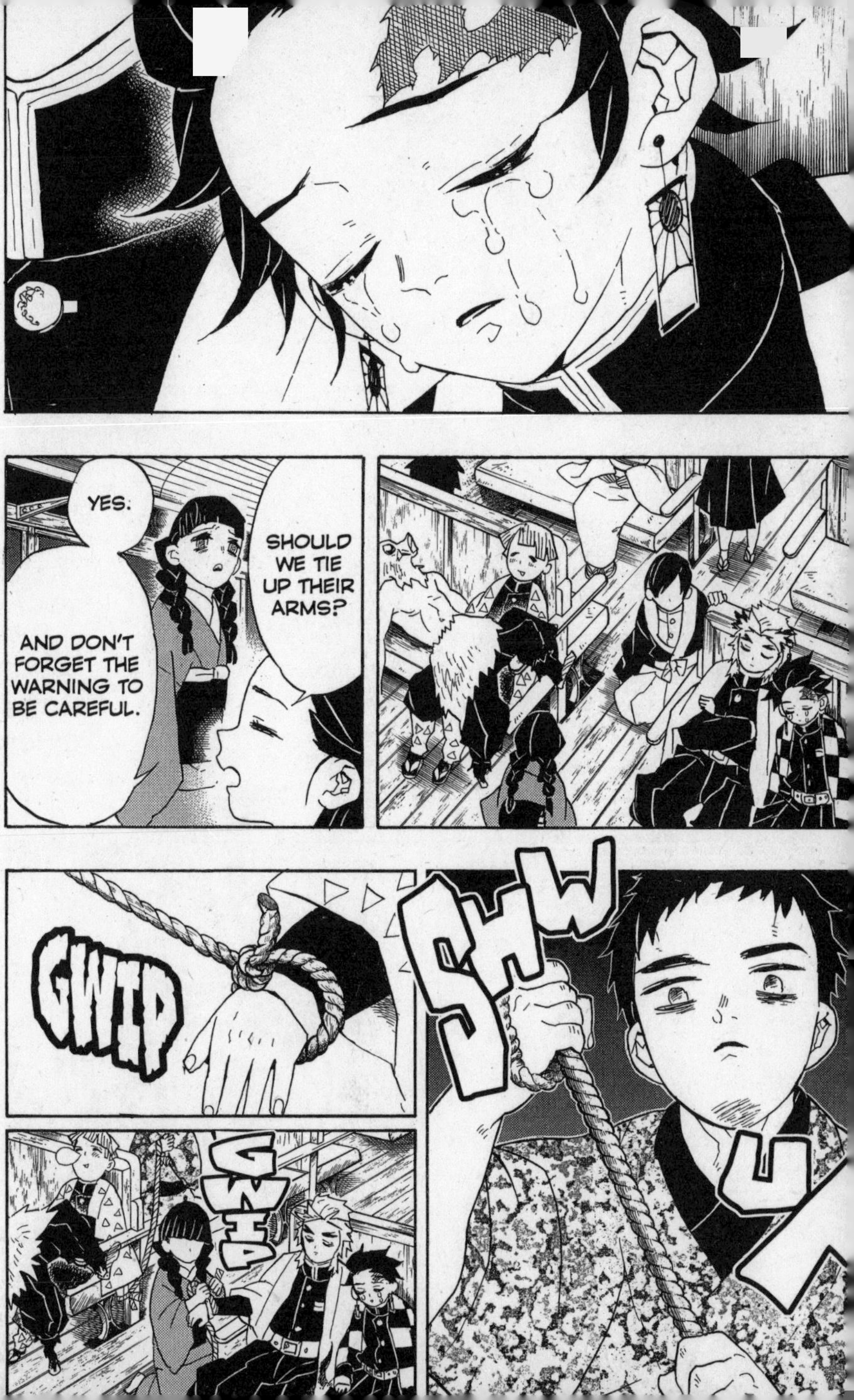
SHOULD WE TIE UP THEIR ARMS?
YES.
AND DON'T FORGET THE WARNING TO BE CAREFUL.
SHW
U
GWIP
GWIP

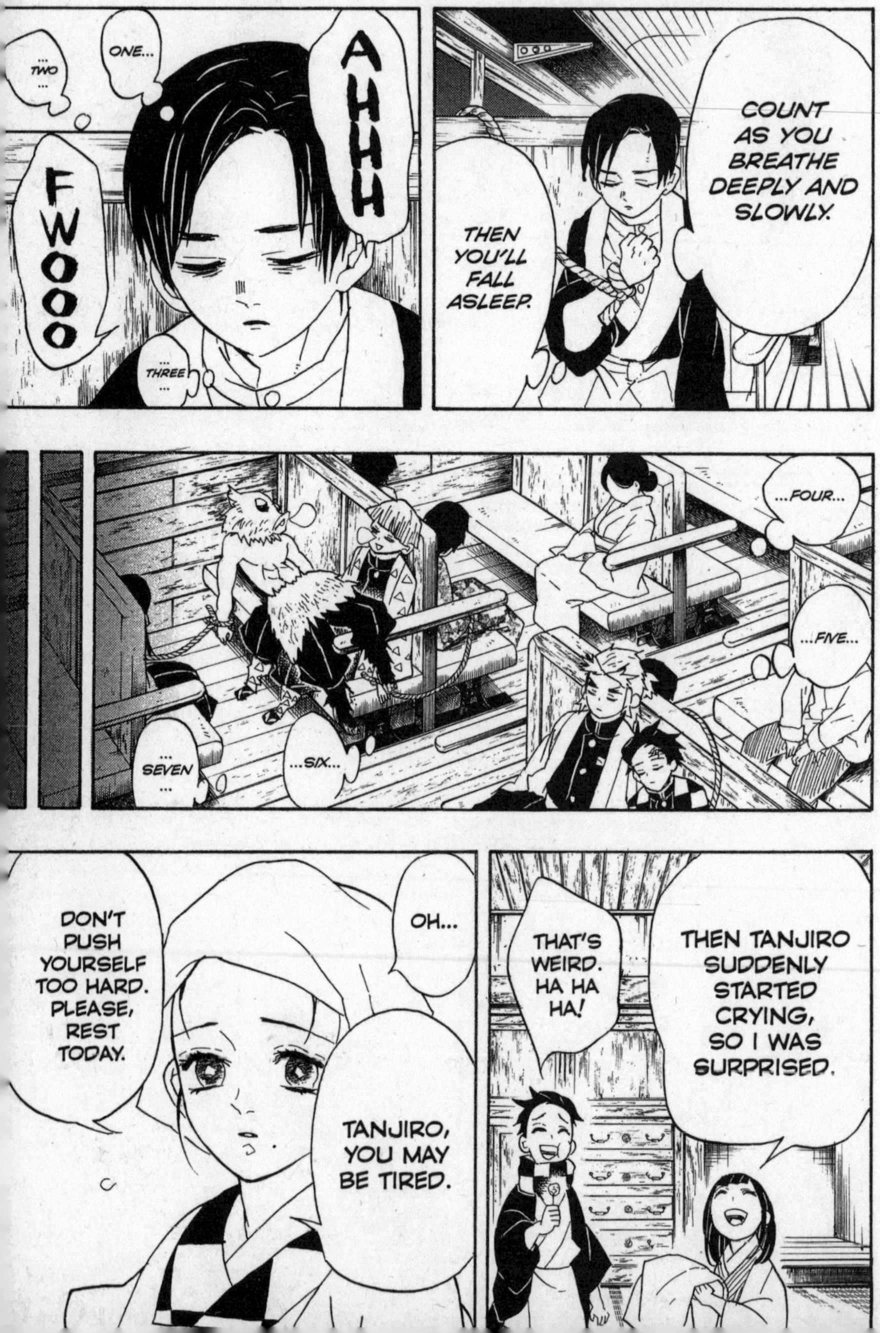
COUNT AS YOU BREATHE DEEPLY AND SLOWLY.
THEN YOU'LL FALL ASLEEP.
AHHH
ONE...
...TWO...
FWOOO
...THREE...
...FOUR...
...FIVE...
...SIX...
...SEVEN...
THEN TANJIRO SUDDENLY STARTED CRYING, SO I WAS SURPRISED.
THAT'S WEIRD. HA HA HA!
OH...
TANJIRO, YOU MAY BE TIRED.
DON'T PUSH YOURSELF TOO HARD. PLEASE, REST TODAY.

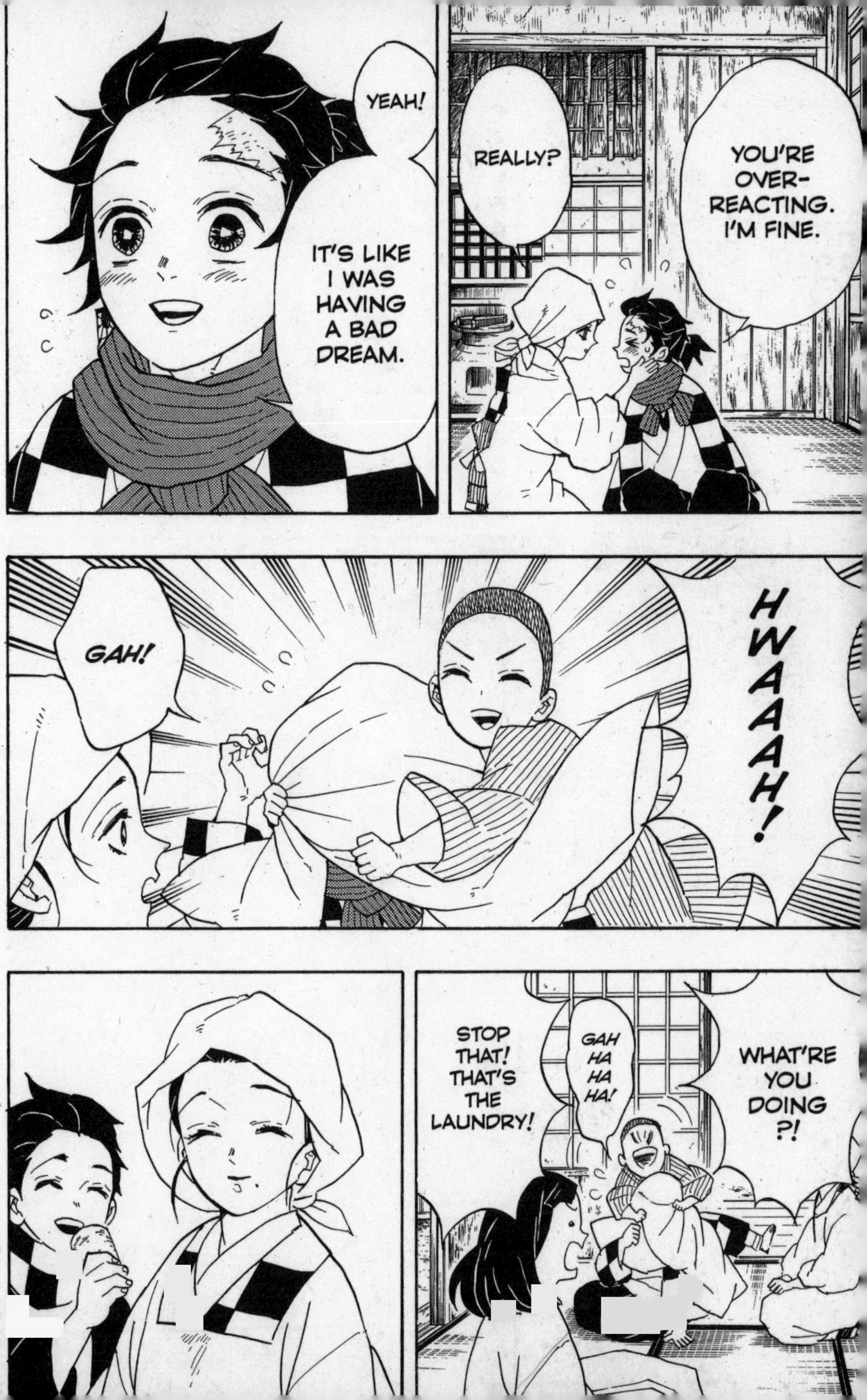
YOU'RE OVER-REACTING. I'M FINE.
REALLY?
YEAH!
IT'S LIKE I WAS HAVING A BAD DREAM.
HWAAAAH!
GAH!
WHAT'RE YOU DOING?!
GAH HA HA HA!
STOP THAT! THAT'S THE LAUNDRY!

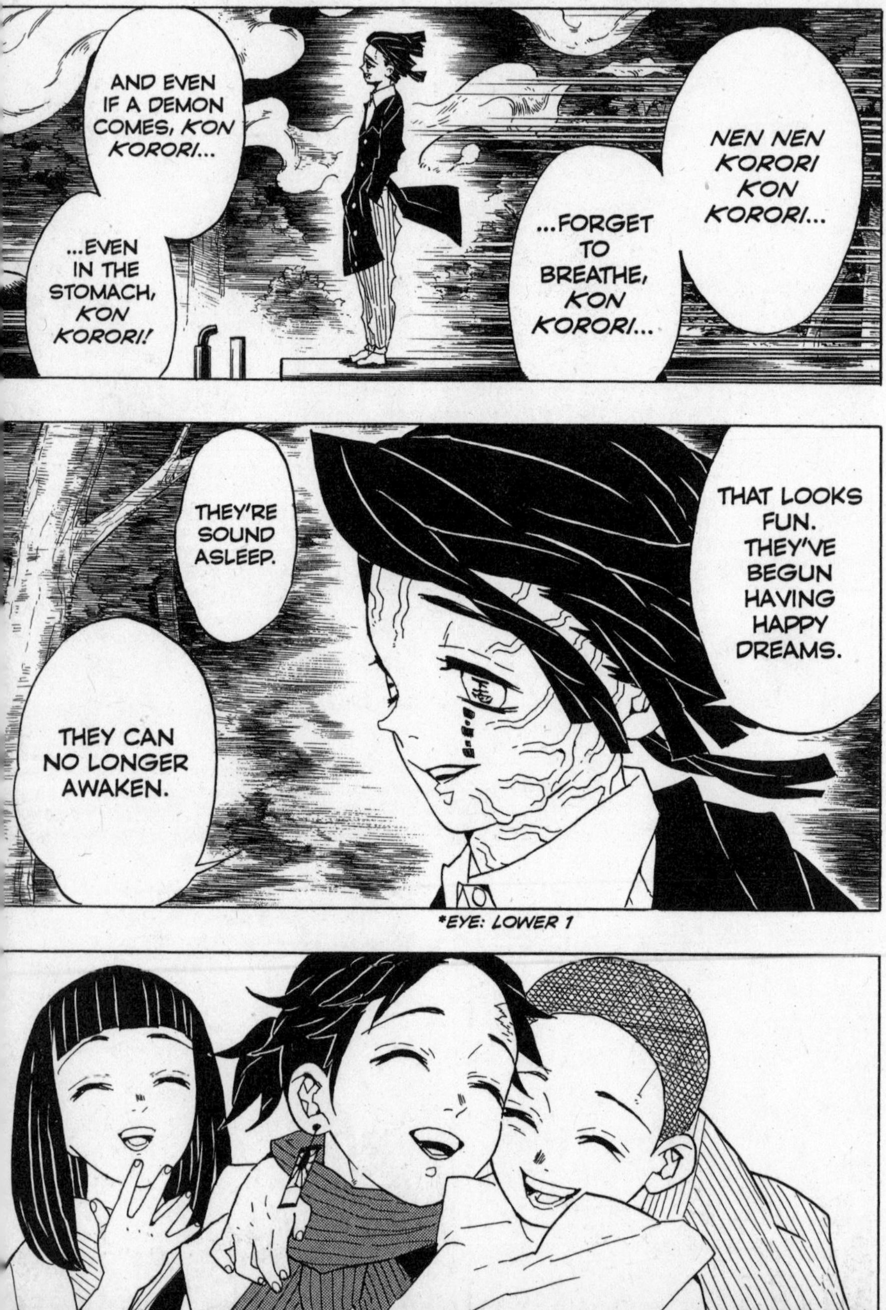
NEN NEN KORORI KON KORORI...
...FORGET TO BREATHE, KON KORORI...
AND EVEN IF A DEMON COMES, KON KORORI...
...EVEN IN THE STOMACH, KON KORORI!
THAT LOOKS FUN. THEY'VE BEGUN HAVING HAPPY DREAMS.
THEY'RE SOUND ASLEEP.
THEY CAN NO LONGER AWAKEN.

*EYE: LOWER 1

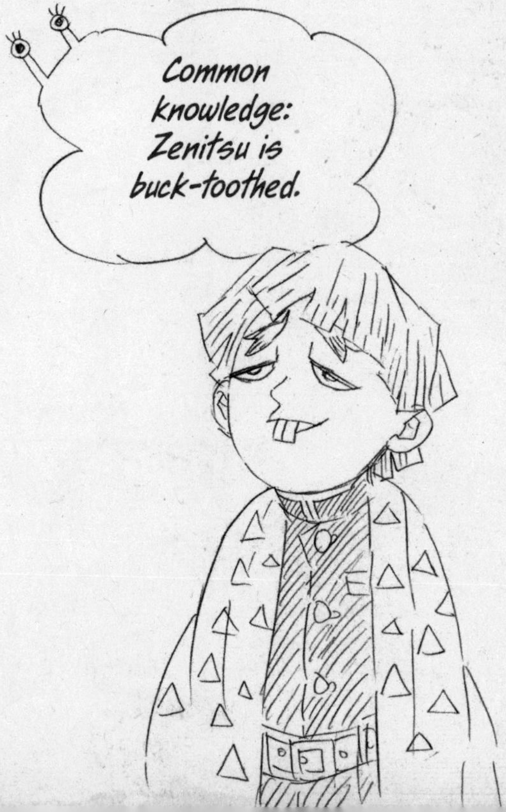
Common knowledge: Zenitsu is buck-toothed.

CHAPTER 56: WAKE UP

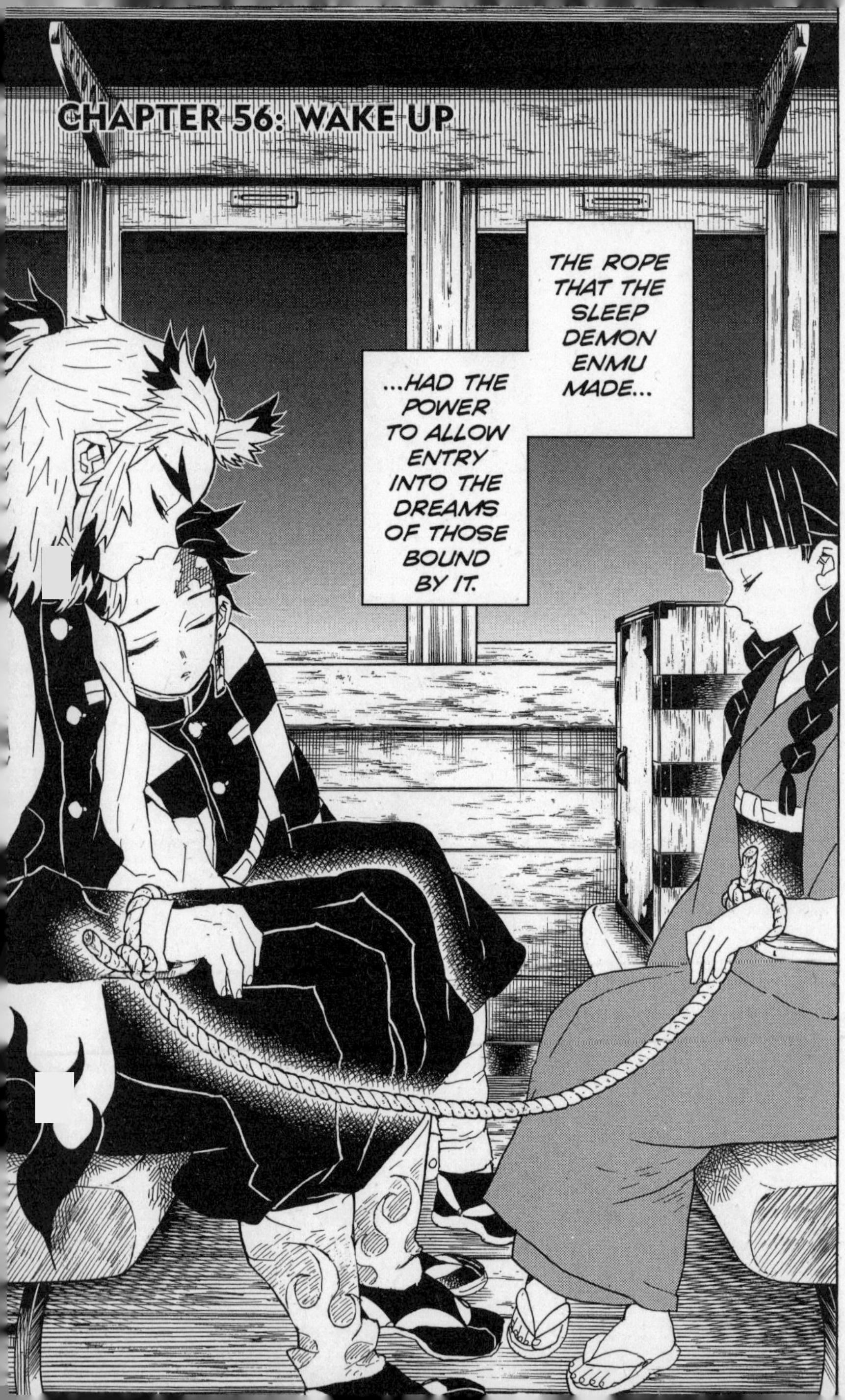
THE ROPE THAT THE SLEEP DEMON ENMU MADE...
...HAD THE POWER TO ALLOW ENTRY INTO THE DREAMS OF THOSE BOUND BY IT.

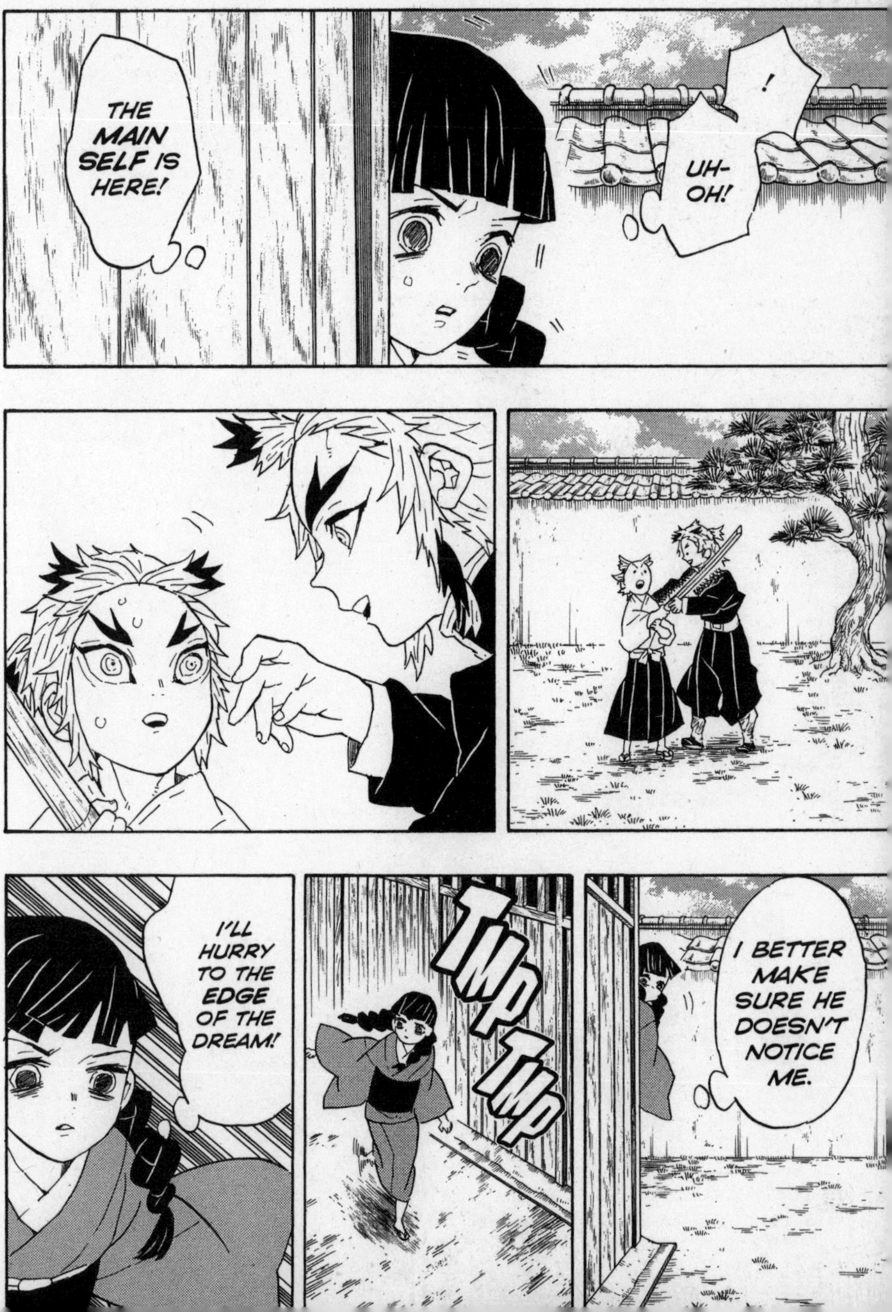
!
UH-OH!
THE MAIN SELF IS HERE!
I BETTER MAKE SURE HE DOESN'T NOTICE ME.
TMP TMP
I'LL HURRY TO THE EDGE OF THE DREAM!

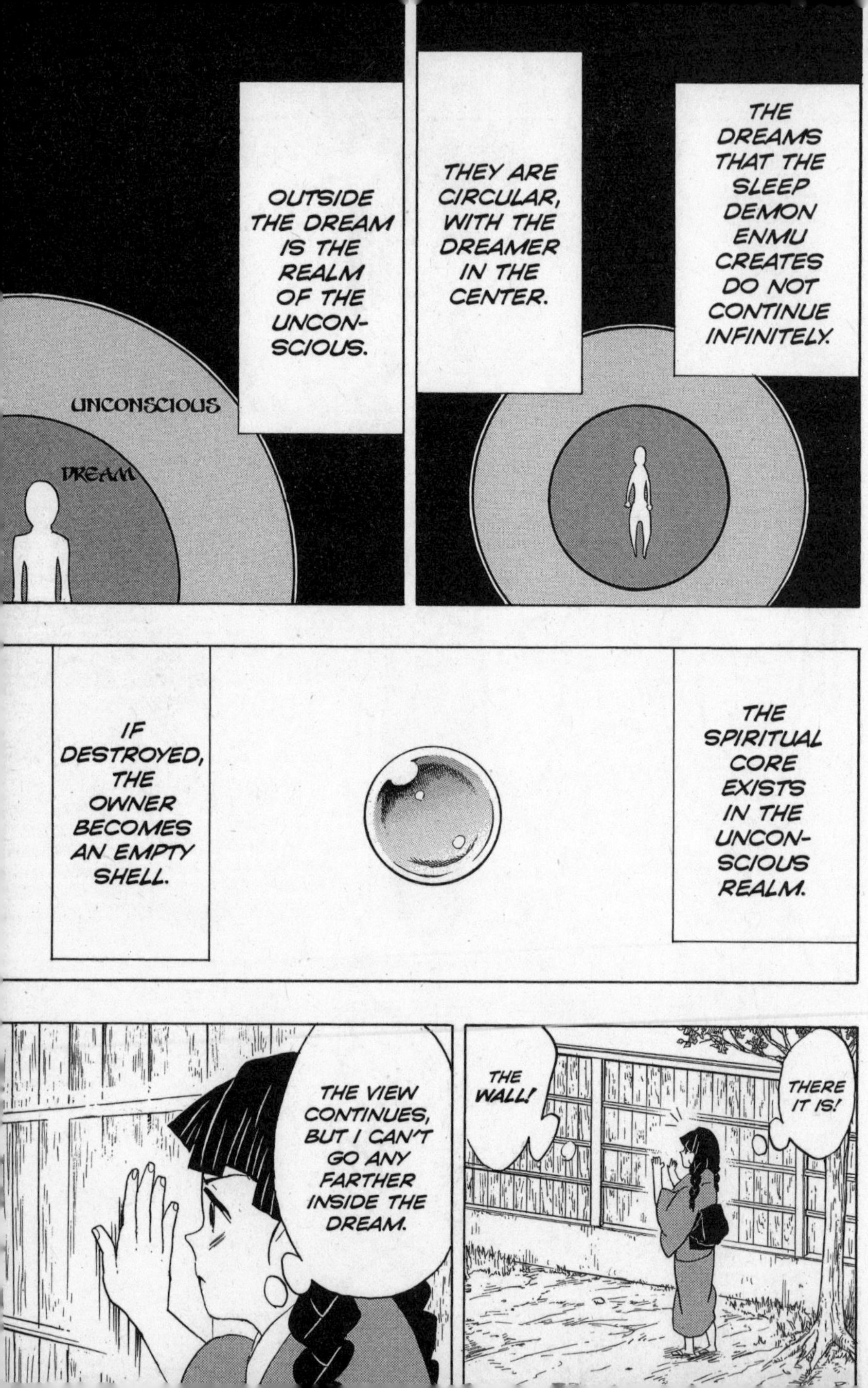

THE DREAMS THAT THE SLEEP DEMON ENMU CREATES DO NOT CONTINUE INFINITELY.
THEY ARE CIRCULAR, WITH THE DREAMER IN THE CENTER.
OUTSIDE THE DREAM IS THE REALM OF THE UNCON-SCIOUS.
UNCONSCIOUS
DREAM
THE SPIRITUAL CORE EXISTS IN THE UNCON-SCIOUS REALM.
IF DESTROYED, THE OWNER BECOMES AN EMPTY SHELL.
THERE IT IS!
THE WALL!
THE VIEW CONTINUES, BUT I CAN'T GO ANY FARTHER INSIDE THE DREAM.

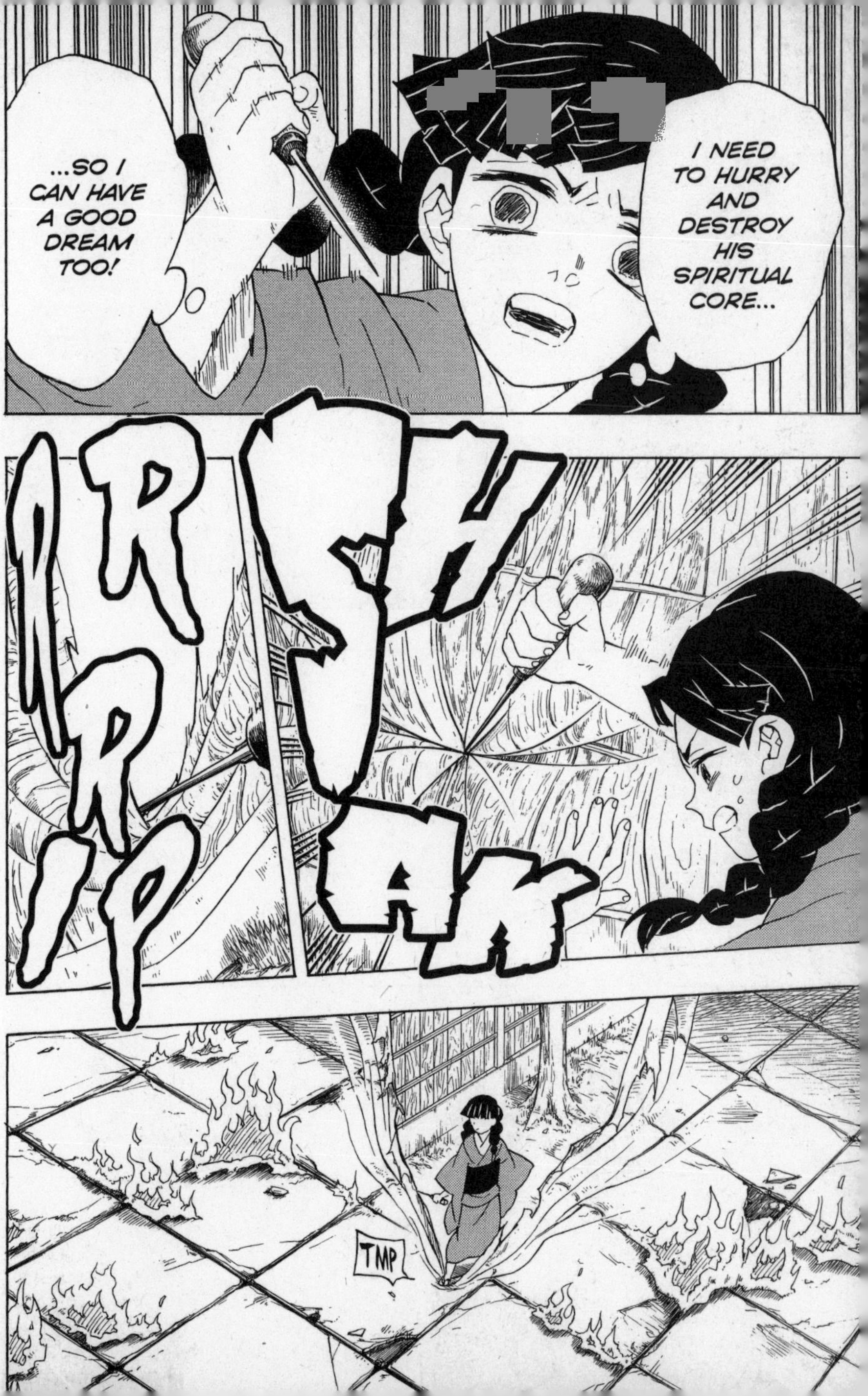
I NEED TO HURRY AND DESTROY HIS SPIRITUAL CORE...
...SO I CAN HAVE A GOOD DREAM TOO!
TMP

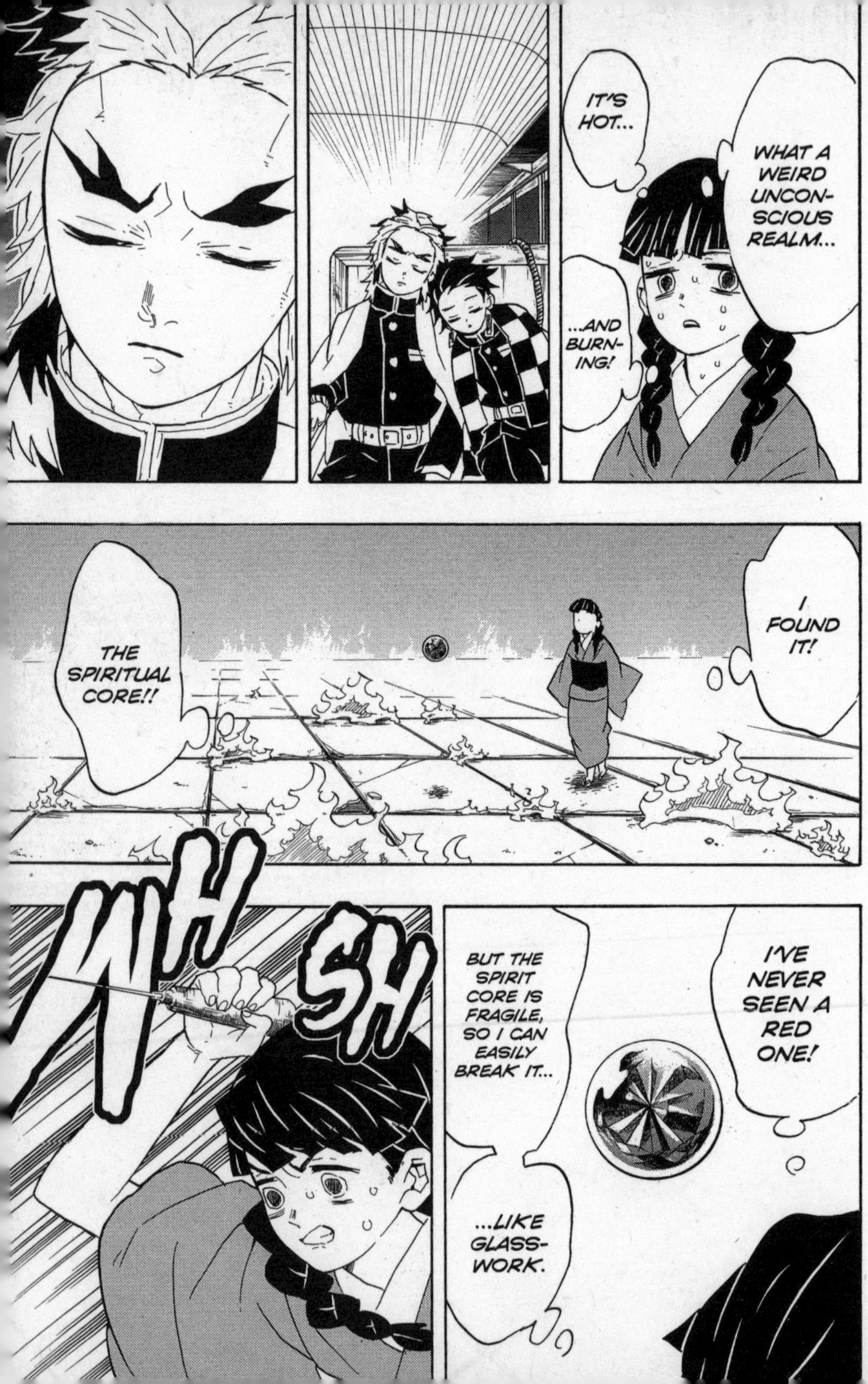
WHAT A WEIRD UNCON-SCIOUS REALM...
IT'S HOT...
...AND BURN-ING!
I FOUND IT!
THE SPIRITUAL CORE!!
I'VE NEVER SEEN A RED ONE!
BUT THE SPIRIT CORE IS FRAGILE, SO I CAN EASILY BREAK IT...
...LIKE GLASS-WORK.
WH
SH

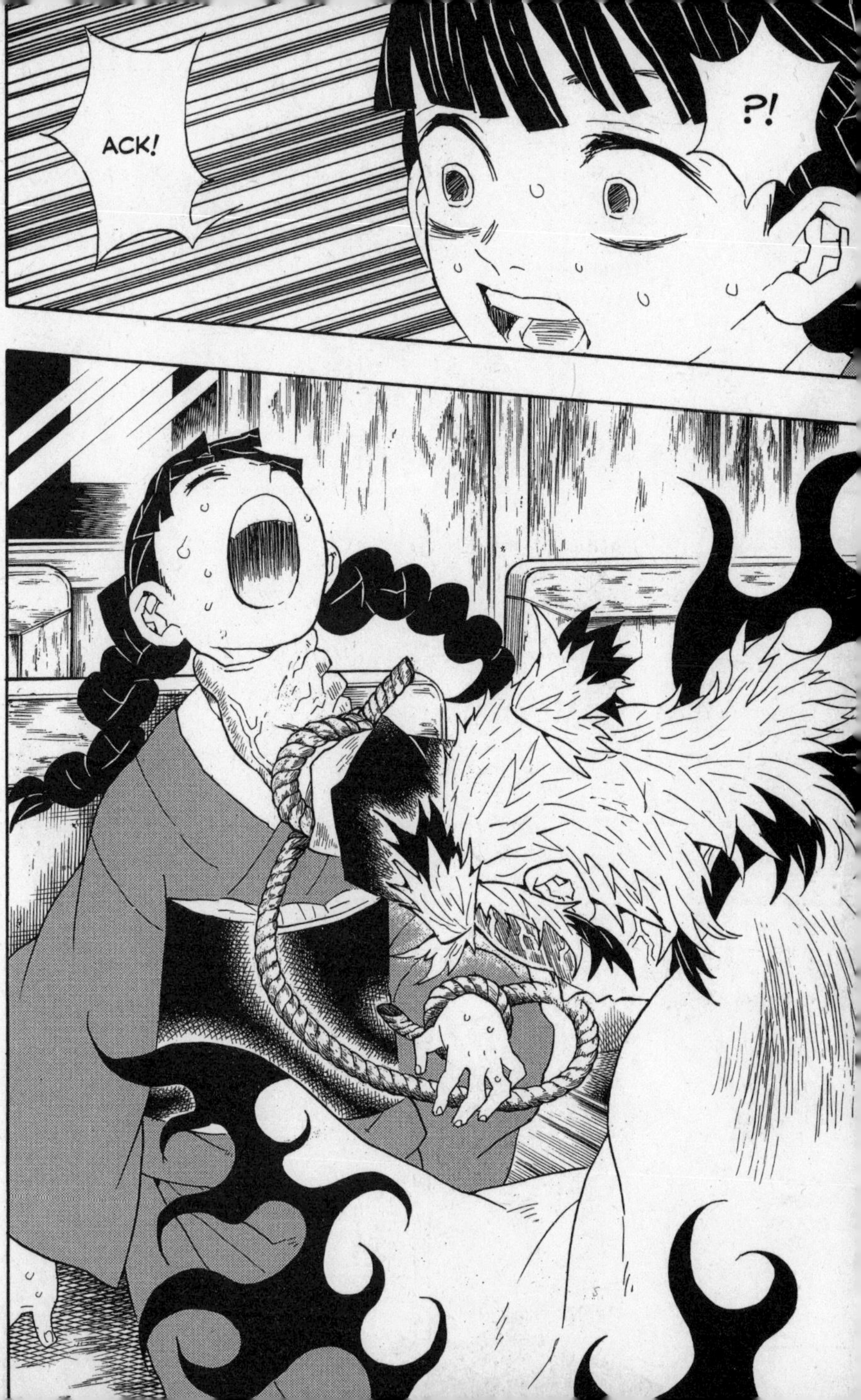
?!
ACK!

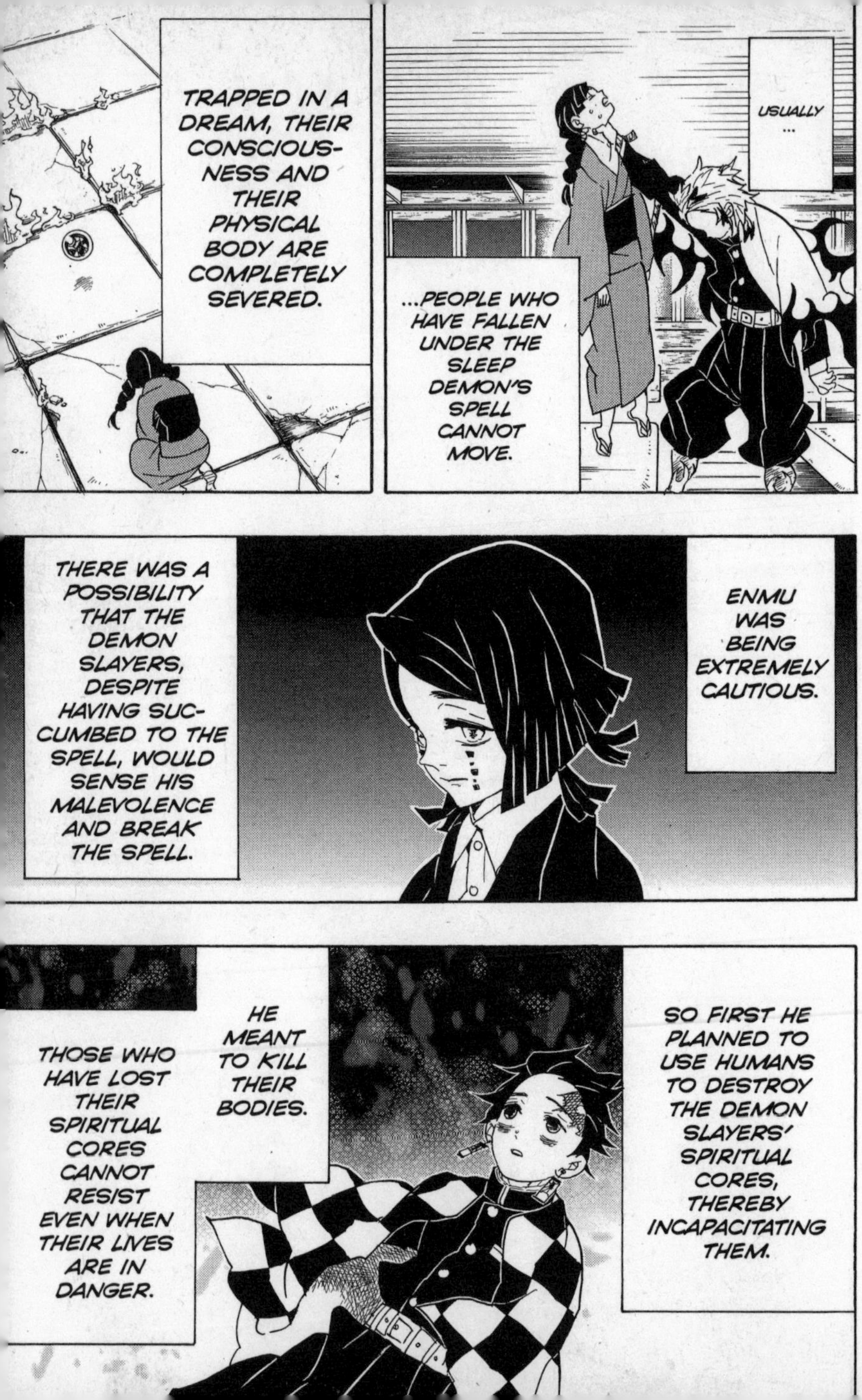
USUALLY ...
...PEOPLE WHO HAVE FALLEN UNDER THE SLEEP DEMON'S SPELL CANNOT MOVE.
TRAPPED IN A DREAM, THEIR CONSCIOUSNESS AND THEIR PHYSICAL BODY ARE COMPLETELY SEVERED.
ENMU WAS BEING EXTREMELY CAUTIOUS.
THERE WAS A POSSIBILITY THAT THE DEMON SLAYERS, DESPITE HAVING SUCCUMBED TO THE SPELL, WOULD SENSE HIS MALEVOLENCE AND BREAK THE SPELL.
SO FIRST HE PLANNED TO USE HUMANS TO DESTROY THE DEMON SLAYERS' SPIRITUAL CORES, THEREBY INCAPACITATING THEM.
HE MEANT TO KILL THEIR BODIES.
THOSE WHO HAVE LOST THEIR SPIRITUAL CORES CANNOT RESIST EVEN WHEN THEIR LIVES ARE IN DANGER.

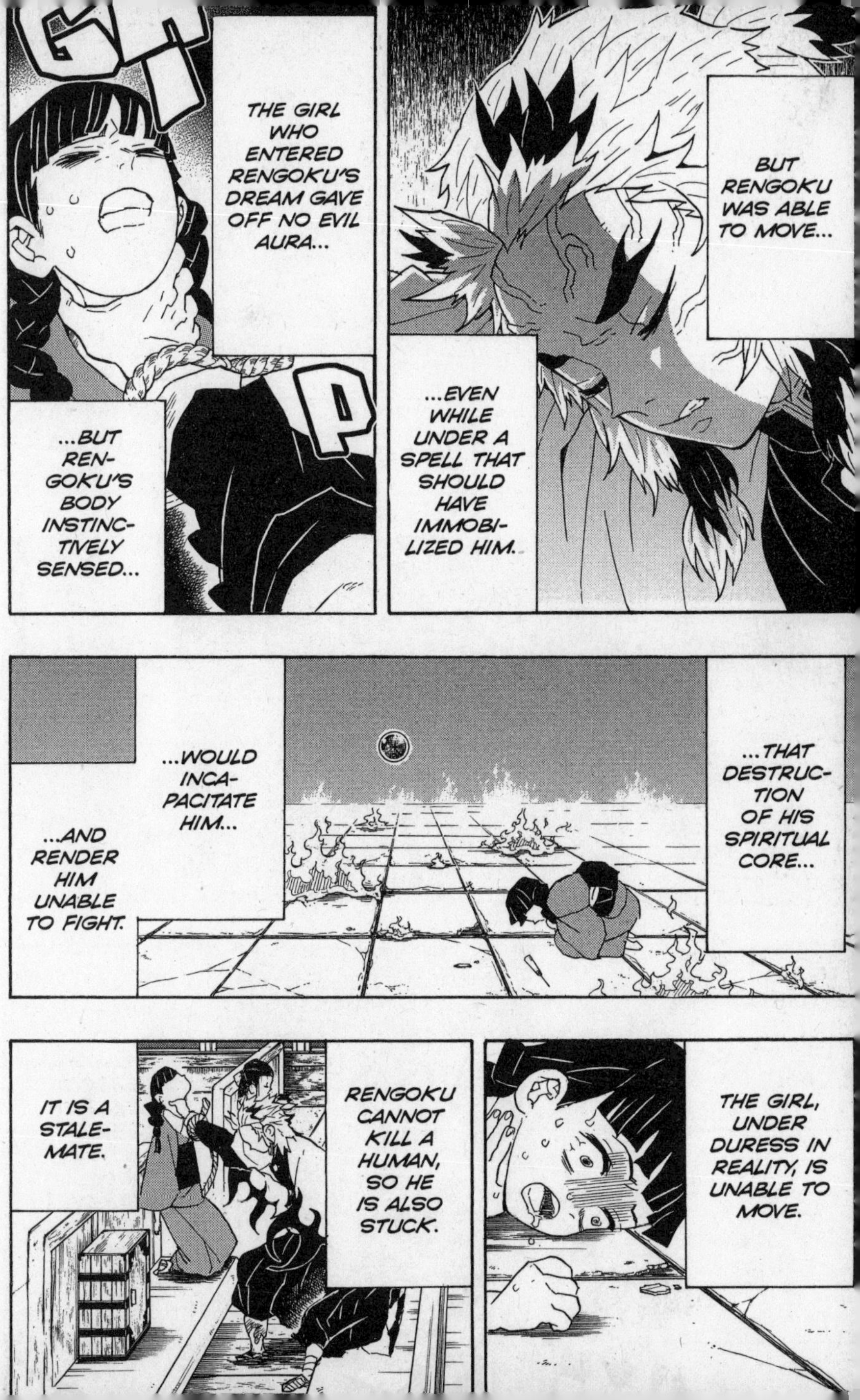
BUT RENGOKU WAS ABLE TO MOVE...
...EVEN WHILE UNDER A SPELL THAT SHOULD HAVE IMMOBILIZED HIM.
THE GIRL WHO ENTERED RENGOKU'S DREAM GAVE OFF NO EVIL AURA...
...BUT RENGOKU'S BODY INSTINCTIVELY SENSED...
...THAT DESTRUCTION OF HIS SPIRITUAL CORE...
...WOULD INCAPACITATE HIM...
...AND RENDER HIM UNABLE TO FIGHT.
THE GIRL, UNDER DURESS IN REALITY, IS UNABLE TO MOVE.
RENGOKU CANNOT KILL A HUMAN, SO HE IS ALSO STUCK.
IT IS A STALEMATE.

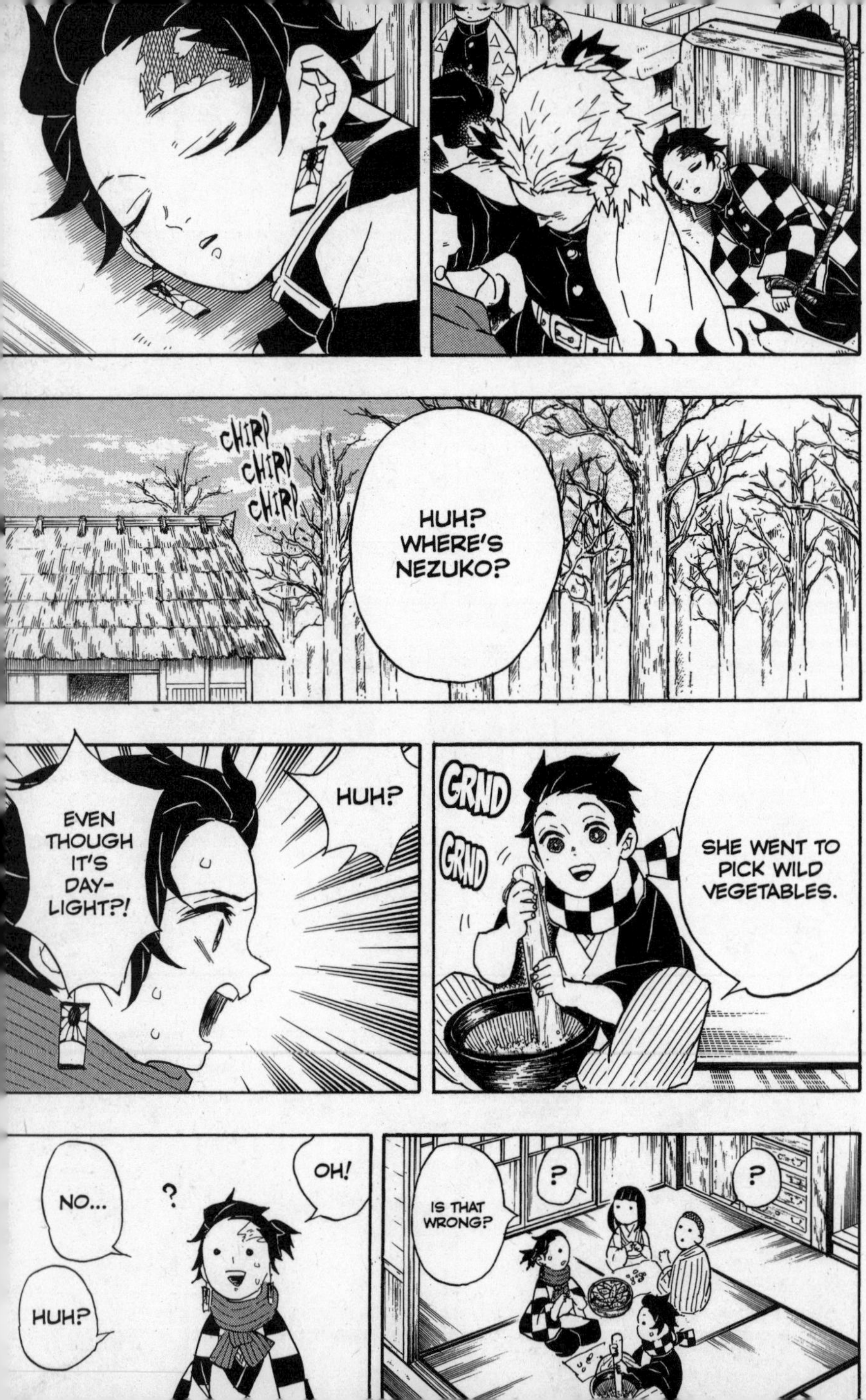
CHIRP
CHIRP
CHIRP
HUH? WHERE'S NEZUKO?
SHE WENT TO PICK WILD VEGETABLES.
GRND
GRND
HUH?
EVEN THOUGH IT'S DAY-LIGHT?!
?
?
IS THAT WRONG?
OH!
?
NO...
HUH?

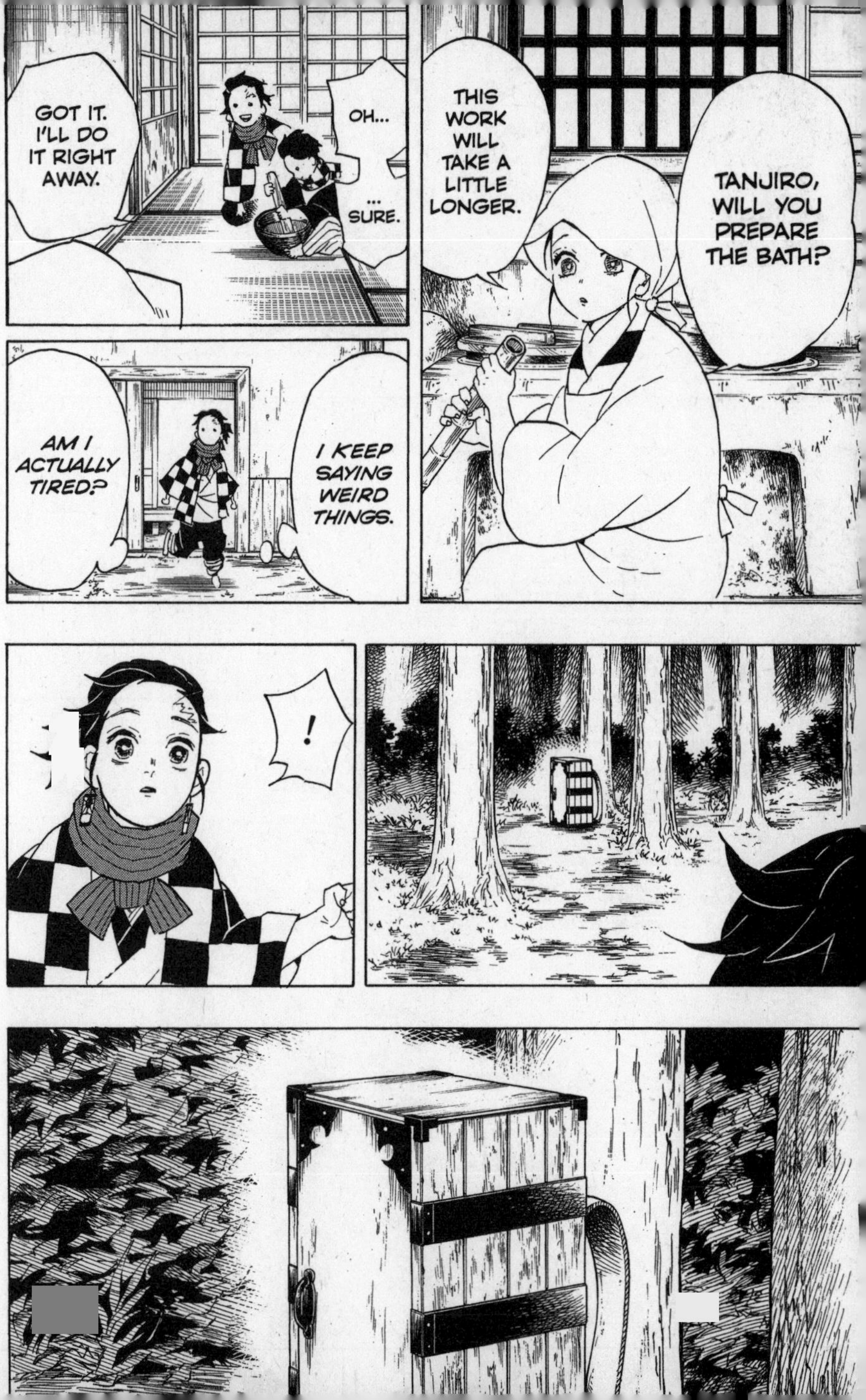
TANJIRO, WILL YOU PREPARE THE BATH?
THIS WORK WILL TAKE A LITTLE LONGER.
OH...
... SURE.
GOT IT. I'LL DO IT RIGHT AWAY.
I KEEP SAYING WEIRD THINGS.
AM I ACTUALLY TIRED?
!

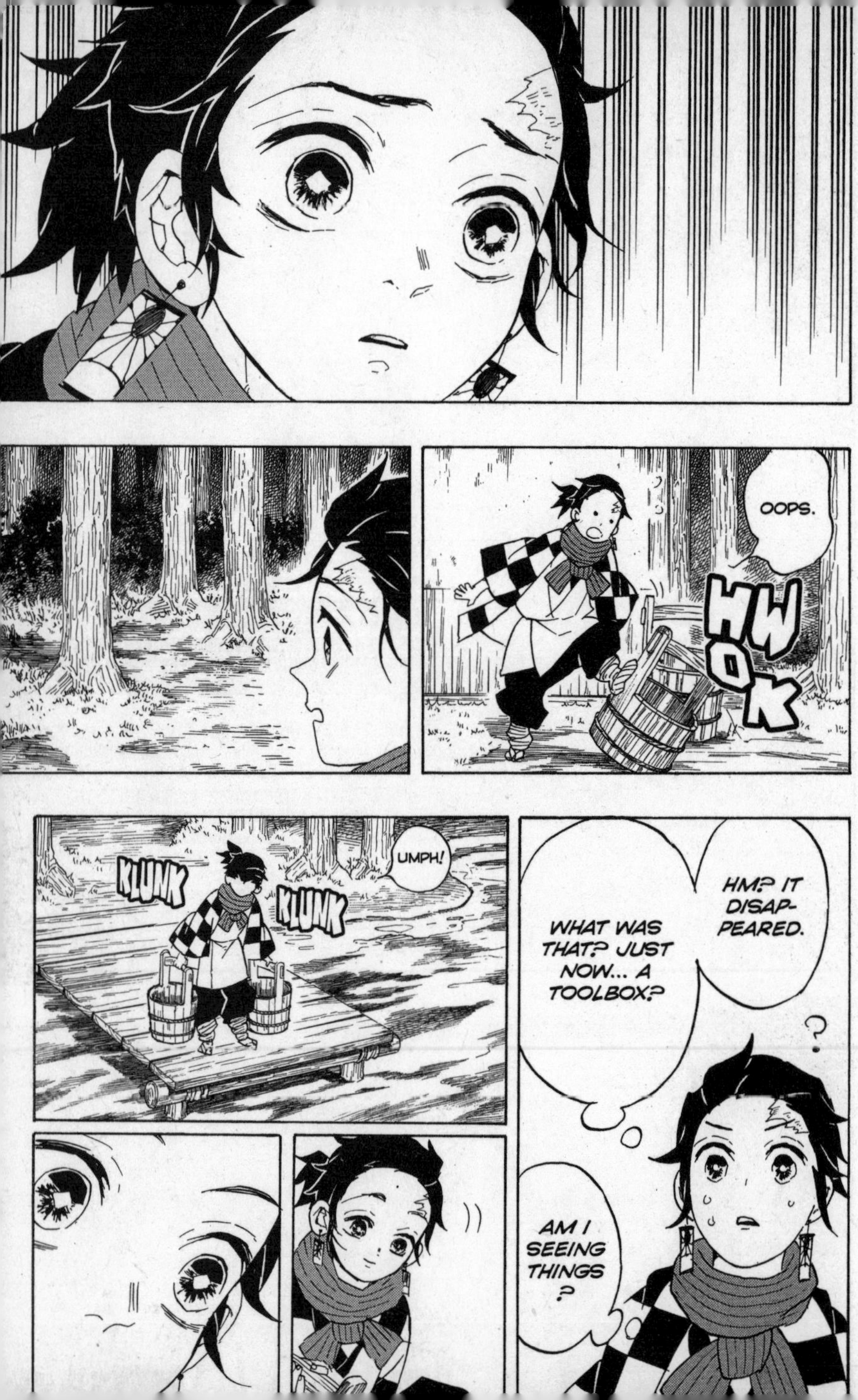
OOPS.
HWOK
HM? IT DISAP-PEARED.
WHAT WAS THAT? JUST NOW... A TOOLBOX?
AM I SEEING THINGS?
UMPH!
KLUNK
KLUNK

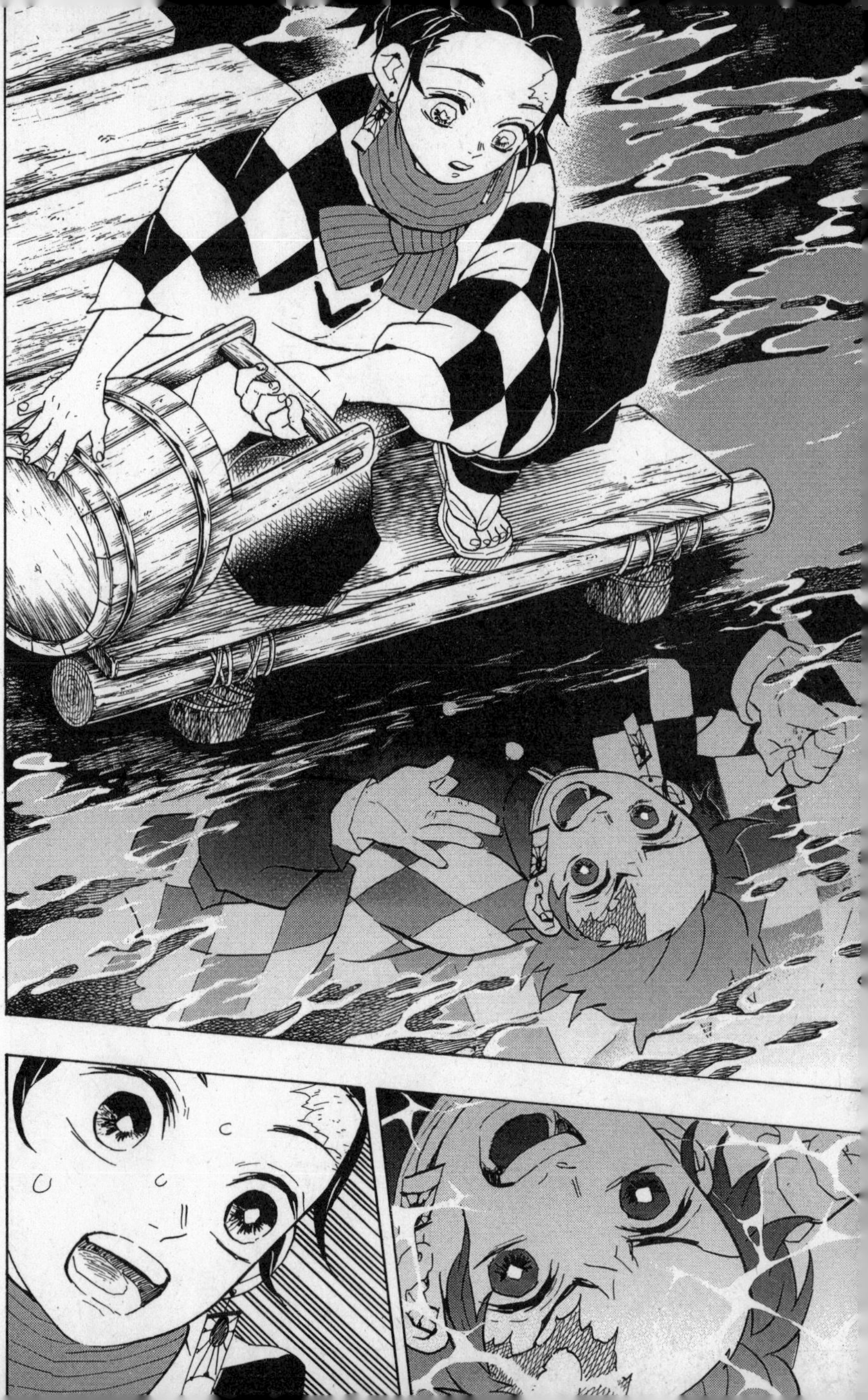

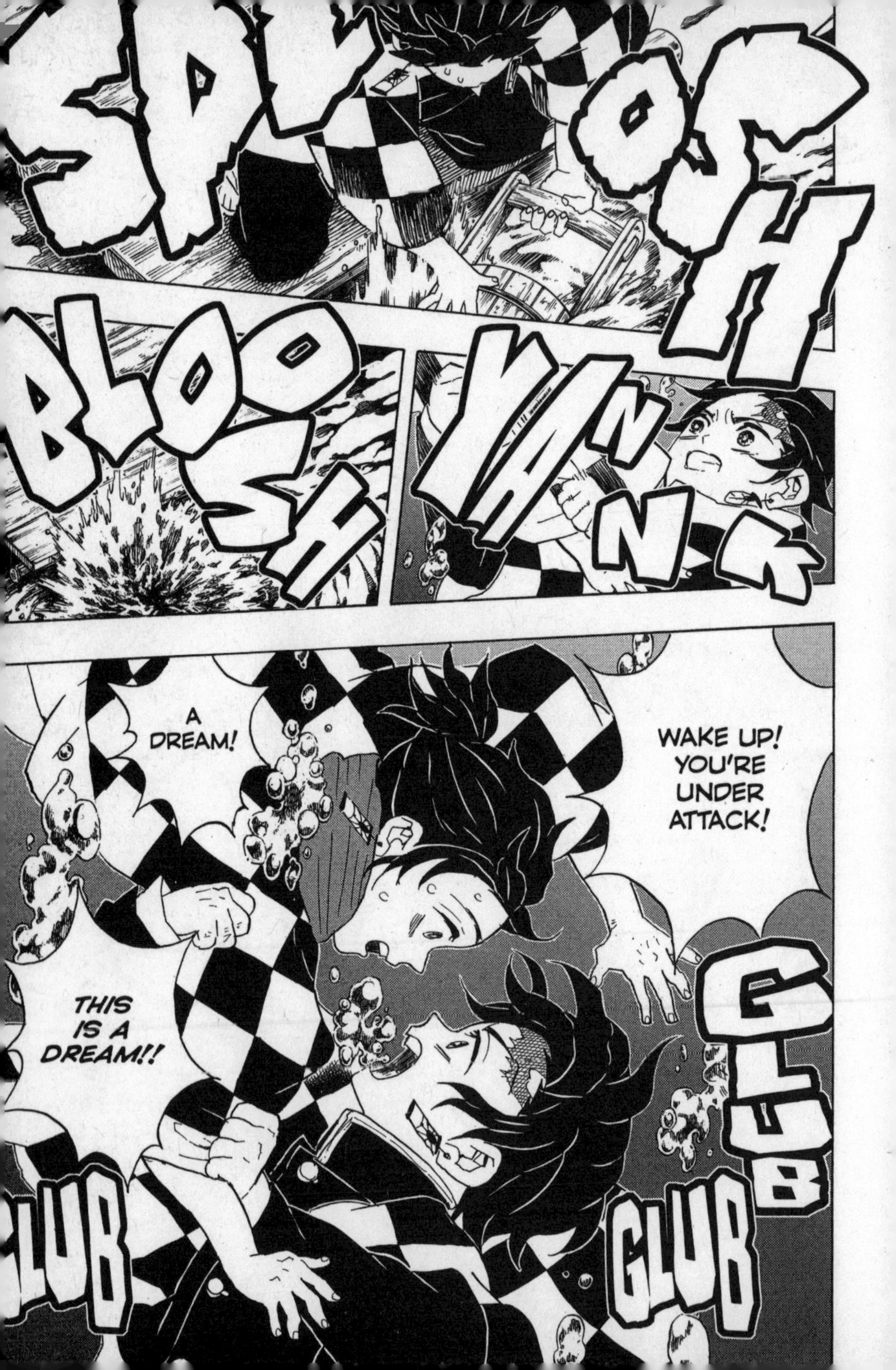
SPLOSH
YANNK
BLOOSH
WAKE UP! YOU'RE UNDER ATTACK!
GLUB
GLUB
A DREAM!
THIS IS A DREAM!!
GLUB

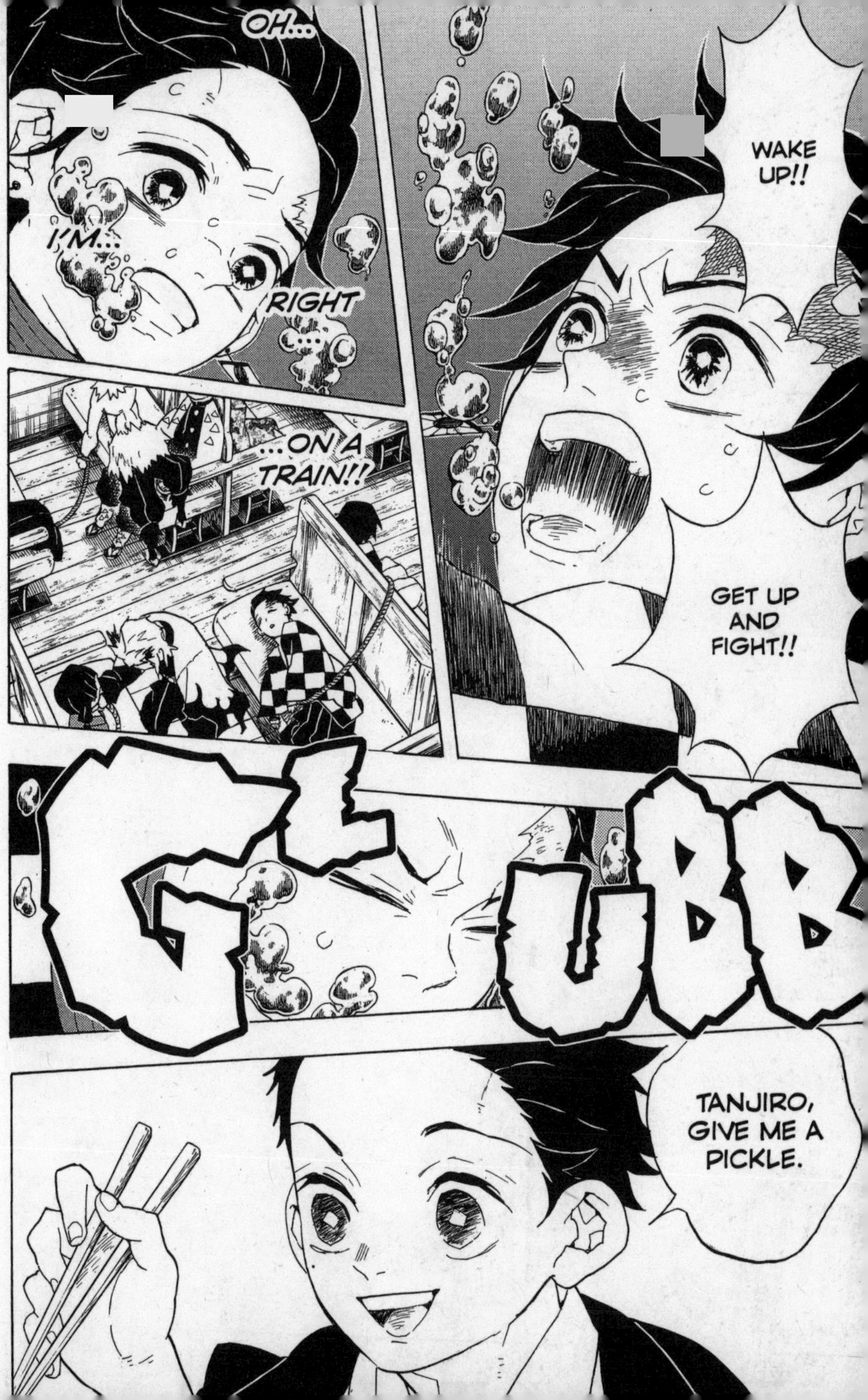
WAKE UP!!
GET UP AND FIGHT!!
OH...
I'M... RIGHT...
...ON A TRAIN!!
GLUBB
TANJIRO, GIVE ME A PICKLE.

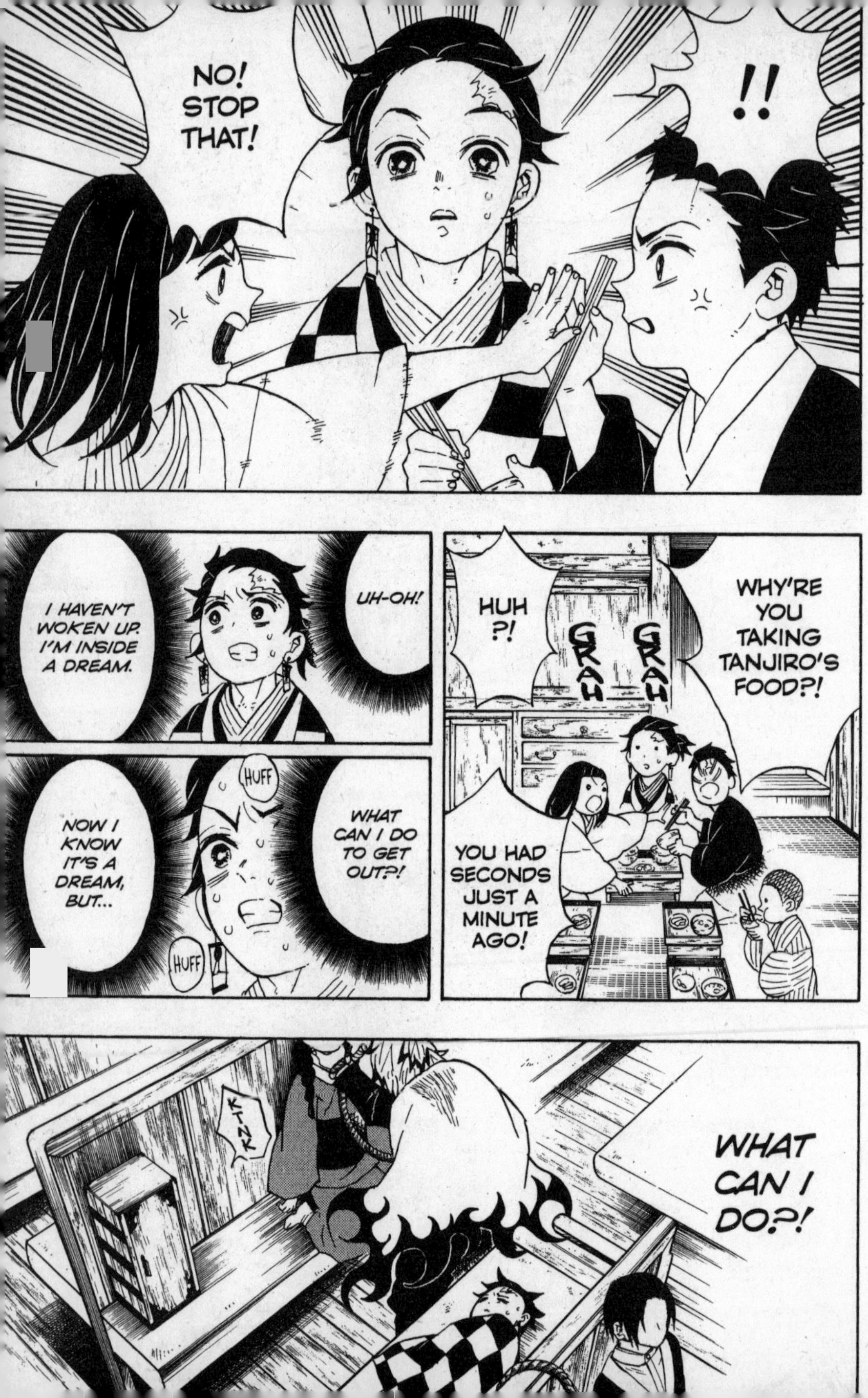
!!
NO! STOP THAT!
WHY'RE YOU TAKING TANJIRO'S FOOD?!
HUH?!
GRAH
GRAH
YOU HAD SECONDS JUST A MINUTE AGO!
UH-OH!
I HAVEN'T WOKEN UP. I'M INSIDE A DREAM.
HUFF
WHAT CAN I DO TO GET OUT?!
NOW I KNOW IT'S A DREAM, BUT...
HUFF
WHAT CAN I DO?!
K-TNK

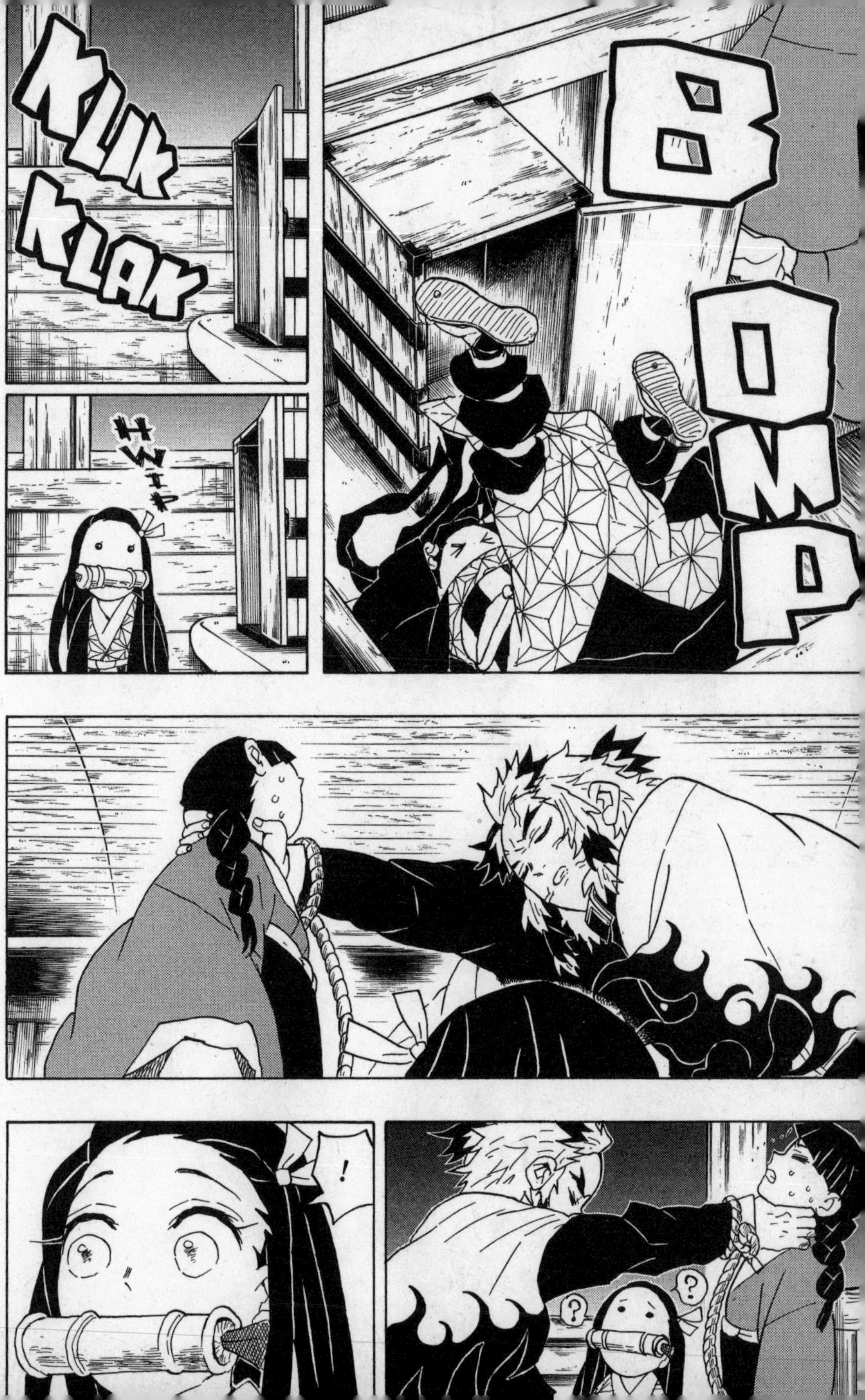
BOMP
KLIK KLAK
HWIP
?
?
!

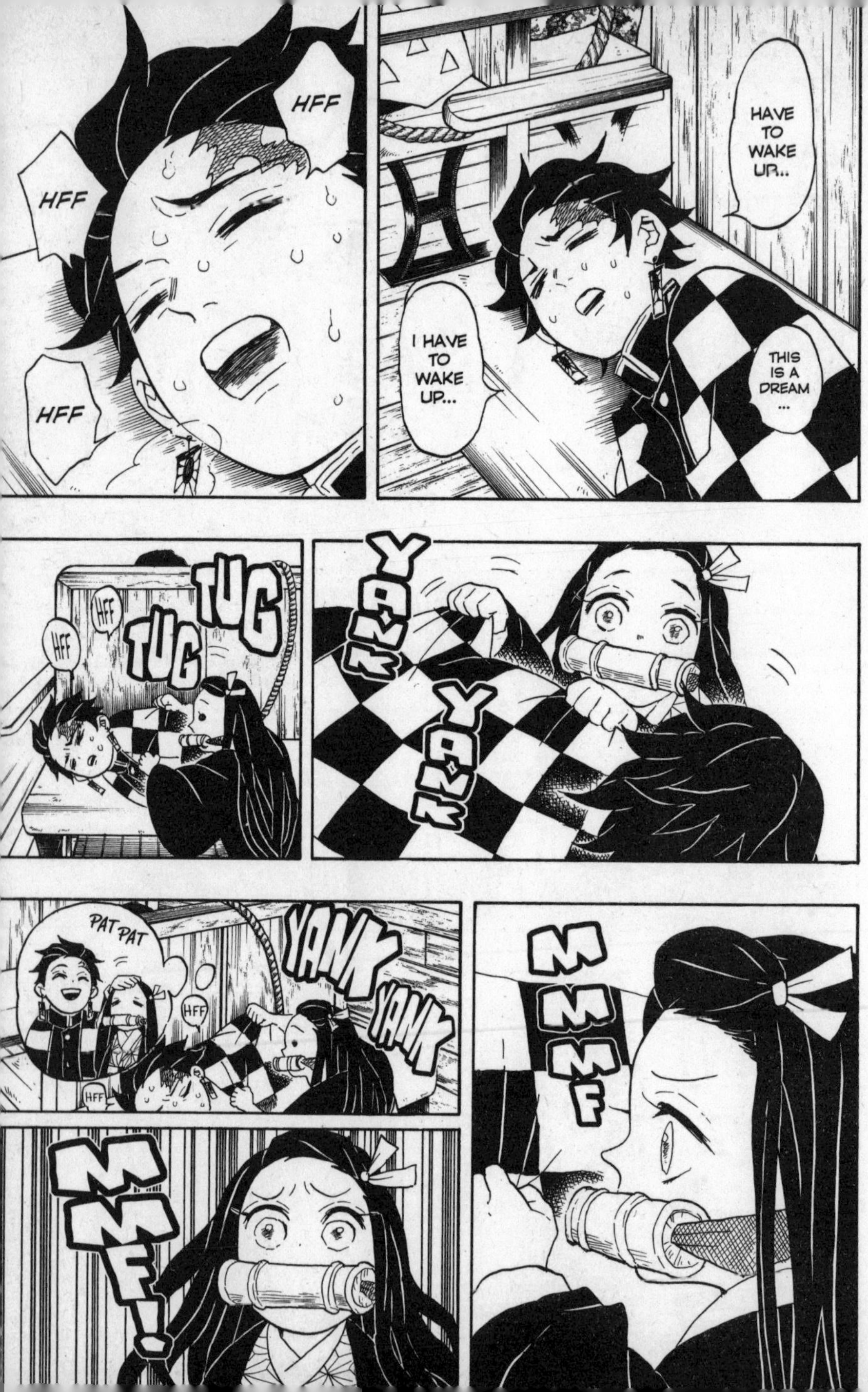
HAVE TO WAKE UP...
THIS IS A DREAM ...
I HAVE TO WAKE UP...
HFF
HFF
HFF
YANK
YANK
TUG
TUG
HFF
HFF
MMMF
YANK
YANK
PAT PAT
HFF
HFF
MMF!

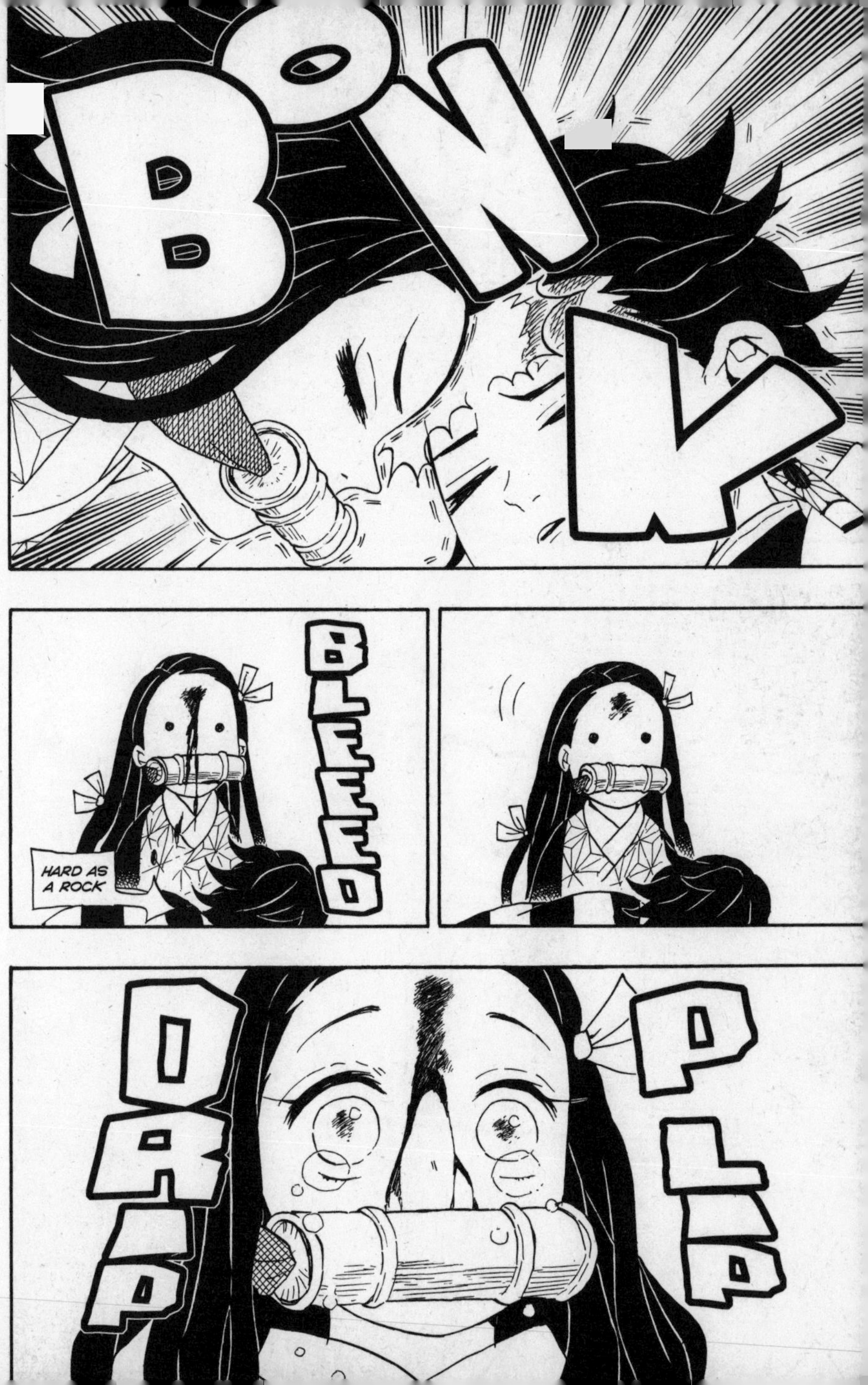
BONK
BLEEED
HARD AS A ROCK
PLP
DRP

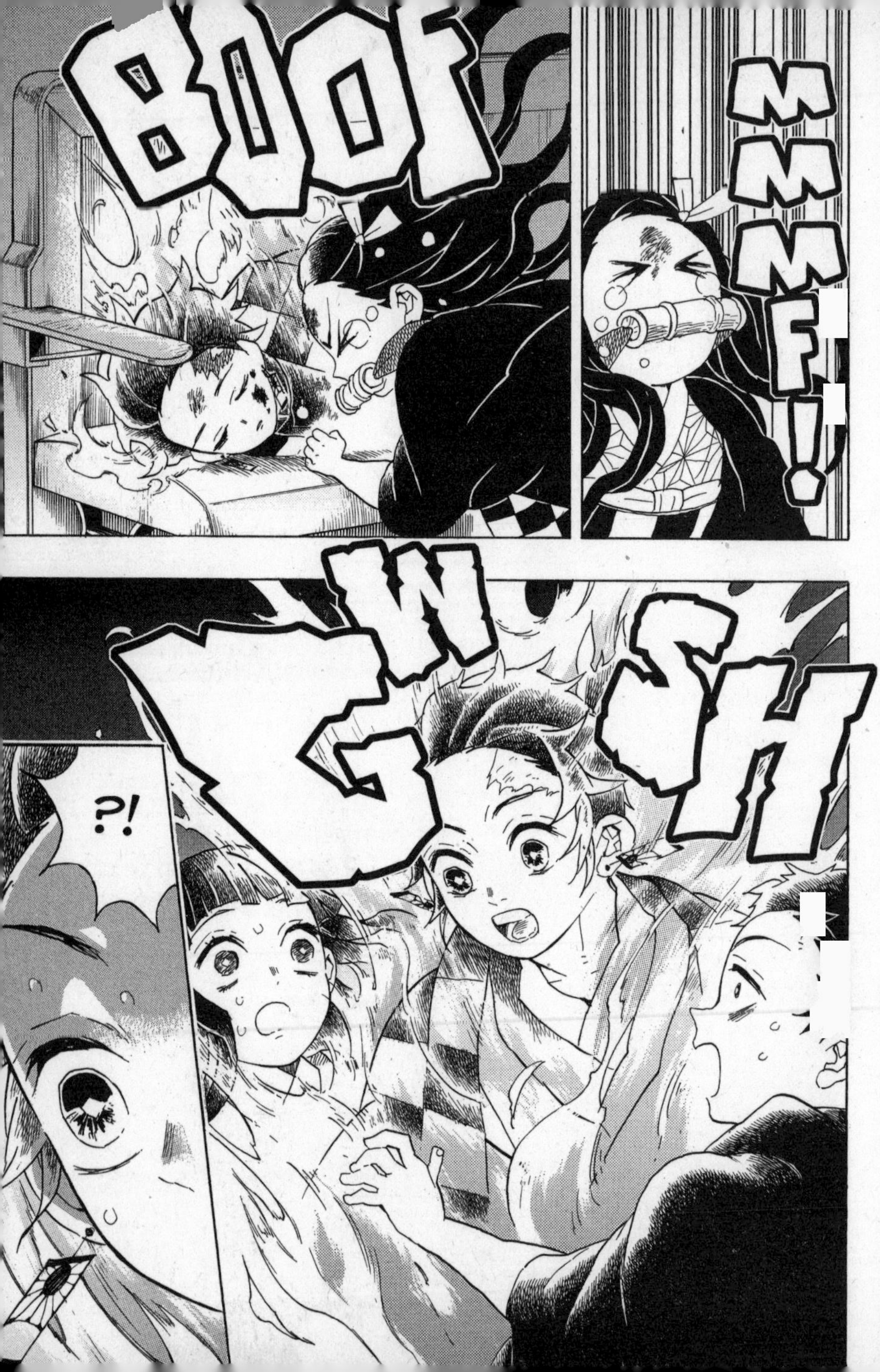
MMMF!
BOOF
?!

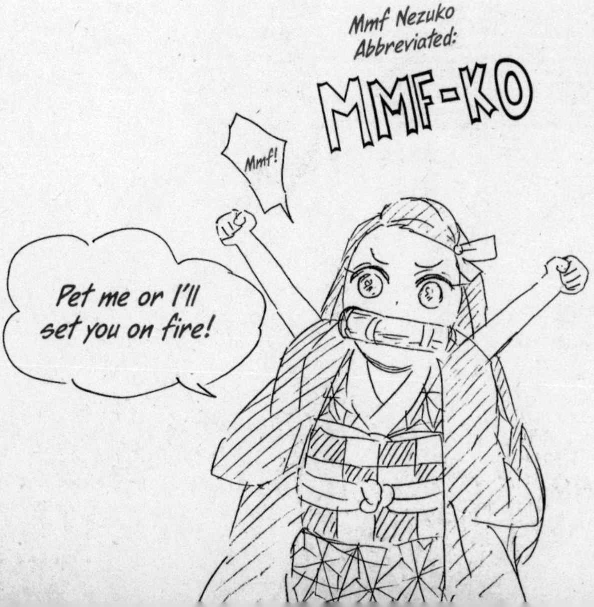
Mmf Nezuko Abbreviated:
MMF-KO
Mmf!
Pet me or I'll set you on fire!

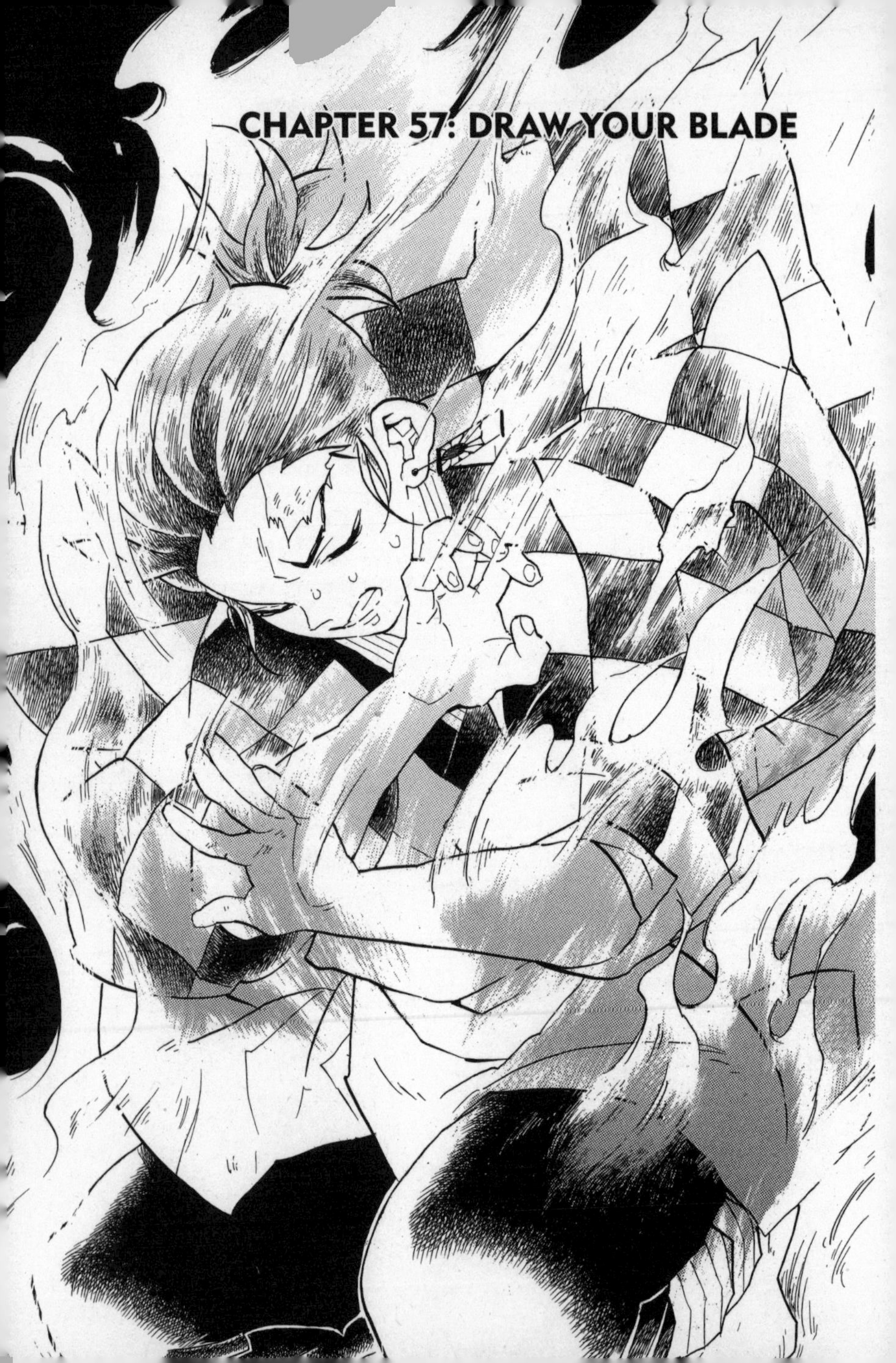
CHAPTER 57: DRAW YOUR BLADE

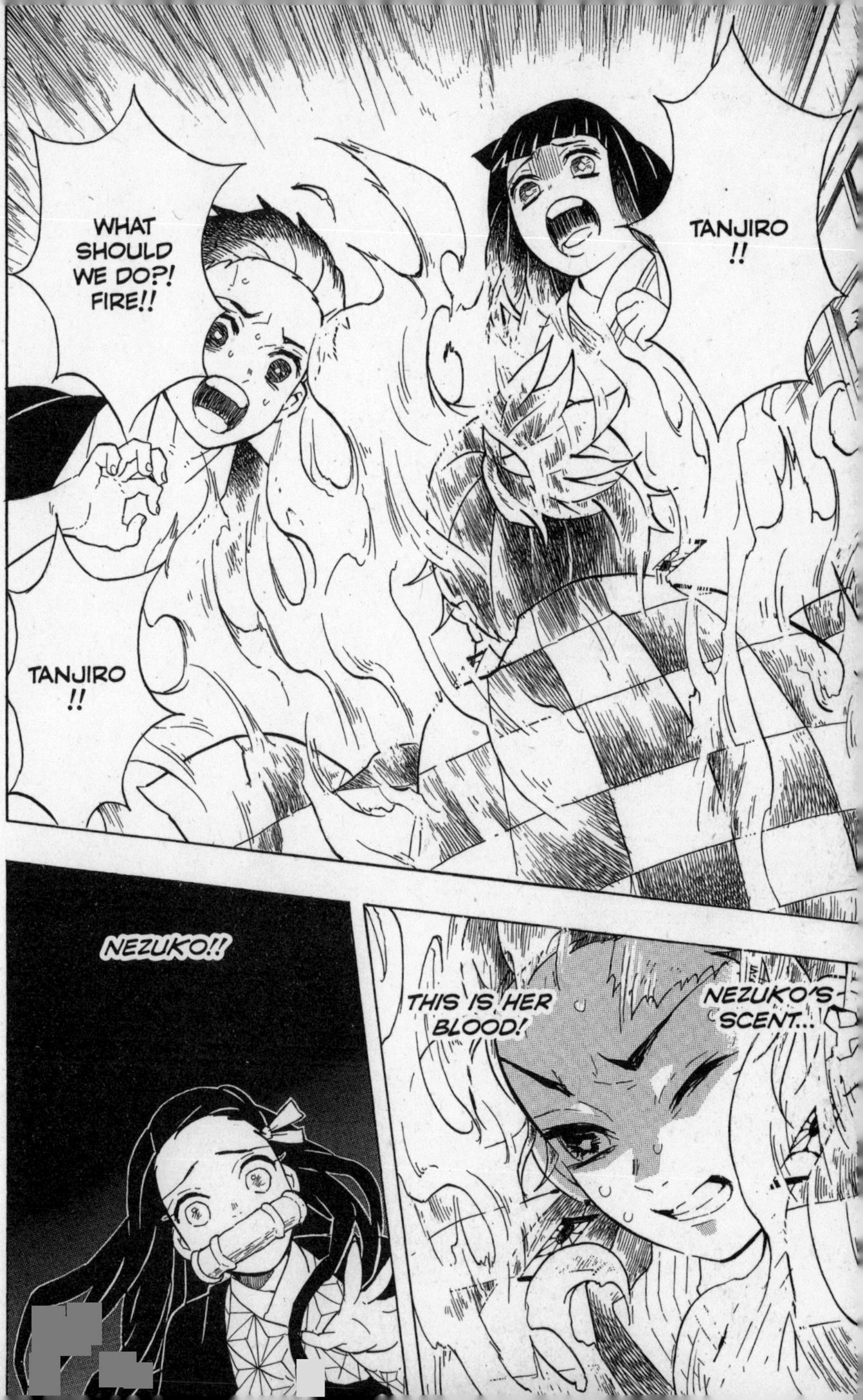
TANJIRO !!
WHAT SHOULD WE DO?! FIRE!!
TANJIRO !!
NEZUKO'S SCENT...
THIS IS HER BLOOD!
NEZUKO!!

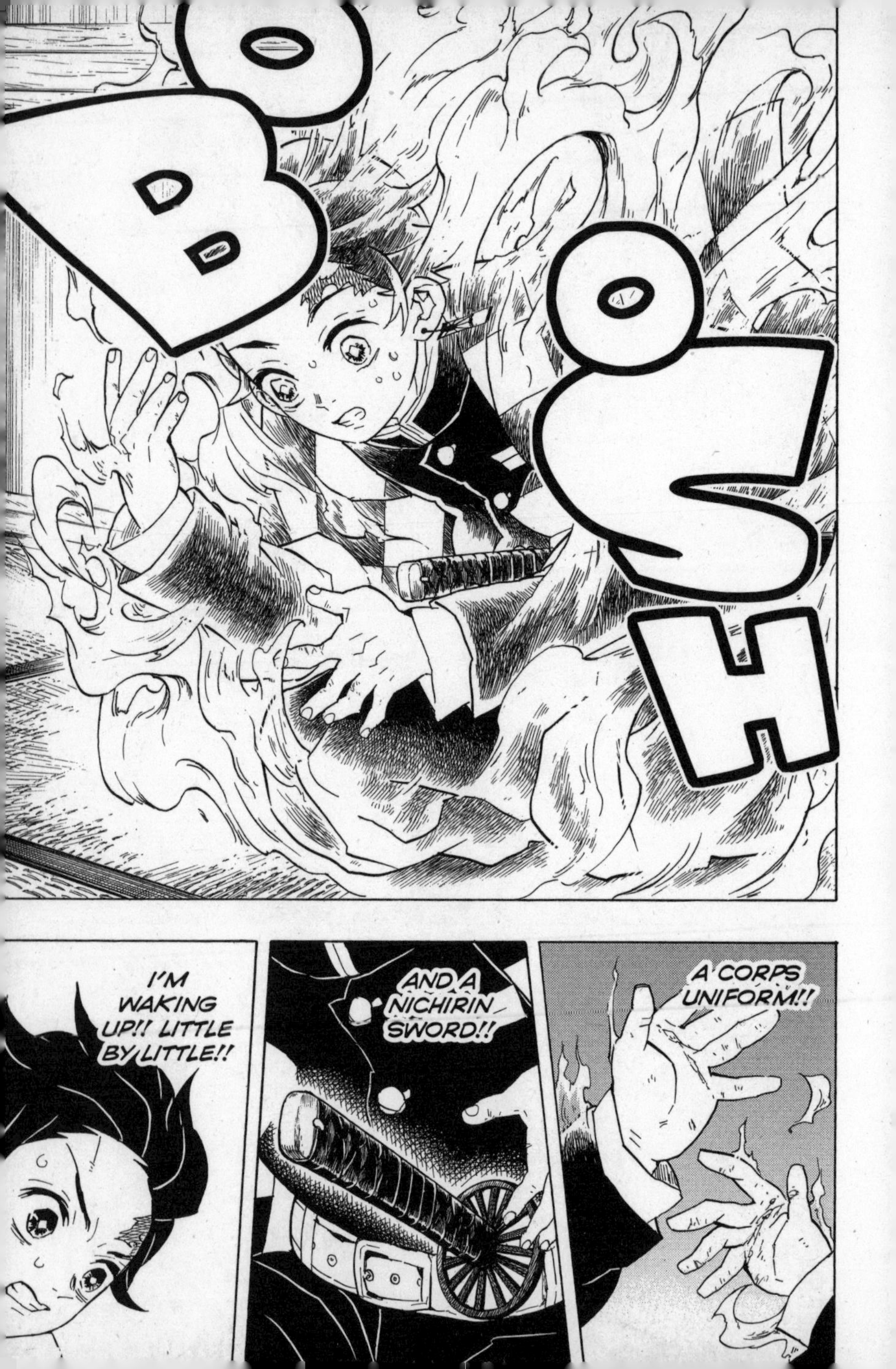
BOOSH
A CORPS UNIFORM!!
AND A NICHIRIN SWORD!!
I'M WAKING UP!! LITTLE BY LITTLE!!

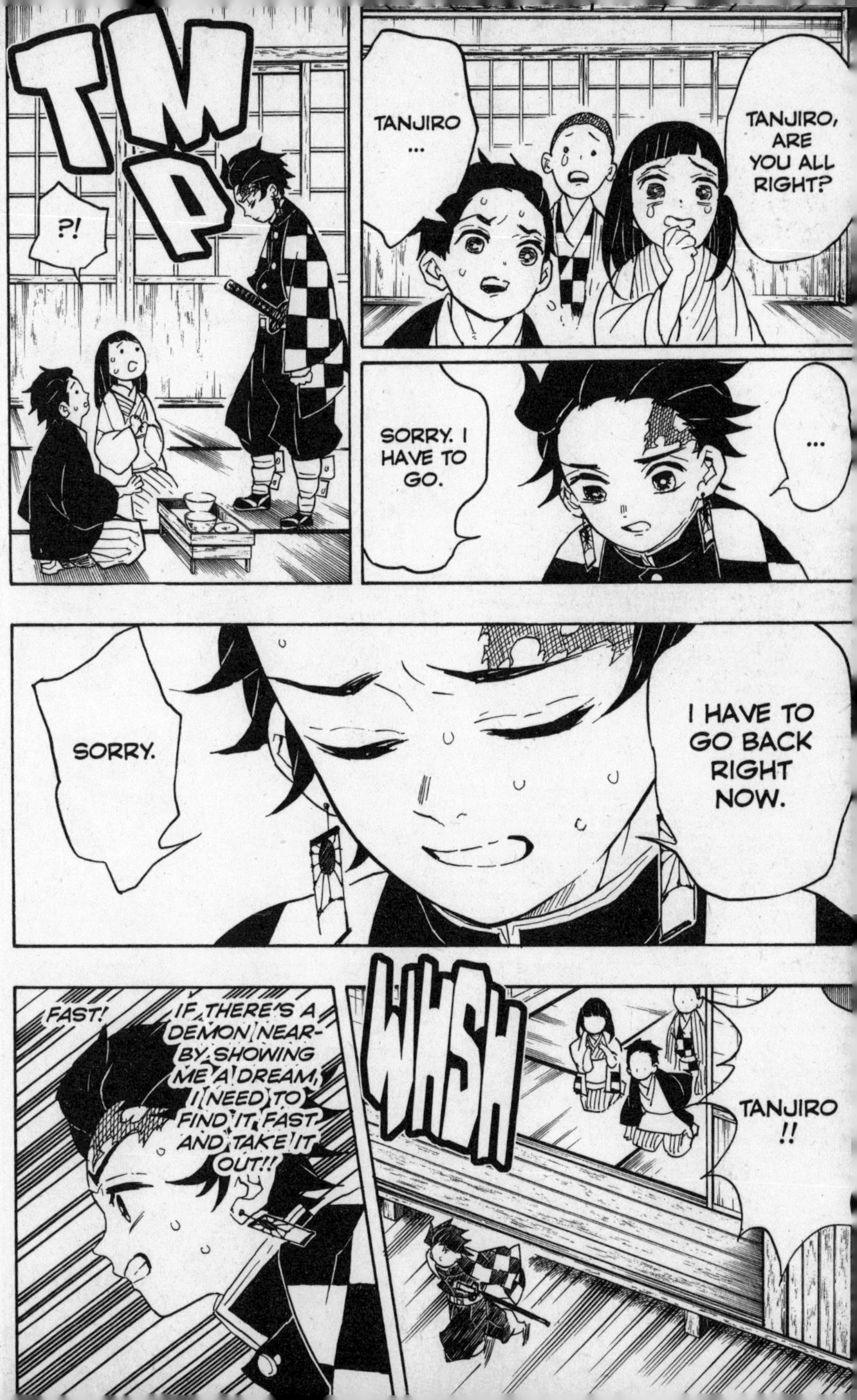
TANJIRO, ARE YOU ALL RIGHT?
TANJIRO ...
...
SORRY. I HAVE TO GO.
TMP
?!
I HAVE TO GO BACK RIGHT NOW.
SORRY.
TANJIRO !!
WHSH
IF THERE'S A DEMON NEARBY SHOWING ME A DREAM, I NEED TO FIND IT FAST AND TAKE IT OUT!!
FAST!

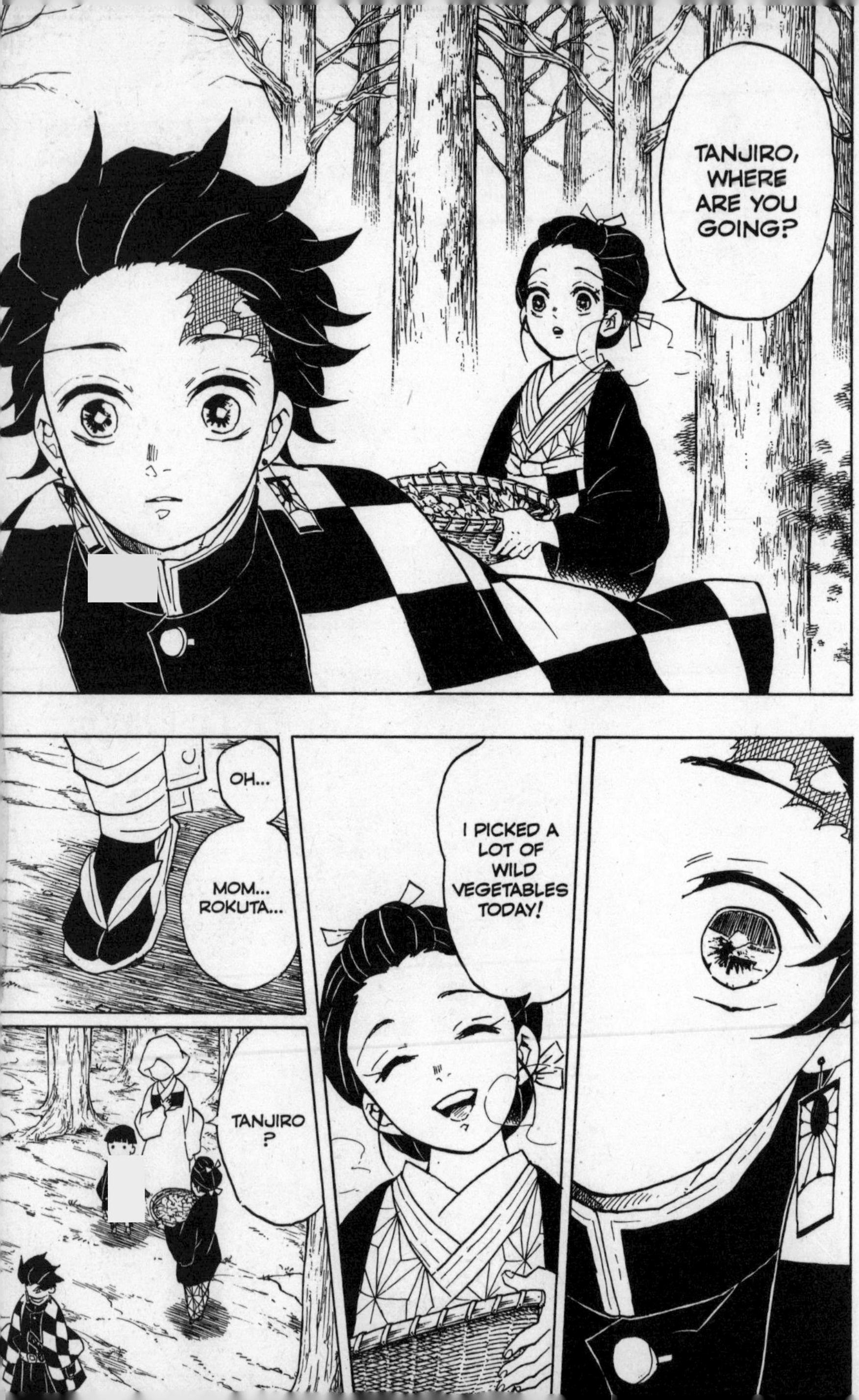
TANJIRO, WHERE ARE YOU GOING?
I PICKED A LOT OF WILD VEGETABLES TODAY!
OH...
MOM... ROKUTA...
TANJIRO ?

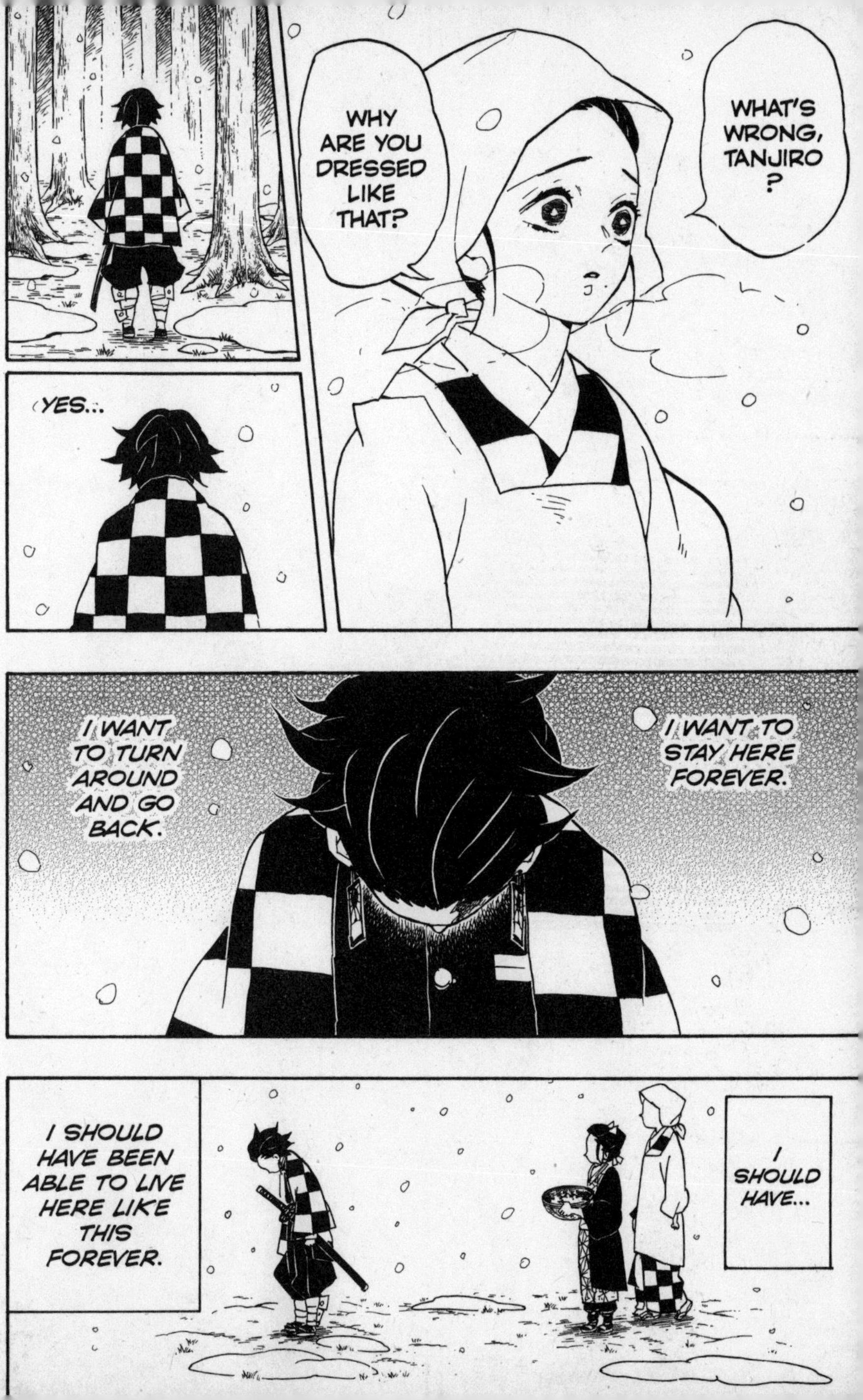
WHAT'S WRONG, TANJIRO?
WHY ARE YOU DRESSED LIKE THAT?
YES...
I WANT TO STAY HERE FOREVER.
I WANT TO TURN AROUND AND GO BACK.
I SHOULD HAVE...
I SHOULD HAVE BEEN ABLE TO LIVE HERE LIKE THIS FOREVER.

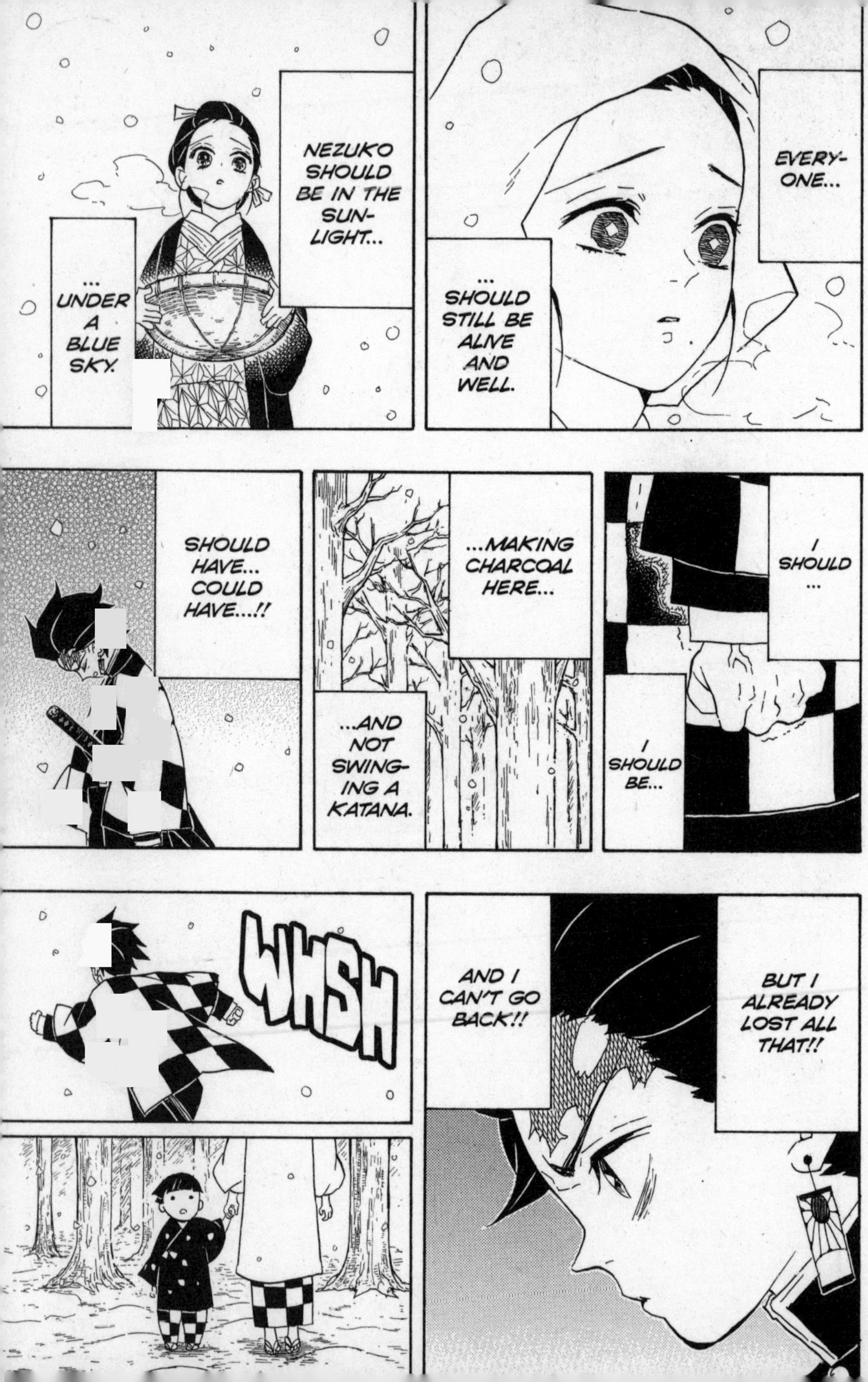
EVERY-ONE...
...SHOULD STILL BE ALIVE AND WELL.
NEZUKO SHOULD BE IN THE SUN-LIGHT...
...UNDER A BLUE SKY.
I SHOULD...
I SHOULD BE...
...MAKING CHARCOAL HERE...
...AND NOT SWING-ING A KATANA.
SHOULD HAVE... COULD HAVE...!!
BUT I ALREADY LOST ALL THAT!!
AND I CAN'T GO BACK!!
WHSH

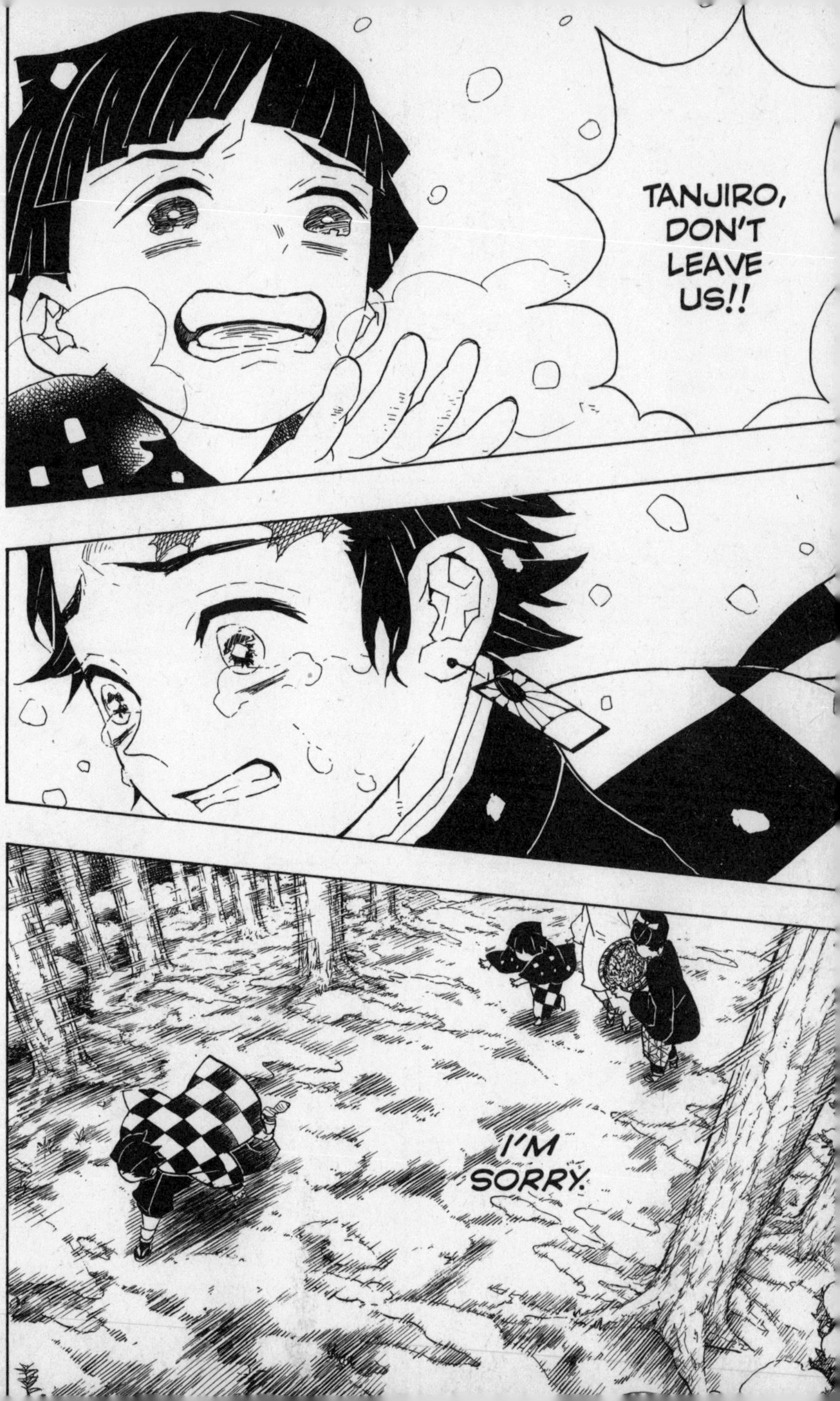

TANJIRO, DON'T LEAVE US!!
I'M SORRY.

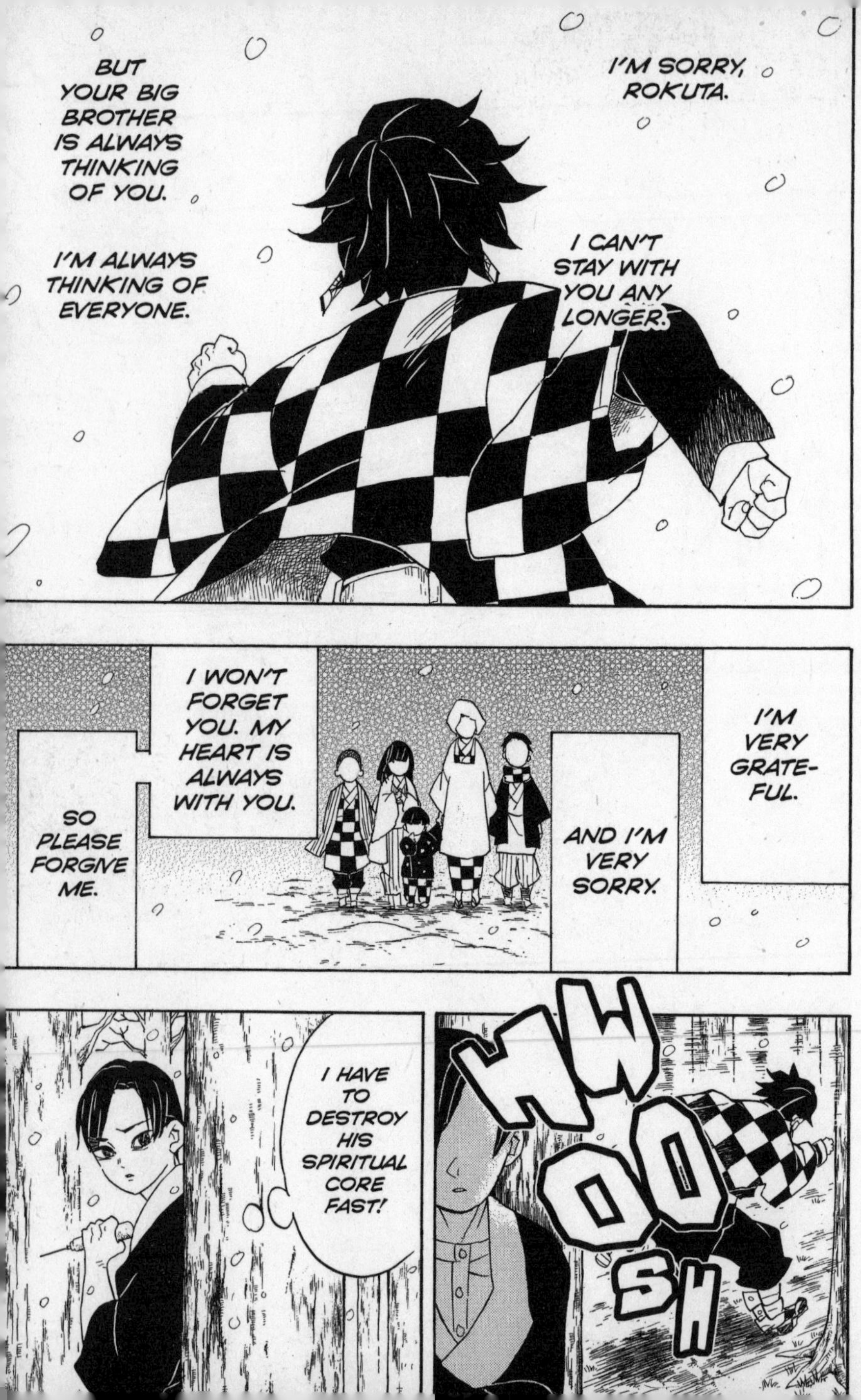
I'M SORRY, ROKUTA.
I CAN'T STAY WITH YOU ANY LONGER.
BUT YOUR BIG BROTHER IS ALWAYS THINKING OF YOU.
I'M ALWAYS THINKING OF EVERYONE.
I'M VERY GRATE-FUL.
AND I'M VERY SORRY.
I WON'T FORGET YOU. MY HEART IS ALWAYS WITH YOU.
SO PLEASE FORGIVE ME.
WHOOSH
I HAVE TO DESTROY HIS SPIRITUAL CORE FAST!

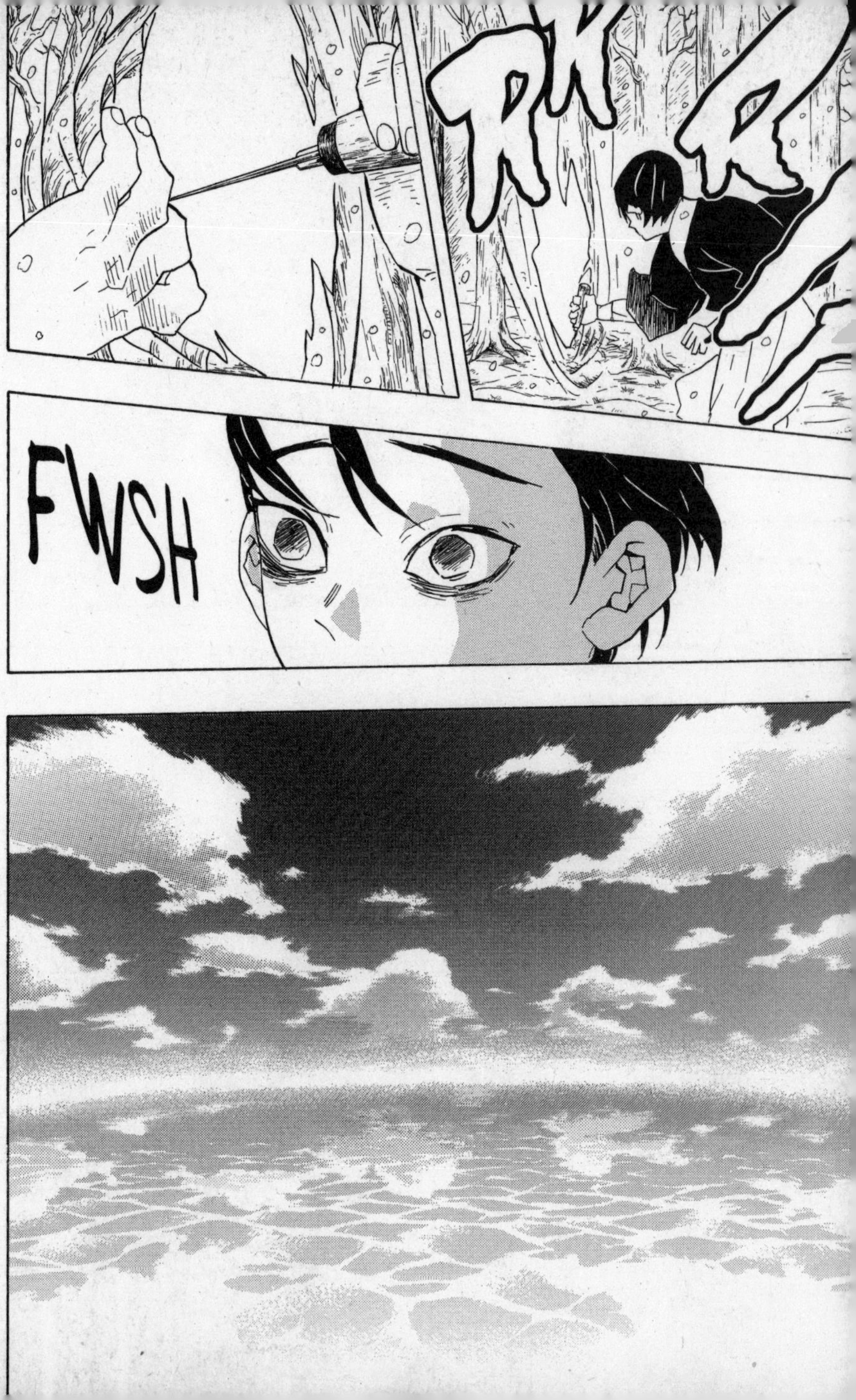
FWSH

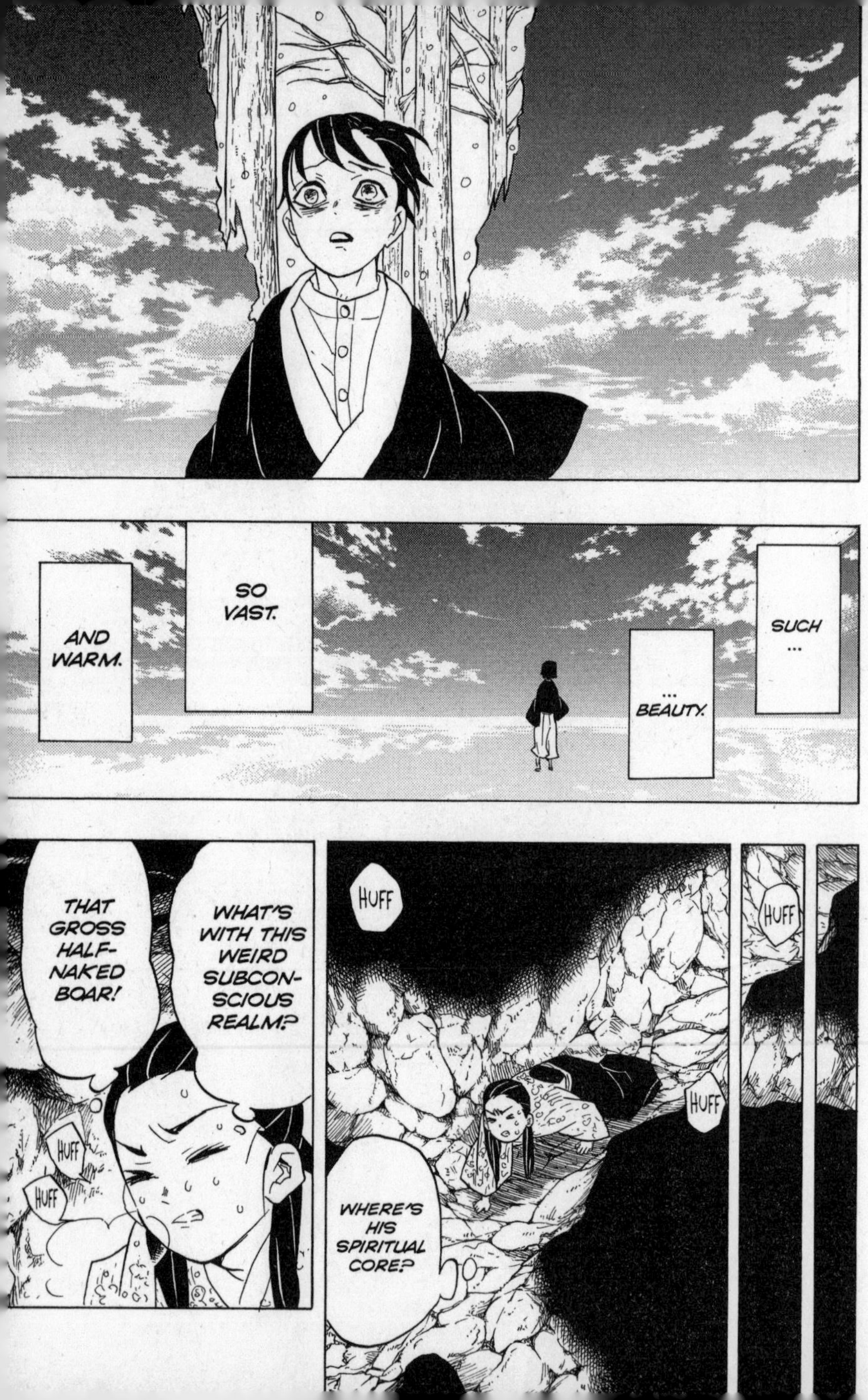
SUCH ...
... BEAUTY.
SO VAST.
AND WARM.
HUFF
HUFF
HUFF
WHERE'S HIS SPIRITUAL CORE?
WHAT'S WITH THIS WEIRD SUBCON-SCIOUS REALM?
THAT GROSS HALF-NAKED BOAR!
HUFF
HUFF

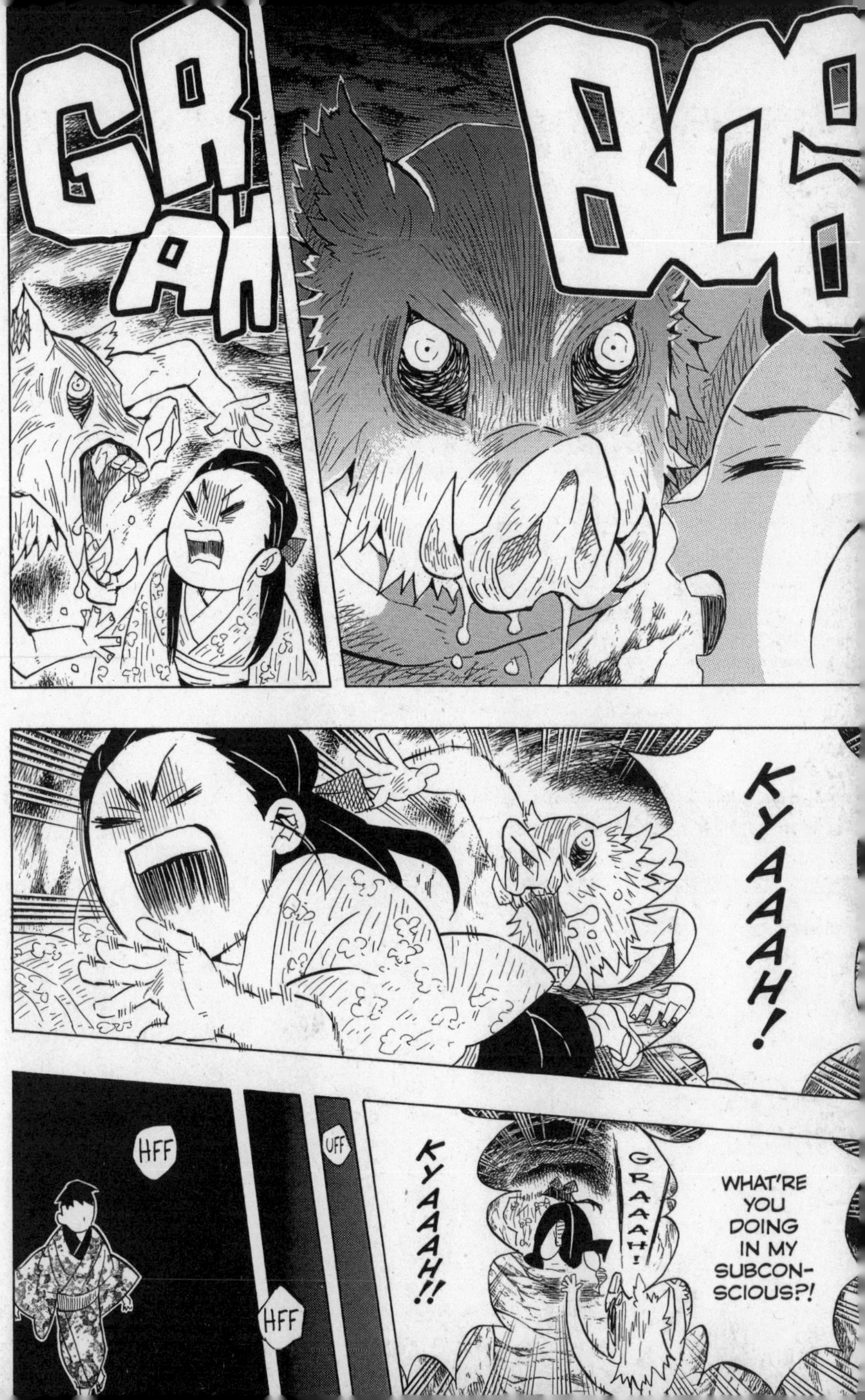

GRAH
KYAAAAH!
WHAT'RE YOU DOING IN MY SUBCON-SCIOUS?!
GRAAAH!
KYAAAAH!!
UFF
HFF
HFF

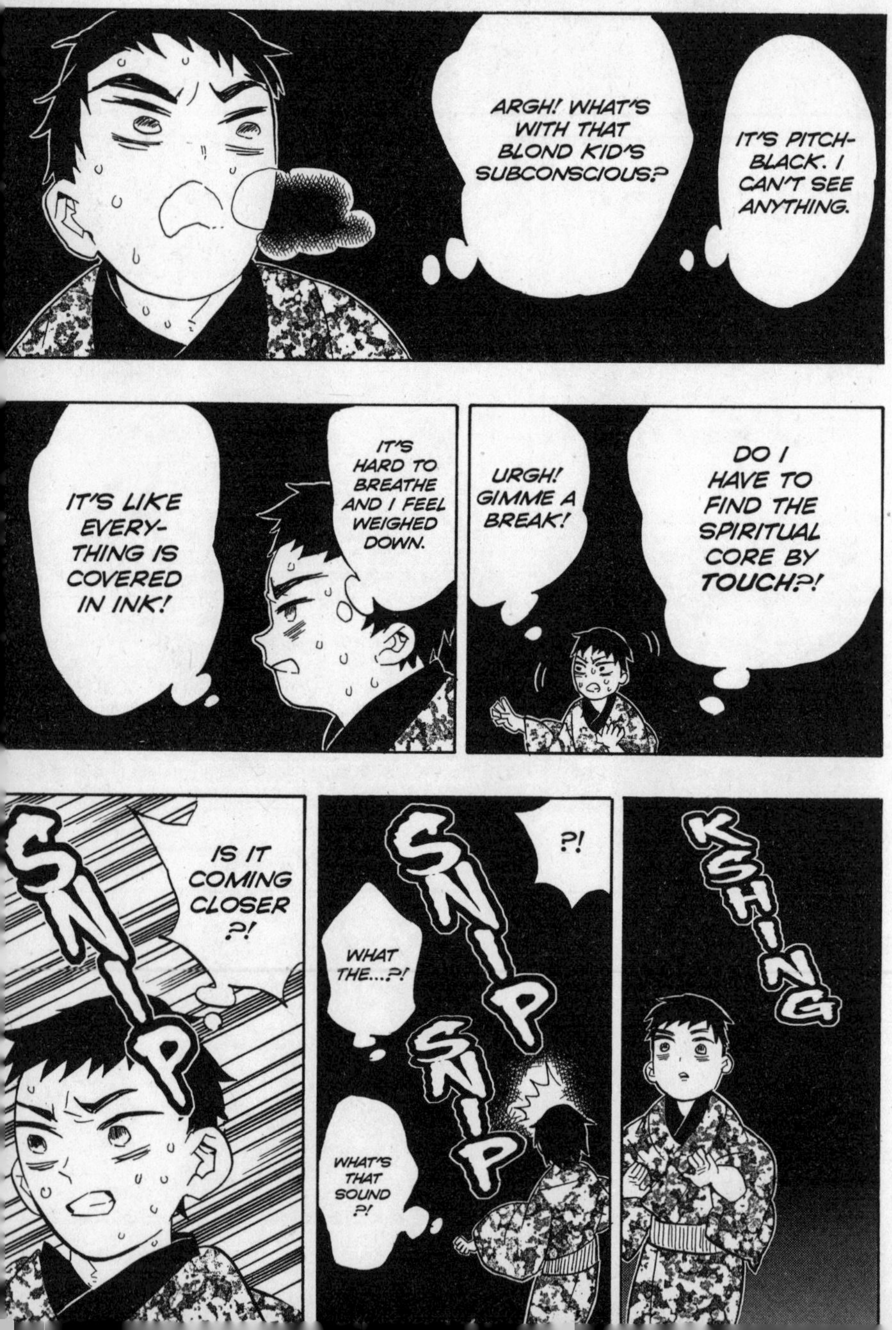
IT'S PITCH-BLACK. I CAN'T SEE ANYTHING.
ARGH! WHAT'S WITH THAT BLOND KID'S SUBCONSCIOUS?
DO I HAVE TO FIND THE SPIRITUAL CORE BY TOUCH?!
URGH! GIMME A BREAK!
IT'S HARD TO BREATHE AND I FEEL WEIGHED DOWN.
IT'S LIKE EVERYTHING IS COVERED IN INK!
KSHING
?!
SNIP
WHAT THE...?!
SNIP
WHAT'S THAT SOUND ?!
IS IT COMING CLOSER ?!
SNIP

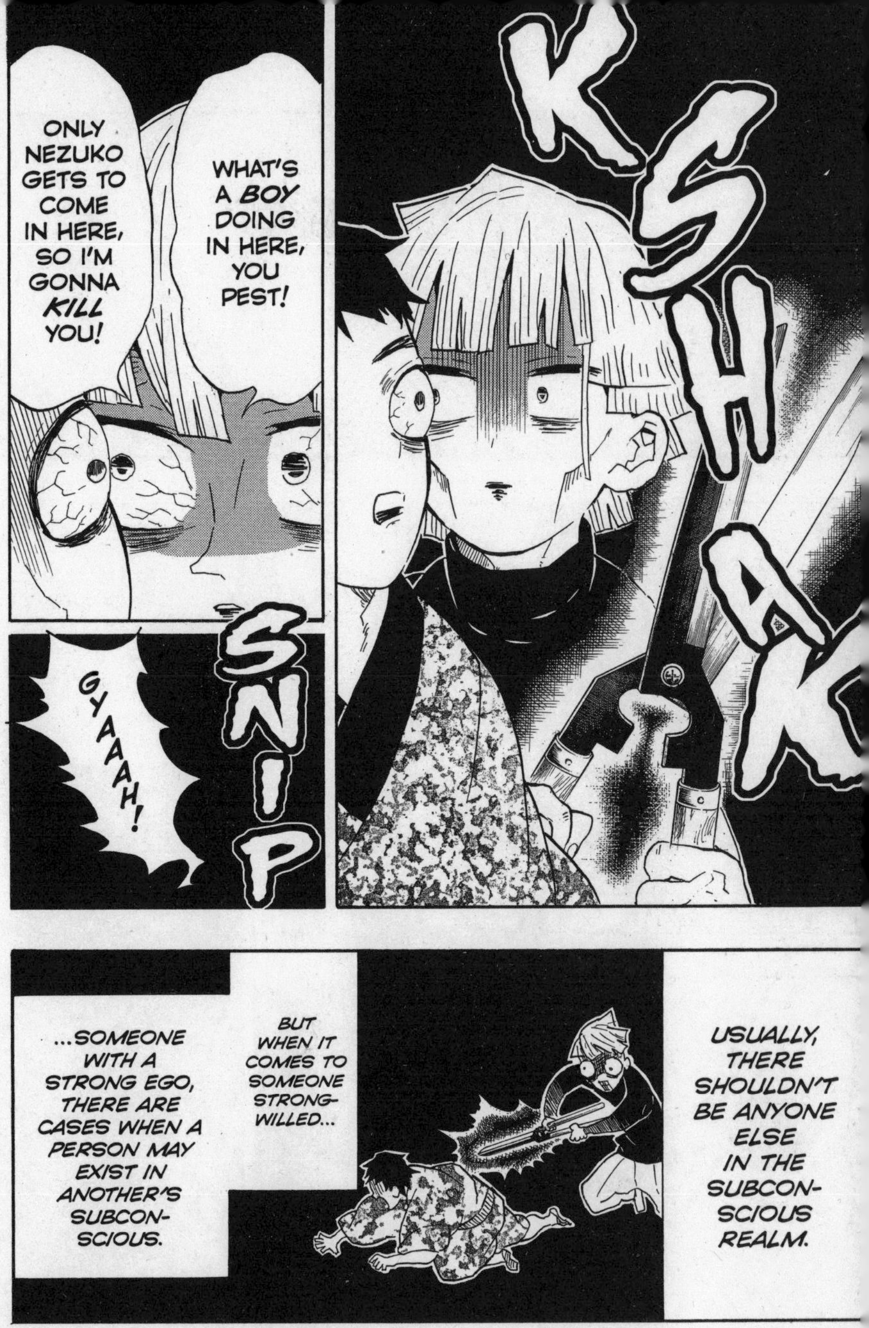
KSHAAK
WHAT'S A BOY DOING IN HERE, YOU PEST!
ONLY NEZUKO GETS TO COME IN HERE, SO I'M GONNA KILL YOU!
SNIP
GYAAAH!
USUALLY, THERE SHOULDN'T BE ANYONE ELSE IN THE SUBCONSCIOUS REALM.
BUT WHEN IT COMES TO SOMEONE STRONG-WILLED...
...SOMEONE WITH A STRONG EGO, THERE ARE CASES WHEN A PERSON MAY EXIST IN ANOTHER'S SUBCONSCIOUS.

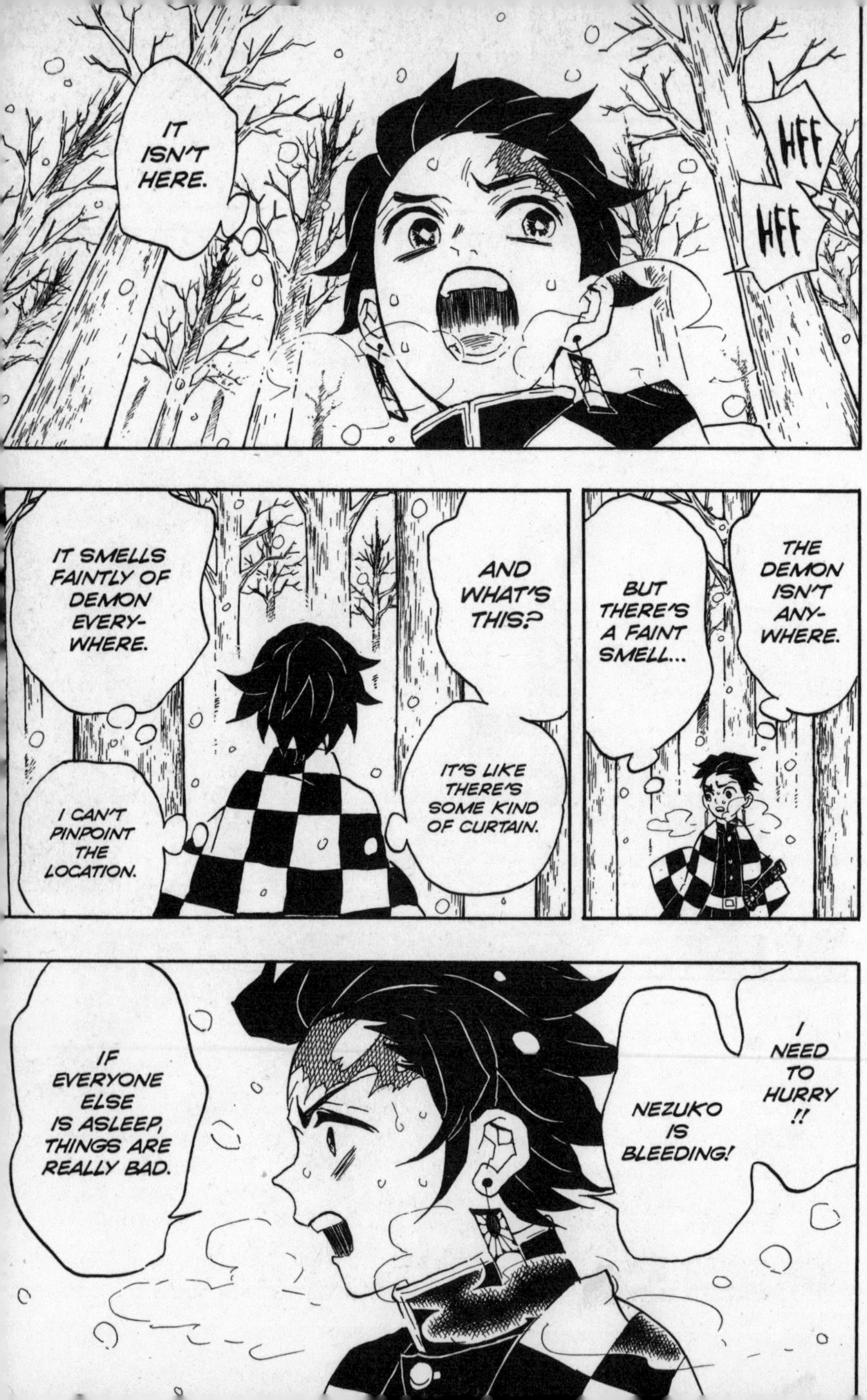
HFF
HFF
IT ISN'T HERE.
THE DEMON ISN'T ANYWHERE.
BUT THERE'S A FAINT SMELL...
AND WHAT'S THIS?
IT'S LIKE THERE'S SOME KIND OF CURTAIN.
IT SMELLS FAINTLY OF DEMON EVERYWHERE.
I CAN'T PINPOINT THE LOCATION.
I NEED TO HURRY!!
NEZUKO IS BLEEDING!
IF EVERYONE ELSE IS ASLEEP, THINGS ARE REALLY BAD.

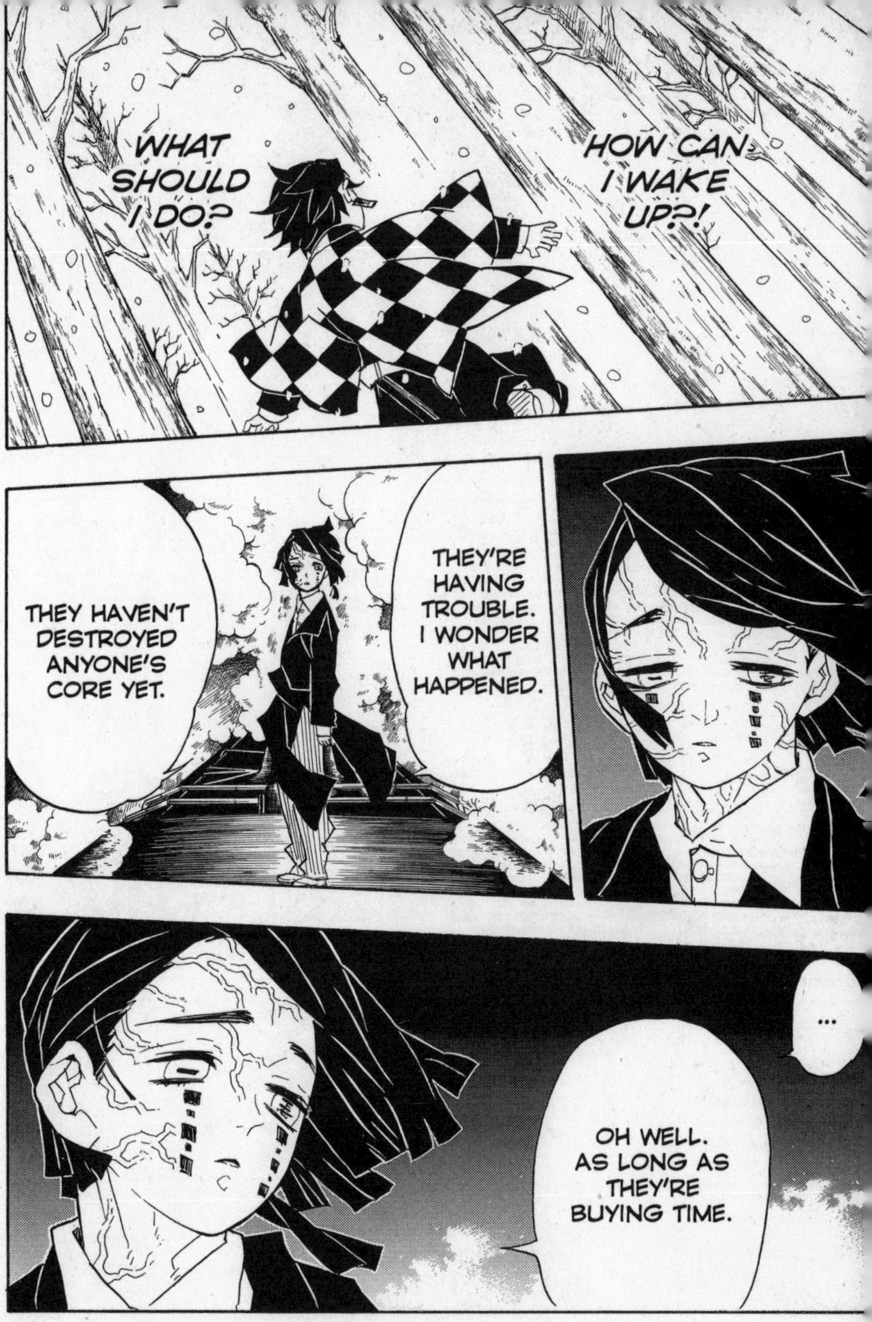
HOW CAN I WAKE UP?!
WHAT SHOULD I DO?
THEY'RE HAVING TROUBLE. I WONDER WHAT HAPPENED.
THEY HAVEN'T DESTROYED ANYONE'S CORE YET.
...
OH WELL. AS LONG AS THEY'RE BUYING TIME.

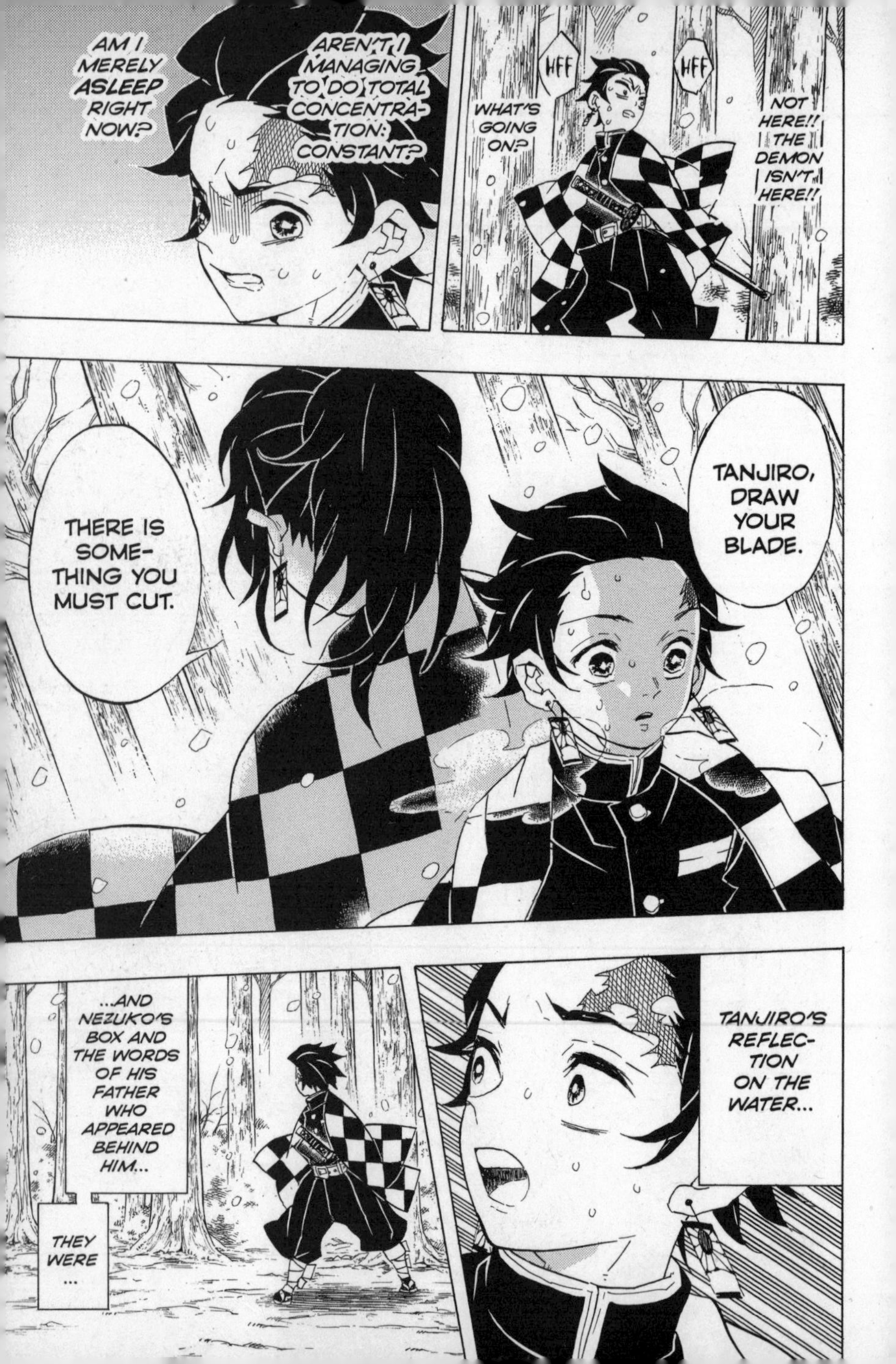
HFF
HFF
NOT HERE!! THE DEMON ISN'T HERE!!
WHAT'S GOING ON?
AREN'T I MANAGING TO DO TOTAL CONCENTRATION: CONSTANT?
AM I MERELY ASLEEP RIGHT NOW?
TANJIRO, DRAW YOUR BLADE.
THERE IS SOMETHING YOU MUST CUT.
TANJIRO'S REFLECTION ON THE WATER...
...AND NEZUKO'S BOX AND THE WORDS OF HIS FATHER WHO APPEARED BEHIND HIM...
THEY WERE ...

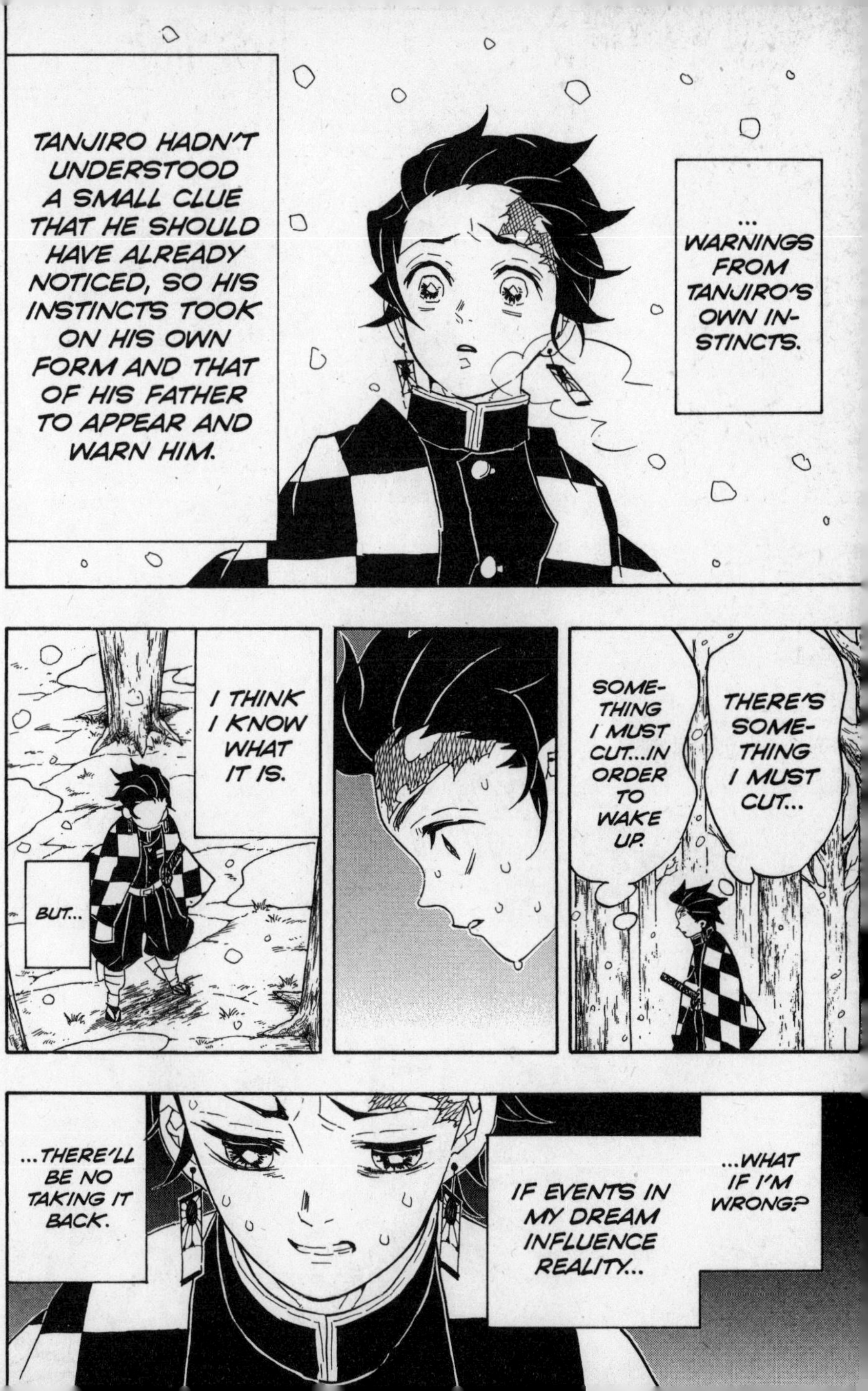
...WARNINGS FROM TANJIRO'S OWN INSTINCTS.
TANJIRO HADN'T UNDERSTOOD A SMALL CLUE THAT HE SHOULD HAVE ALREADY NOTICED, SO HIS INSTINCTS TOOK ON HIS OWN FORM AND THAT OF HIS FATHER TO APPEAR AND WARN HIM.
THERE'S SOMETHING I MUST CUT...
SOMETHING I MUST CUT...IN ORDER TO WAKE UP.
I THINK I KNOW WHAT IT IS.
BUT...
...WHAT IF I'M WRONG?
IF EVENTS IN MY DREAM INFLUENCE REALITY...
...THERE'LL BE NO TAKING IT BACK.

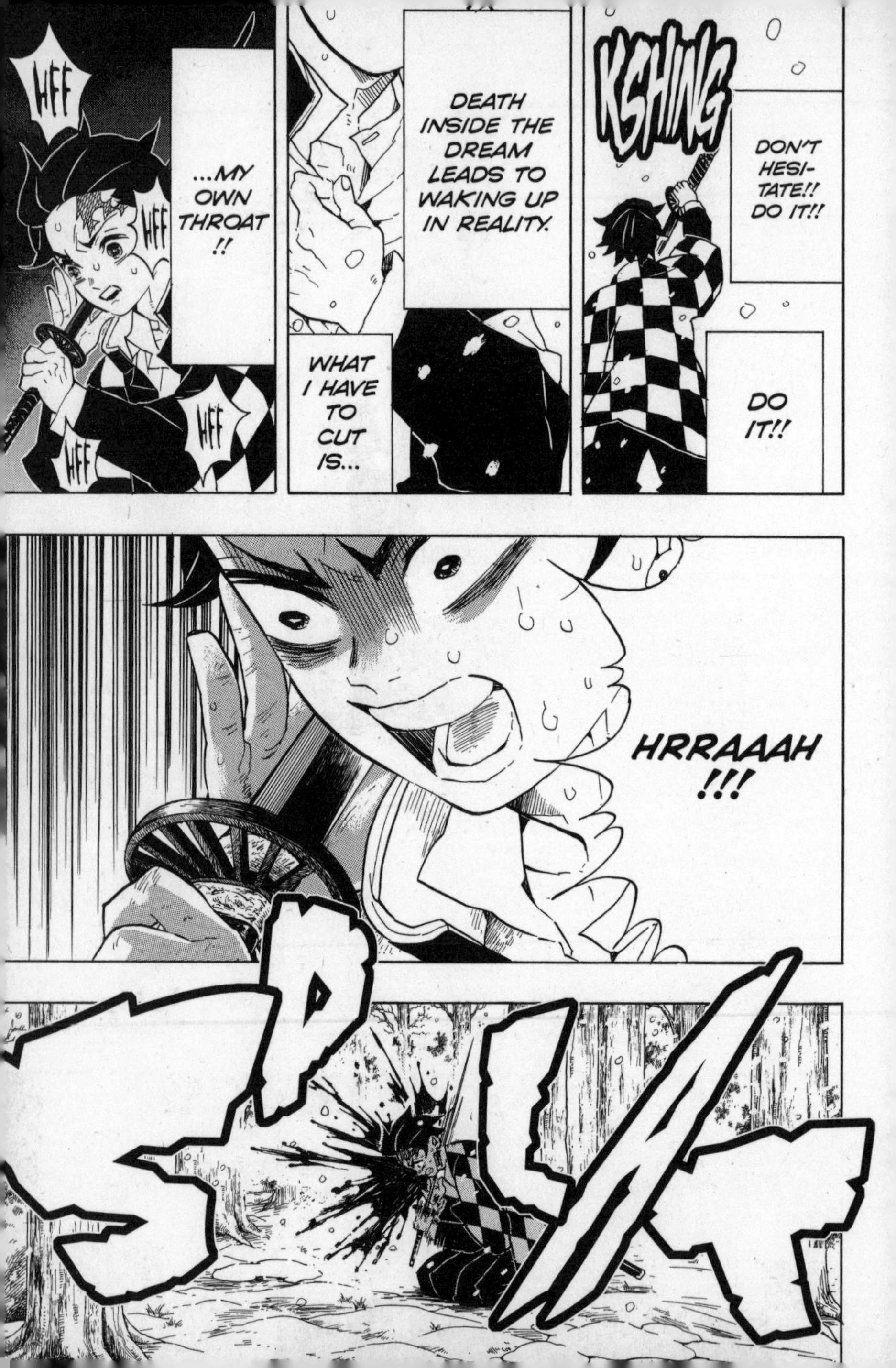
KSHING
DON'T HESI-TATE!! DO IT!!
DO IT!!
DEATH INSIDE THE DREAM LEADS TO WAKING UP IN REALITY.
WHAT I HAVE TO CUT IS...
...MY OWN THROAT!!
HFF
HFF
HFF
HFF
HRRAAAH!!!

Inosuke's Ideal Self-Image

Spikes

Breathes fire

About three meters
tall when standing up

CHAPTER 58: GOOD MORNING

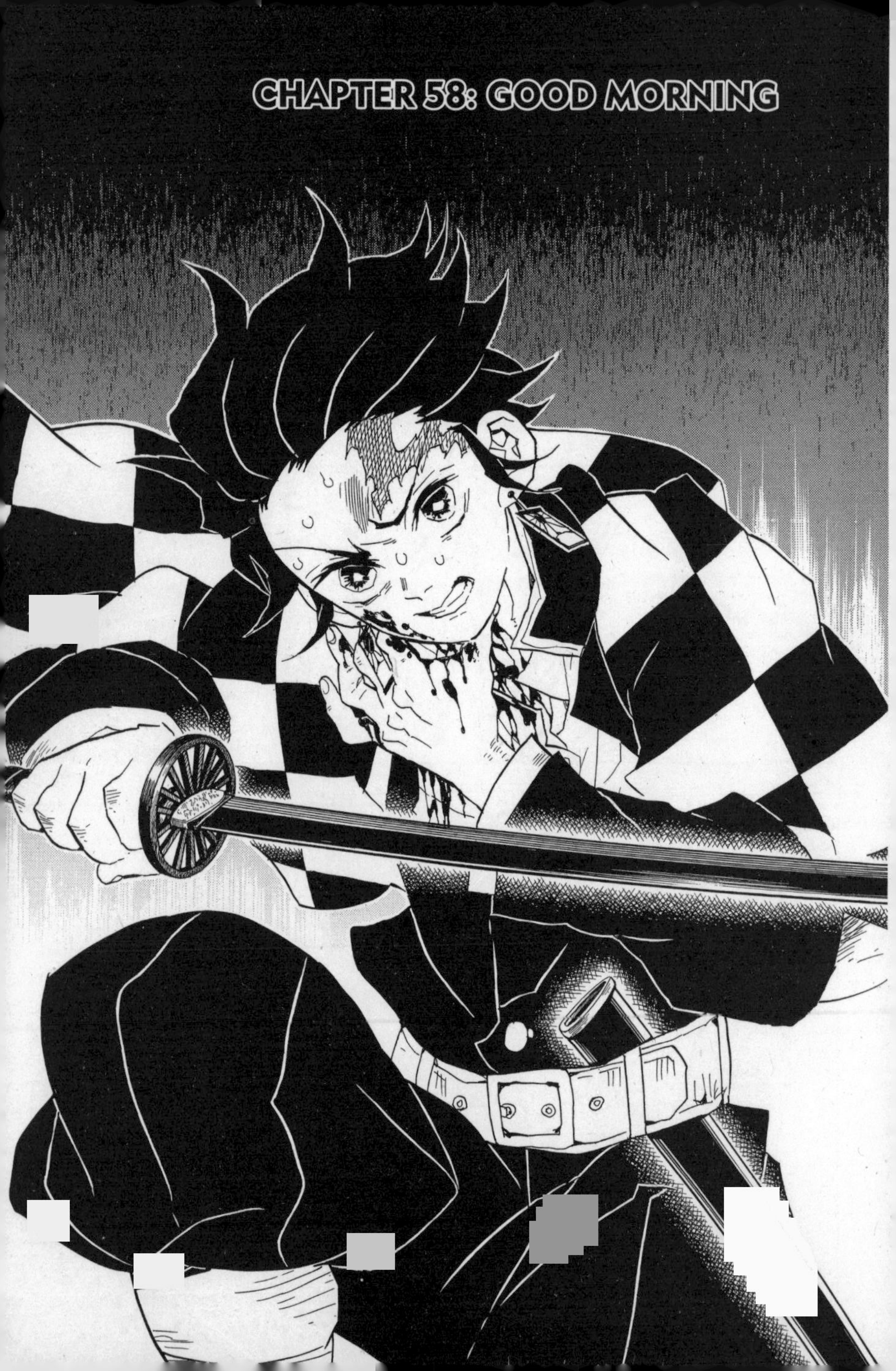

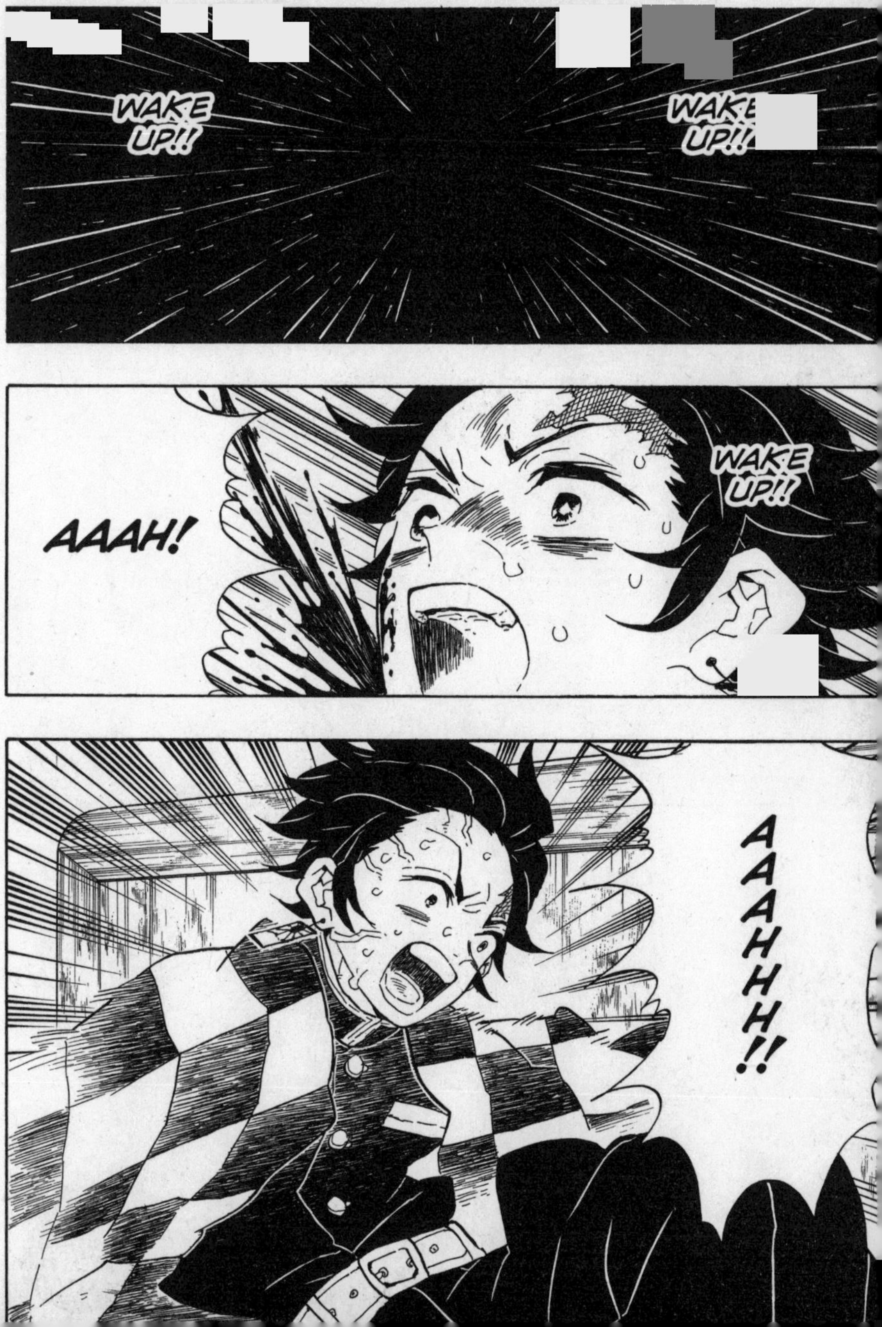
WAKE UP!!
WAKE UP!!
WAKE UP!!
AAAH!
AAAHHH!!

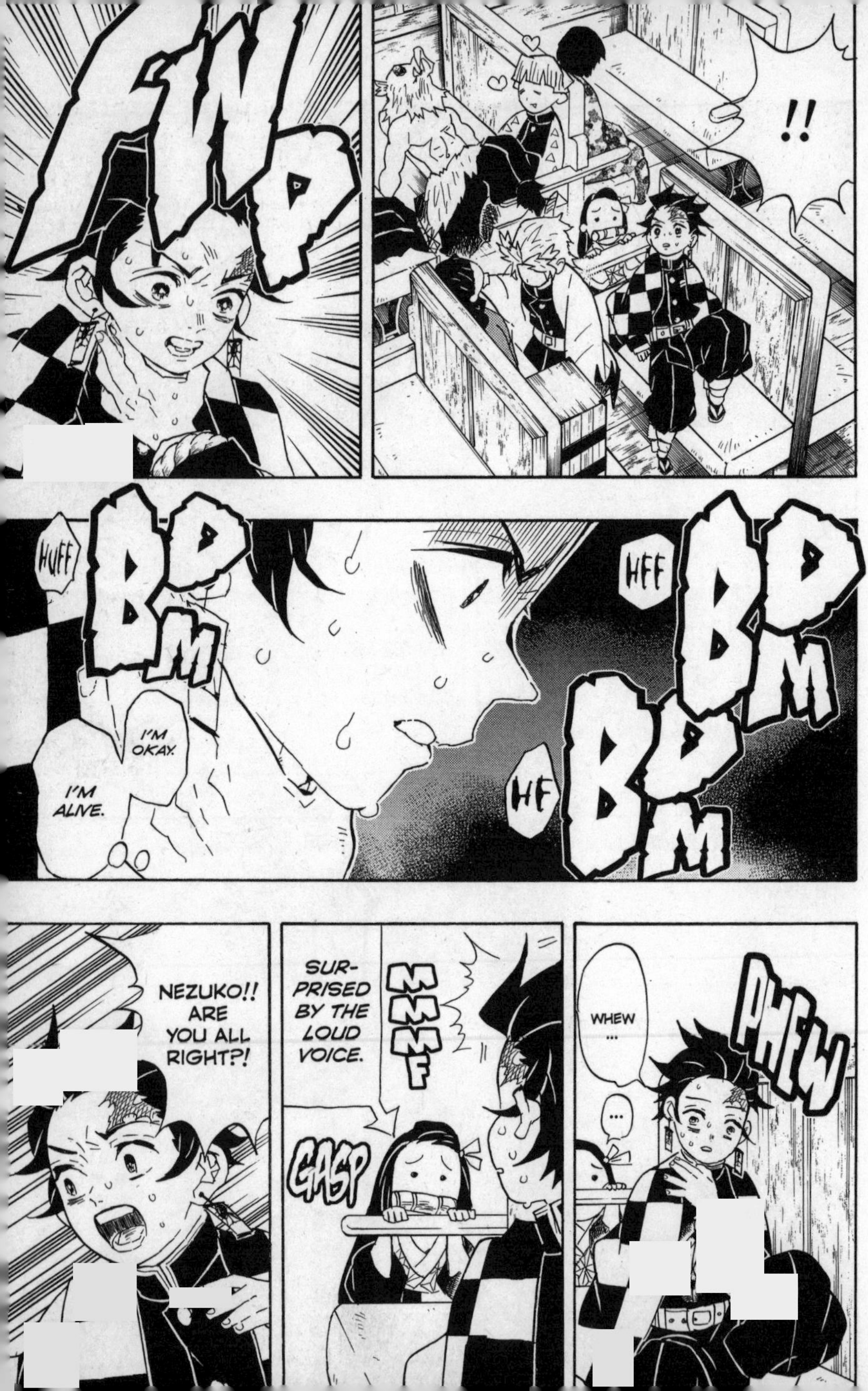
!!
FWP
HFF
BDM
HF
BDM
HUFF
BDM
I'M OKAY.
I'M ALIVE.
PHEW
WHEW...
...
SUR-PRISED BY THE LOUD VOICE.
MMMF
GASP
NEZUKO!! ARE YOU ALL RIGHT?!

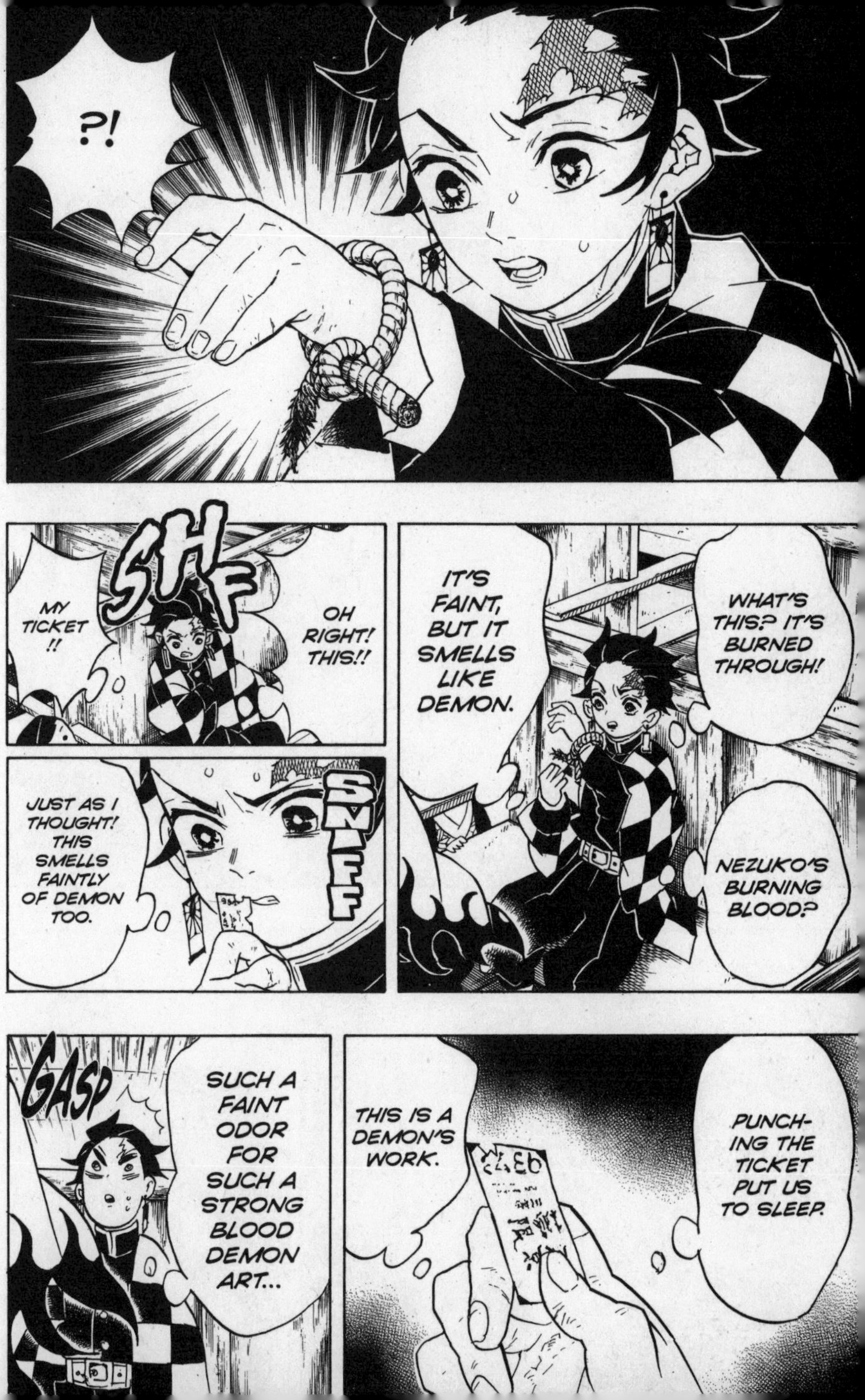
?!
WHAT'S THIS? IT'S BURNED THROUGH!
IT'S FAINT, BUT IT SMELLS LIKE DEMON.
NEZUKO'S BURNING BLOOD?
OH RIGHT! THIS!!
SHF
MY TICKET!!
SNIFF
JUST AS I THOUGHT! THIS SMELLS FAINTLY OF DEMON TOO.
PUNCHING THE TICKET PUT US TO SLEEP.
THIS IS A DEMON'S WORK.
SUCH A FAINT ODOR FOR SUCH A STRONG BLOOD DEMON ART...
GASP

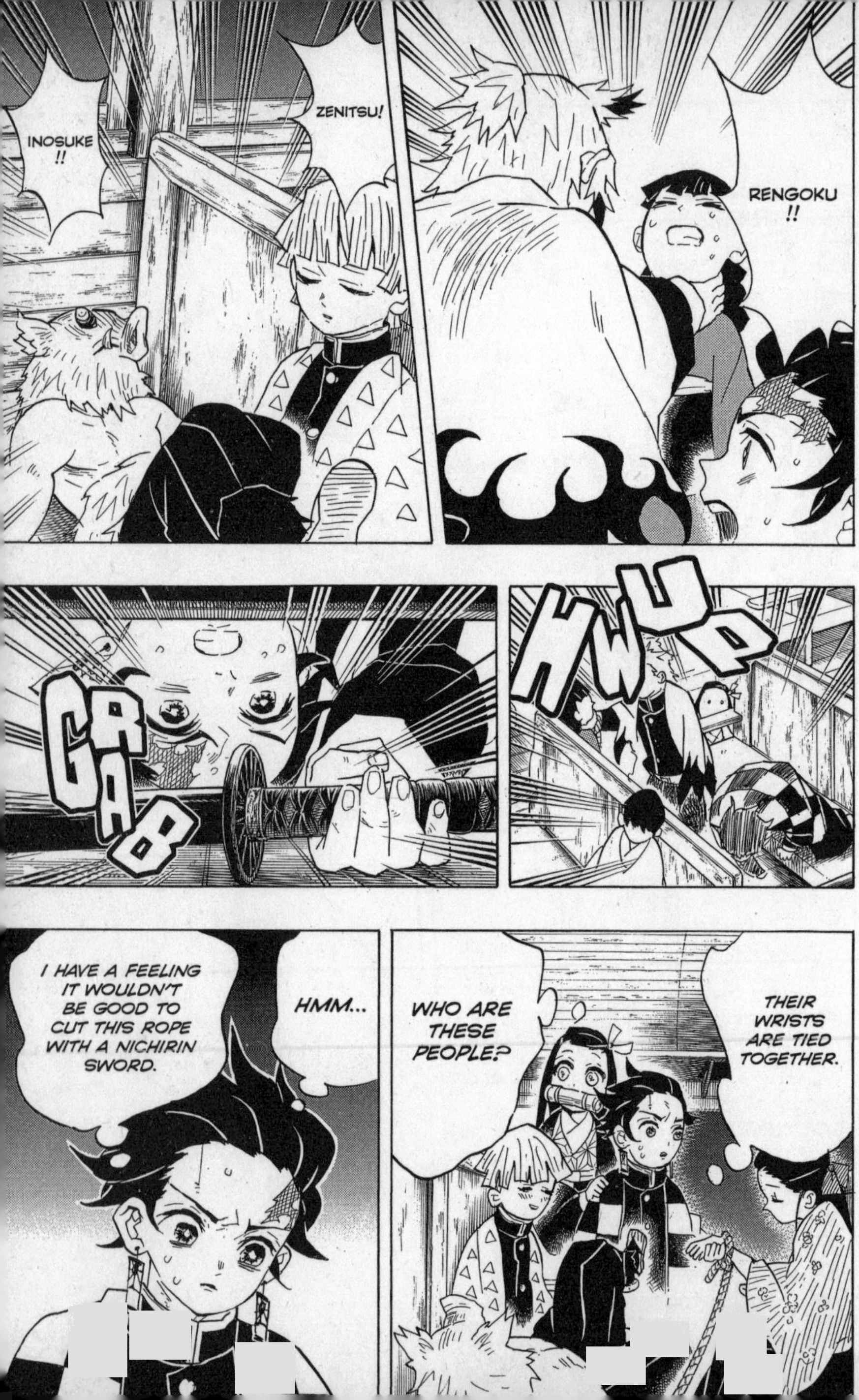
RENGOKU !!
ZENITSU!
INOSUKE !!
HWUP
GRAB
THEIR WRISTS ARE TIED TOGETHER.
WHO ARE THESE PEOPLE?
HMM...
I HAVE A FEELING IT WOULDN'T BE GOOD TO CUT THIS ROPE WITH A NICHIRIN SWORD.

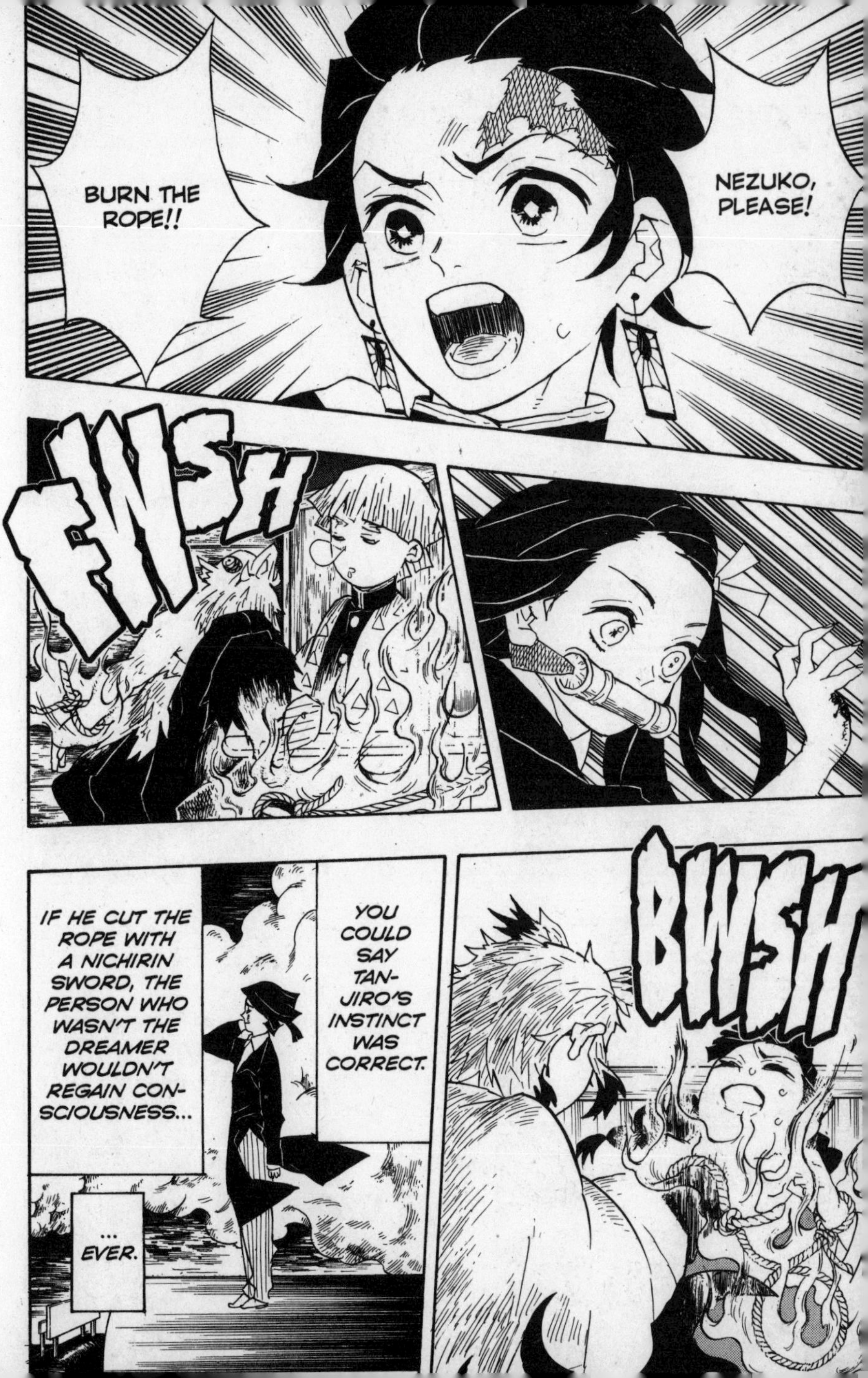
NEZUKO, PLEASE!
BURN THE ROPE!!
FWSH
BWSH
YOU COULD SAY TAN-JIRO'S INSTINCT WAS CORRECT.
IF HE CUT THE ROPE WITH A NICHIRIN SWORD, THE PERSON WHO WASN'T THE DREAMER WOULDN'T REGAIN CON-SCIOUSNESS...
... EVER.

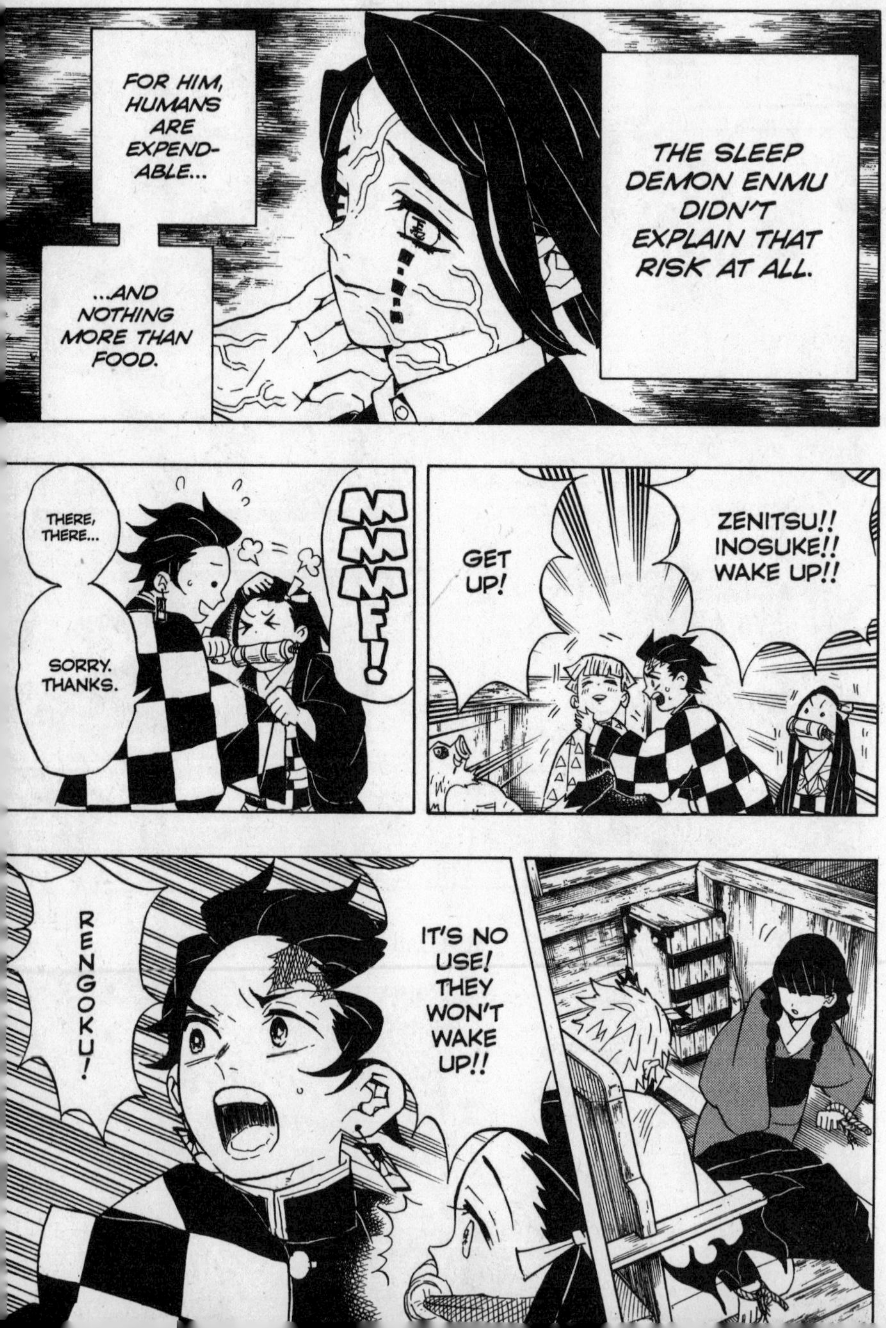
THE SLEEP DEMON ENMU DIDN'T EXPLAIN THAT RISK AT ALL.
FOR HIM, HUMANS ARE EXPEND-ABLE...
...AND NOTHING MORE THAN FOOD.
ZENITSU!! INOSUKE!! WAKE UP!!
GET UP!
MMMF!
THERE, THERE...
SORRY. THANKS.
IT'S NO USE! THEY WON'T WAKE UP!!
RENGOKU!

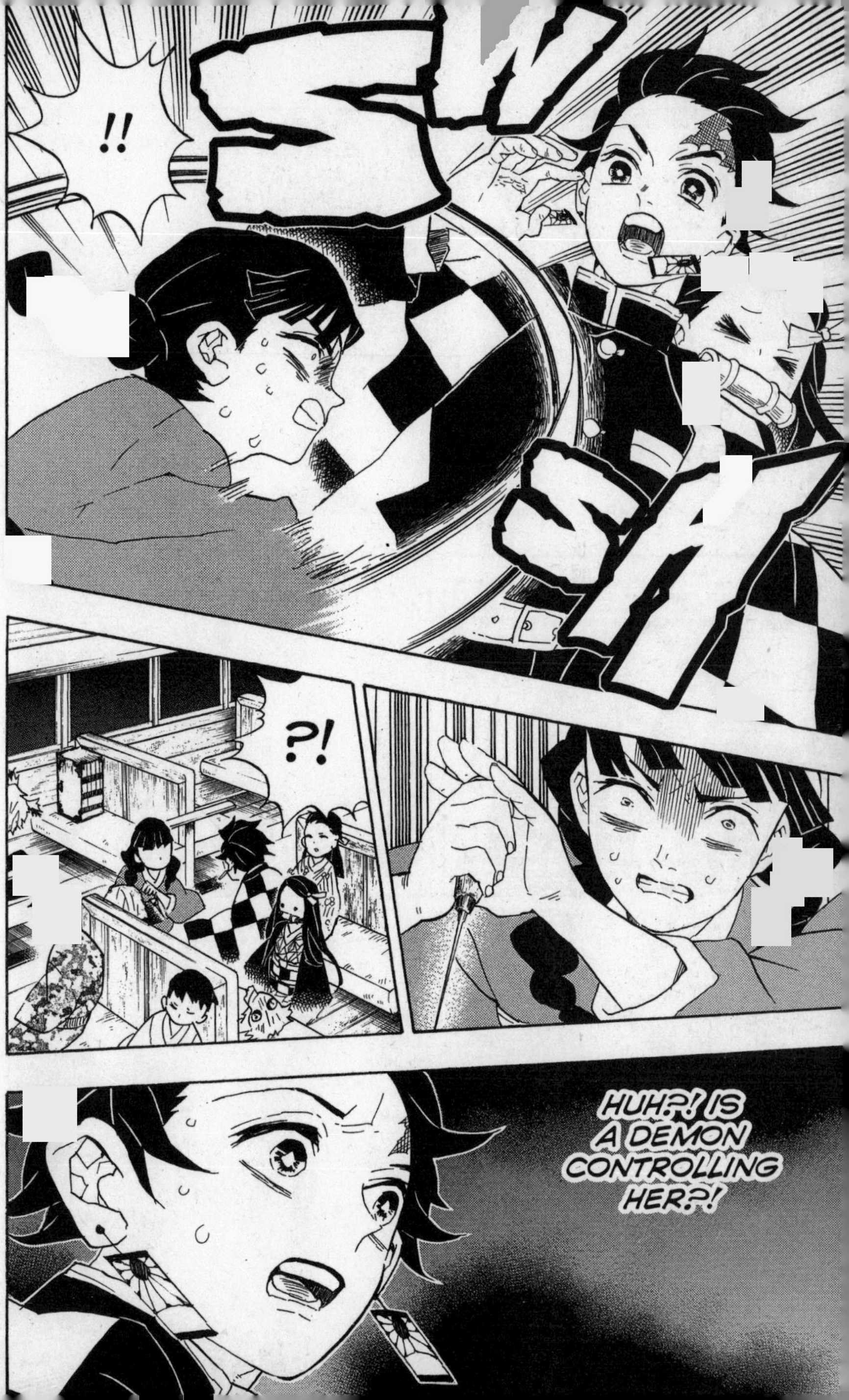
!!
SW
SH
?!
HUH?! IS A DEMON CONTROLLING HER?!

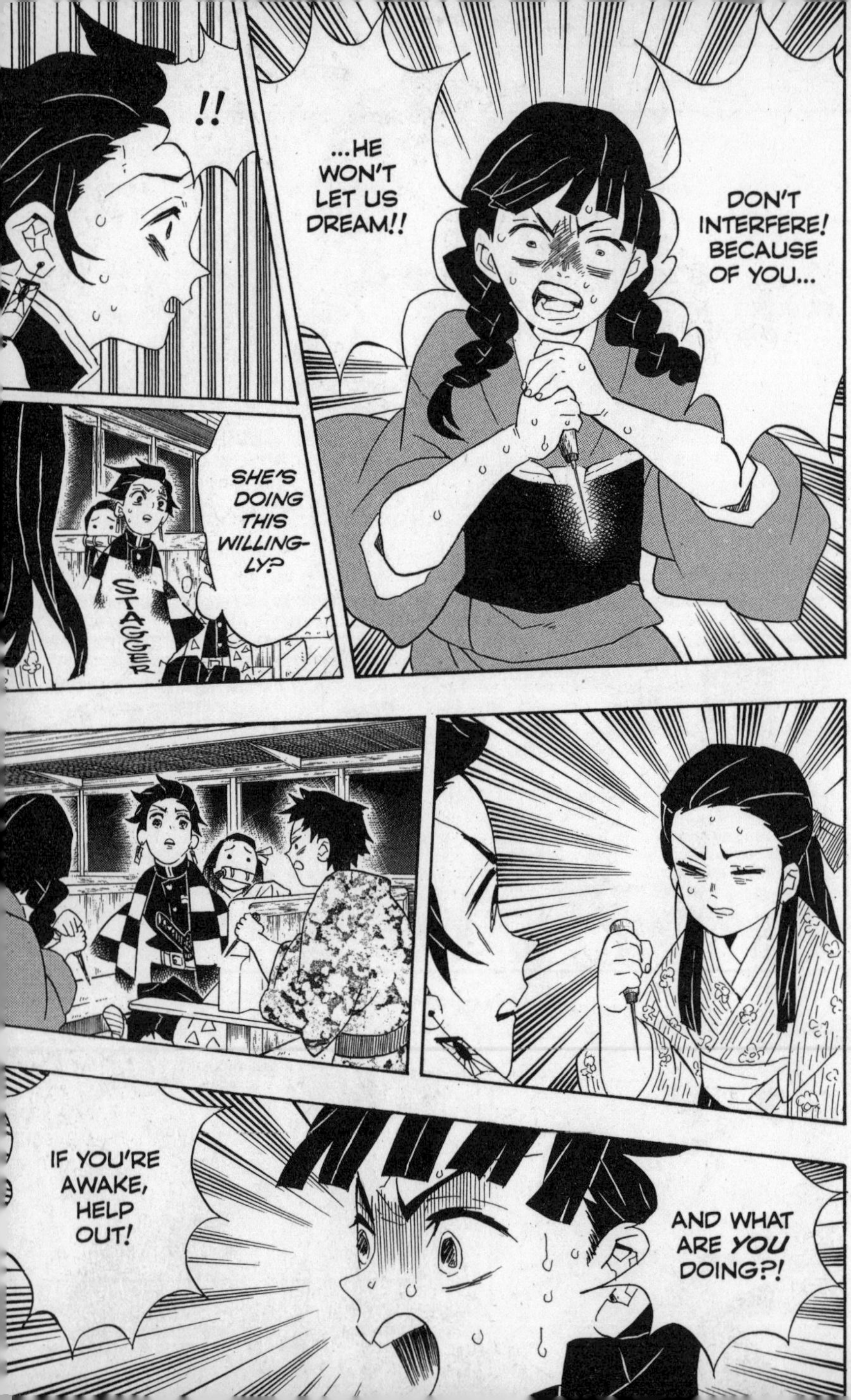
DON'T INTERFERE! BECAUSE OF YOU...
...HE WON'T LET US DREAM!!
!!
SHE'S DOING THIS WILLING-LY?
STAGGER
AND WHAT ARE YOU DOING?!
IF YOU'RE AWAKE, HELP OUT!

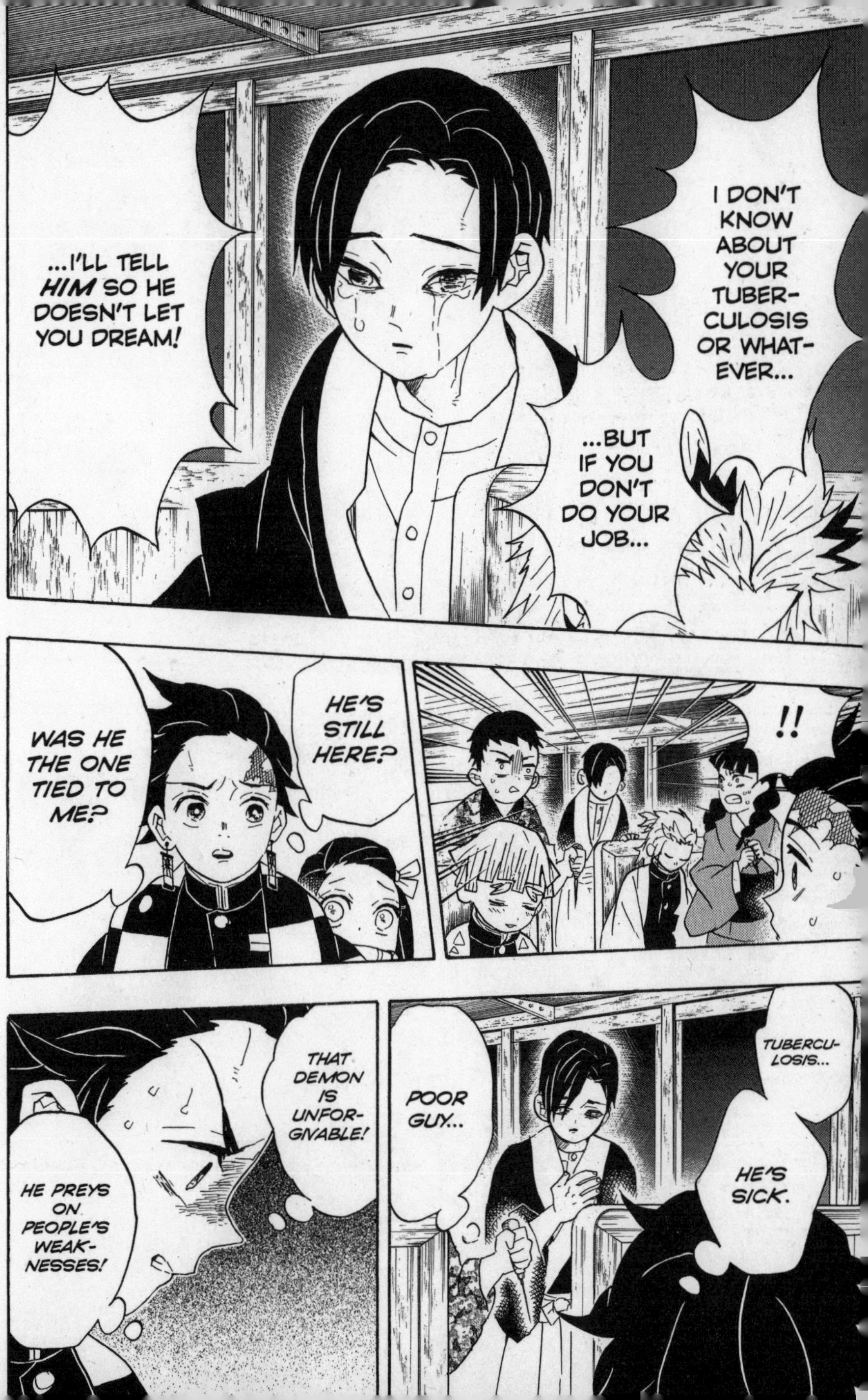
I DON'T KNOW ABOUT YOUR TUBERCULOSIS OR WHATEVER...
...BUT IF YOU DON'T DO YOUR JOB...
...I'LL TELL *HIM* SO HE DOESN'T LET YOU DREAM!
!!
HE'S STILL HERE?
WAS HE THE ONE TIED TO ME?
TUBERCULOSIS...
HE'S SICK.
POOR GUY...
THAT DEMON IS UNFORGIVABLE!
HE PREYS ON PEOPLE'S WEAKNESSES!

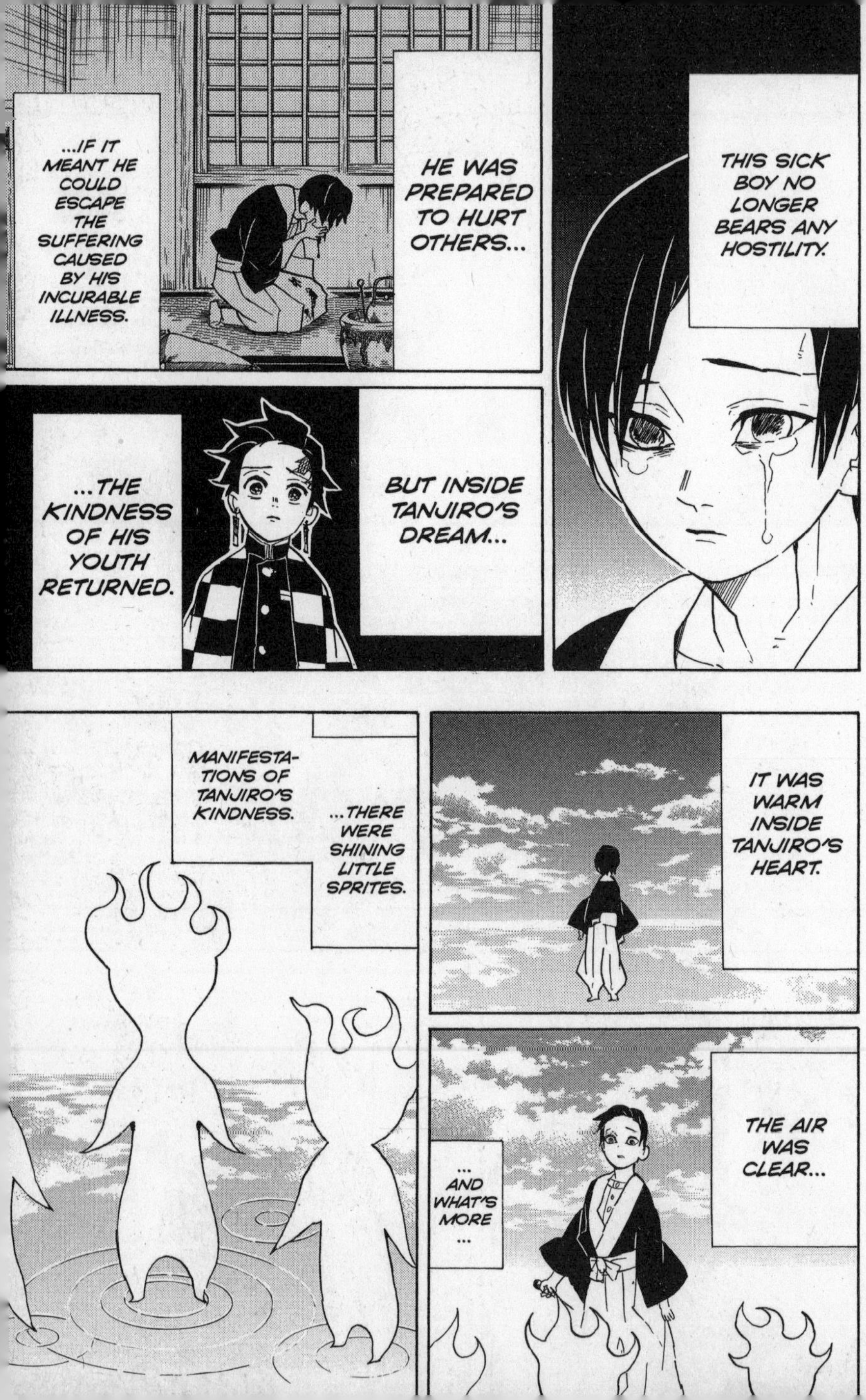
THIS SICK BOY NO LONGER BEARS ANY HOSTILITY.
HE WAS PREPARED TO HURT OTHERS...
...IF IT MEANT HE COULD ESCAPE THE SUFFERING CAUSED BY HIS INCURABLE ILLNESS.
BUT INSIDE TANJIRO'S DREAM...
...THE KINDNESS OF HIS YOUTH RETURNED.
IT WAS WARM INSIDE TANJIRO'S HEART.
THE AIR WAS CLEAR...
... AND WHAT'S MORE ...
...THERE WERE SHINING LITTLE SPRITES.
MANIFESTATIONS OF TANJIRO'S KINDNESS.

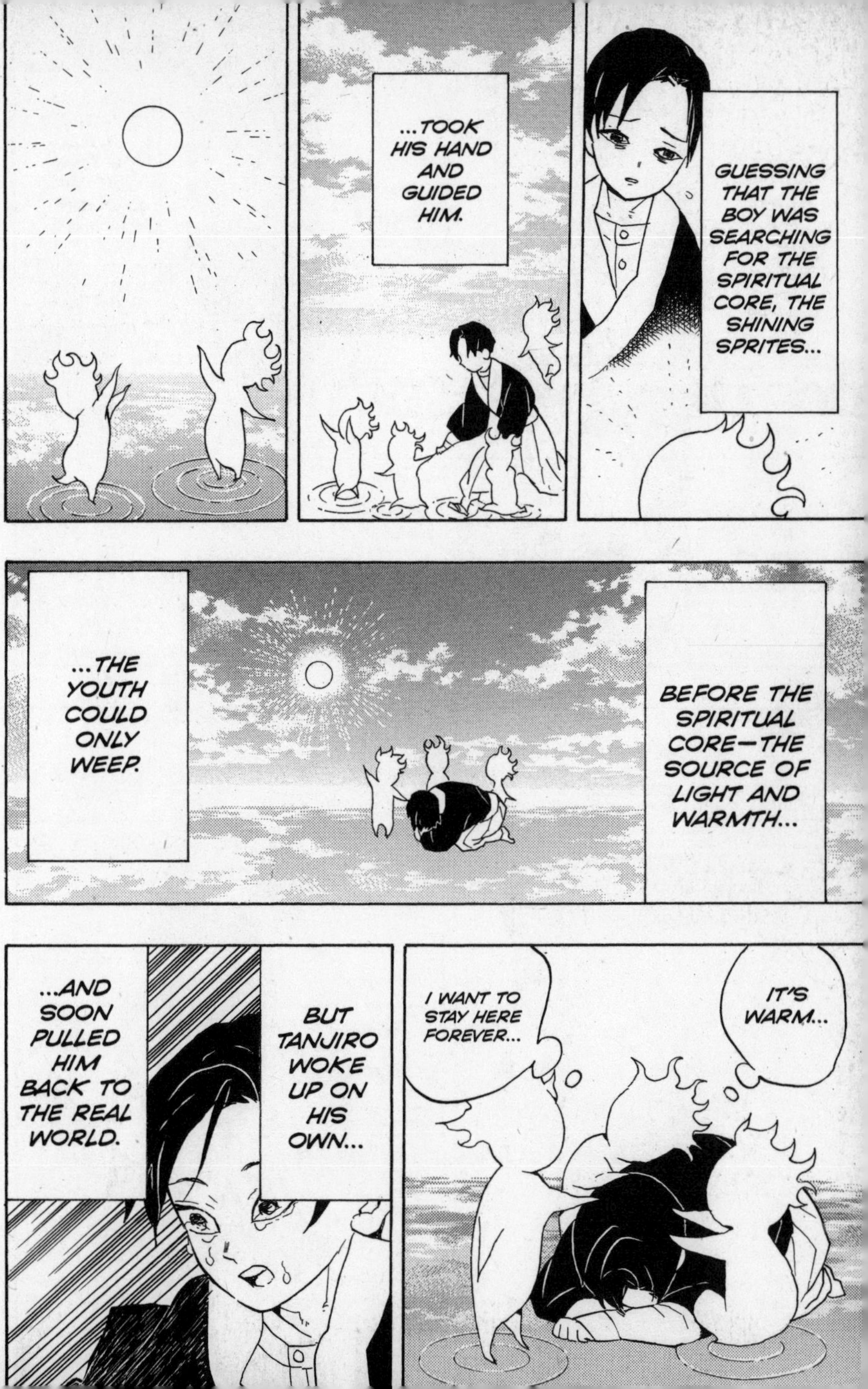
GUESSING THAT THE BOY WAS SEARCHING FOR THE SPIRITUAL CORE, THE SHINING SPRITES...
...TOOK HIS HAND AND GUIDED HIM.
BEFORE THE SPIRITUAL CORE—THE SOURCE OF LIGHT AND WARMTH...
...THE YOUTH COULD ONLY WEEP.
IT'S WARM...
I WANT TO STAY HERE FOREVER...
BUT TANJIRO WOKE UP ON HIS OWN...
...AND SOON PULLED HIM BACK TO THE REAL WORLD.

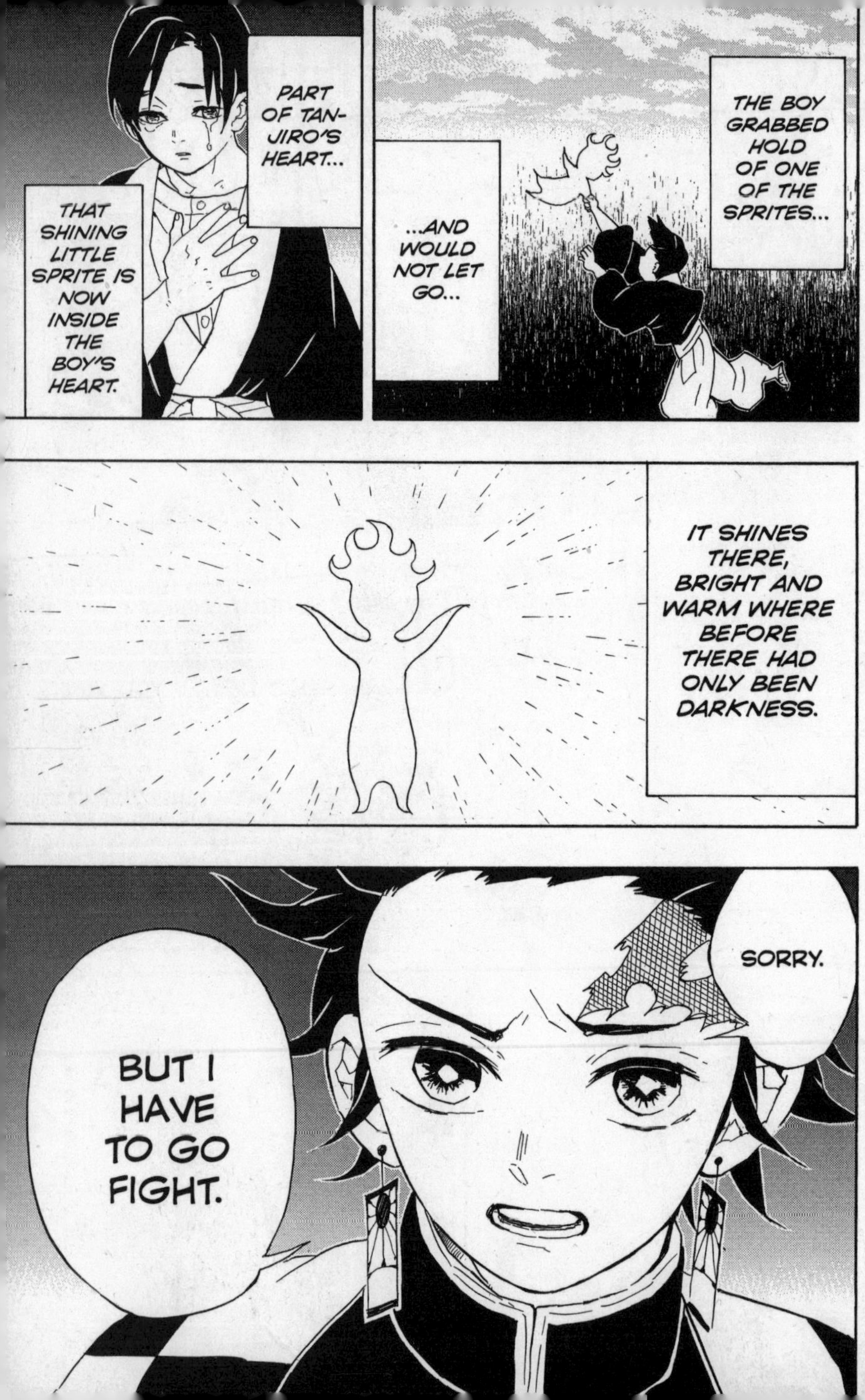
THE BOY GRABBED HOLD OF ONE OF THE SPRITES...
...AND WOULD NOT LET GO...
PART OF TANJIRO'S HEART...
THAT SHINING LITTLE SPRITE IS NOW INSIDE THE BOY'S HEART.
IT SHINES THERE, BRIGHT AND WARM WHERE BEFORE THERE HAD ONLY BEEN DARKNESS.
SORRY.
BUT I HAVE TO GO FIGHT.

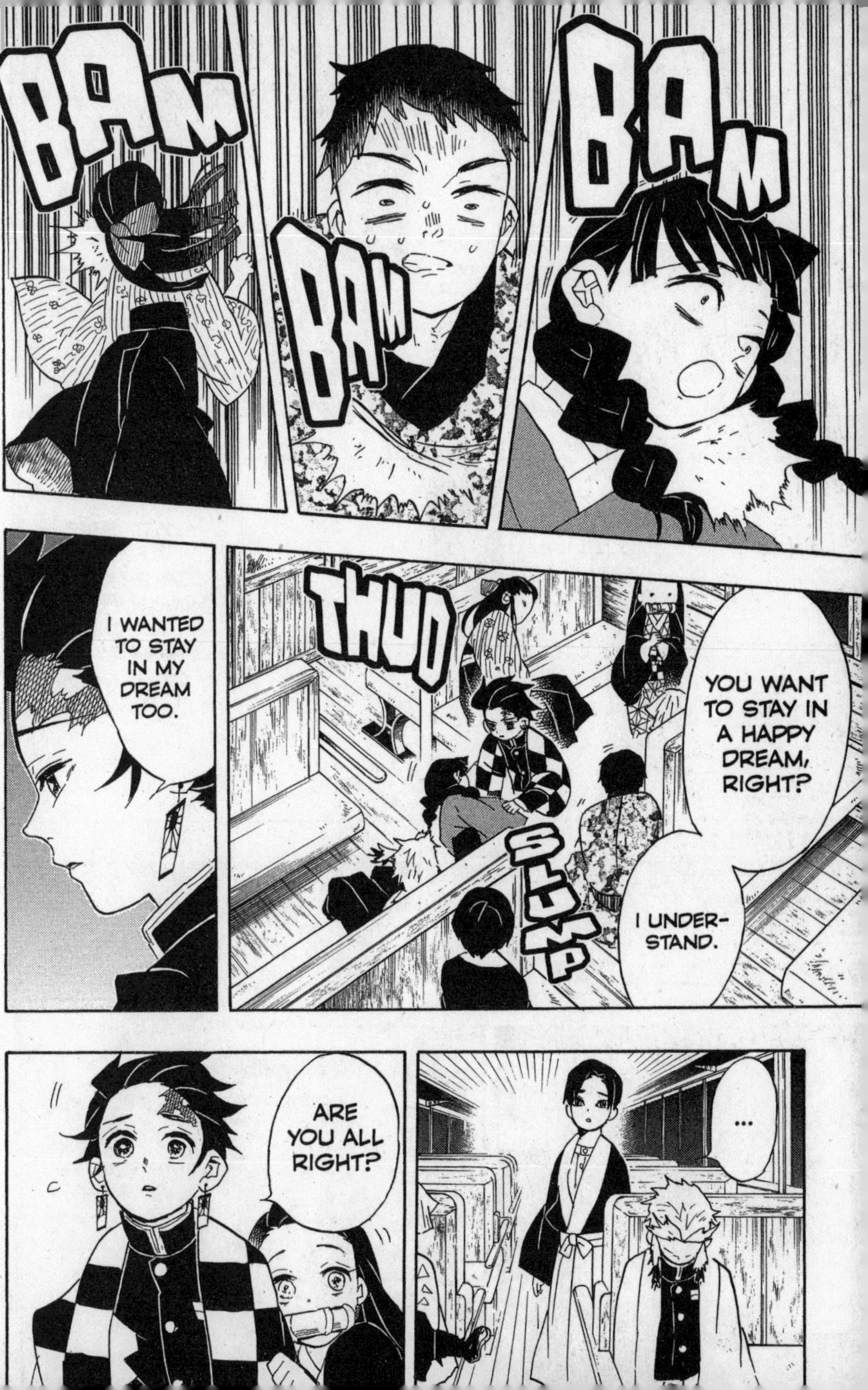
BAM
BAM
BAM
YOU WANT TO STAY IN A HAPPY DREAM, RIGHT?
THUD
I UNDER-STAND.
SLUMP
I WANTED TO STAY IN MY DREAM TOO.
...
ARE YOU ALL RIGHT?

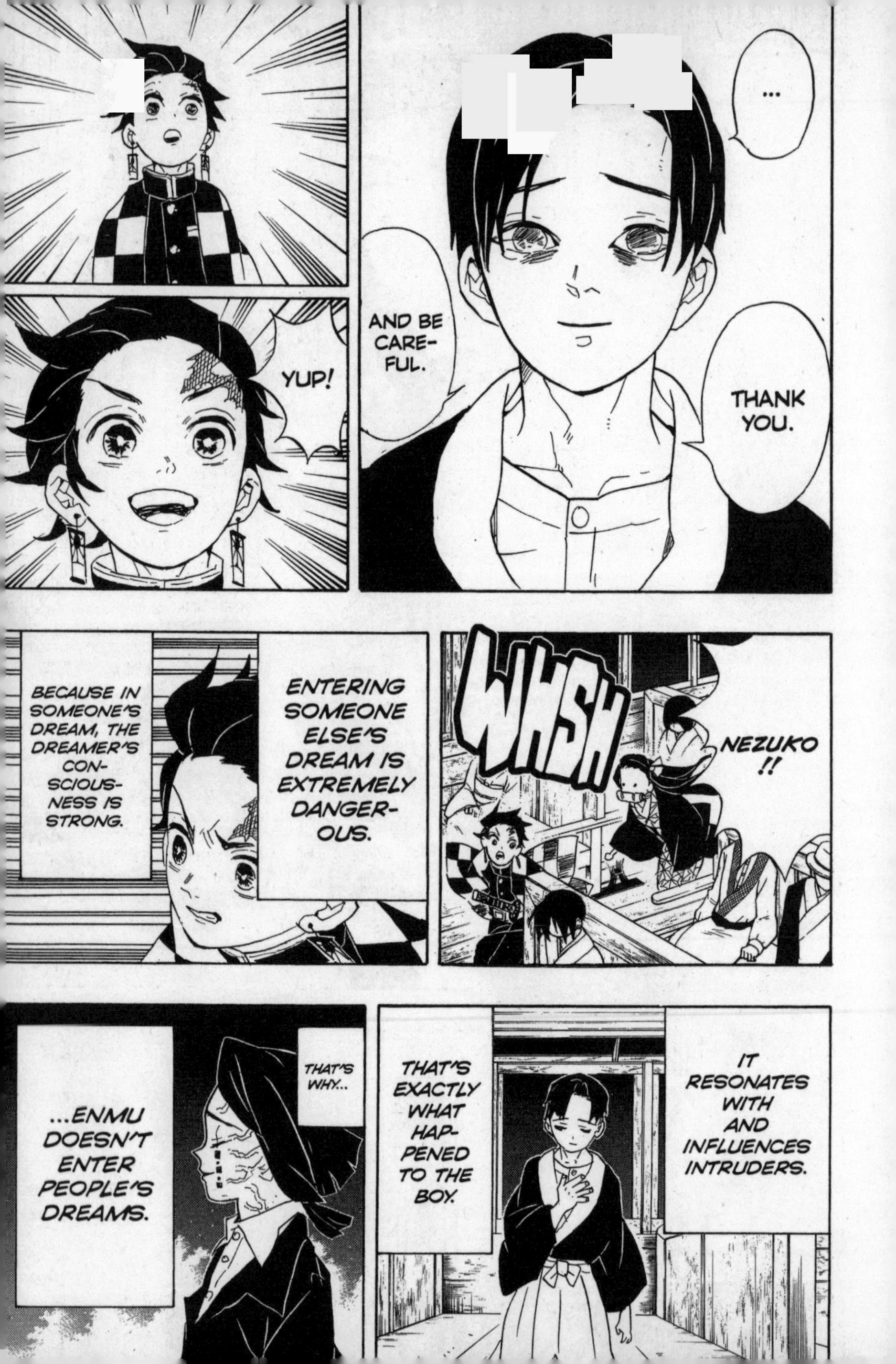
...
THANK YOU.
AND BE CARE-FUL.
YUP!
WHSH
NEZUKO!!
ENTERING SOMEONE ELSE'S DREAM IS EXTREMELY DANGER-OUS.
BECAUSE IN SOMEONE'S DREAM, THE DREAMER'S CON-SCIOUS-NESS IS STRONG.
IT RESONATES WITH AND INFLUENCES INTRUDERS.
THAT'S EXACTLY WHAT HAP-PENED TO THE BOY.
THAT'S WHY...
...ENMU DOESN'T ENTER PEOPLE'S DREAMS.

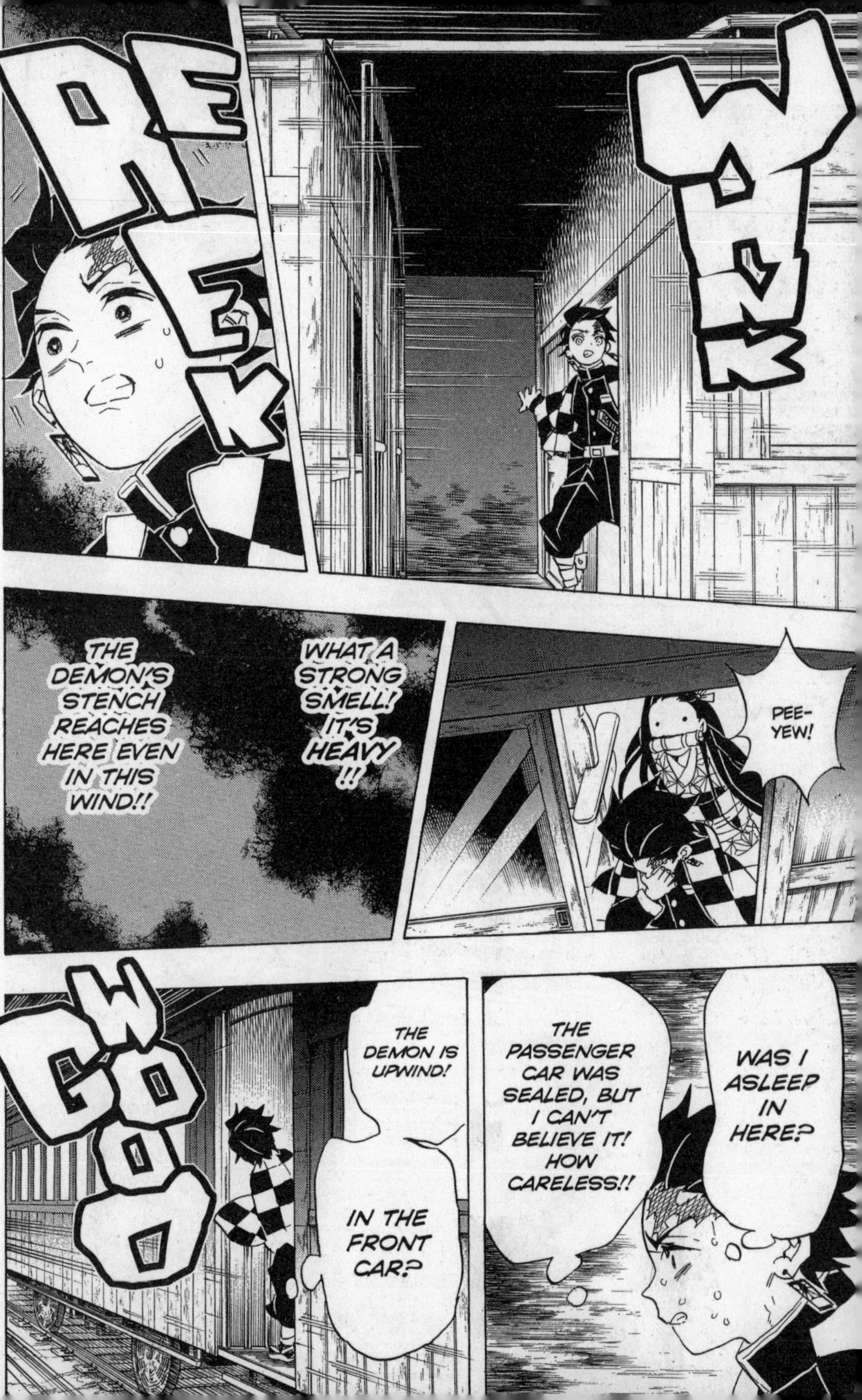
PEE-YEW!
WHAT A STRONG SMELL! IT'S HEAVY!!
THE DEMON'S STENCH REACHES HERE EVEN IN THIS WIND!!
WAS I ASLEEP IN HERE?
THE PASSENGER CAR WAS SEALED, BUT I CAN'T BELIEVE IT! HOW CARELESS!!
THE DEMON IS UPWIND!
IN THE FRONT CAR?

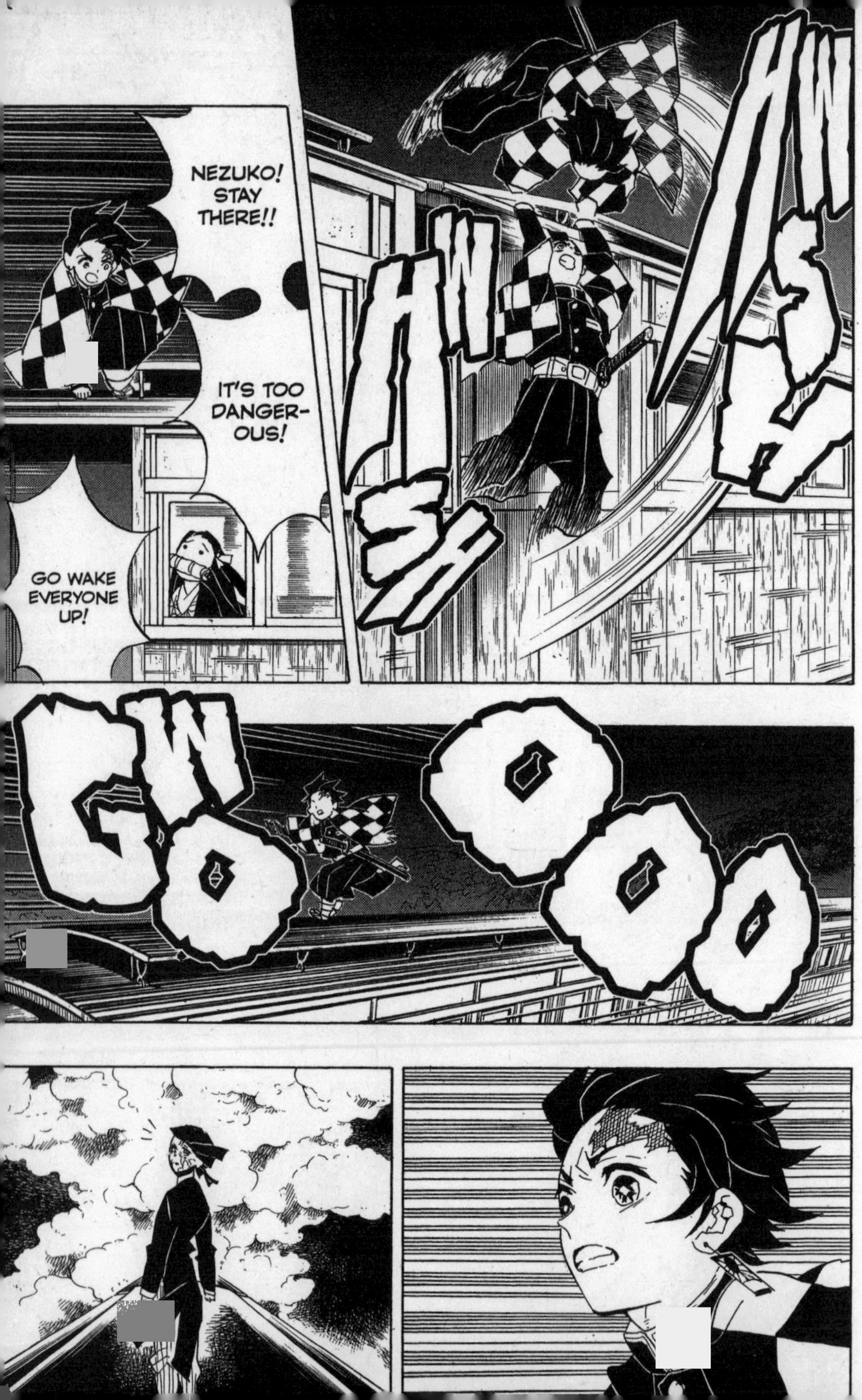
NEZUKO! STAY THERE!!
IT'S TOO DANGER-OUS!
GO WAKE EVERYONE UP!
GWOOOO

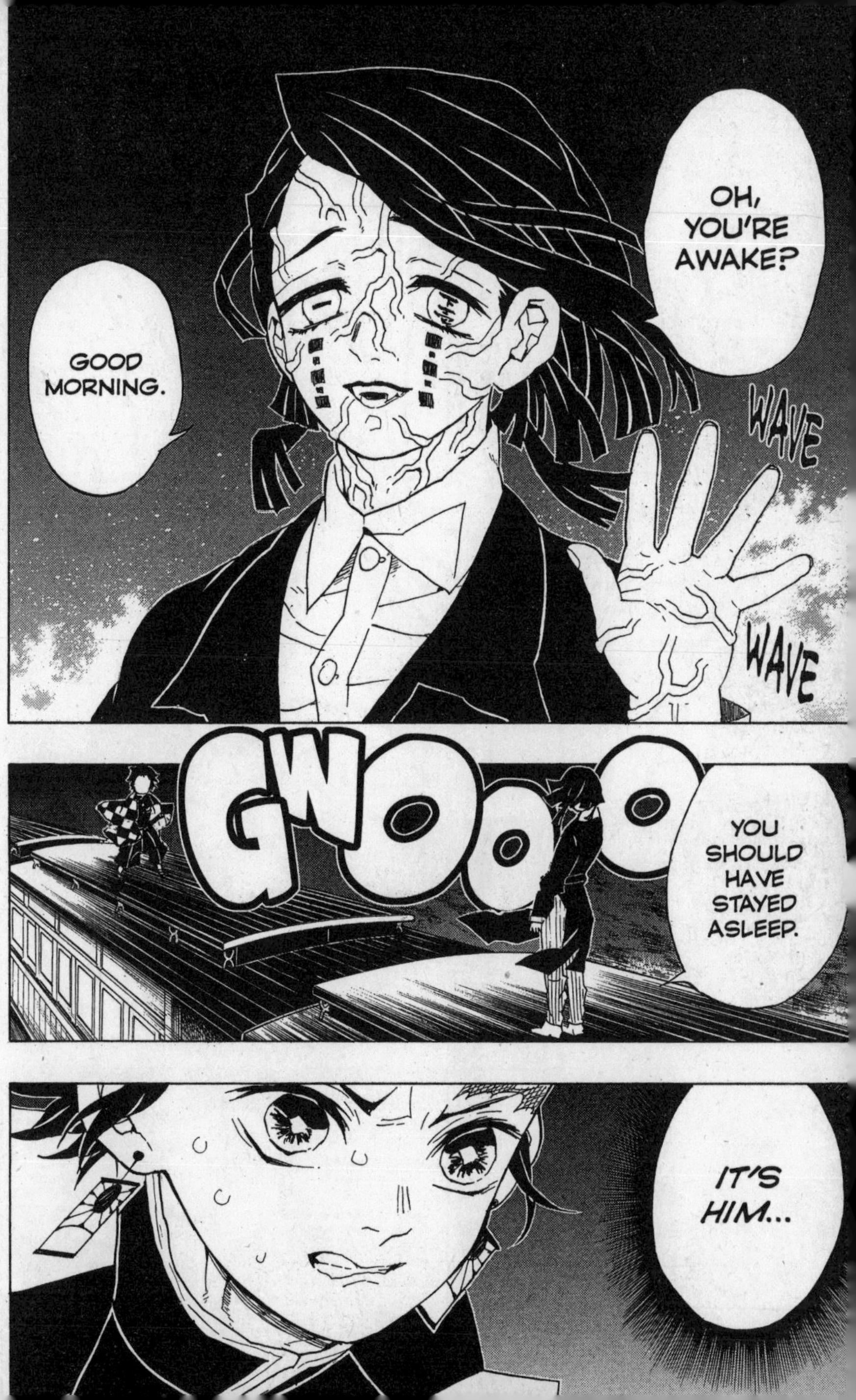
OH, YOU'RE AWAKE?
GOOD MORNING.
WAVE
WAVE
YOU SHOULD HAVE STAYED ASLEEP.
GWOOO
IT'S HIM...

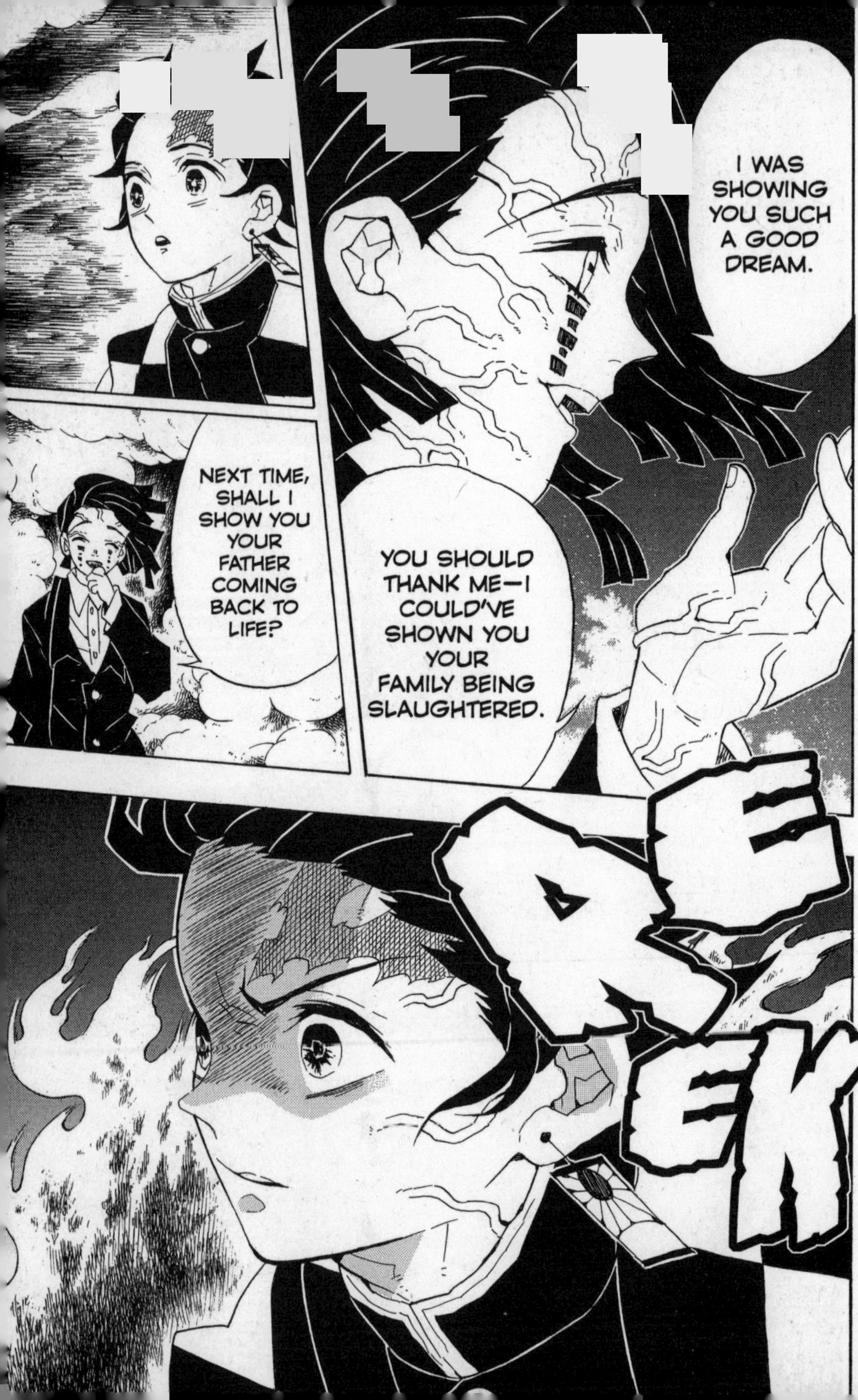
I WAS SHOWING YOU SUCH A GOOD DREAM.
YOU SHOULD THANK ME—I COULD'VE SHOWN YOU YOUR FAMILY BEING SLAUGHTERED.
NEXT TIME, SHALL I SHOW YOU YOUR FATHER COMING BACK TO LIFE?

The awl Enmu made. It seems he used one of his bones for the handle and the point is made from his tooth!
Scary!

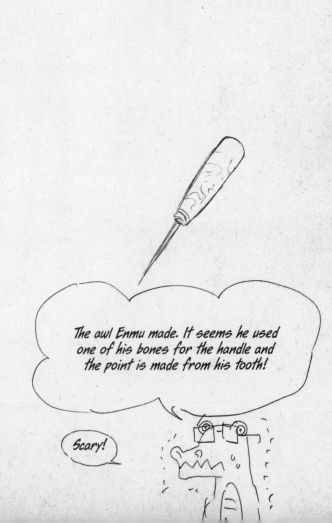

CHAPTER 59: INSULT

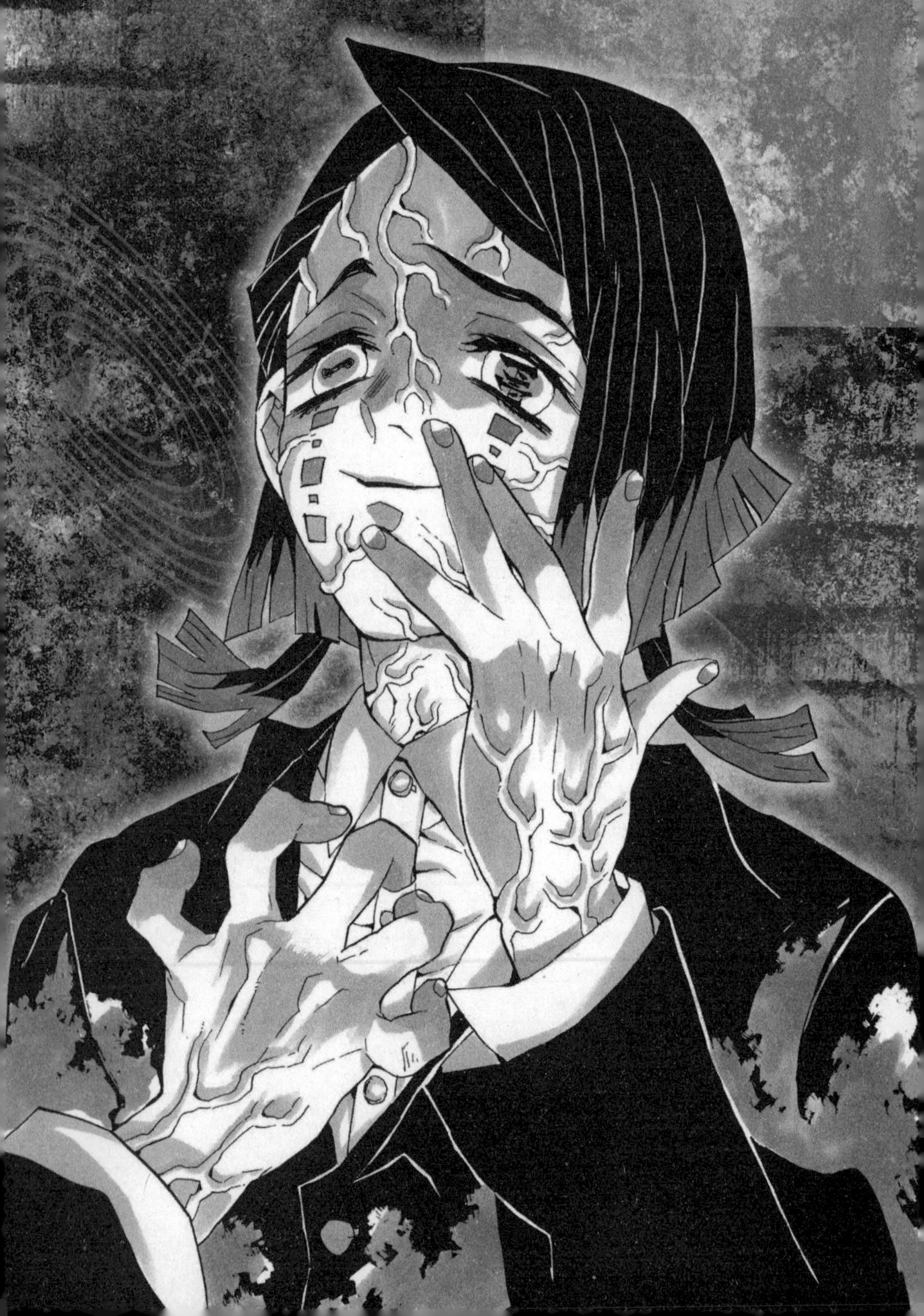

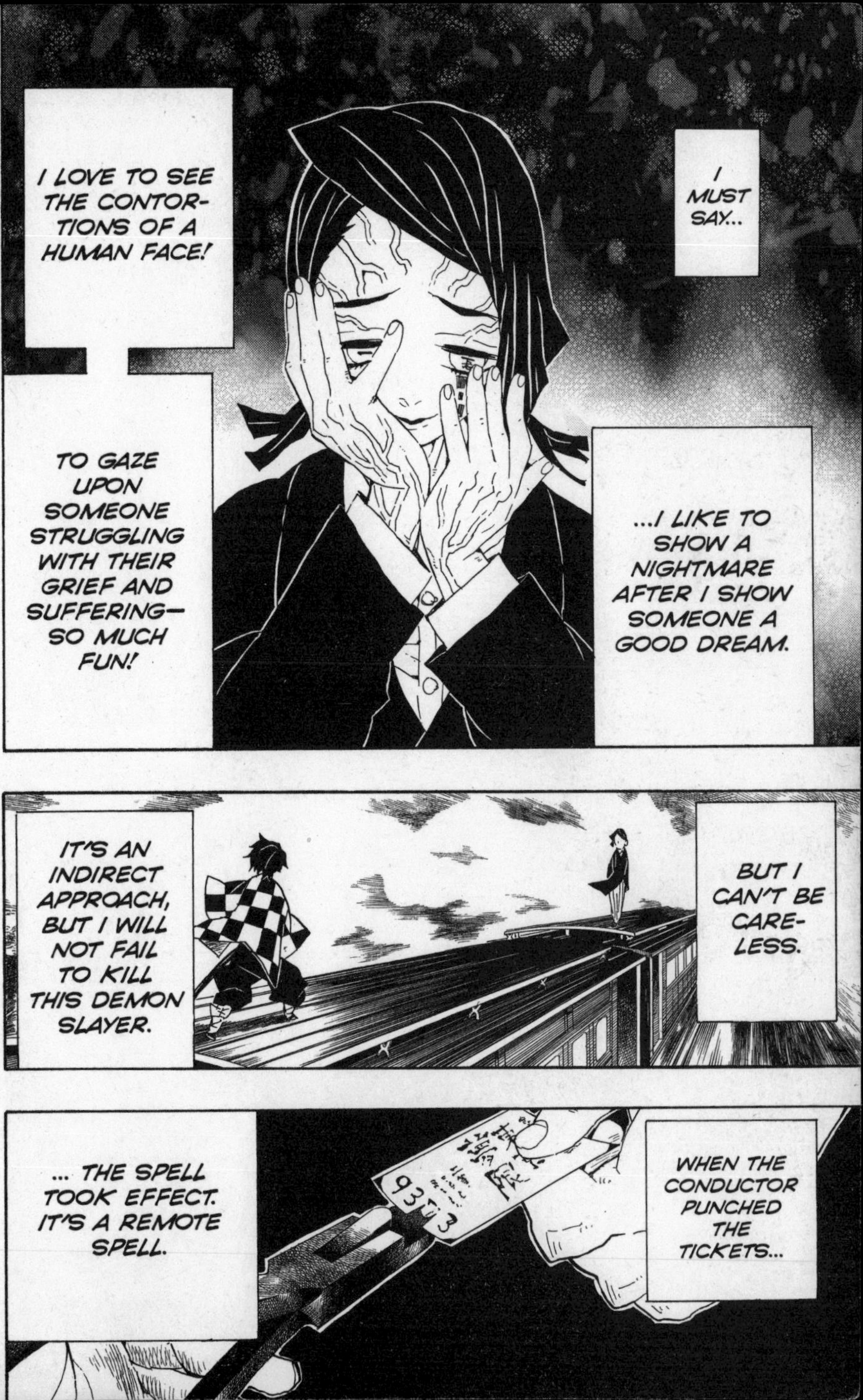
I MUST SAY...
...I LIKE TO SHOW A NIGHTMARE AFTER I SHOW SOMEONE A GOOD DREAM.
I LOVE TO SEE THE CONTORTIONS OF A HUMAN FACE!
TO GAZE UPON SOMEONE STRUGGLING WITH THEIR GRIEF AND SUFFERING—SO MUCH FUN!
BUT I CAN'T BE CARELESS.
IT'S AN INDIRECT APPROACH, BUT I WILL NOT FAIL TO KILL THIS DEMON SLAYER.
WHEN THE CONDUCTOR PUNCHED THE TICKETS...
... THE SPELL TOOK EFFECT. IT'S A REMOTE SPELL.

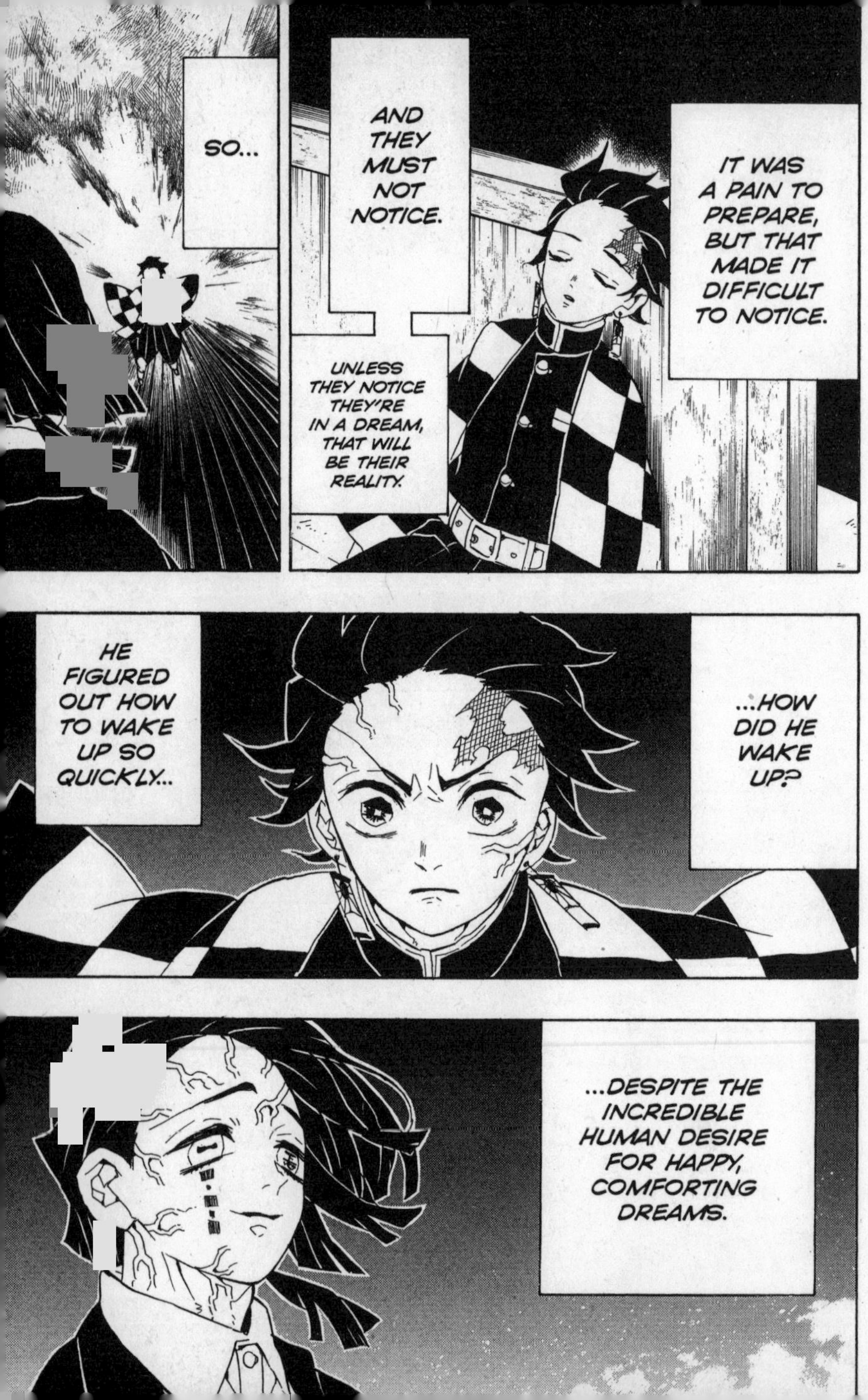
IT WAS A PAIN TO PREPARE, BUT THAT MADE IT DIFFICULT TO NOTICE.
AND THEY MUST NOT NOTICE.
UNLESS THEY NOTICE THEY'RE IN A DREAM, THAT WILL BE THEIR REALITY.
SO...
...HOW DID HE WAKE UP?
HE FIGURED OUT HOW TO WAKE UP SO QUICKLY...
...DESPITE THE INCREDIBLE HUMAN DESIRE FOR HAPPY, COMFORTING DREAMS.

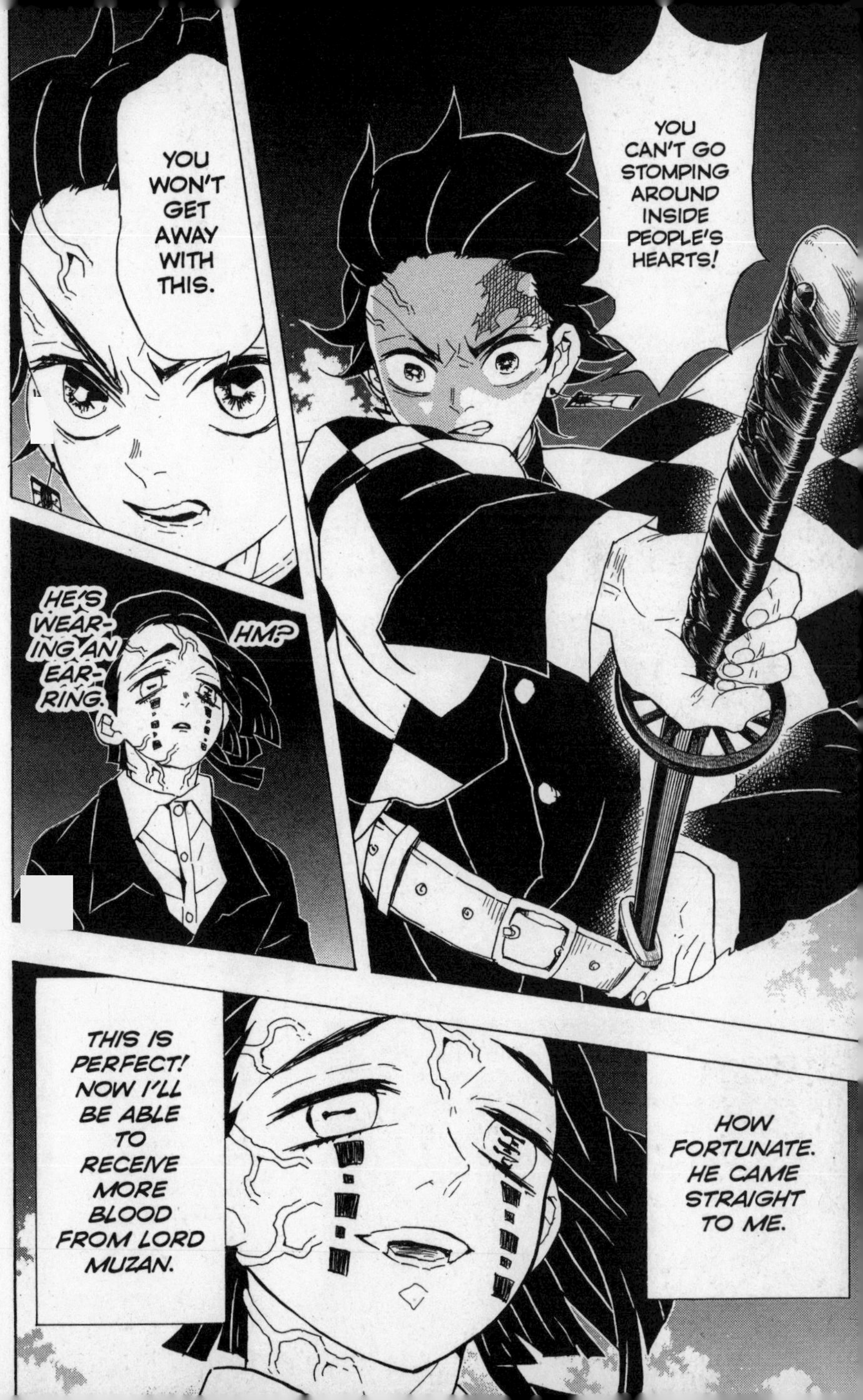
YOU CAN'T GO STOMPING AROUND INSIDE PEOPLE'S HEARTS!
YOU WON'T GET AWAY WITH THIS.
HM?
HE'S WEARING AN EARRING.
HOW FORTUNATE. HE CAME STRAIGHT TO ME.
THIS IS PERFECT! NOW I'LL BE ABLE TO RECEIVE MORE BLOOD FROM LORD MUZAN.

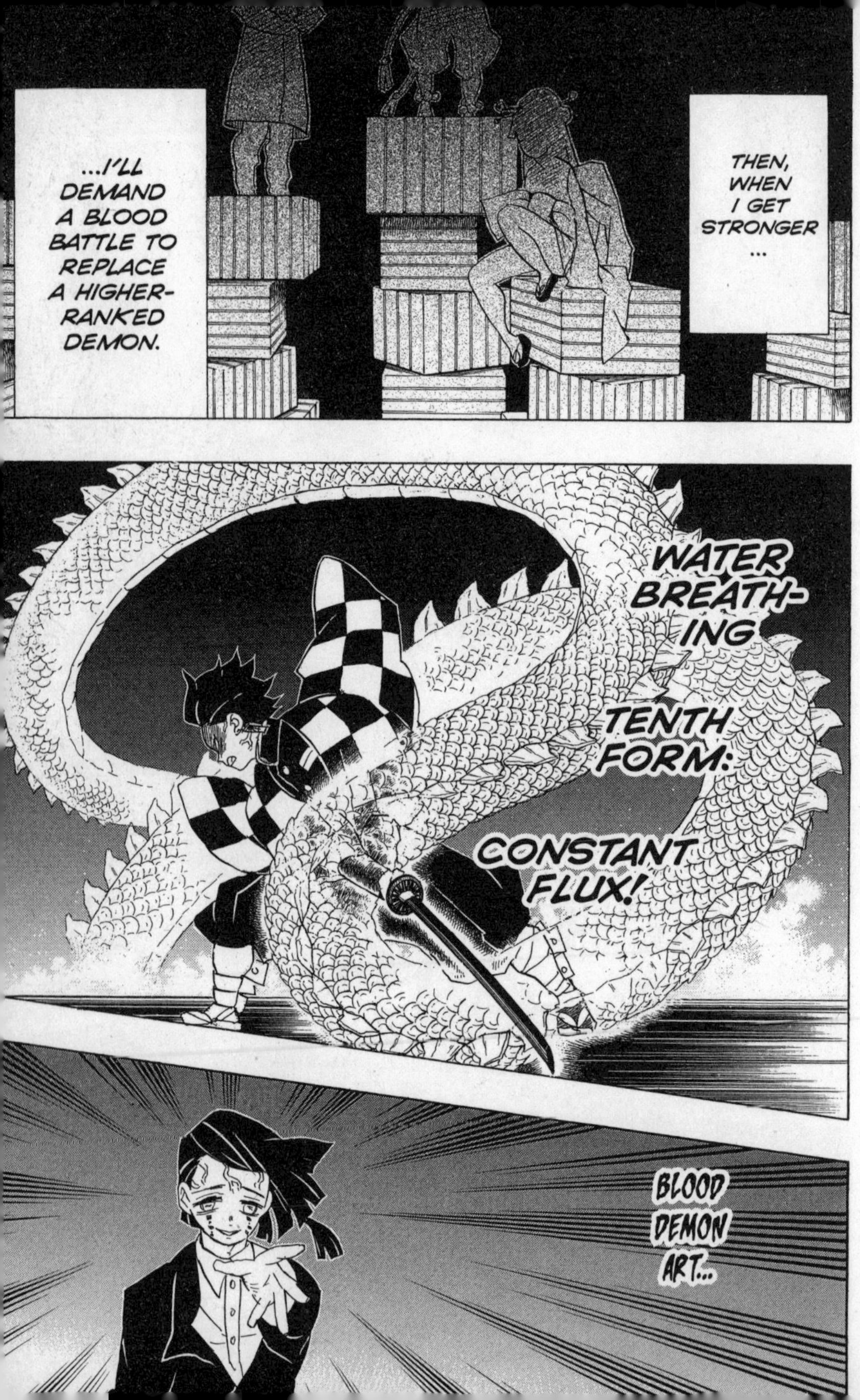
THEN, WHEN I GET STRONGER ...
...I'LL DEMAND A BLOOD BATTLE TO REPLACE A HIGHER-RANKED DEMON.
WATER BREATHING
TENTH FORM:
CONSTANT FLUX!
BLOOD DEMON ART...

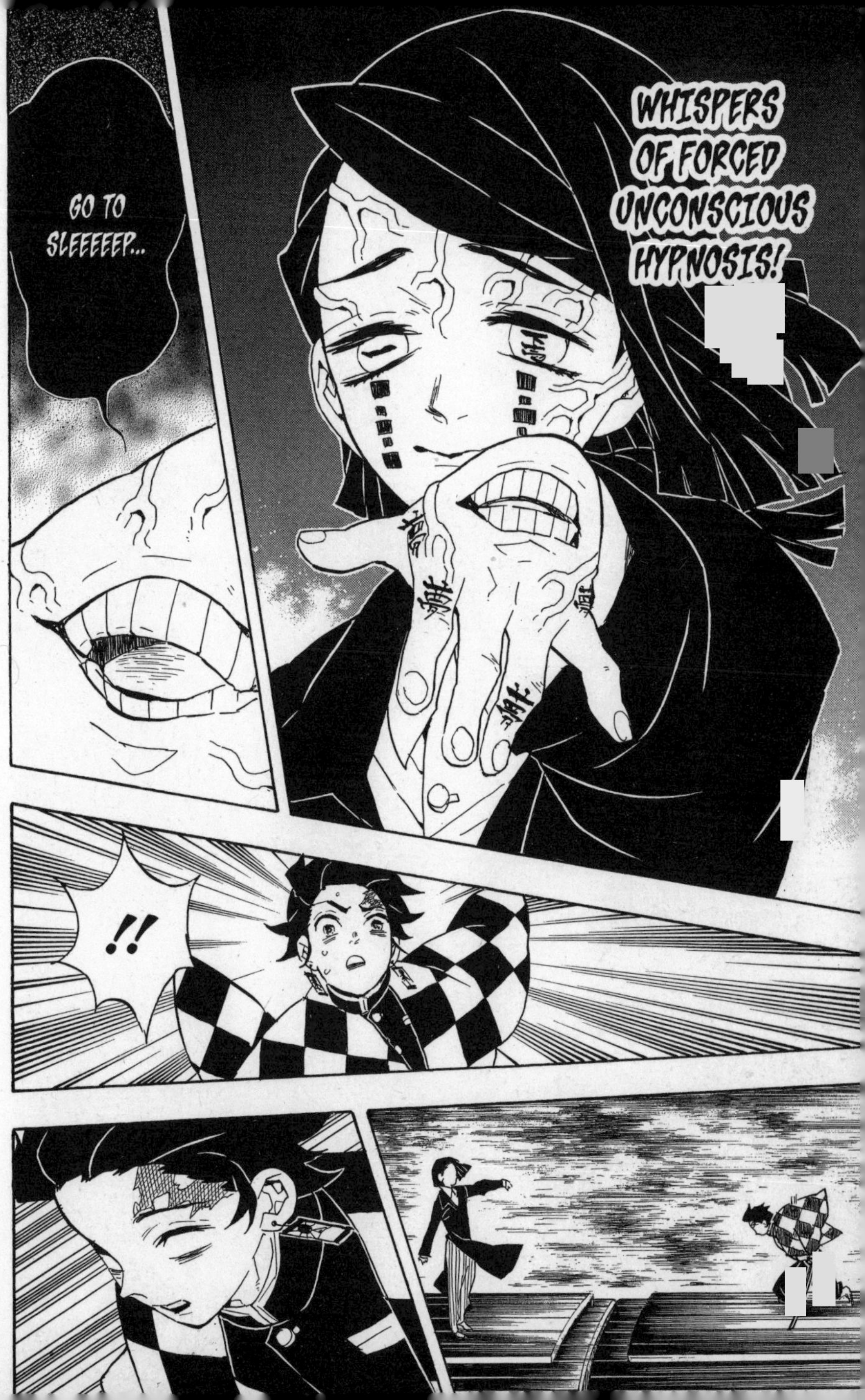
WHISPERS OF FORCED UNCONSCIOUS HYPNOSIS!
GO TO SLEEEEEP...
!!

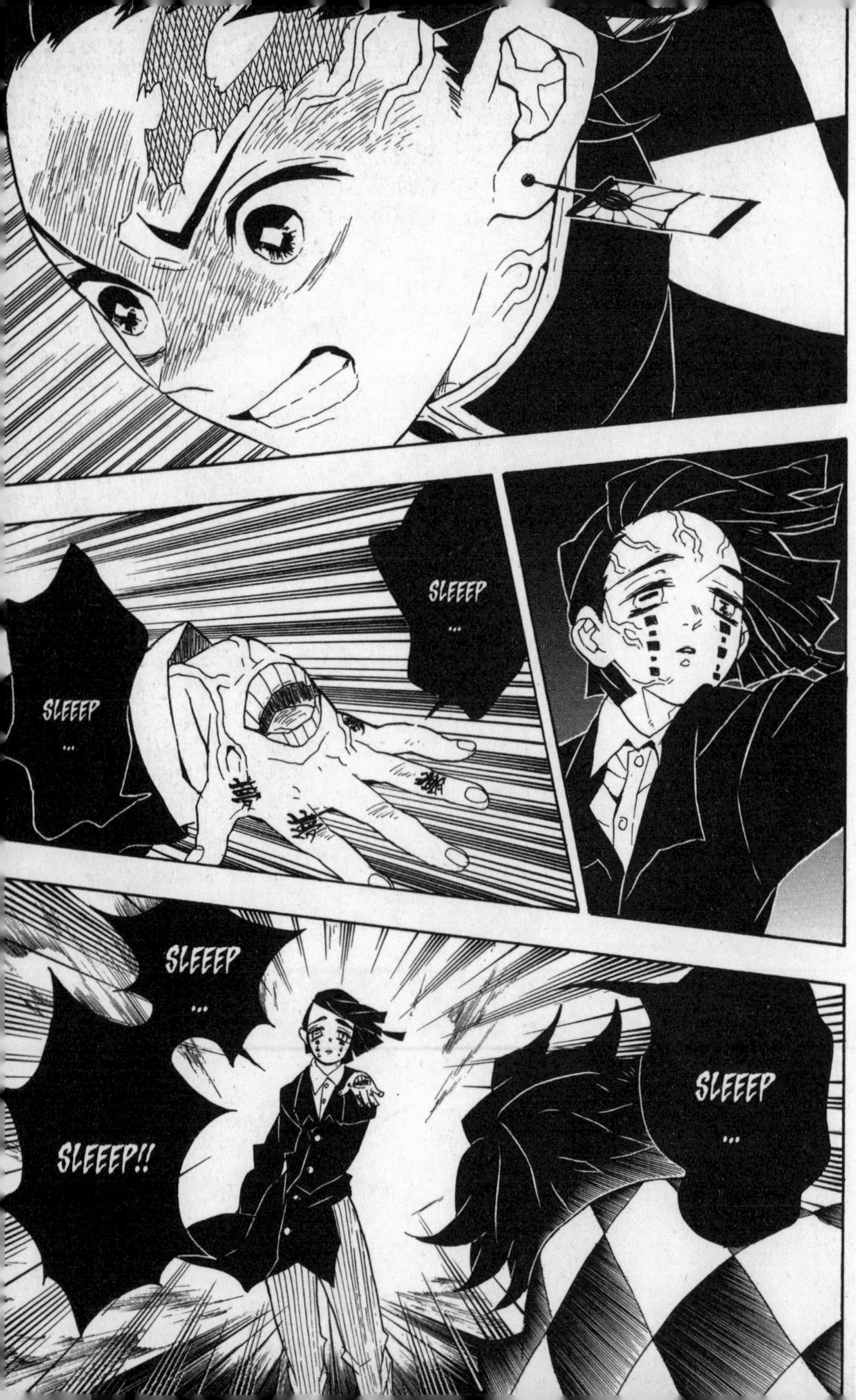
SLEEEP ...
SLEEEP ...
SLEEEP ...
SLEEEP ...
SLEEEP!!

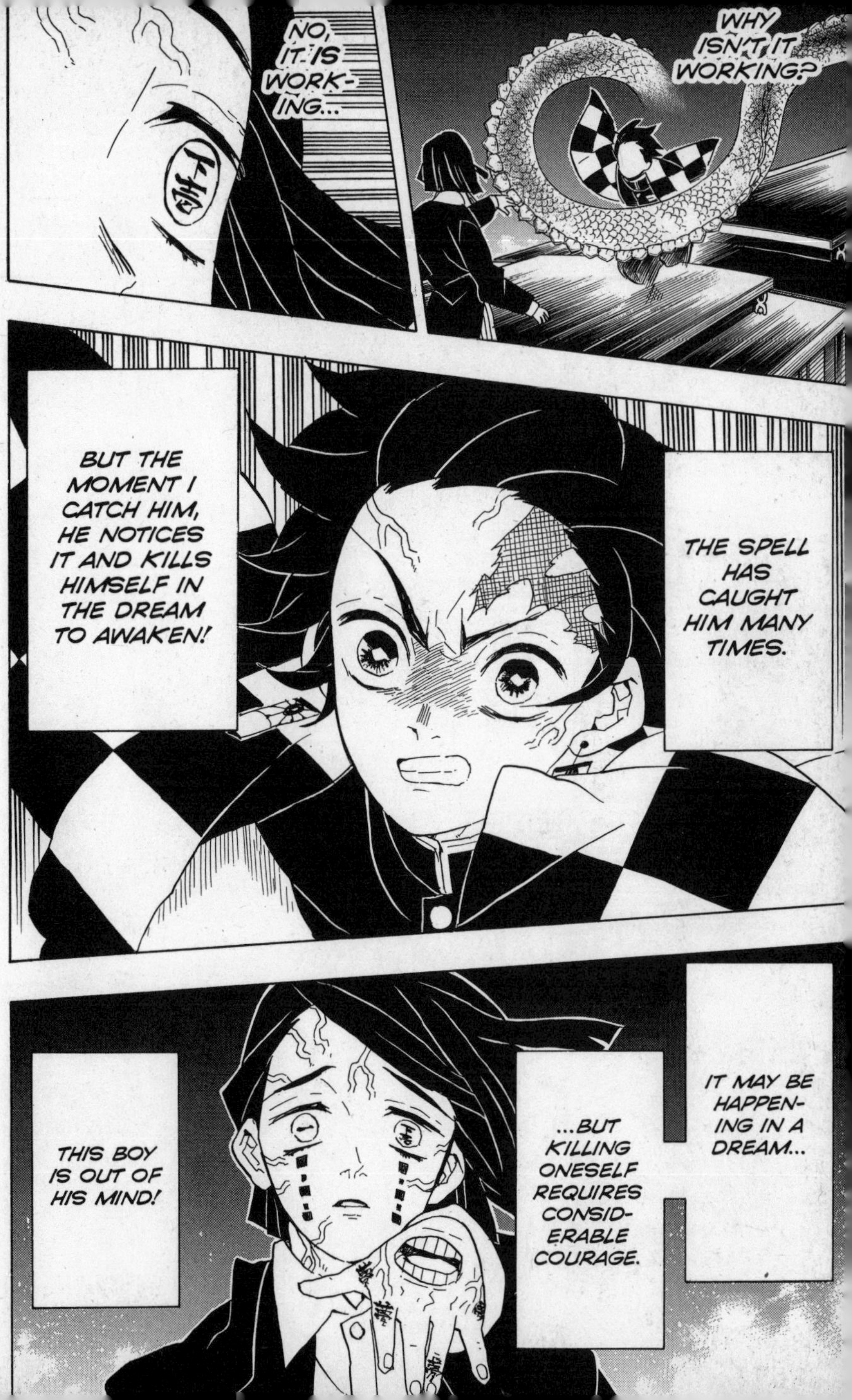
WHY ISN'T IT WORKING?
NO, IT IS WORKING...
THE SPELL HAS CAUGHT HIM MANY TIMES.
BUT THE MOMENT I CATCH HIM, HE NOTICES IT AND KILLS HIMSELF IN THE DREAM TO AWAKEN!
IT MAY BE HAPPENING IN A DREAM...
...BUT KILLING ONESELF REQUIRES CONSIDERABLE COURAGE.
THIS BOY IS OUT OF HIS MIND!

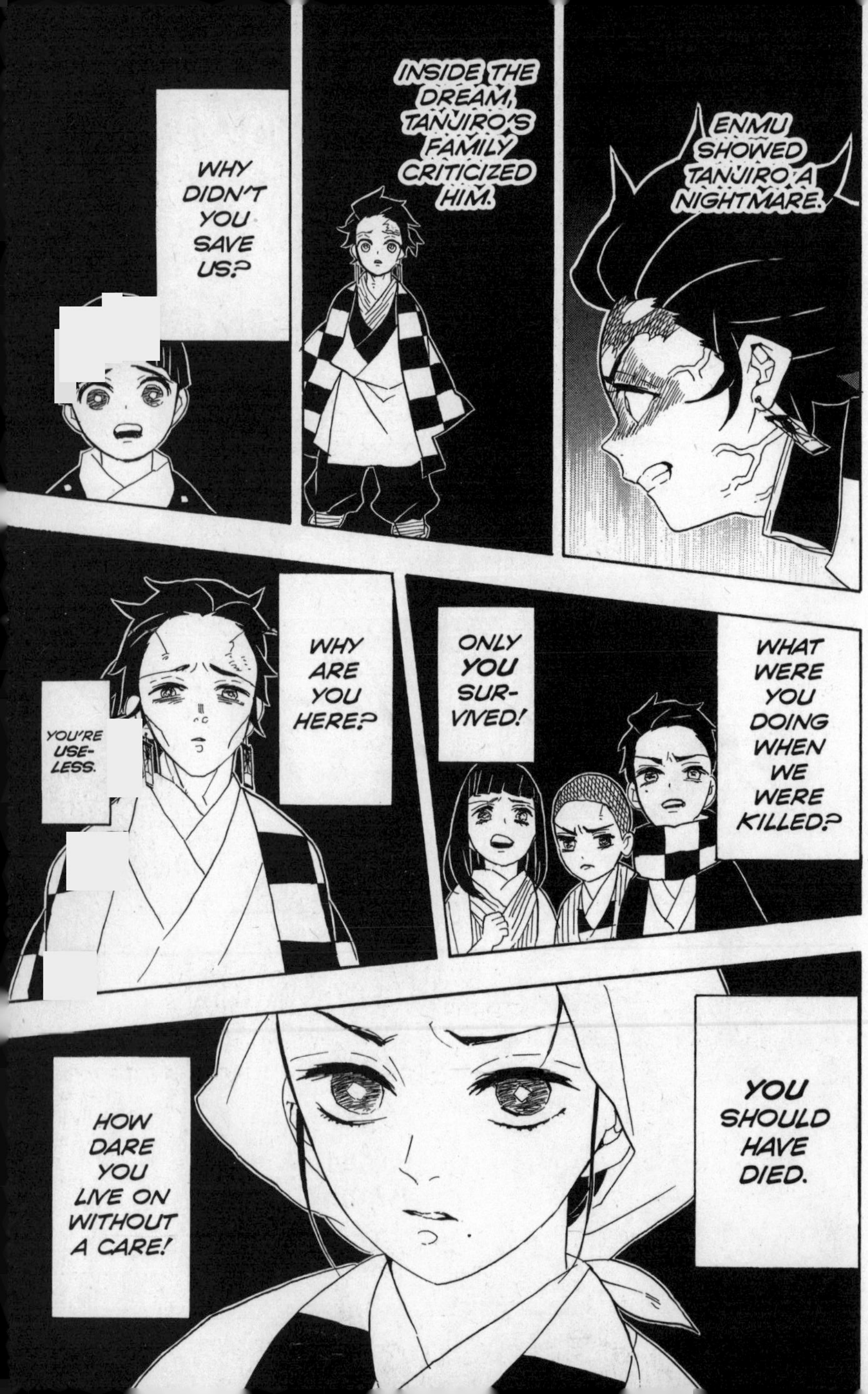
ENMU SHOWED TANJIRO A NIGHTMARE.
INSIDE THE DREAM, TANJIRO'S FAMILY CRITICIZED HIM.
WHY DIDN'T YOU SAVE US?
WHAT WERE YOU DOING WHEN WE WERE KILLED?
ONLY YOU SUR-VIVED!
WHY ARE YOU HERE?
YOU'RE USE-LESS.
YOU SHOULD HAVE DIED.
HOW DARE YOU LIVE ON WITHOUT A CARE!

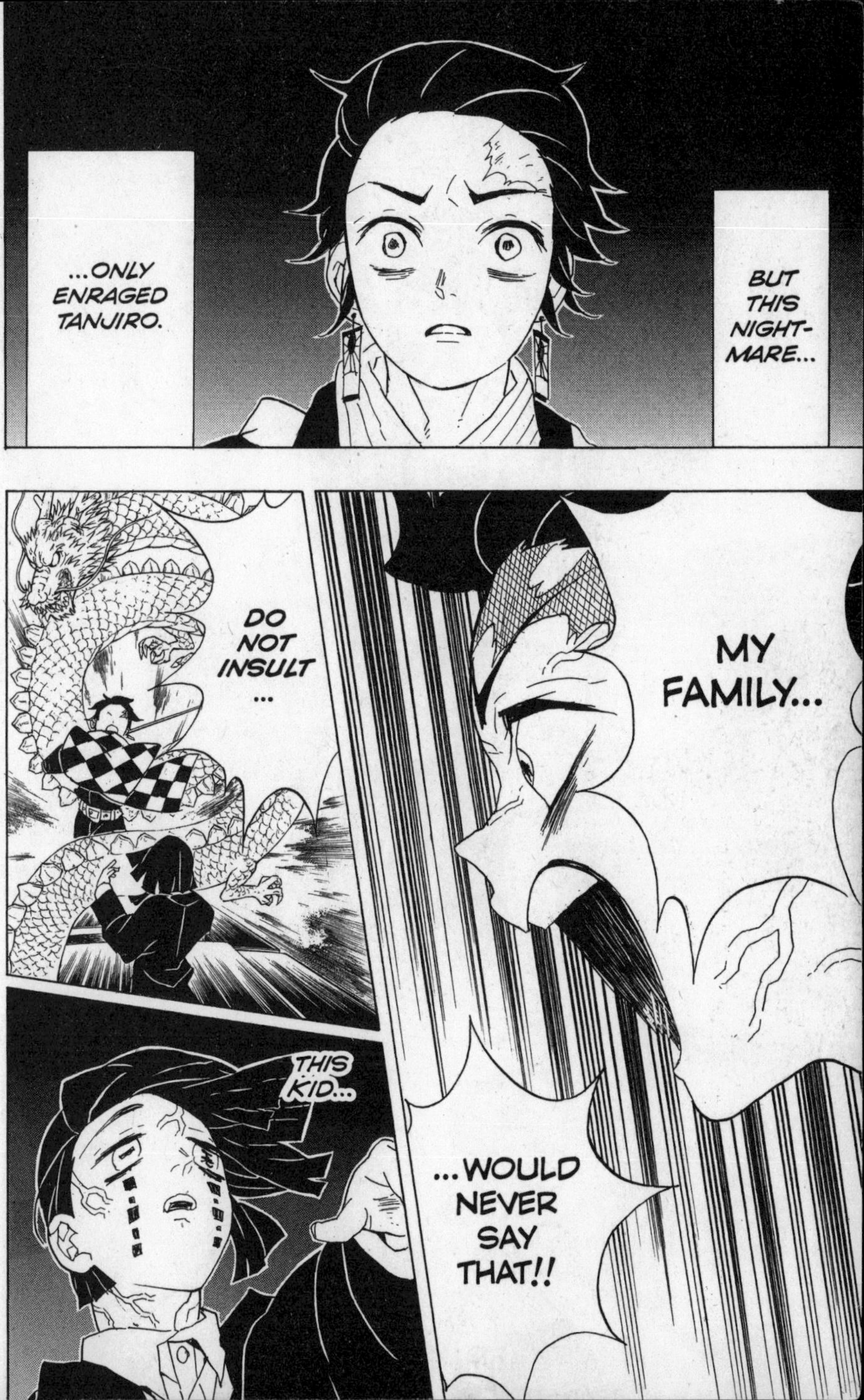
BUT THIS NIGHTMARE...
...ONLY ENRAGED TANJIRO.
MY FAMILY...
...WOULD NEVER SAY THAT!!
DO NOT INSULT ...
THIS KID...

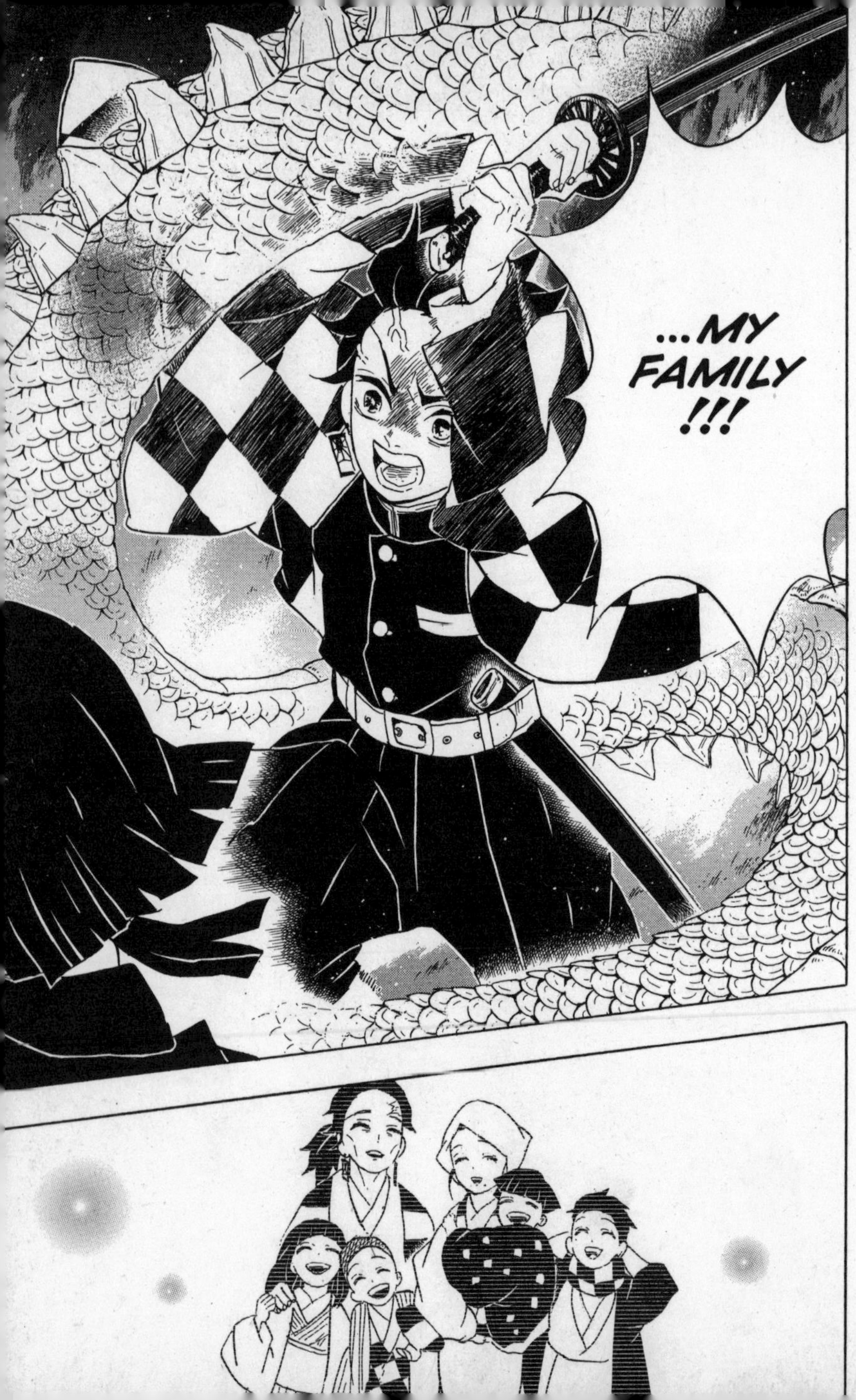
...MY FAMILY !!!

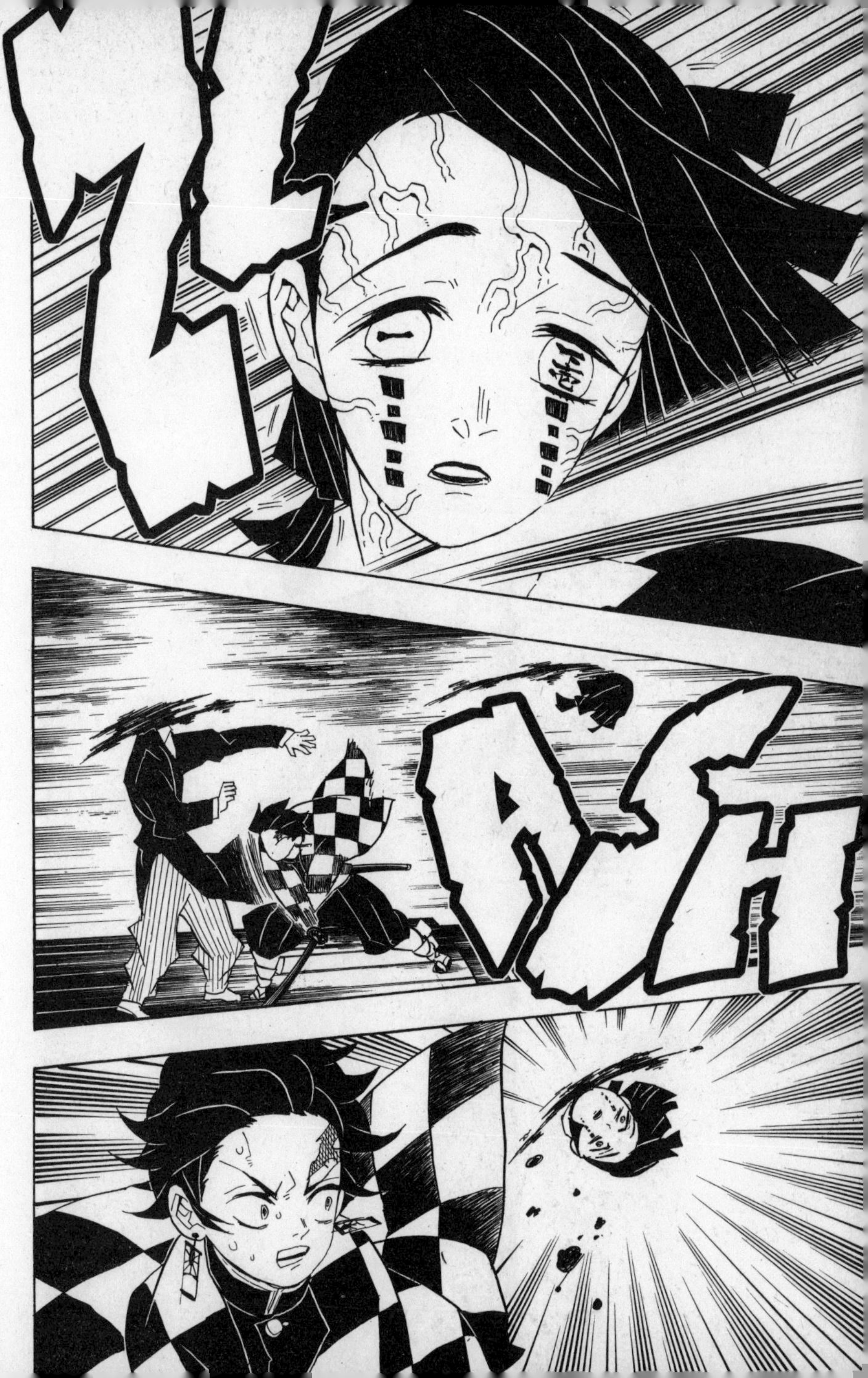
ASH

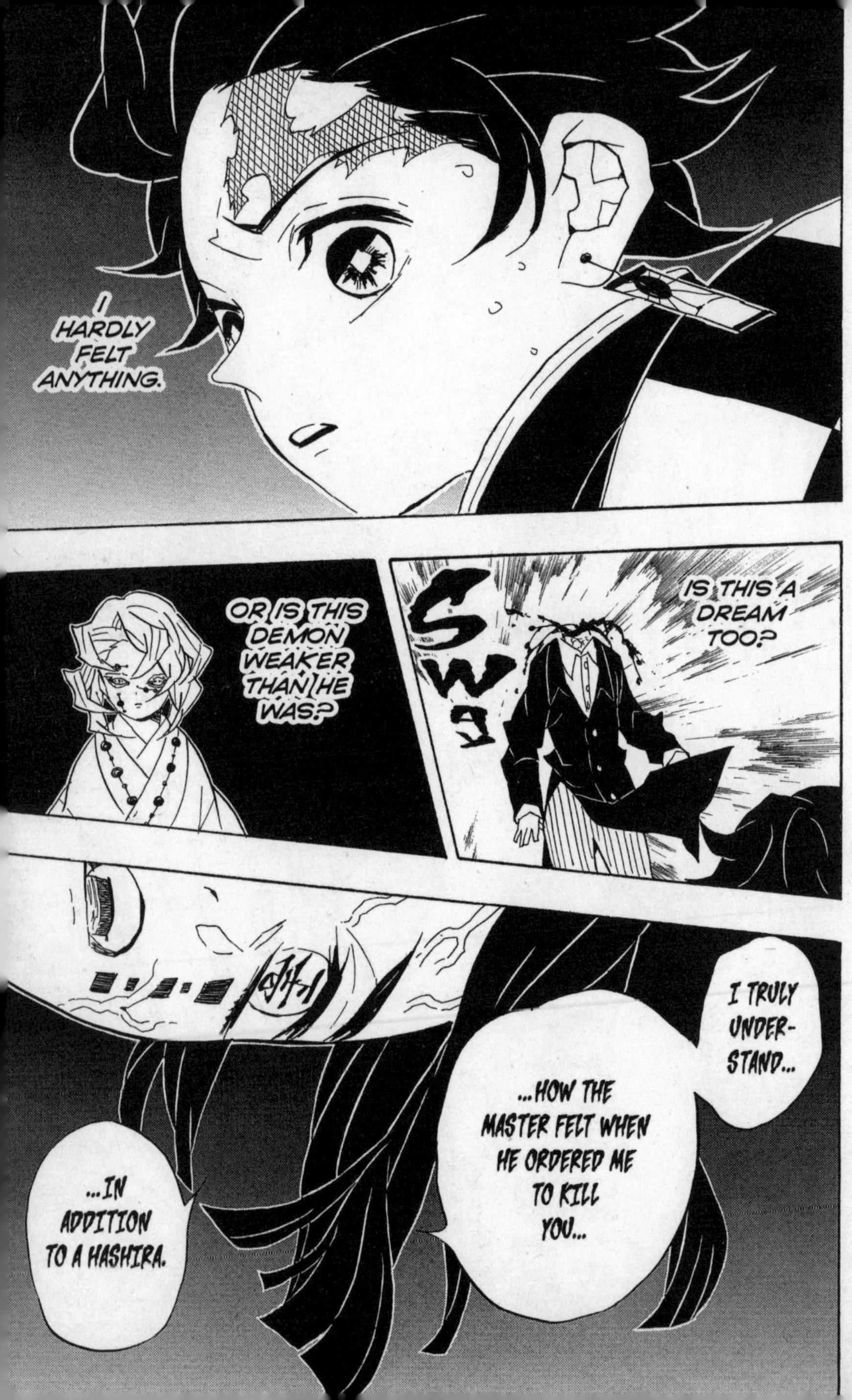
I HARDLY FELT ANYTHING.
SW
IS THIS A DREAM TOO?
OR IS THIS DEMON WEAKER THAN HE WAS?
I TRULY UNDER-STAND...
...HOW THE MASTER FELT WHEN HE ORDERED ME TO KILL YOU...
...IN ADDITION TO A HASHIRA.

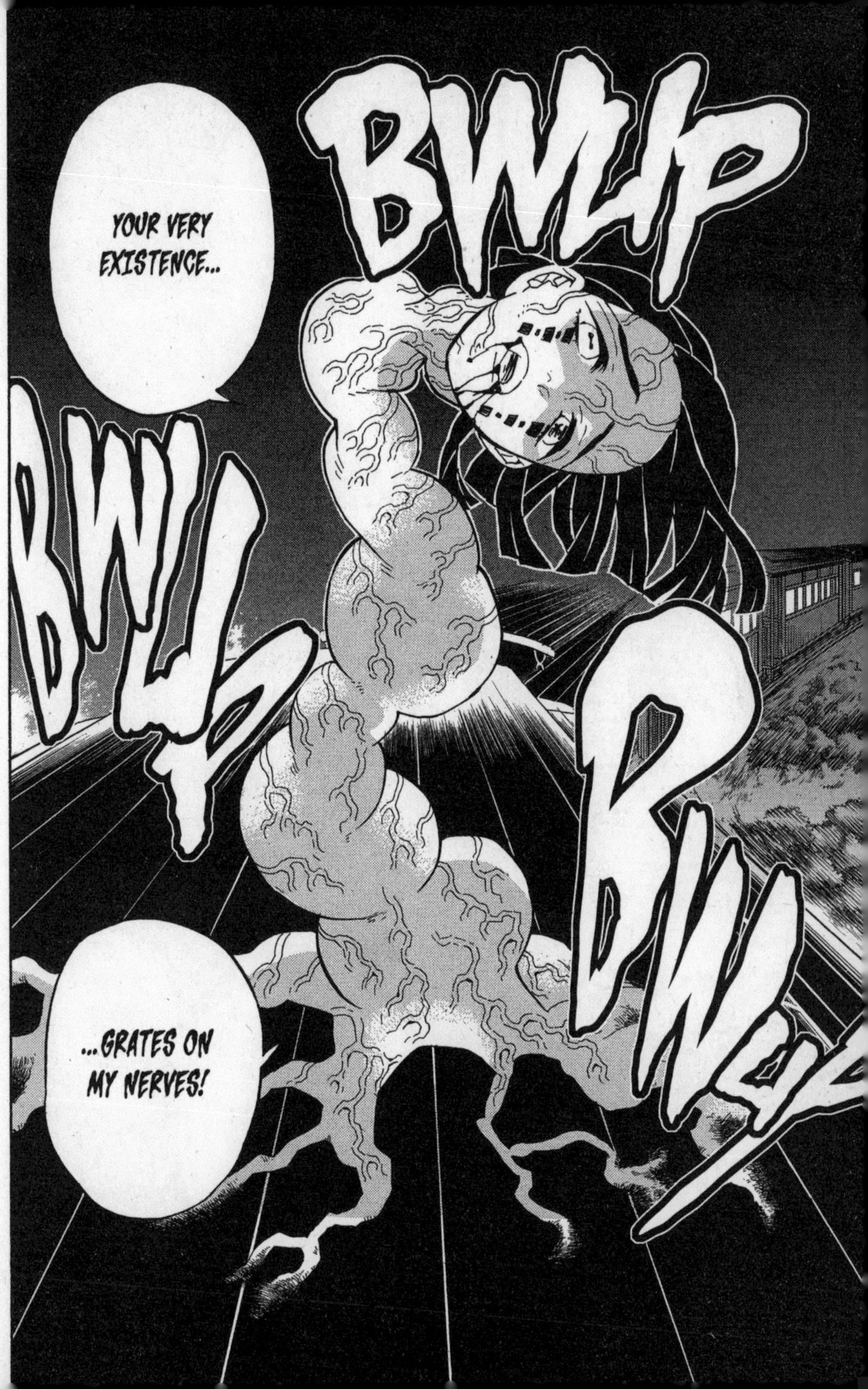
BWUP
YOUR VERY EXISTENCE...
...GRATES ON MY NERVES!

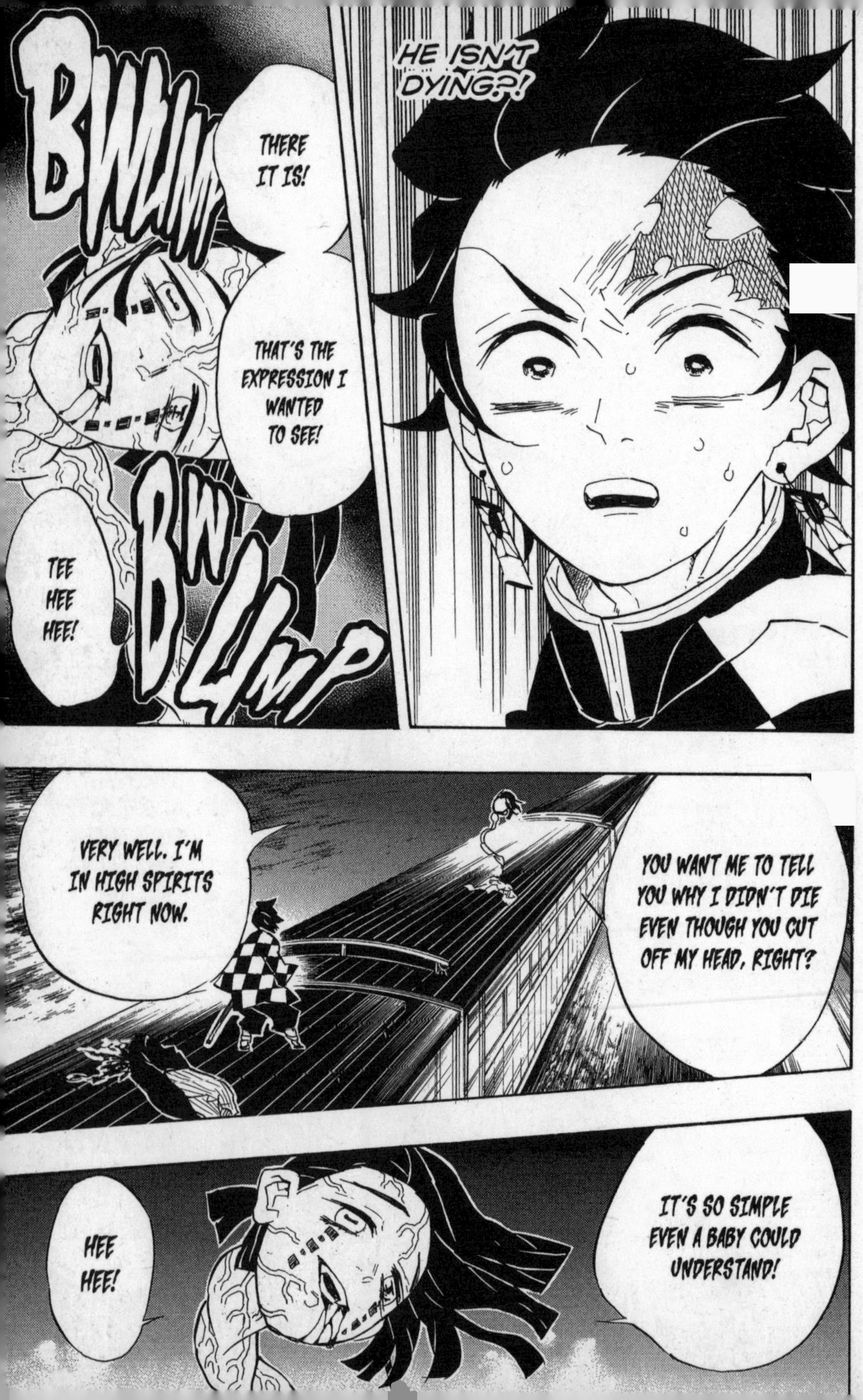
HE ISN'T DYING?!
THERE IT IS!
THAT'S THE EXPRESSION I WANTED TO SEE!
TEE HEE HEE!
YOU WANT ME TO TELL YOU WHY I DIDN'T DIE EVEN THOUGH YOU CUT OFF MY HEAD, RIGHT?
VERY WELL. I'M IN HIGH SPIRITS RIGHT NOW.
IT'S SO SIMPLE EVEN A BABY COULD UNDERSTAND!
HEE HEE!

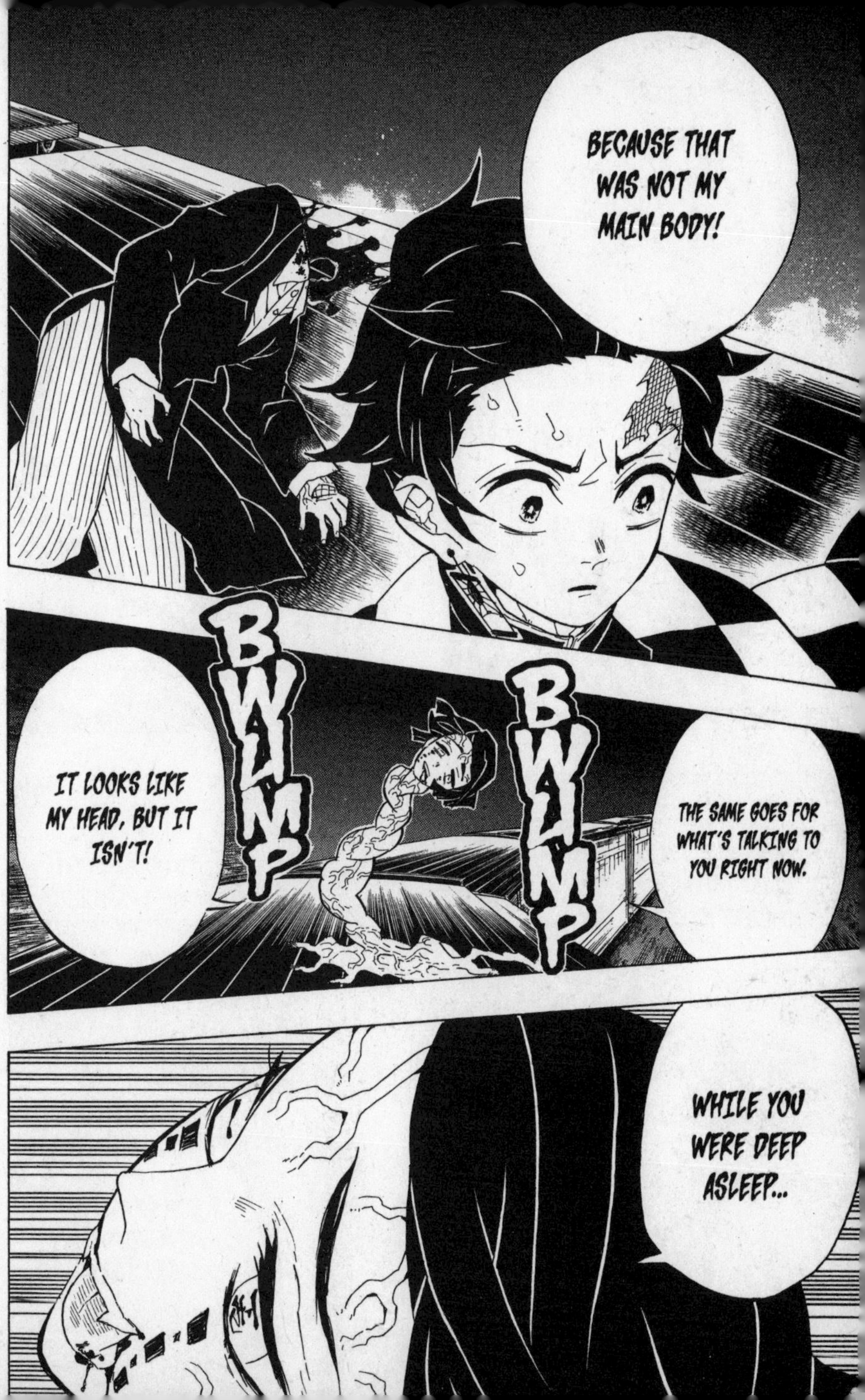
BECAUSE THAT WAS NOT MY MAIN BODY!
BWUMP
IT LOOKS LIKE MY HEAD, BUT IT ISN'T!
BWUMP
THE SAME GOES FOR WHAT'S TALKING TO YOU RIGHT NOW.
WHILE YOU WERE DEEP ASLEEP...

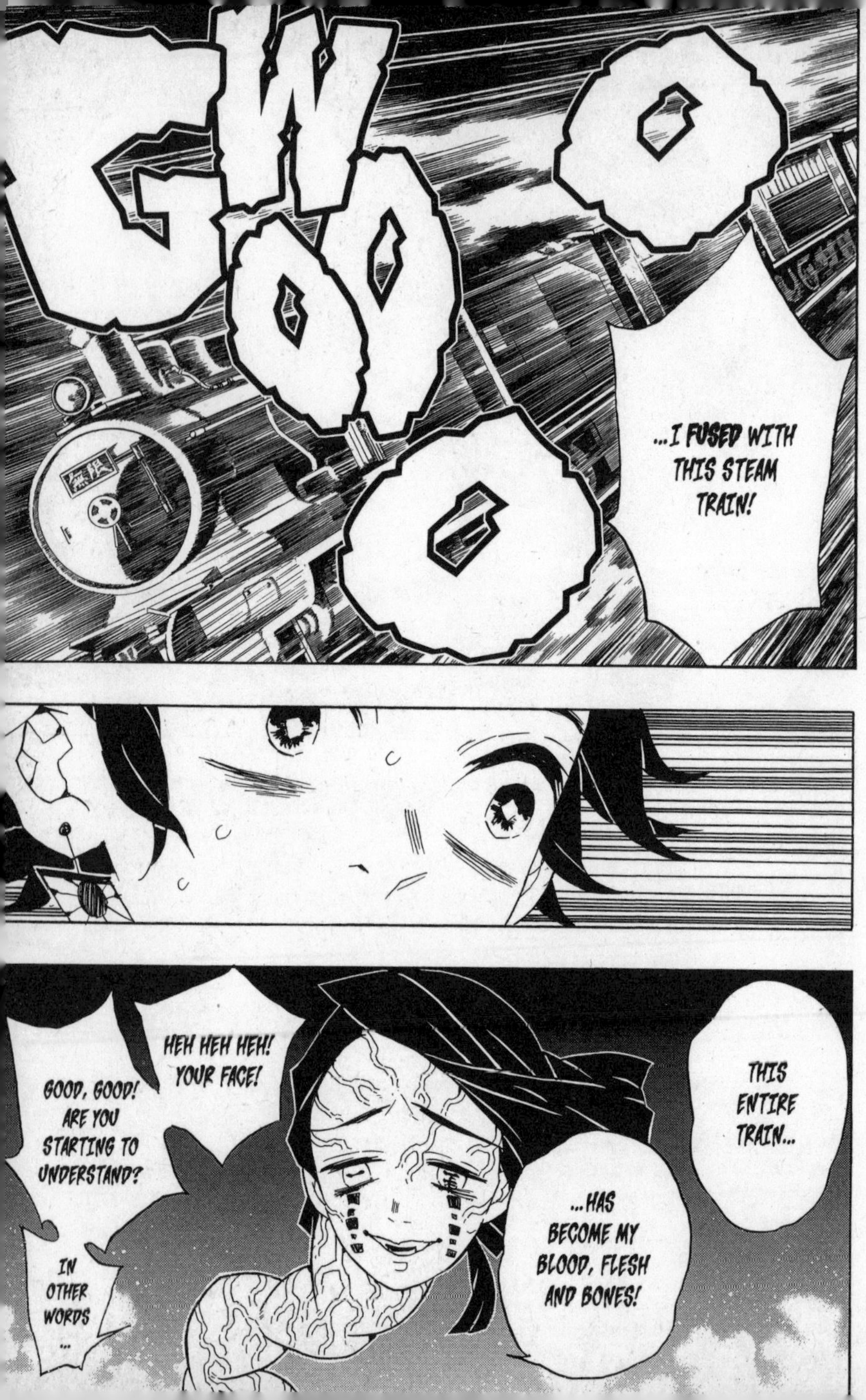
GWOOOO
...I FUSED WITH THIS STEAM TRAIN!
THIS ENTIRE TRAIN...
...HAS BECOME MY BLOOD, FLESH AND BONES!
HEH HEH HEH! YOUR FACE!
GOOD, GOOD! ARE YOU STARTING TO UNDERSTAND?
IN OTHER WORDS ...

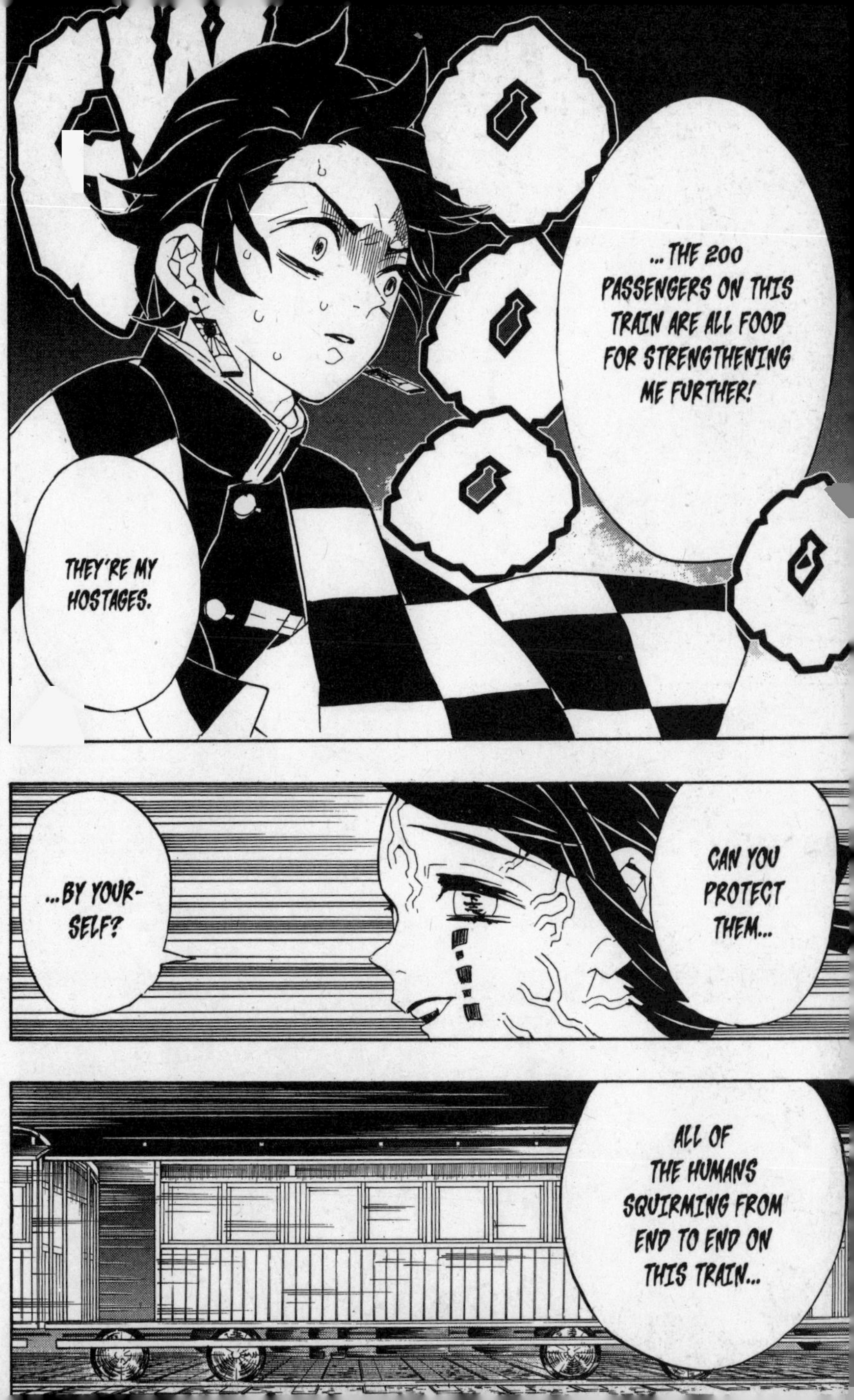
...THE 200 PASSENGERS ON THIS TRAIN ARE ALL FOOD FOR STRENGTHENING ME FURTHER!
THEY'RE MY HOSTAGES.
CAN YOU PROTECT THEM...
...BY YOUR-SELF?
ALL OF THE HUMANS SQUIRMING FROM END TO END ON THIS TRAIN...

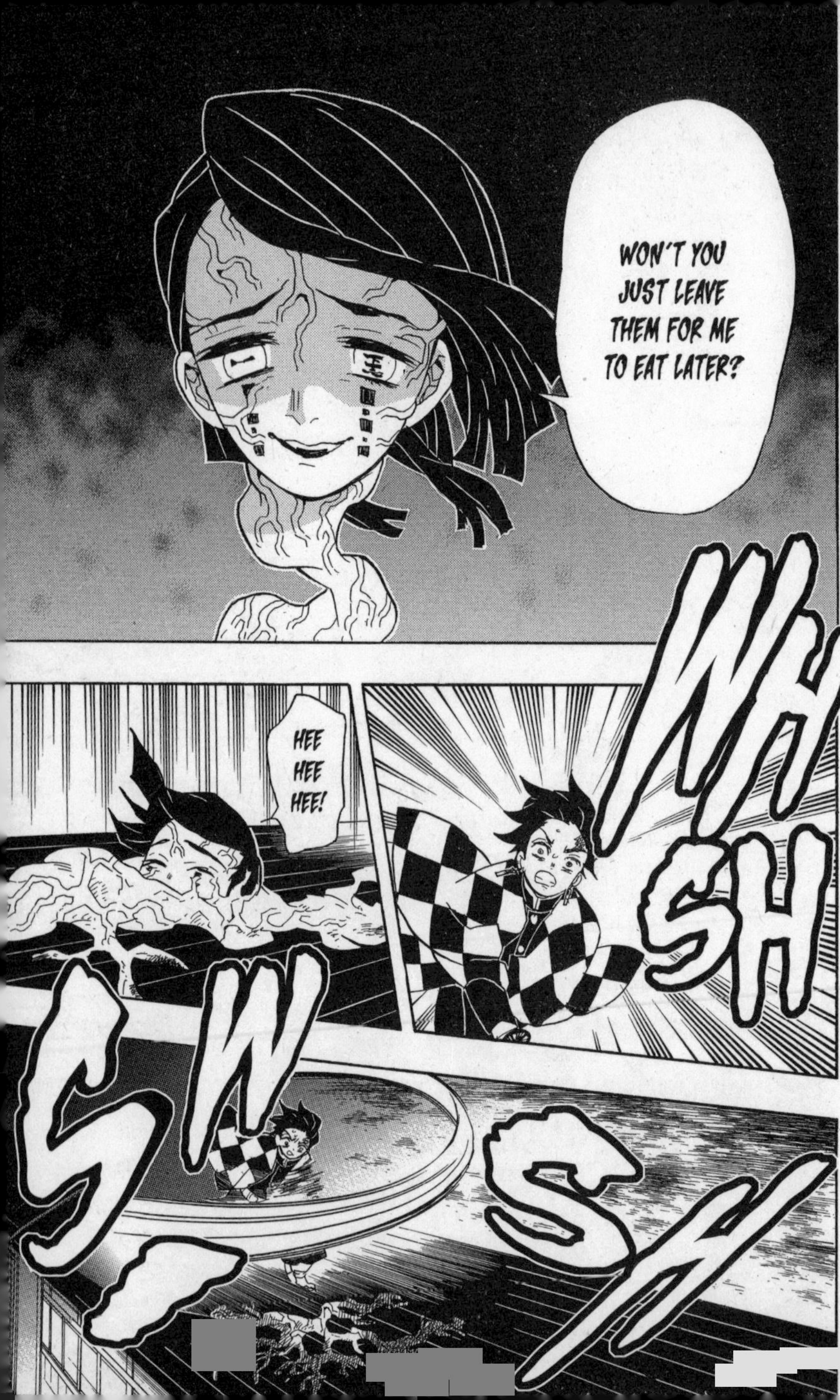
WON'T YOU JUST LEAVE THEM FOR ME TO EAT LATER?
WHSH
HEE HEE HEE!
SWSH

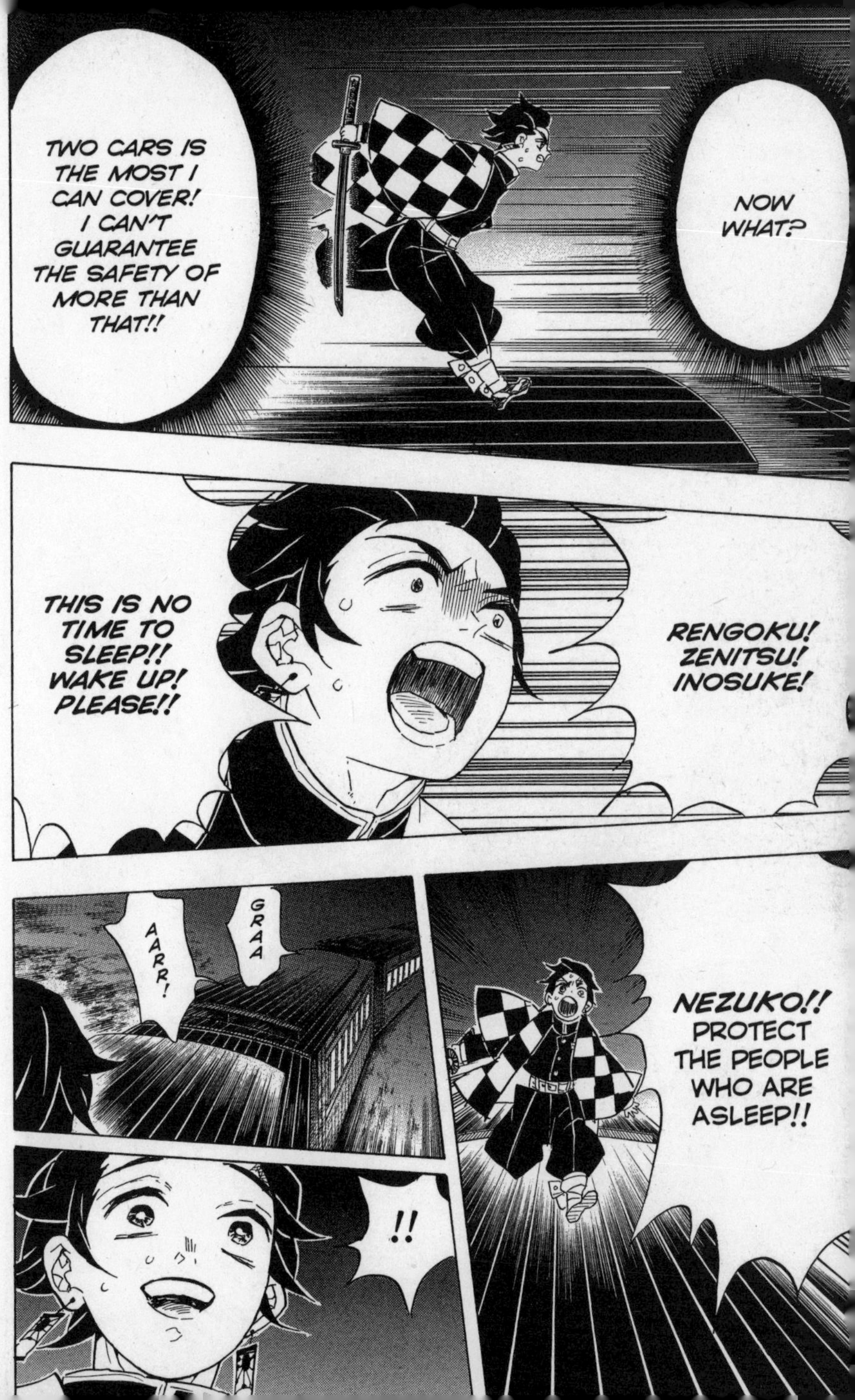
NOW WHAT?
TWO CARS IS THE MOST I CAN COVER! I CAN'T GUARANTEE THE SAFETY OF MORE THAN THAT!!
RENGOKU! ZENITSU! INOSUKE!
THIS IS NO TIME TO SLEEP!! WAKE UP! PLEASE!!
NEZUKO!! PROTECT THE PEOPLE WHO ARE ASLEEP!!
GRAA
AARR!
!!

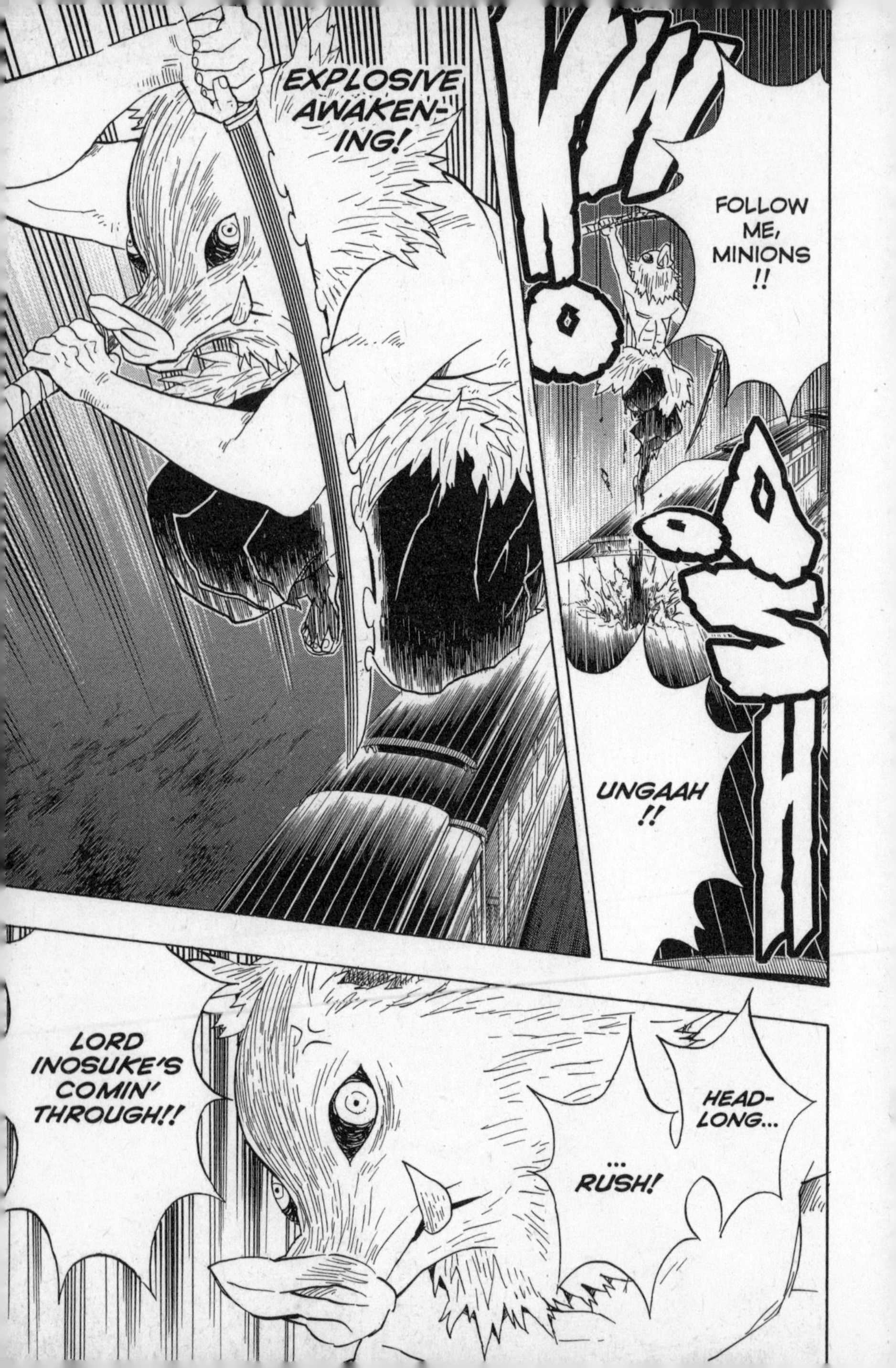
FOLLOW ME, MINIONS!!
WHOOSH
UNGAAH!!
EXPLOSIVE AWAKEN-ING!
HEAD-LONG...
...RUSH!
LORD INOSUKE'S COMIN' THROUGH!!

Taisho Whispers
Deleted Scene

Nezuko burned
Rengoku's and the
others' tickets, so
they woke up. Yahoo!!
Sorry that didn't get
into the main story!

CHAPTER 60: DEFENDING 200 PEOPLE

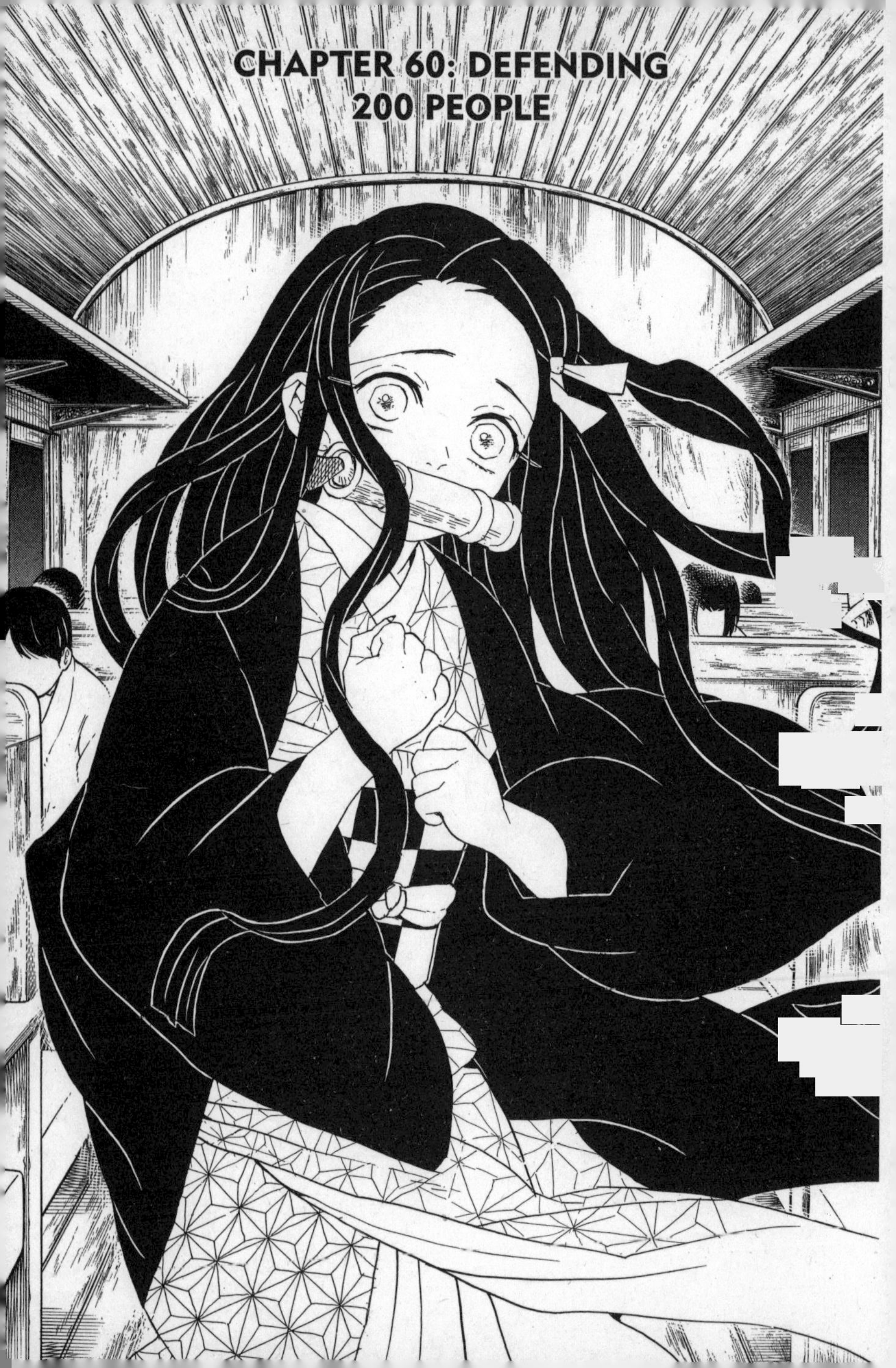

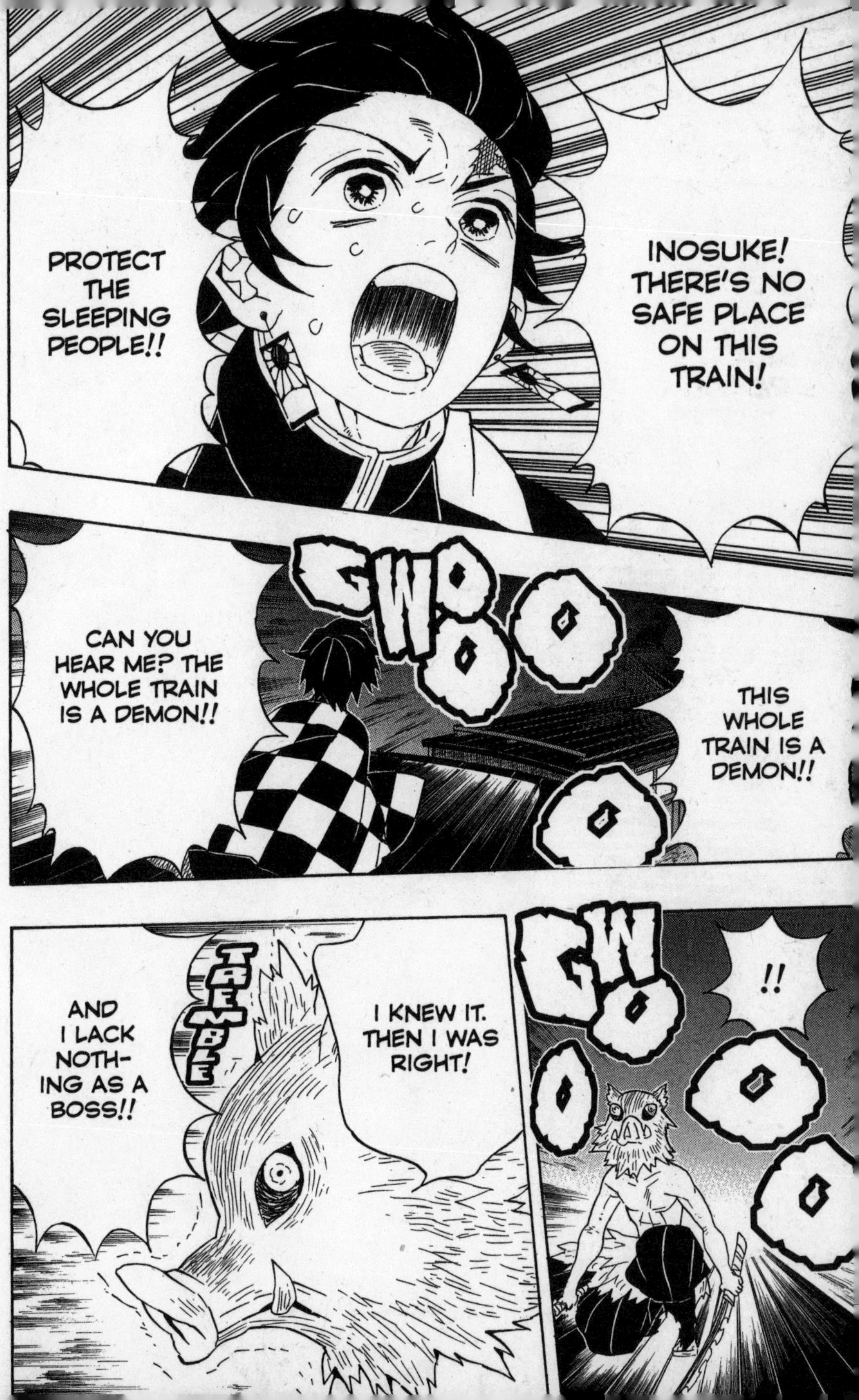
INOSUKE! THERE'S NO SAFE PLACE ON THIS TRAIN!
PROTECT THE SLEEPING PEOPLE!!
GWOOOO
THIS WHOLE TRAIN IS A DEMON!!
CAN YOU HEAR ME? THE WHOLE TRAIN IS A DEMON!!
GWOOOO
!!
I KNEW IT. THEN I WAS RIGHT!
TREMBLE
AND I LACK NOTHING AS A BOSS!!

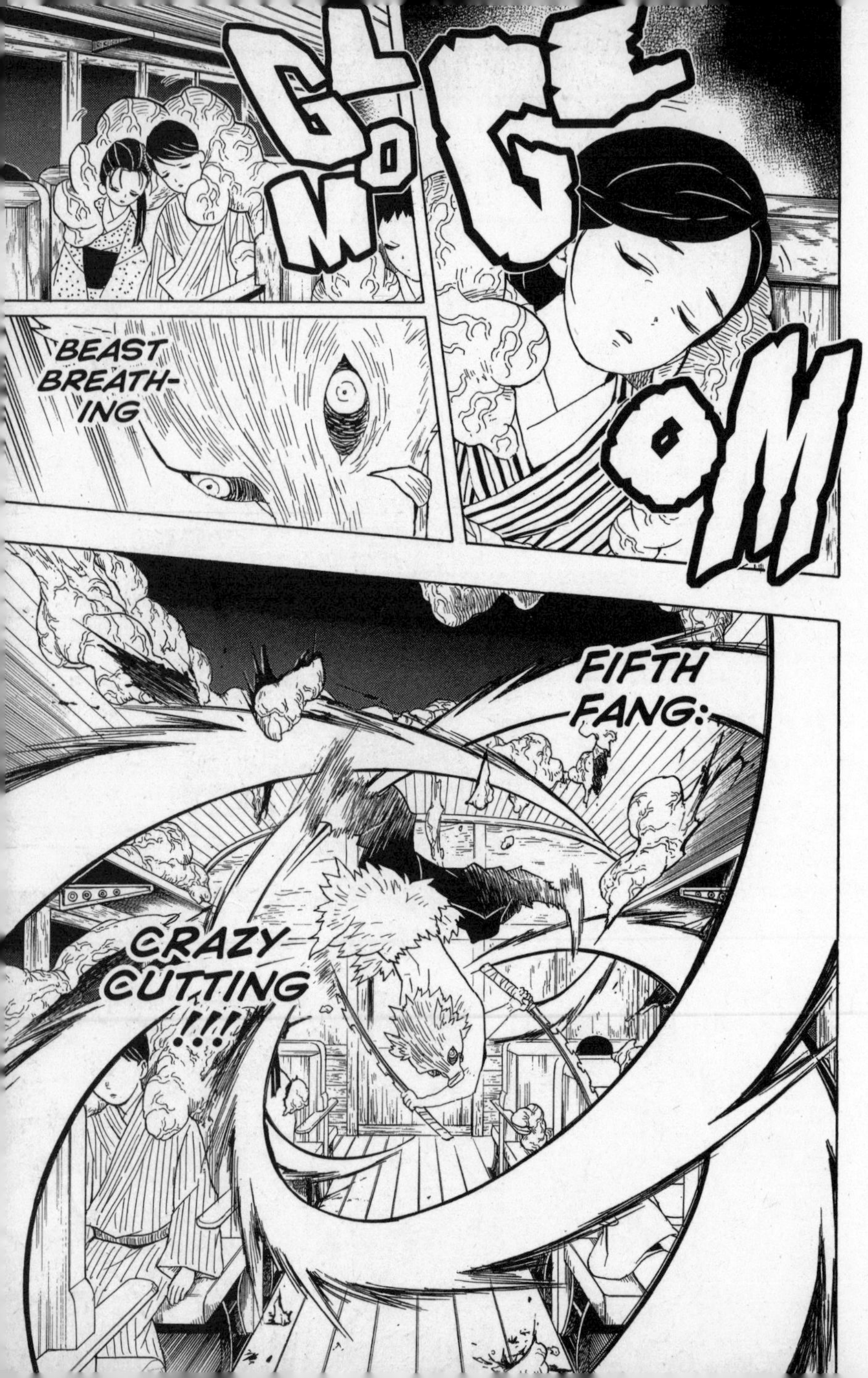

GLOM
GLOM
BEAST BREATHING
FIFTH FANG:
CRAZY CUTTING!!!

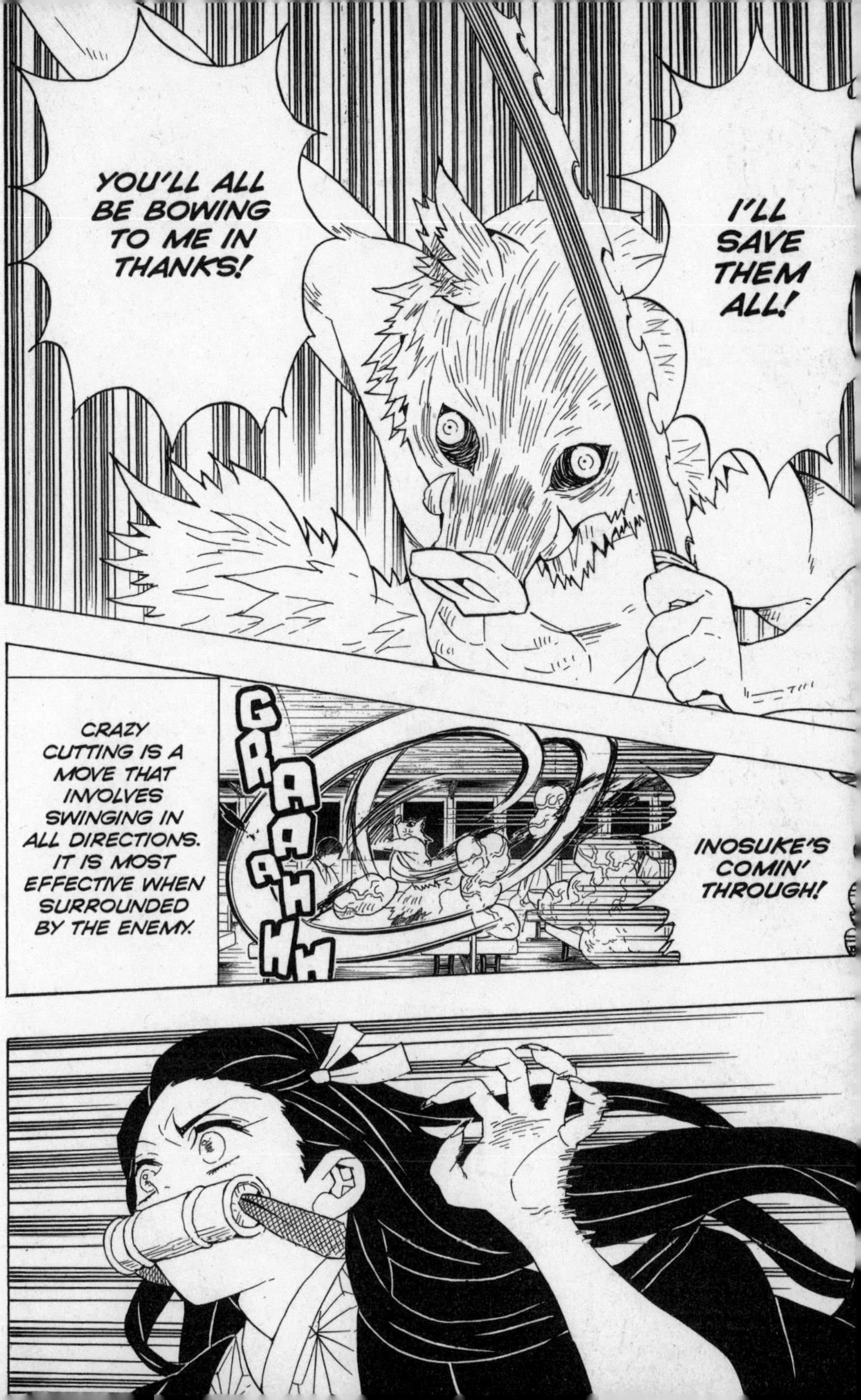
I'LL SAVE THEM ALL!
YOU'LL ALL BE BOWING TO ME IN THANKS!
INOSUKE'S COMIN' THROUGH!
GRAAAHHH
CRAZY CUTTING IS A MOVE THAT INVOLVES SWINGING IN ALL DIRECTIONS. IT IS MOST EFFECTIVE WHEN SURROUNDED BY THE ENEMY.

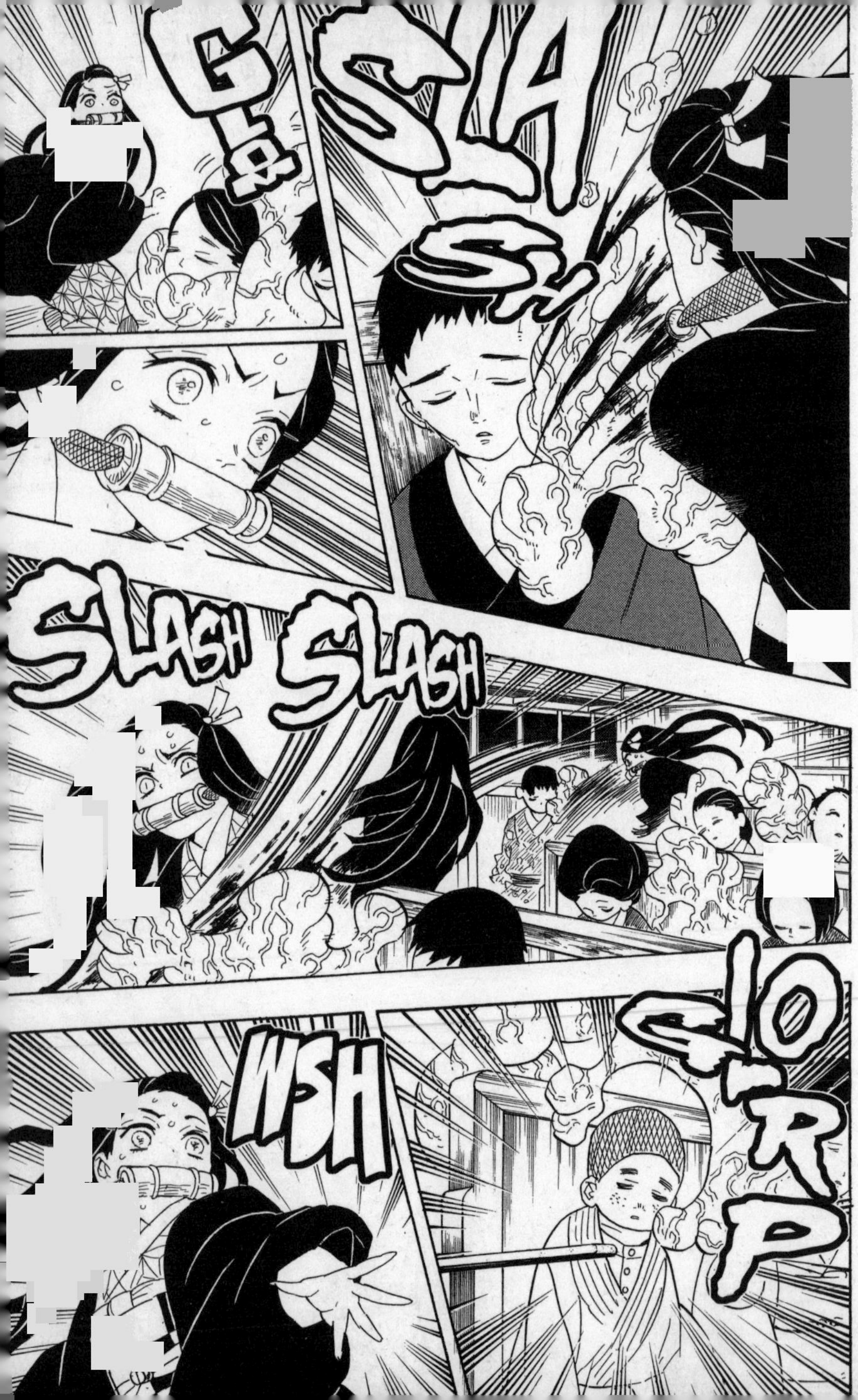

SHA
SH
SLASH
SLASH
GLORP
WSH

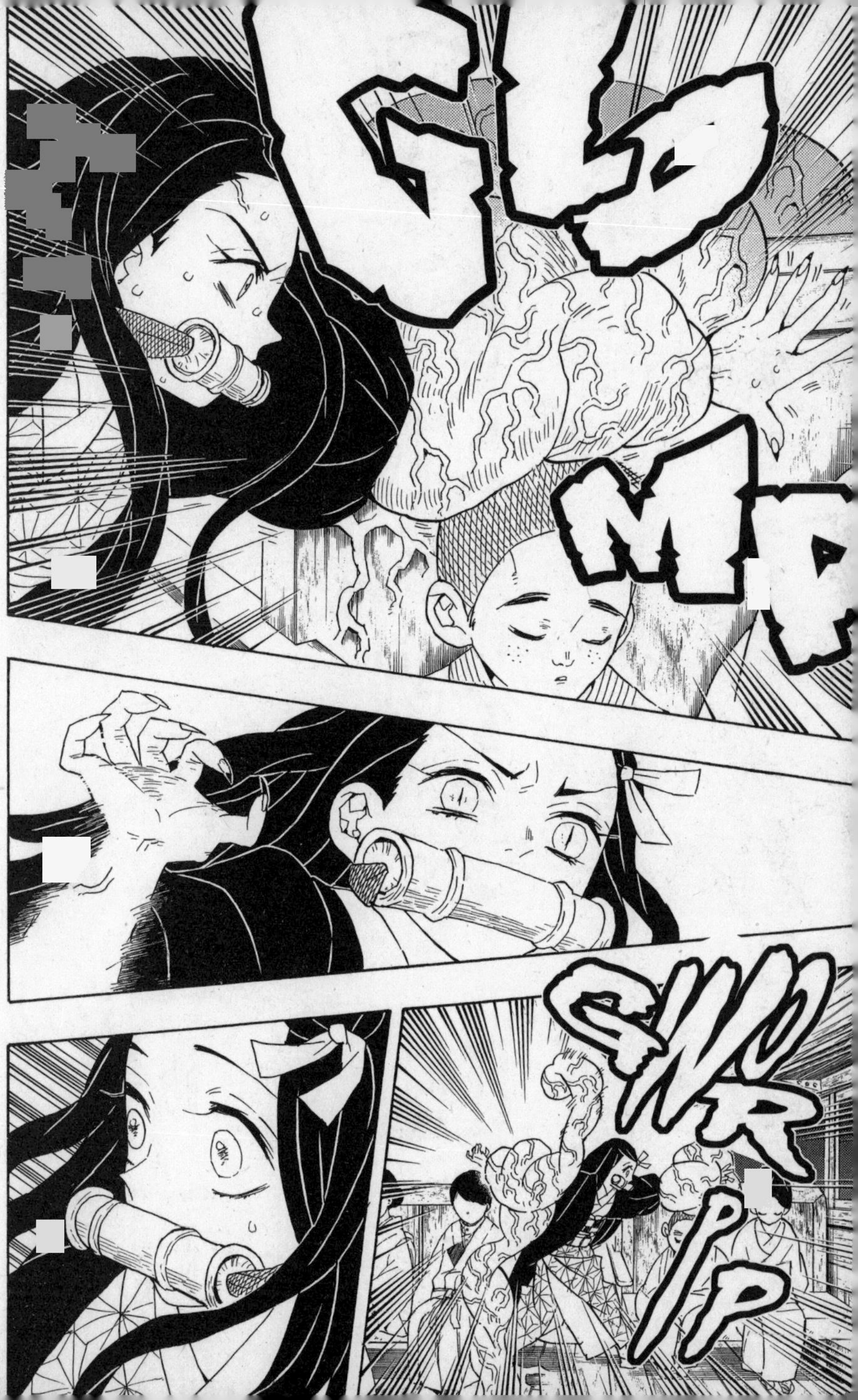
CHOMP
SHRIPP

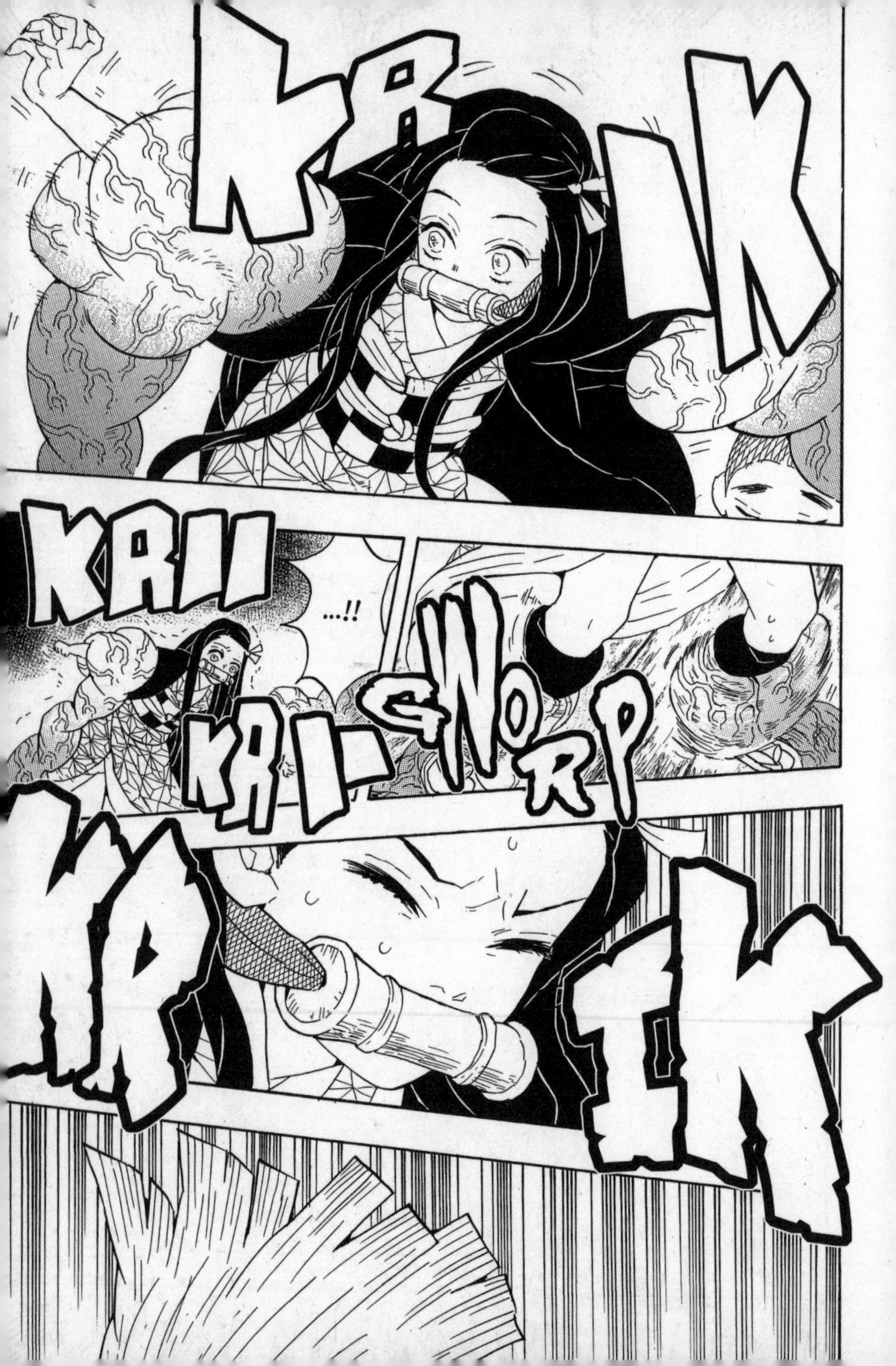
KRIK
KRII
...!!
KRII-
GNORP
KRIK

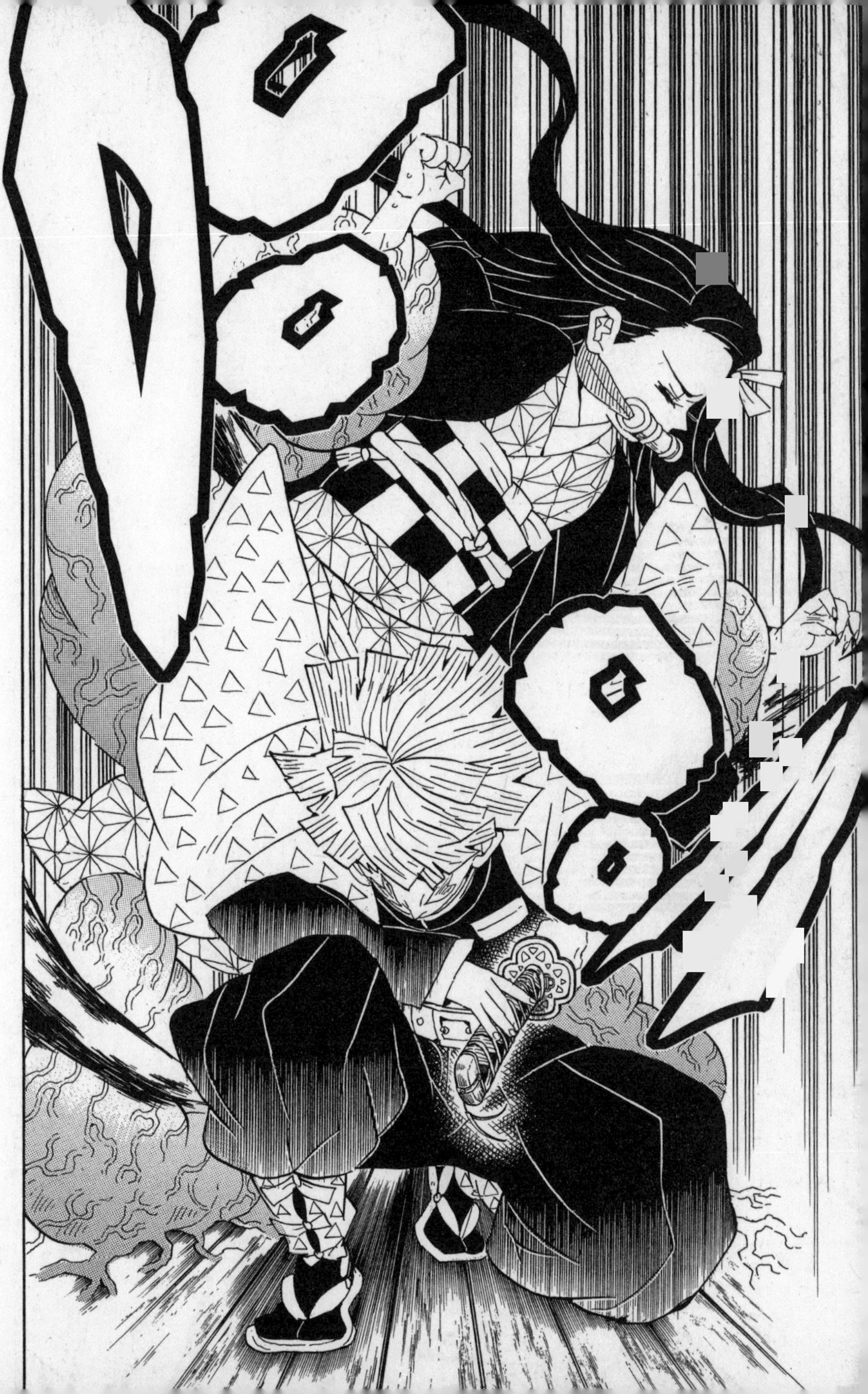

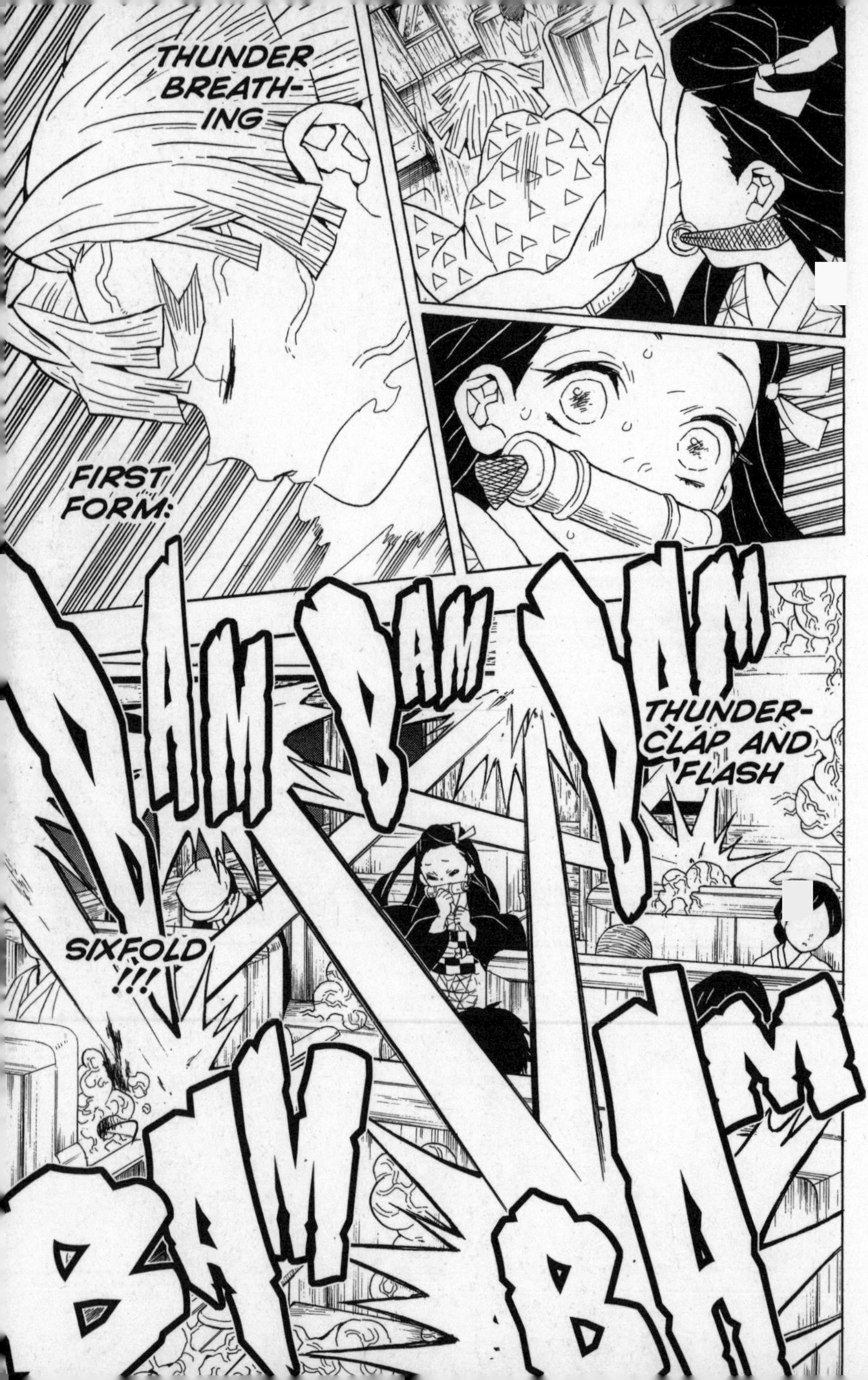
THUNDER BREATHING
FIRST FORM:
BAM
THUNDERCLAP AND FLASH
BAM
BAM
SIXFOLD!!!
BAM
BAM
BAM

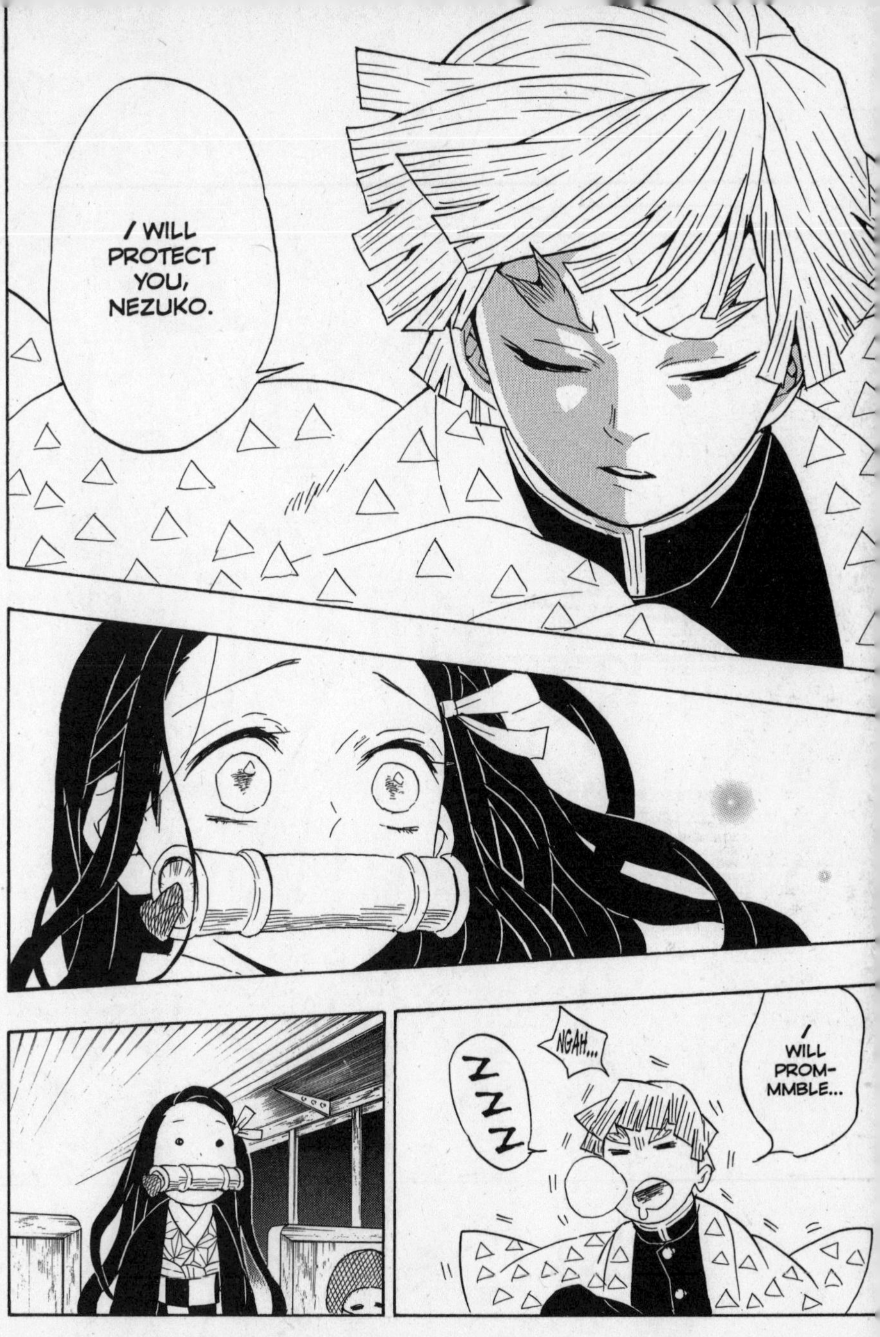
I WILL PROTECT YOU, NEZUKO.
I WILL PROM-MMBLE...
NGAH...
ZZZZ

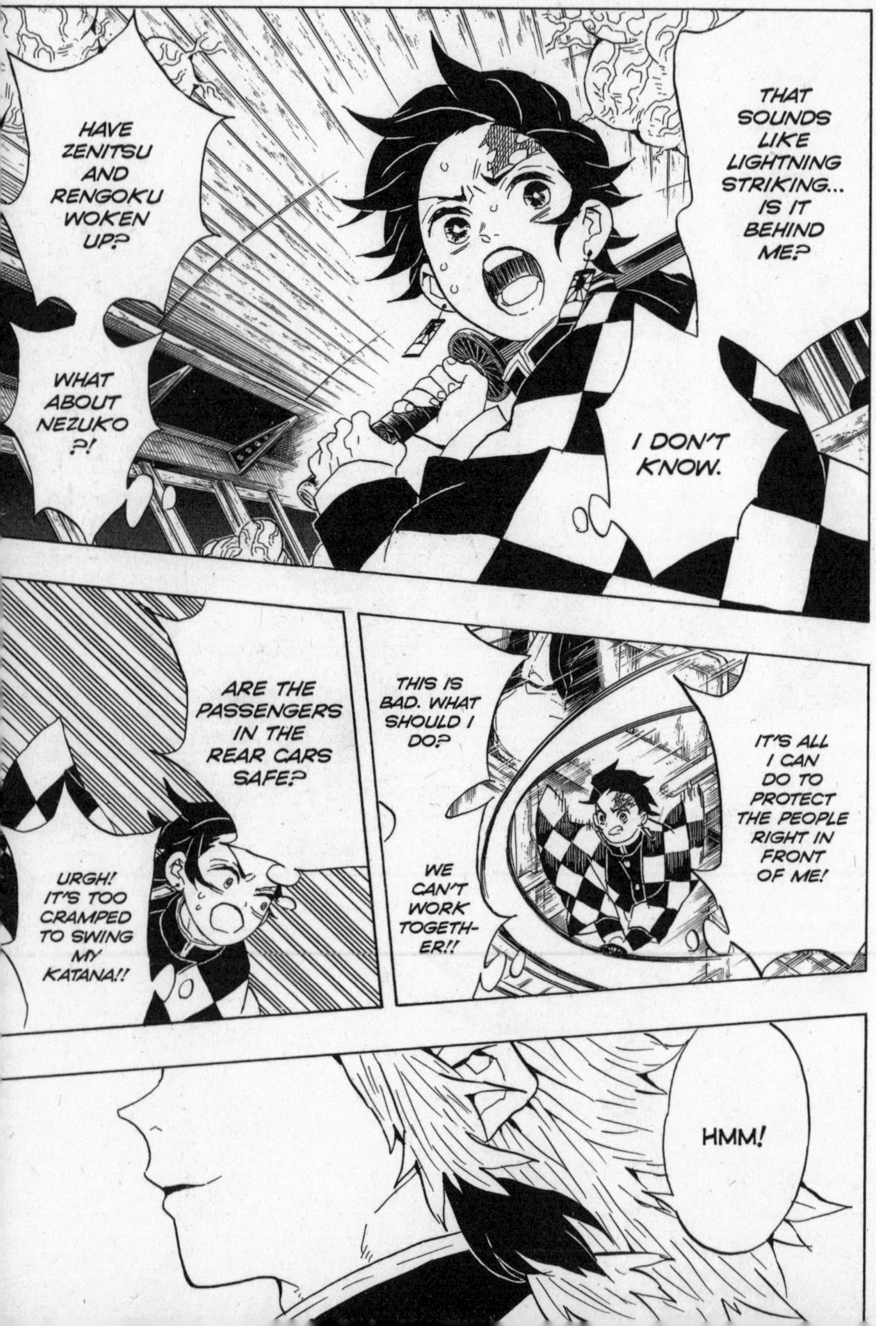
THAT SOUNDS LIKE LIGHTNING STRIKING... IS IT BEHIND ME?
HAVE ZENITSU AND RENGOKU WOKEN UP?
WHAT ABOUT NEZUKO?!
I DON'T KNOW.
IT'S ALL I CAN DO TO PROTECT THE PEOPLE RIGHT IN FRONT OF ME!
THIS IS BAD. WHAT SHOULD I DO?
WE CAN'T WORK TOGETHER!!
ARE THE PASSENGERS IN THE REAR CARS SAFE?
URGH! IT'S TOO CRAMPED TO SWING MY KATANA!!
HMM!

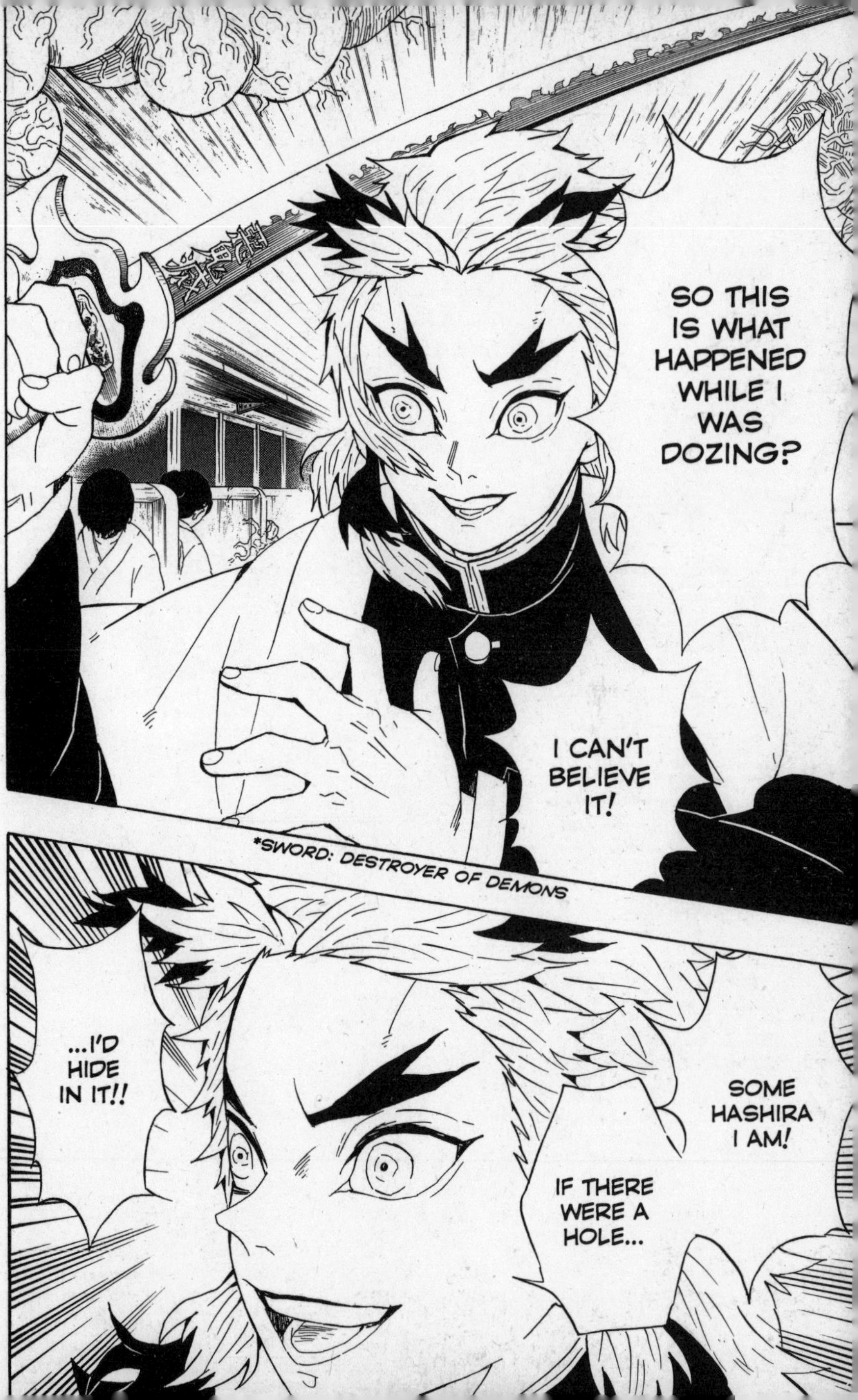
SO THIS IS WHAT HAPPENED WHILE I WAS DOZING?
I CAN'T BELIEVE IT!
*SWORD: DESTROYER OF DEMONS
SOME HASHIRA I AM!
IF THERE WERE A HOLE...
...I'D HIDE IN IT!!

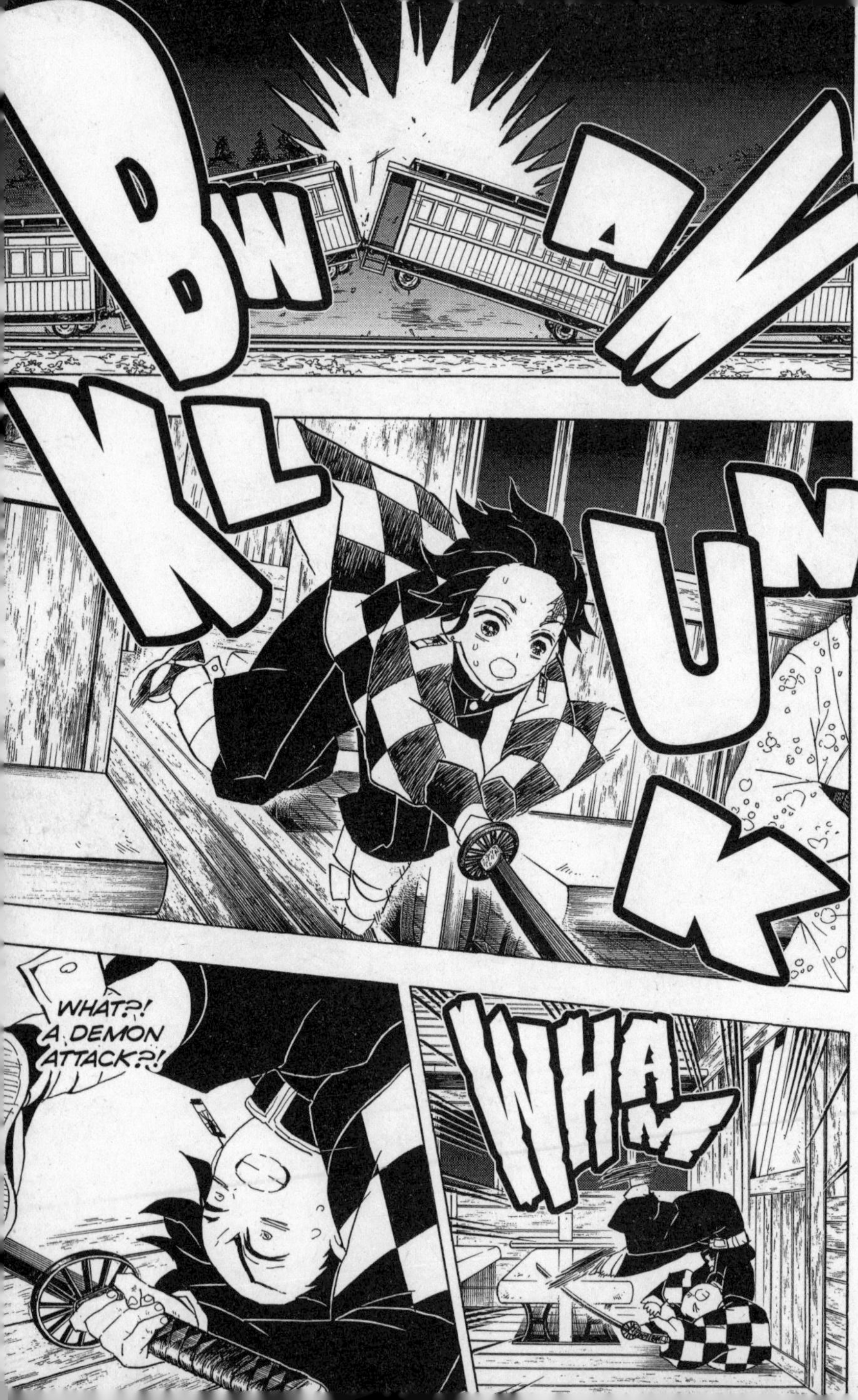
BWAM
KLUNK
WHAM
WHAT?! A DEMON ATTACK?!

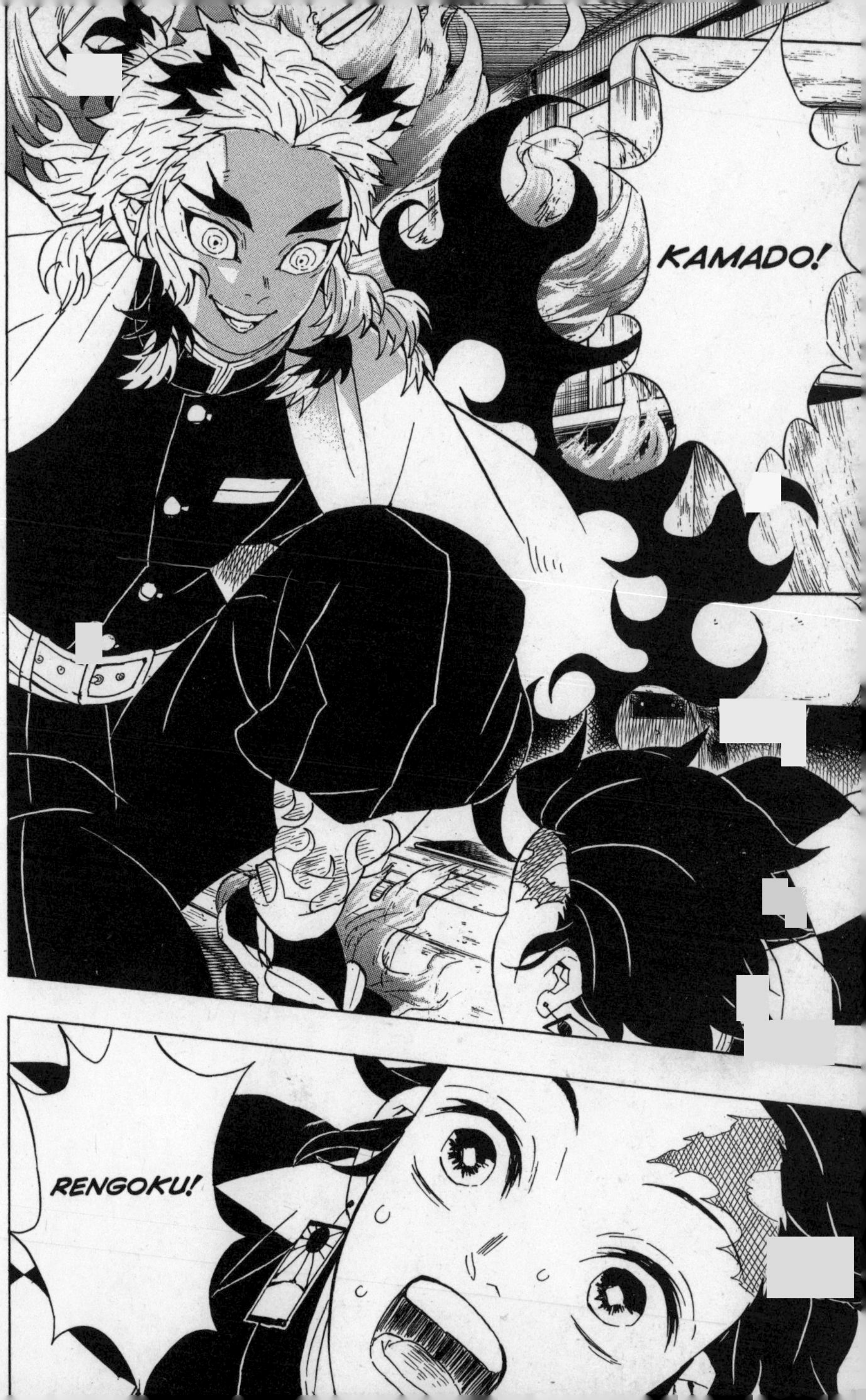
KAMADO!
RENGOKU!

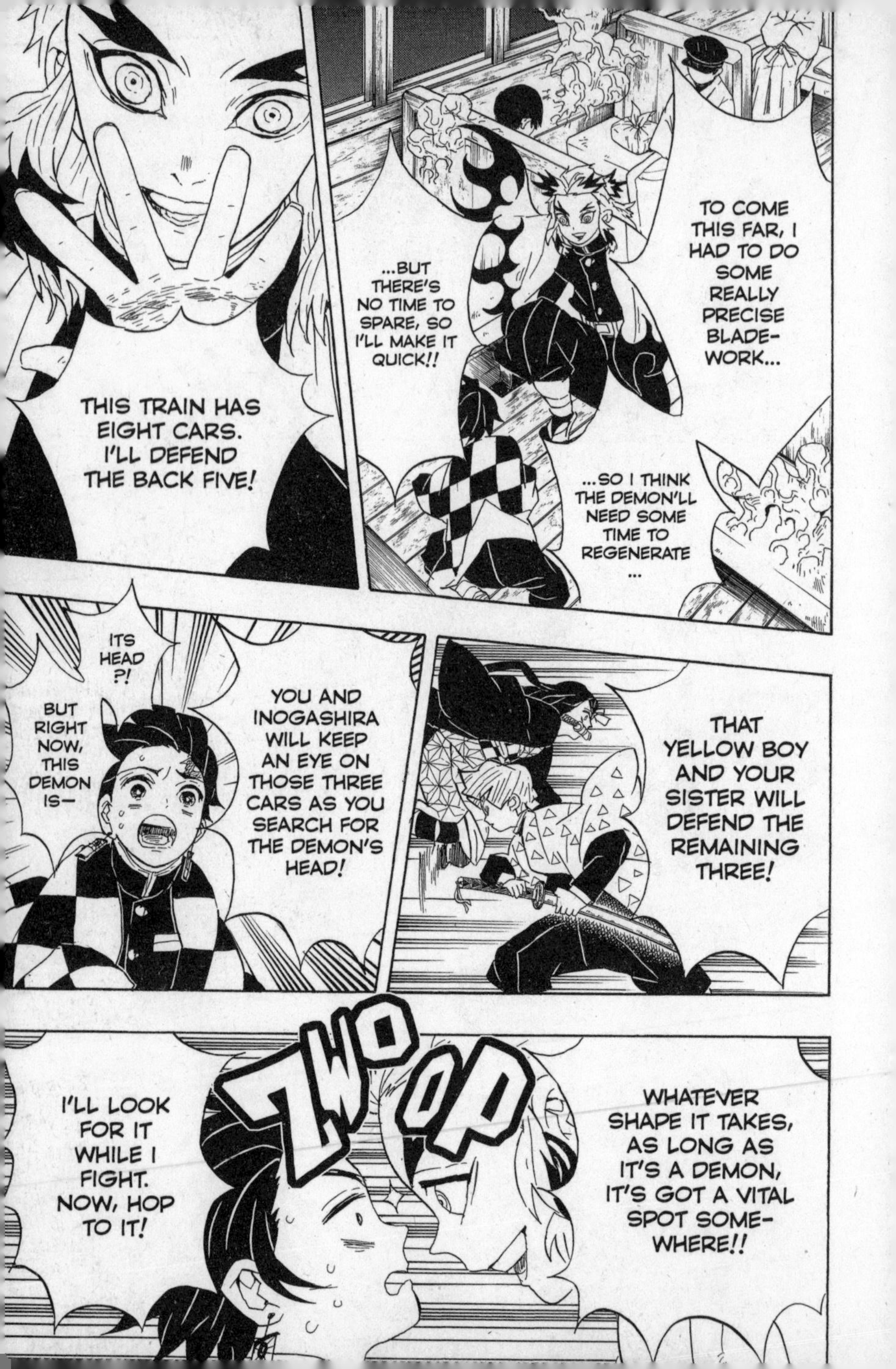
TO COME THIS FAR, I HAD TO DO SOME REALLY PRECISE BLADE-WORK...
...SO I THINK THE DEMON'LL NEED SOME TIME TO REGENERATE ...
...BUT THERE'S NO TIME TO SPARE, SO I'LL MAKE IT QUICK!!
THIS TRAIN HAS EIGHT CARS. I'LL DEFEND THE BACK FIVE!
THAT YELLOW BOY AND YOUR SISTER WILL DEFEND THE REMAINING THREE!
YOU AND INOGASHIRA WILL KEEP AN EYE ON THOSE THREE CARS AS YOU SEARCH FOR THE DEMON'S HEAD!
ITS HEAD ?!
BUT RIGHT NOW, THIS DEMON IS—
WHATEVER SHAPE IT TAKES, AS LONG AS IT'S A DEMON, IT'S GOT A VITAL SPOT SOME-WHERE!!
ZWOOP
I'LL LOOK FOR IT WHILE I FIGHT. NOW, HOP TO IT!

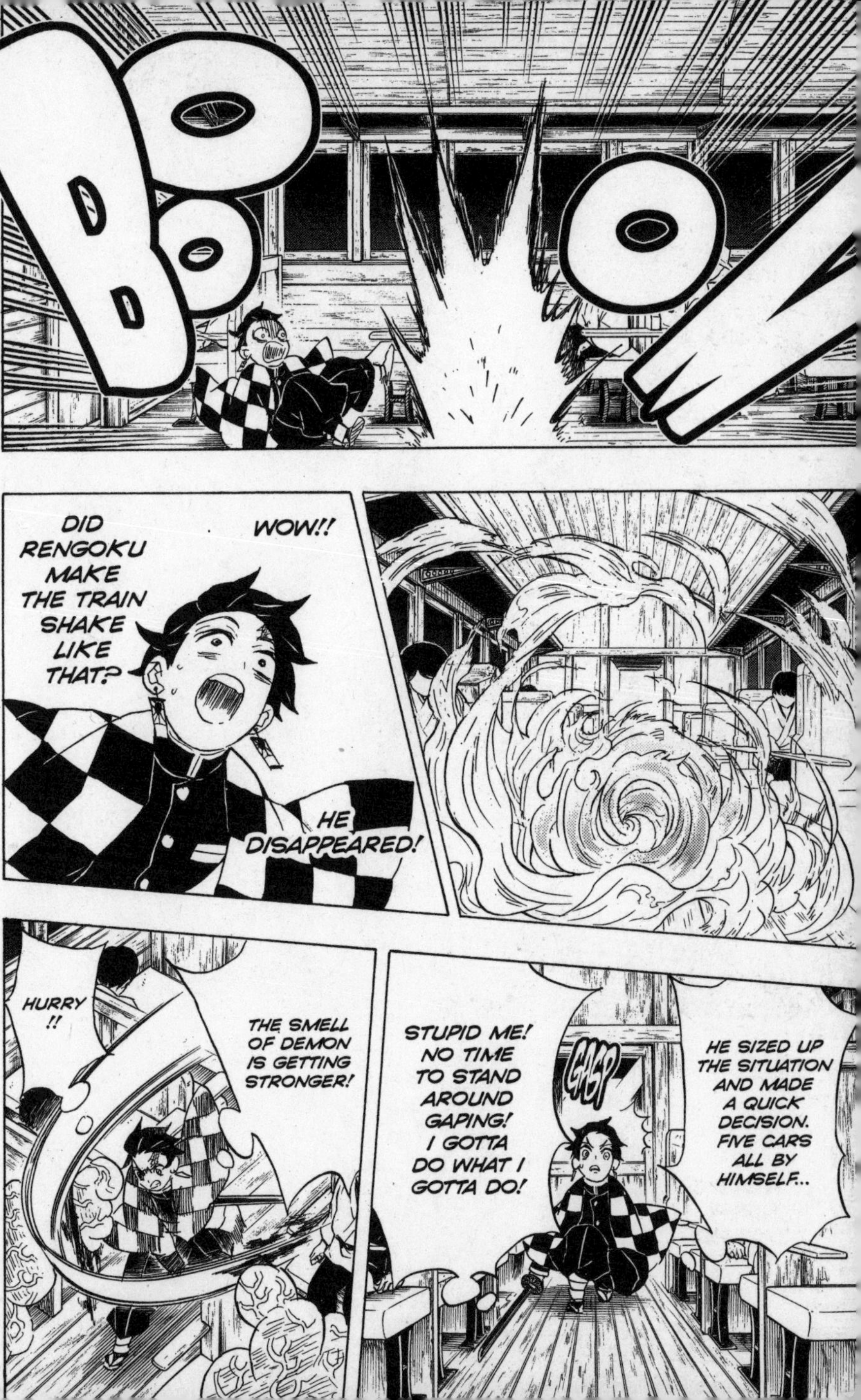
WOW!!
DID RENGOKU MAKE THE TRAIN SHAKE LIKE THAT?
HE DISAPPEARED!
HE SIZED UP THE SITUATION AND MADE A QUICK DECISION. FIVE CARS ALL BY HIMSELF...
GASP
STUPID ME! NO TIME TO STAND AROUND GAPING! I GOTTA DO WHAT I GOTTA DO!
THE SMELL OF DEMON IS GETTING STRONGER!
HURRY!!

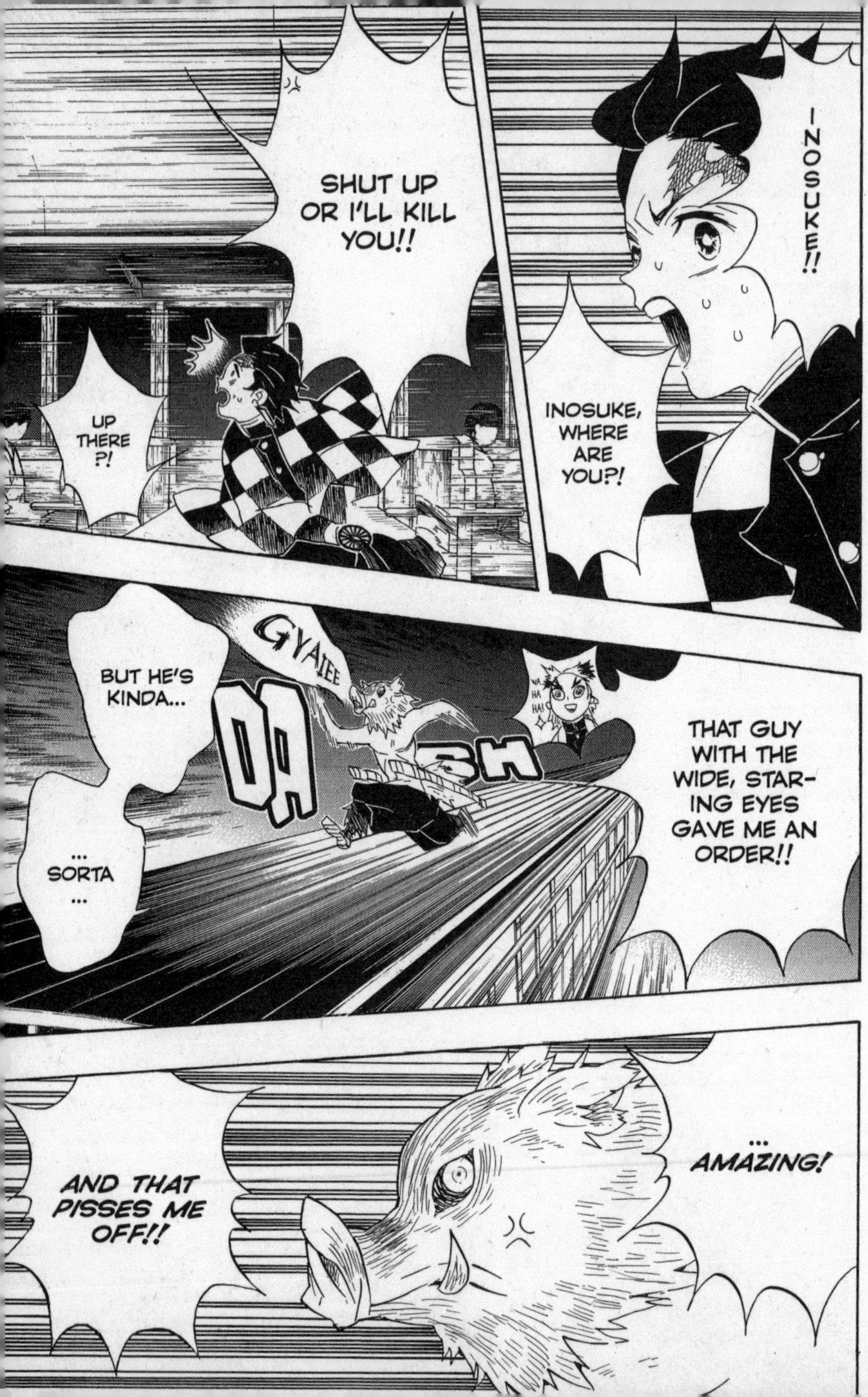
INOSUKE!!
INOSUKE, WHERE ARE YOU?!
SHUT UP OR I'LL KILL YOU!!
UP THERE?!
THAT GUY WITH THE WIDE, STARING EYES GAVE ME AN ORDER!!
WA HA HA!
GYAIEE
DASH
BUT HE'S KINDA...
... SORTA ...
... AMAZING!
AND THAT PISSES ME OFF!!

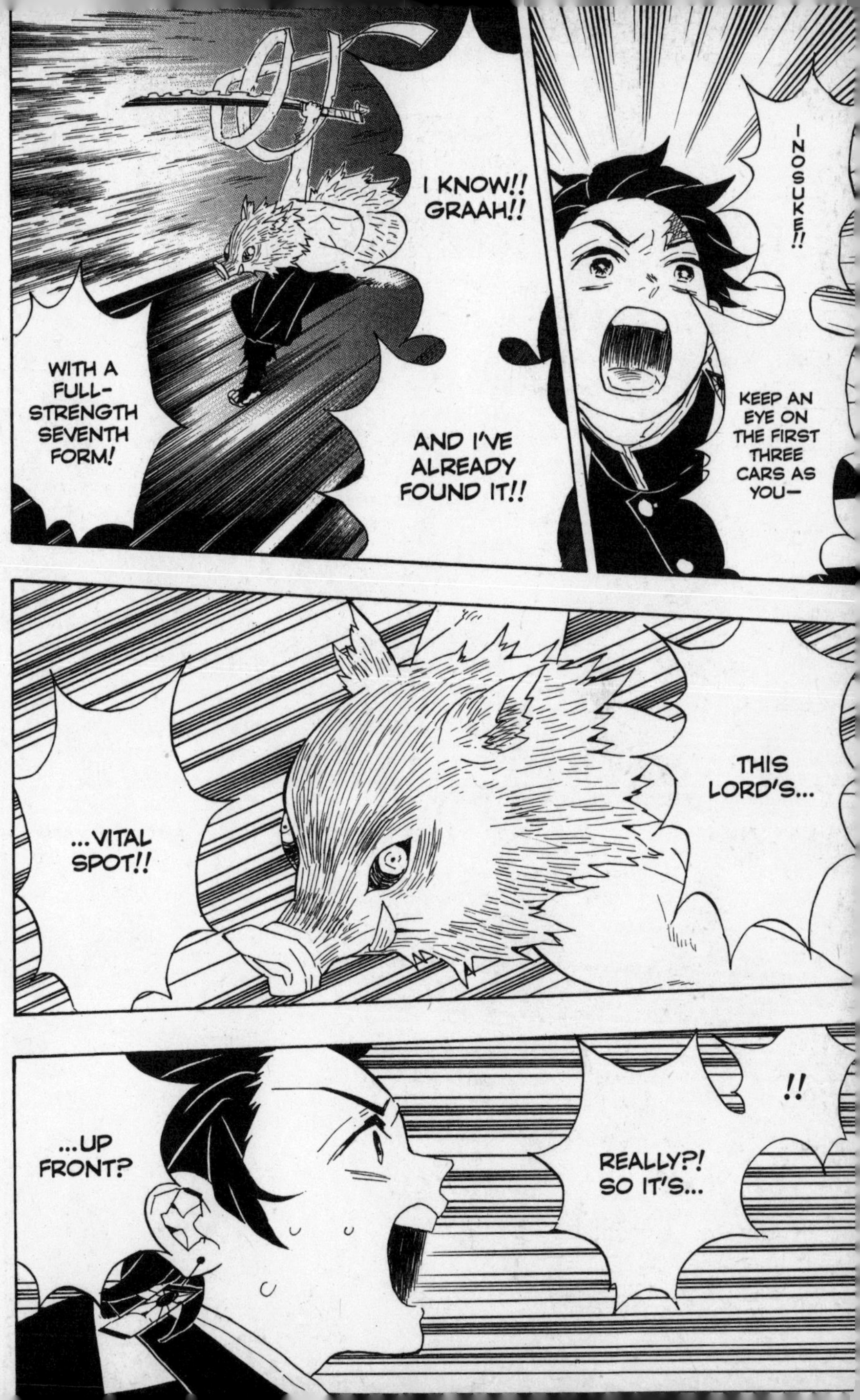
INOSUKE!!
KEEP AN EYE ON THE FIRST THREE CARS AS YOU—
I KNOW!! GRAAH!!
AND I'VE ALREADY FOUND IT!!
WITH A FULL-STRENGTH SEVENTH FORM!
THIS LORD'S...
...VITAL SPOT!!
!!
REALLY?! SO IT'S...
...UP FRONT?

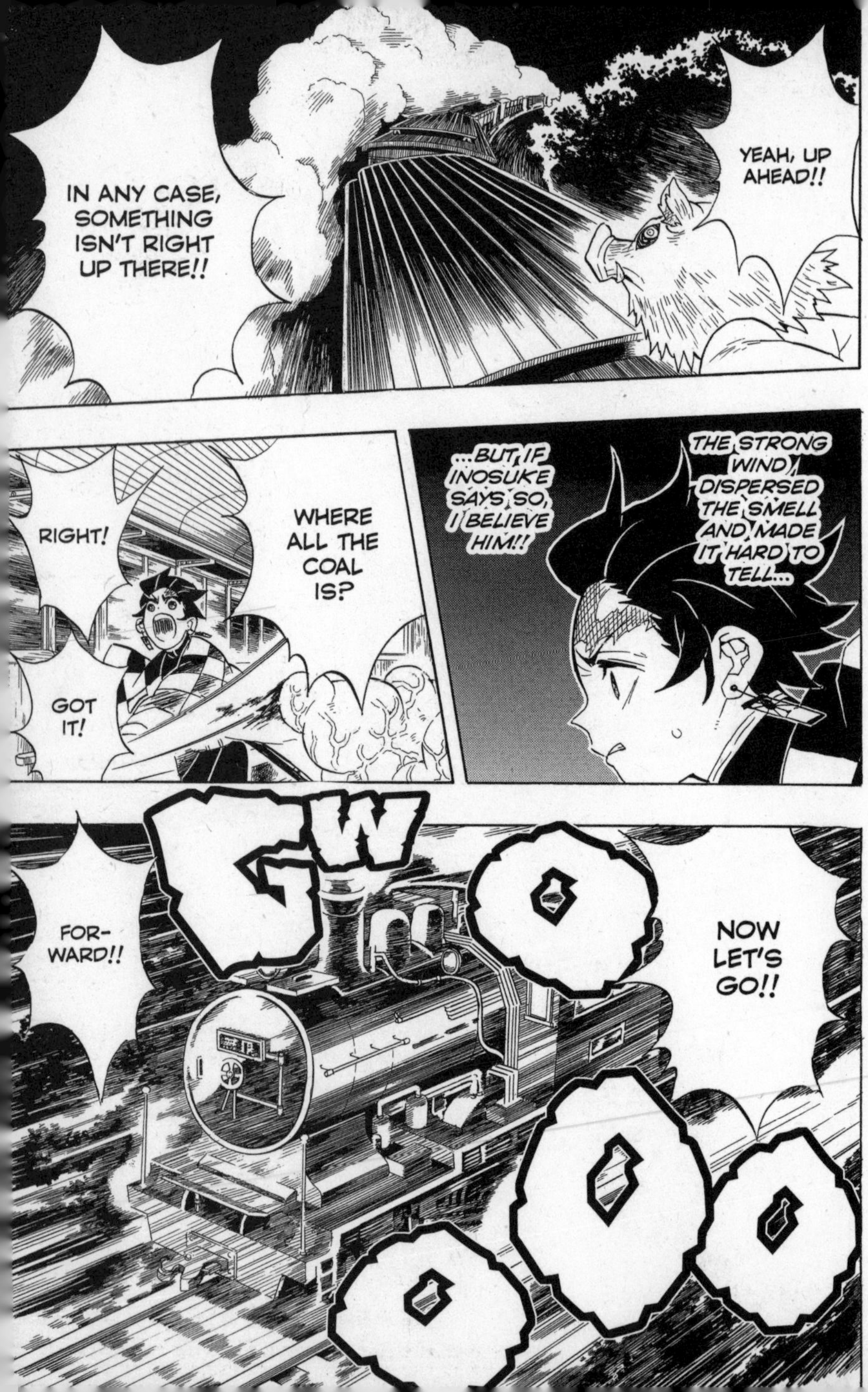
YEAH, UP AHEAD!!
IN ANY CASE, SOMETHING ISN'T RIGHT UP THERE!!
THE STRONG WIND DISPERSED THE SMELL AND MADE IT HARD TO TELL...
...BUT IF INOSUKE SAYS SO, I BELIEVE HIM!!
WHERE ALL THE COAL IS?
RIGHT!
GOT IT!
NOW LET'S GO!!
FOR-WARD!!
GWOOOO

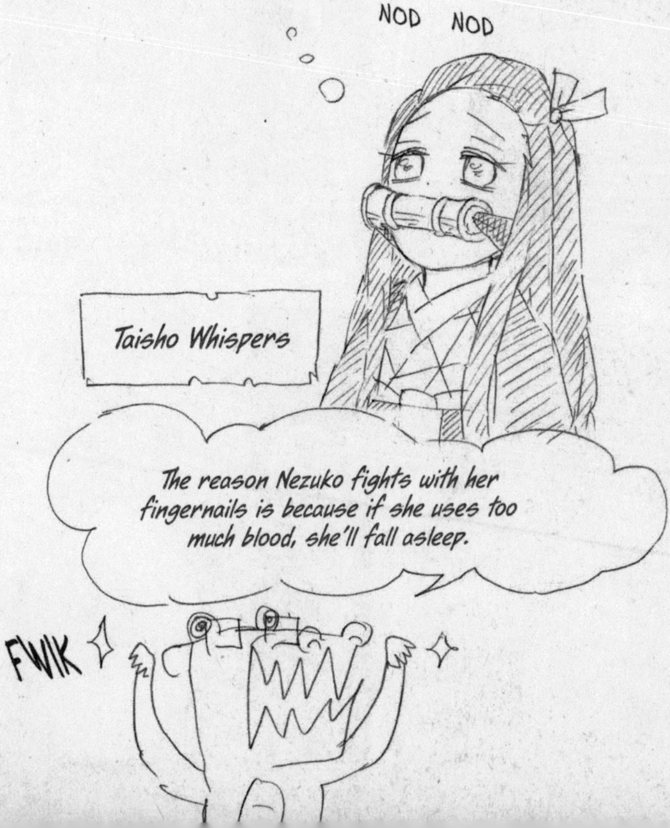
NOD NOD
Taisho Whispers
The reason Nezuko fights with her fingernails is because if she uses too much blood, she'll fall asleep.
FWIK

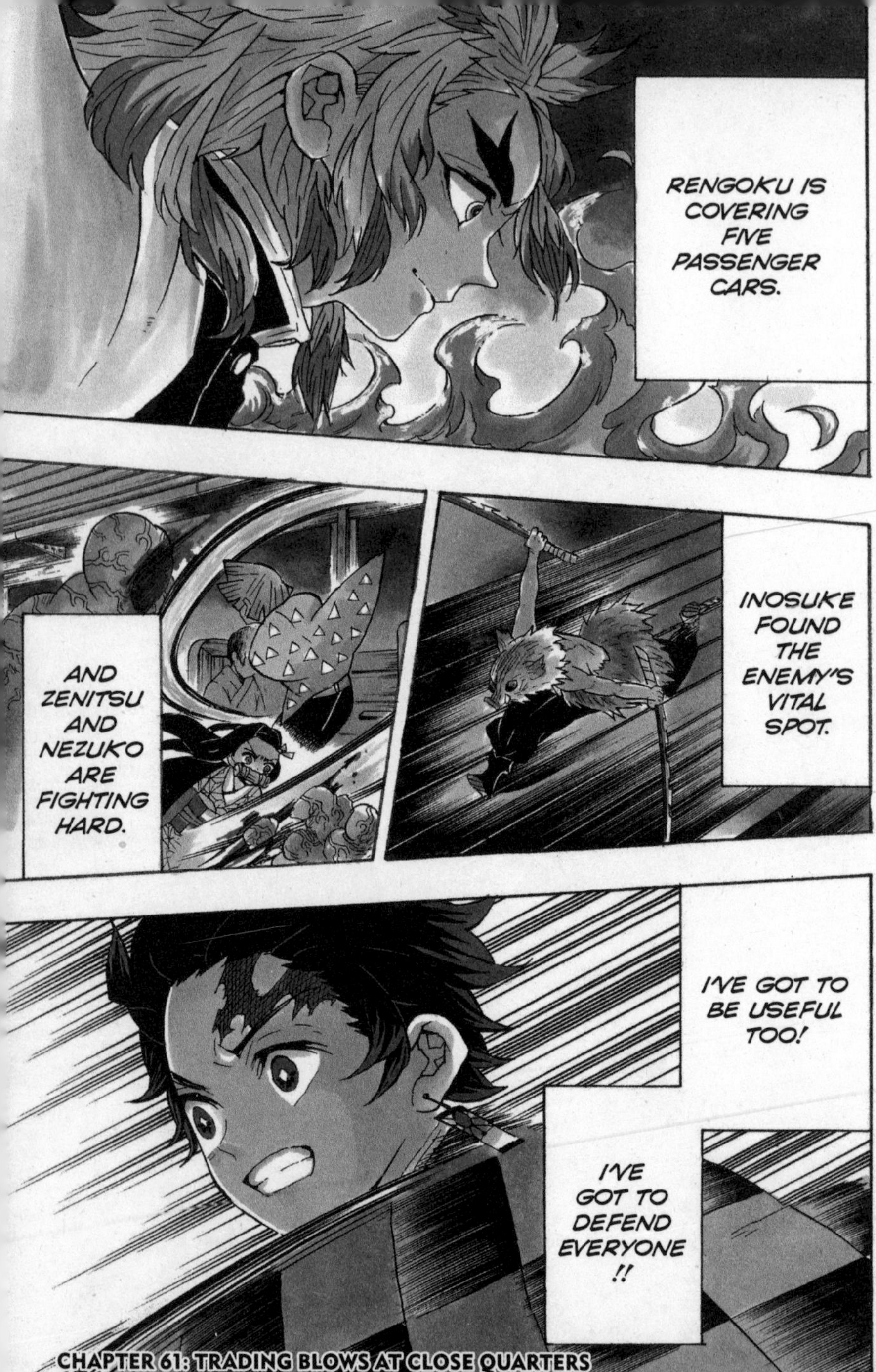
RENGOKU IS COVERING FIVE PASSENGER CARS.
INOSUKE FOUND THE ENEMY'S VITAL SPOT.
AND ZENITSU AND NEZUKO ARE FIGHTING HARD.
I'VE GOT TO BE USEFUL TOO!
I'VE GOT TO DEFEND EVERYONE!!

CHAPTER 61: TRADING BLOWS AT CLOSE QUARTERS

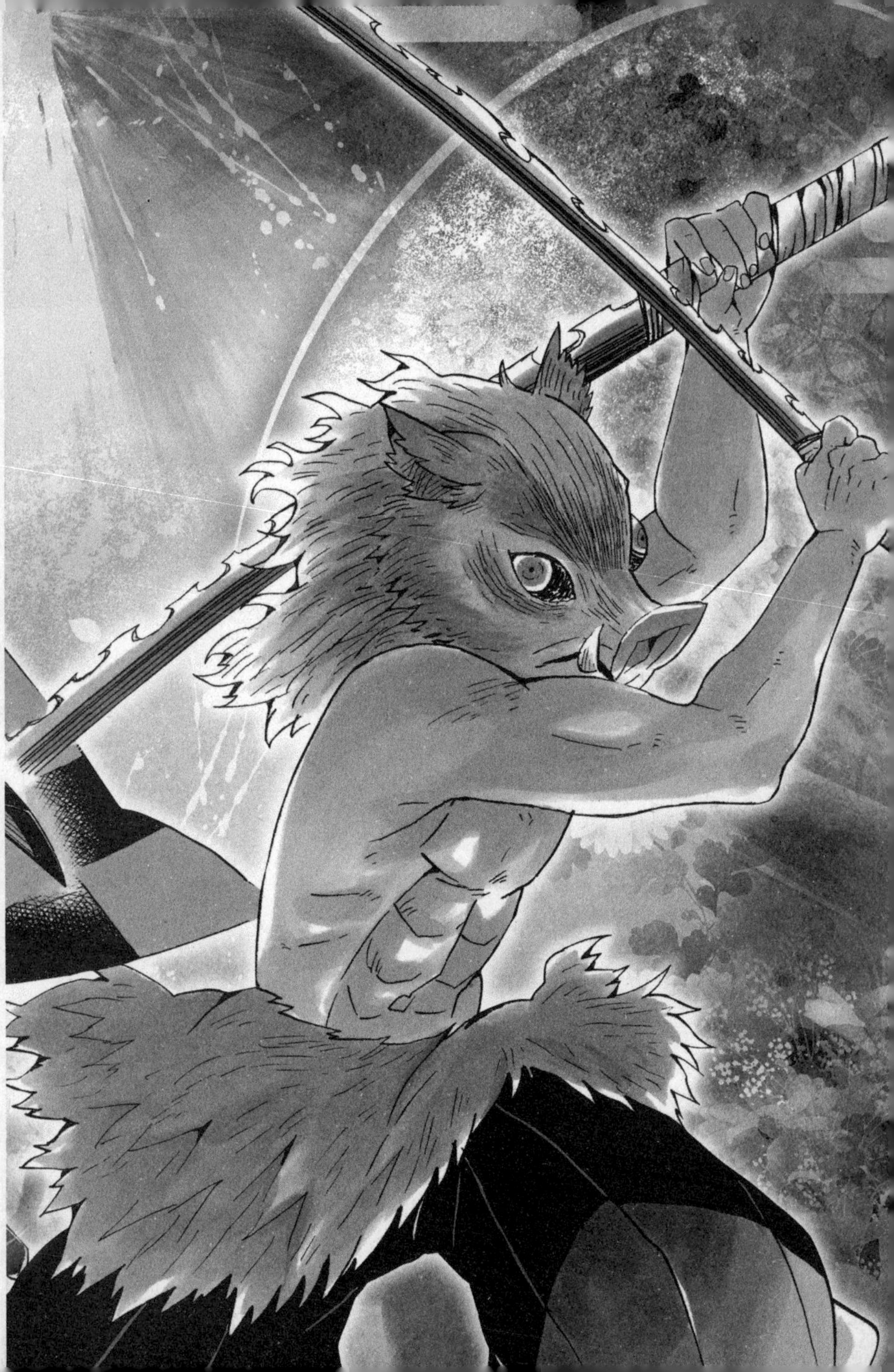

CHAPTER 61: TRADING BLOWS AT CLOSE QUARTERS

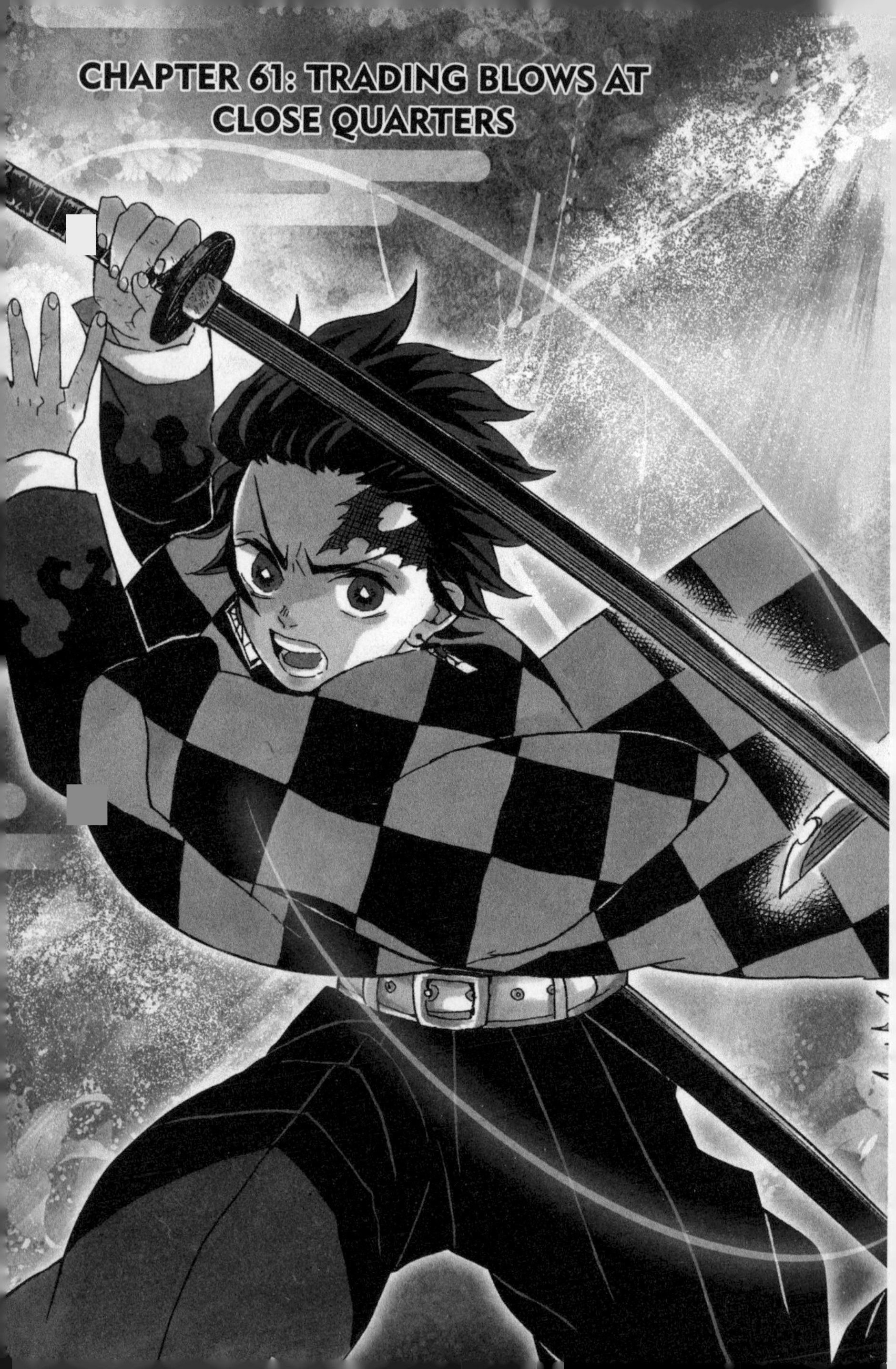

DEMON SLAYER

KIMETSU NO YAIBA

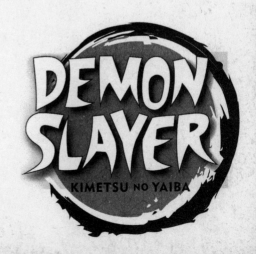

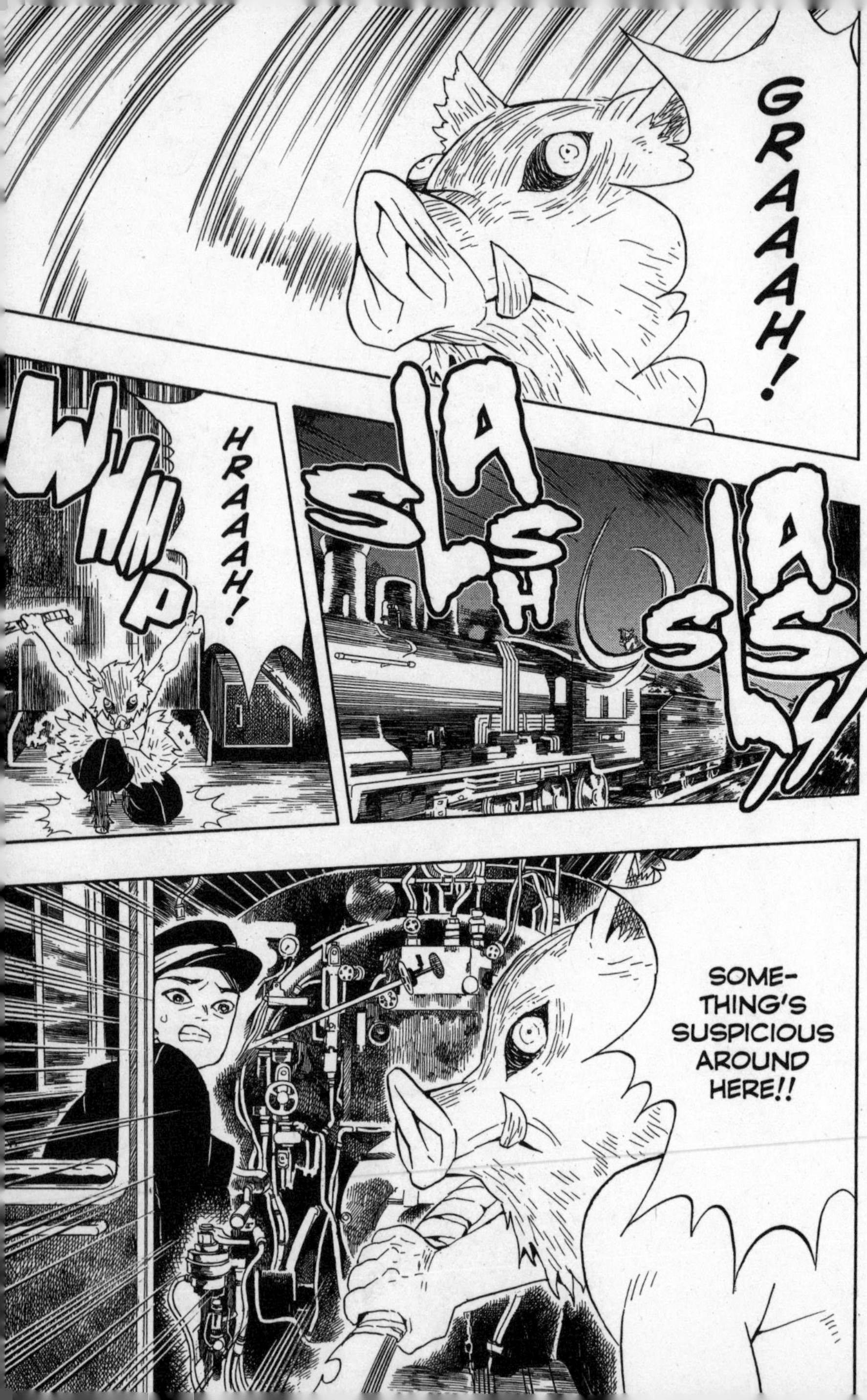
GRAAAAH!
SLASH
SLASH
WHMP
HRAAAAH!
SOME-THING'S SUSPICIOUS AROUND HERE!!

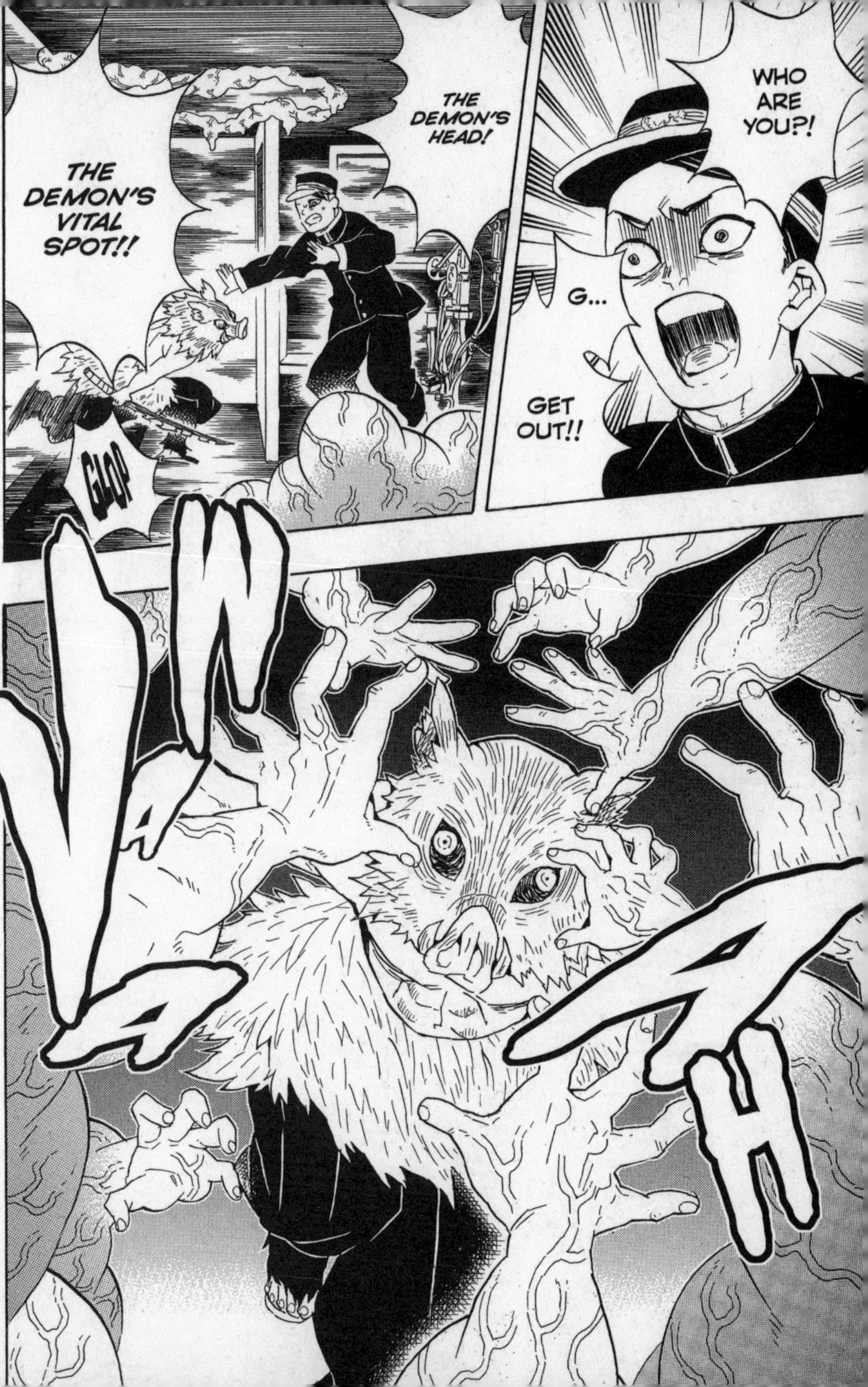
WHO ARE YOU?!
G...
GET OUT!!
THE DEMON'S HEAD!
THE DEMON'S VITAL SPOT!!
GLOP

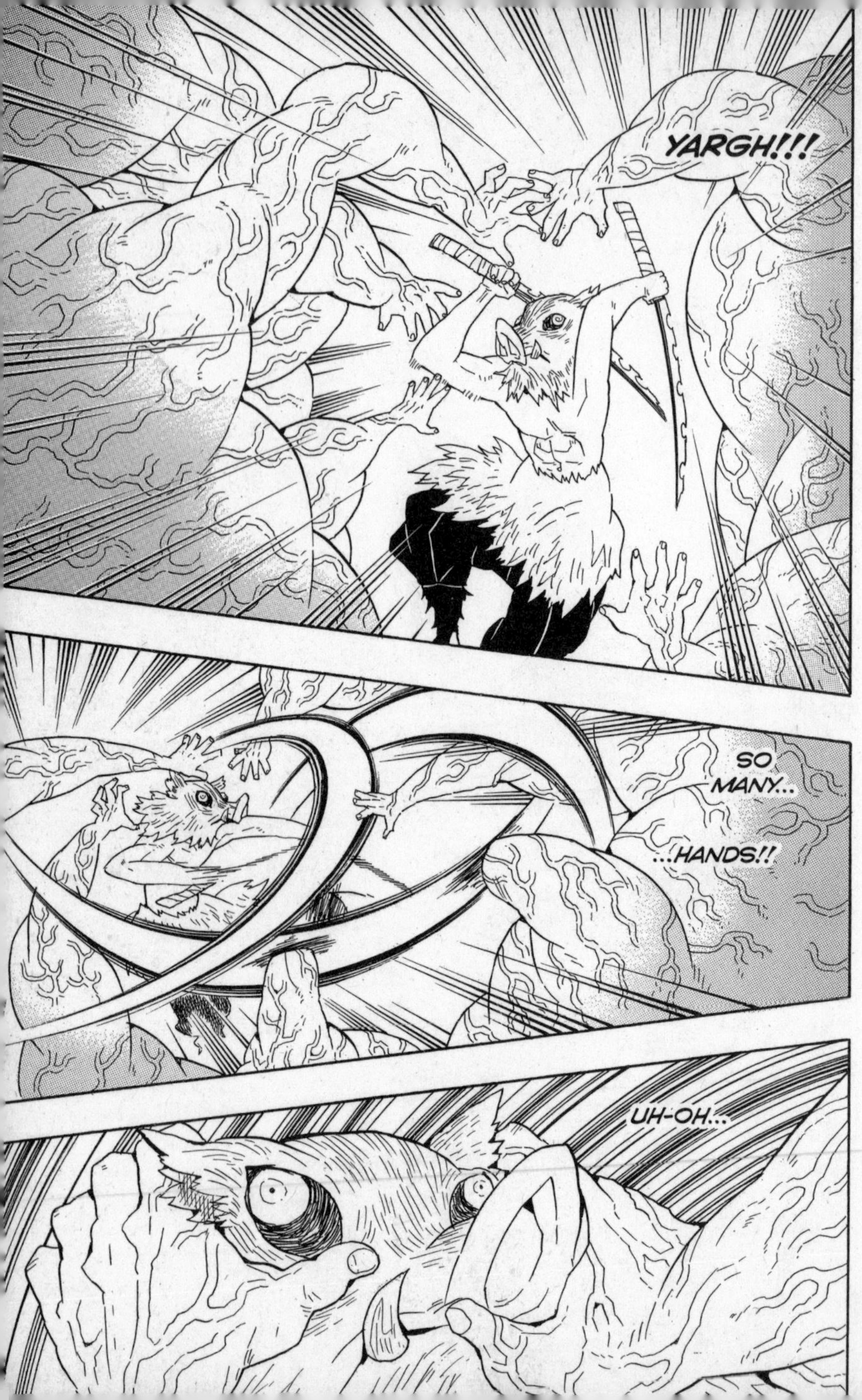
YARGH!!!
SO MANY...
...HANDS!!
UH-OH...

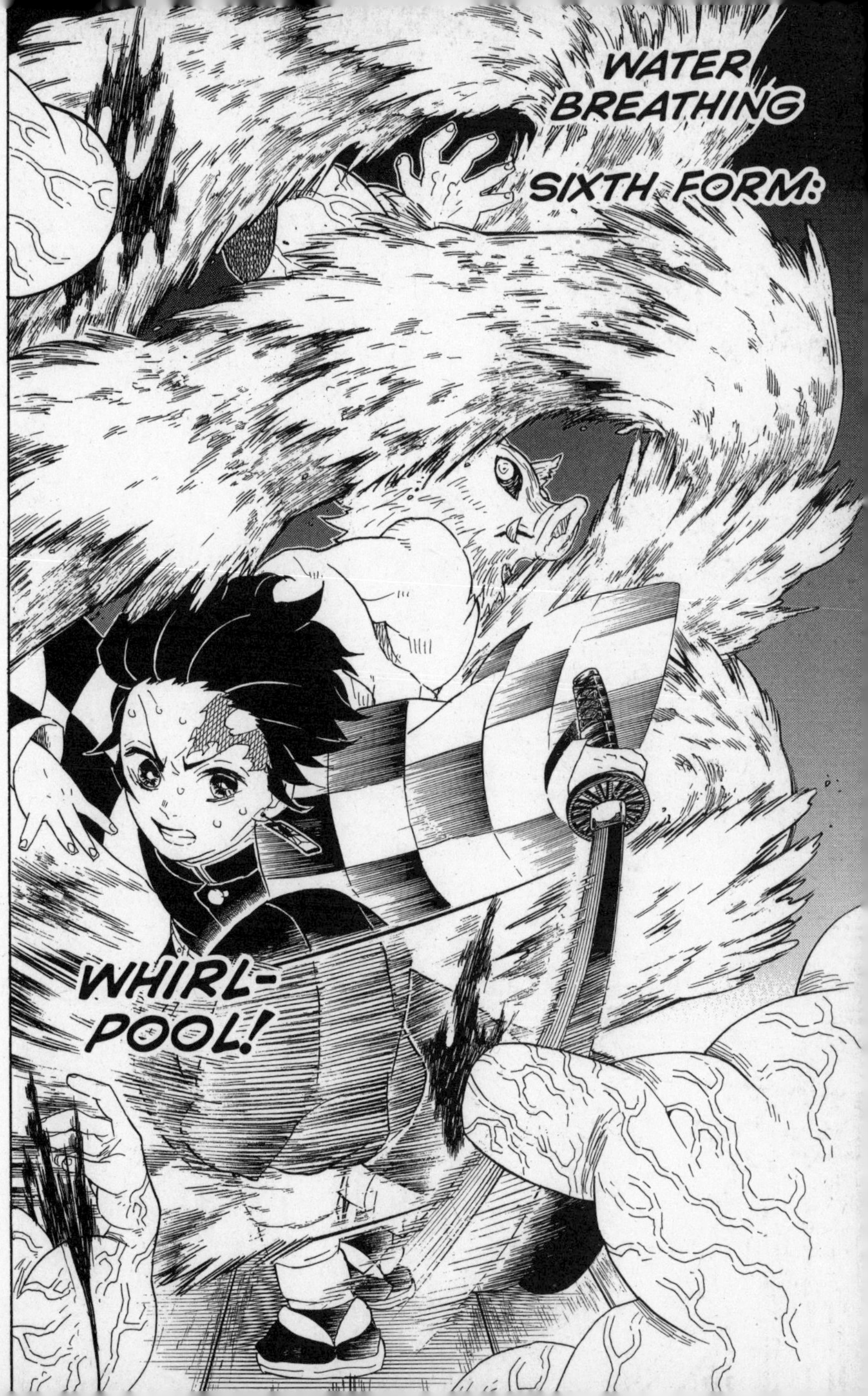
WATER BREATHING
SIXTH FORM:
WHIRL-POOL!

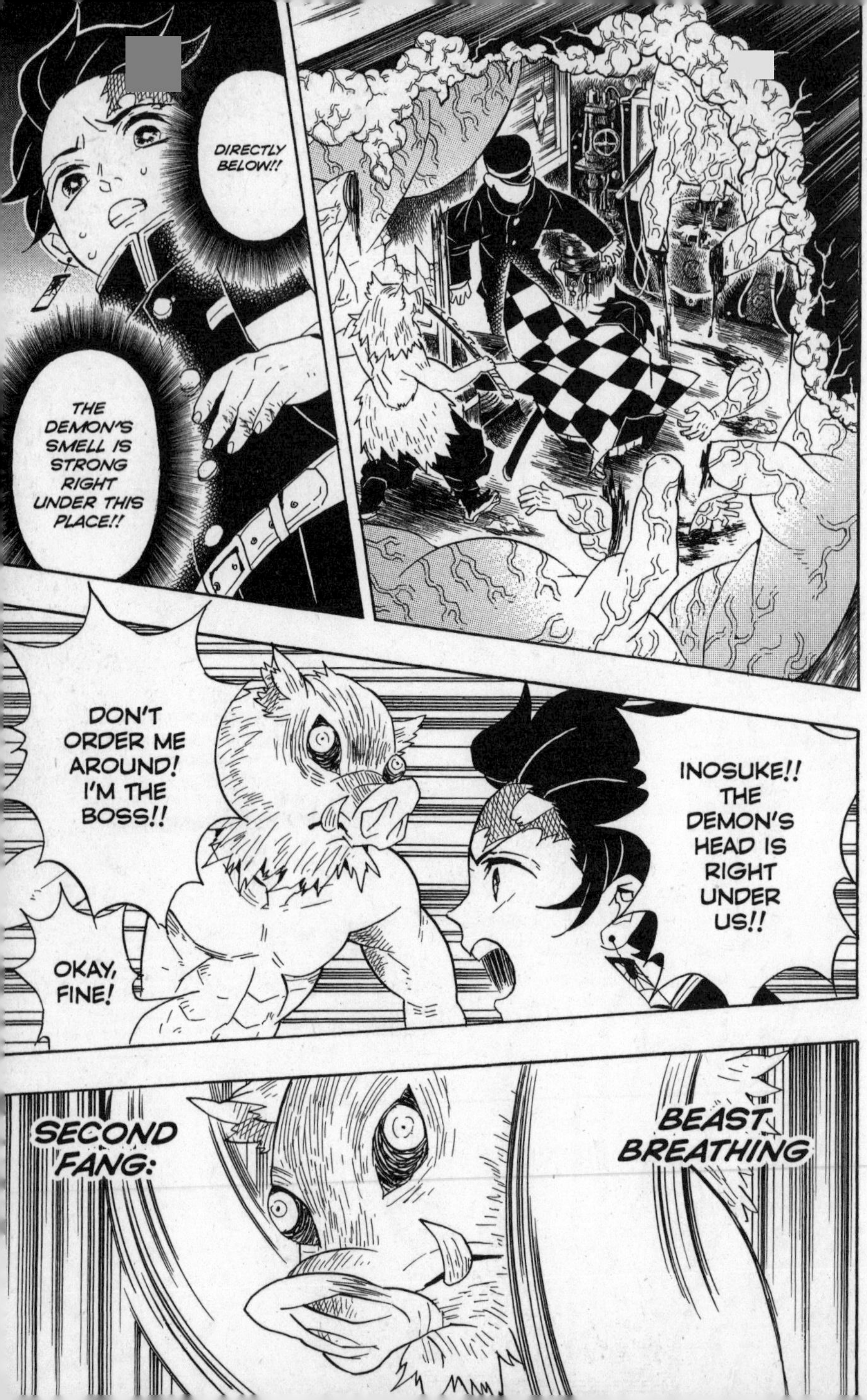
DIRECTLY BELOW!!
THE DEMON'S SMELL IS STRONG RIGHT UNDER THIS PLACE!!
INOSUKE!! THE DEMON'S HEAD IS RIGHT UNDER US!!
DON'T ORDER ME AROUND! I'M THE BOSS!!
OKAY, FINE!
BEAST BREATHING
SECOND FANG:

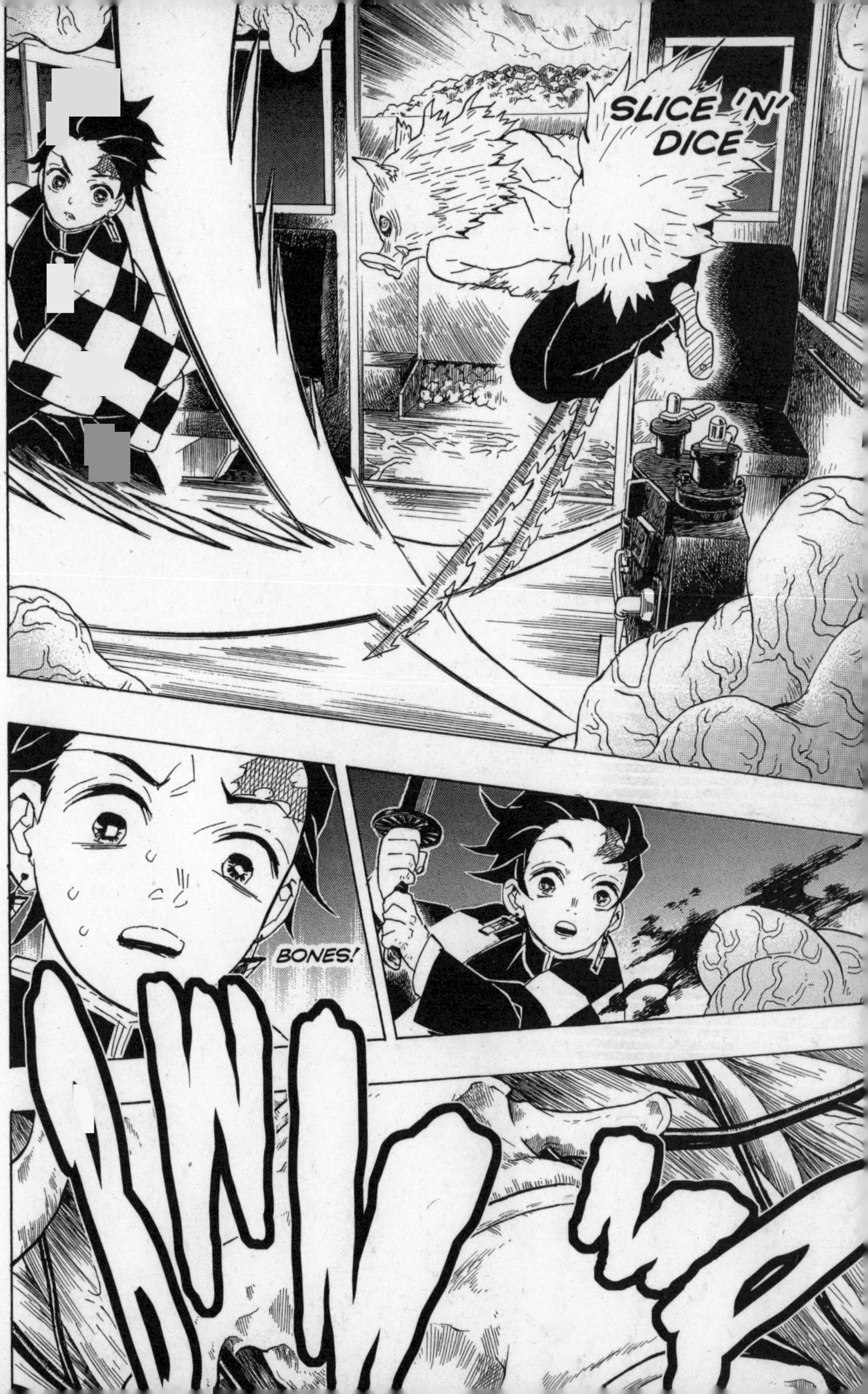
SLICE 'N' DICE
BONES!

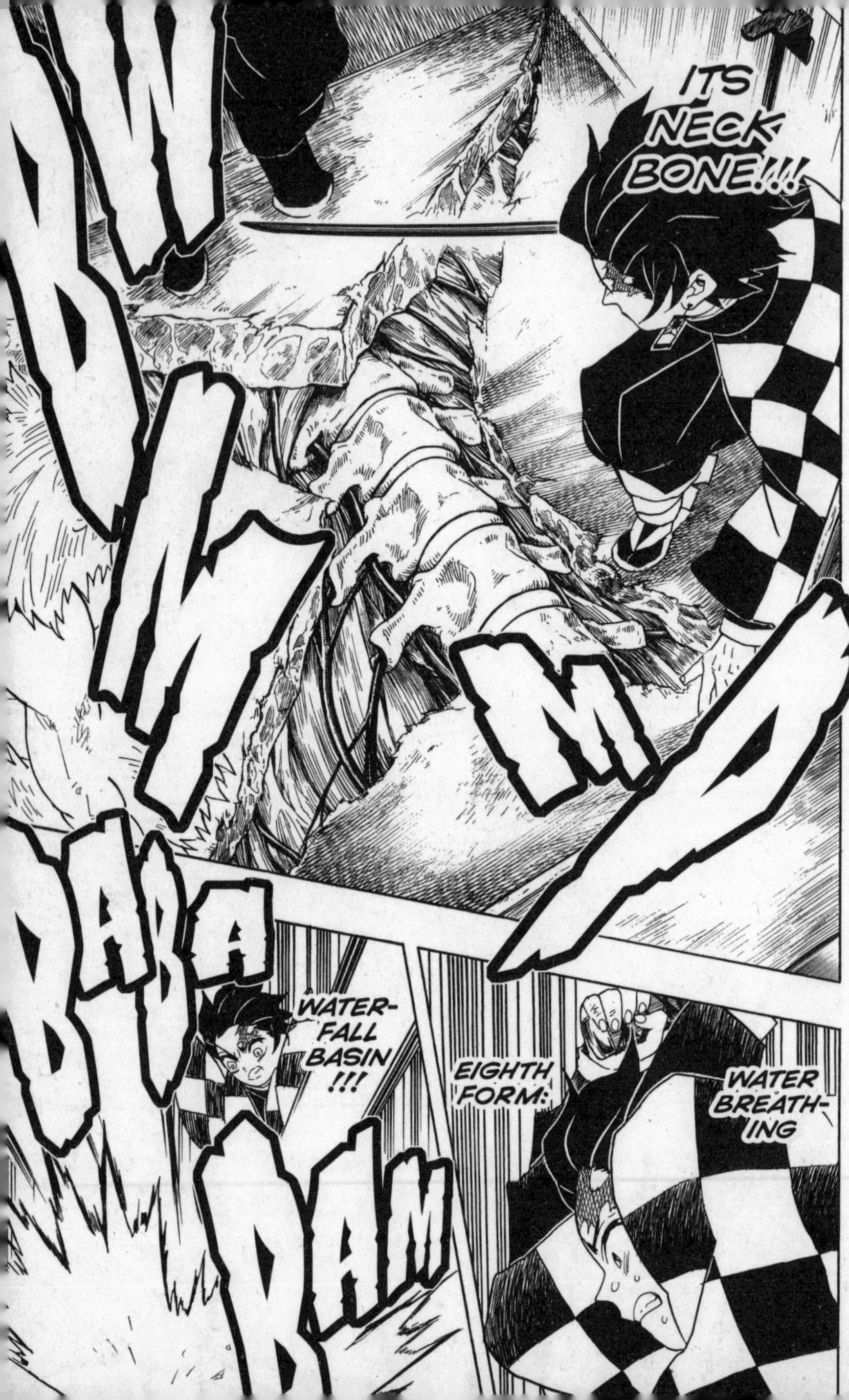
ITS NECK BONE!!!
WATER BREATH-ING
EIGHTH FORM:
WATER-FALL BASIN !!!

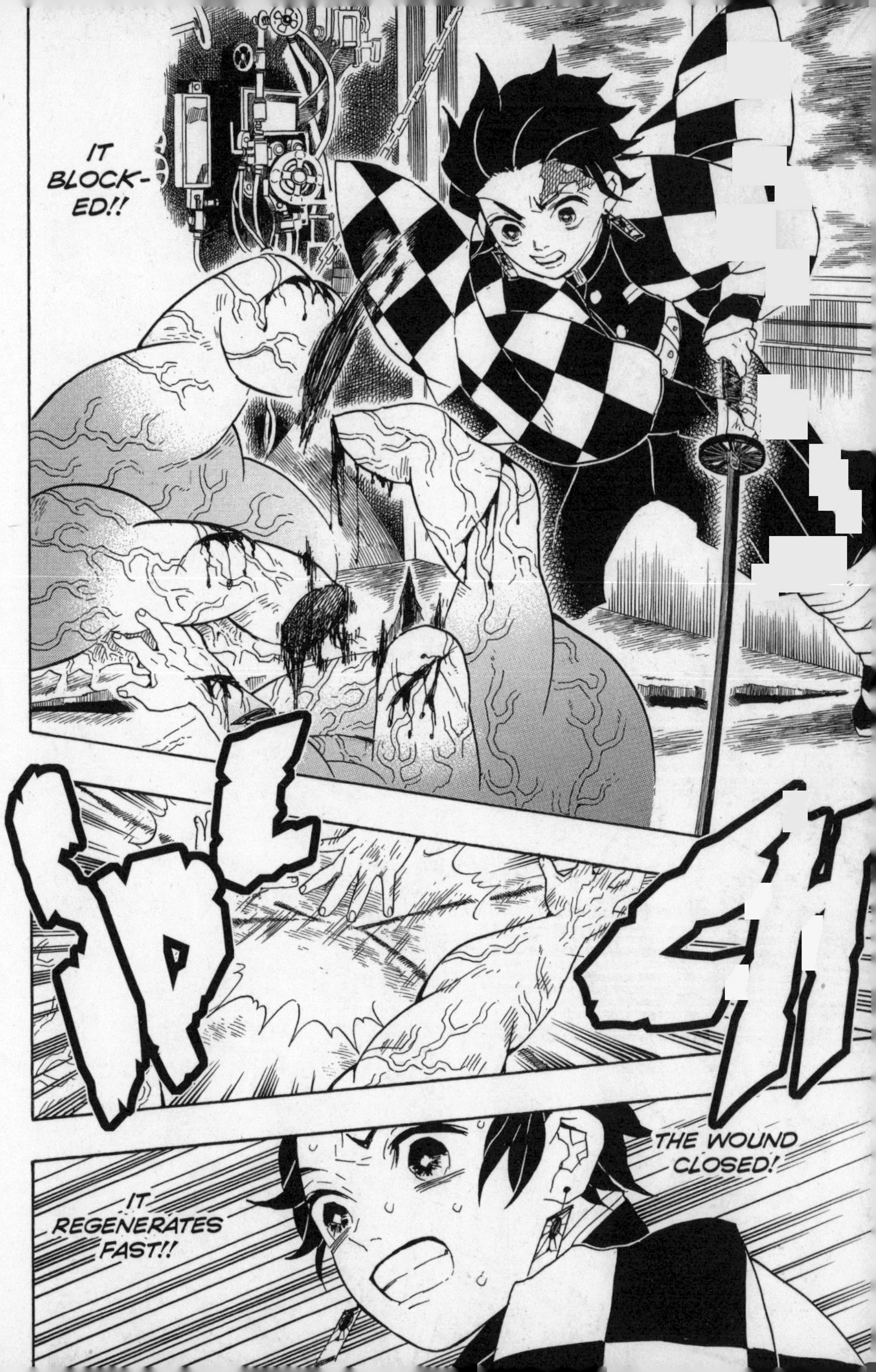
IT BLOCK-ED!!
THE WOUND CLOSED!
IT REGENERATES FAST!!

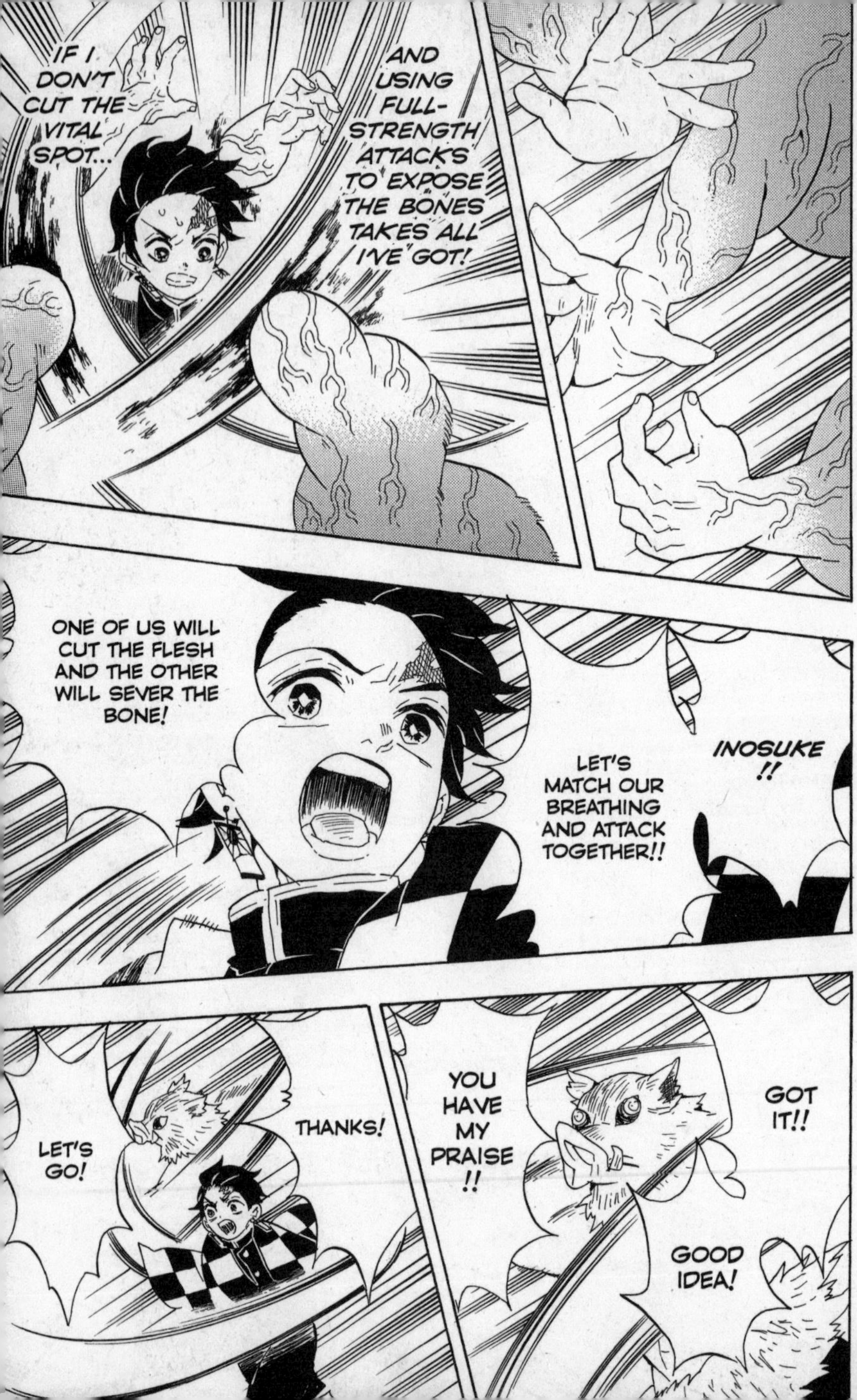
AND USING FULL-STRENGTH ATTACKS TO EXPOSE THE BONES TAKES ALL I'VE GOT!
IF I DON'T CUT THE VITAL SPOT...
INOSUKE!!
LET'S MATCH OUR BREATHING AND ATTACK TOGETHER!!
ONE OF US WILL CUT THE FLESH AND THE OTHER WILL SEVER THE BONE!
GOT IT!!
YOU HAVE MY PRAISE!!
GOOD IDEA!
THANKS!
LET'S GO!

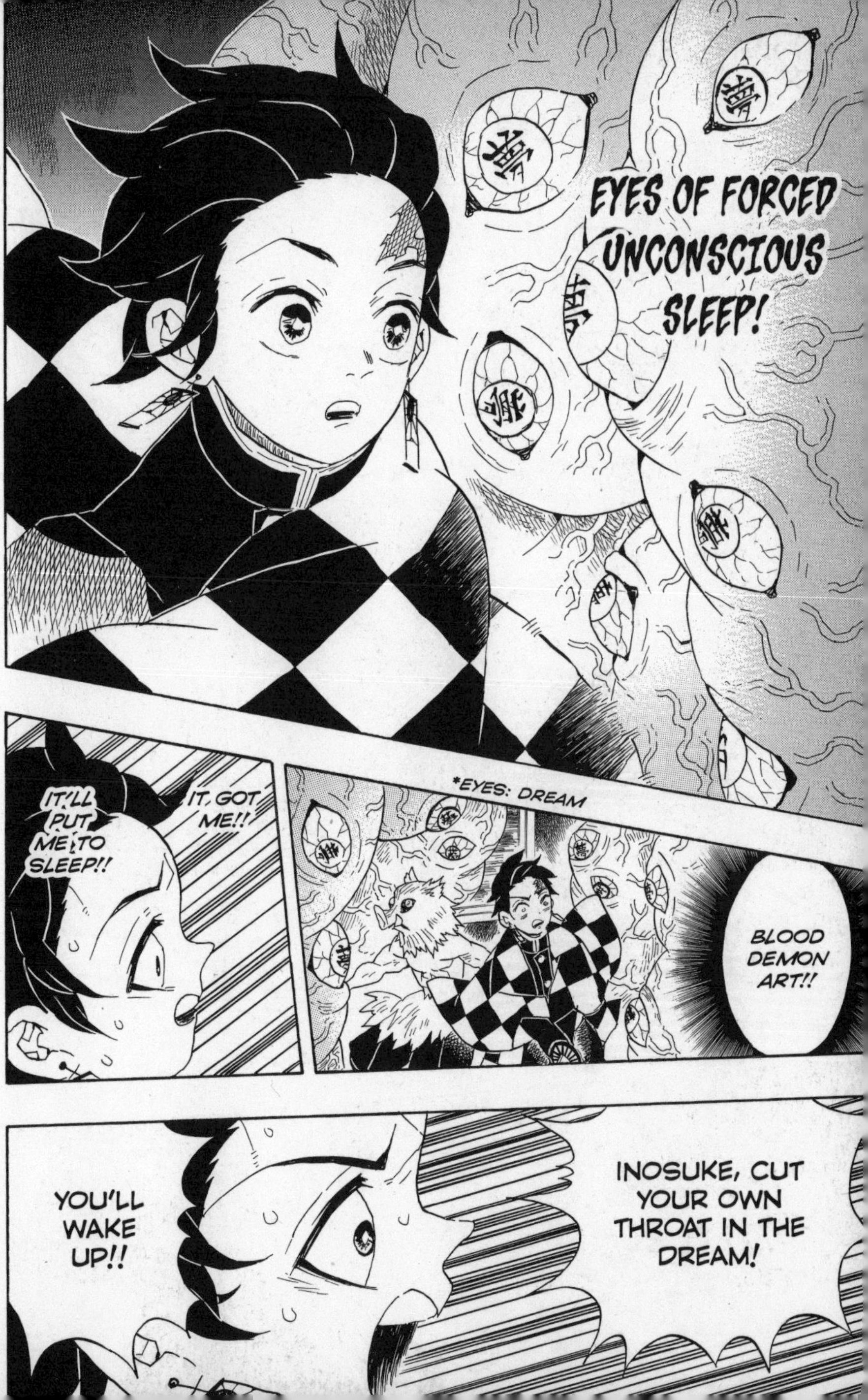
EYES OF FORCED UNCONSCIOUS SLEEP!
*EYES: DREAM
BLOOD DEMON ART!!
IT GOT ME!!
IT'LL PUT ME TO SLEEP!!
INOSUKE, CUT YOUR OWN THROAT IN THE DREAM!
YOU'LL WAKE UP!!

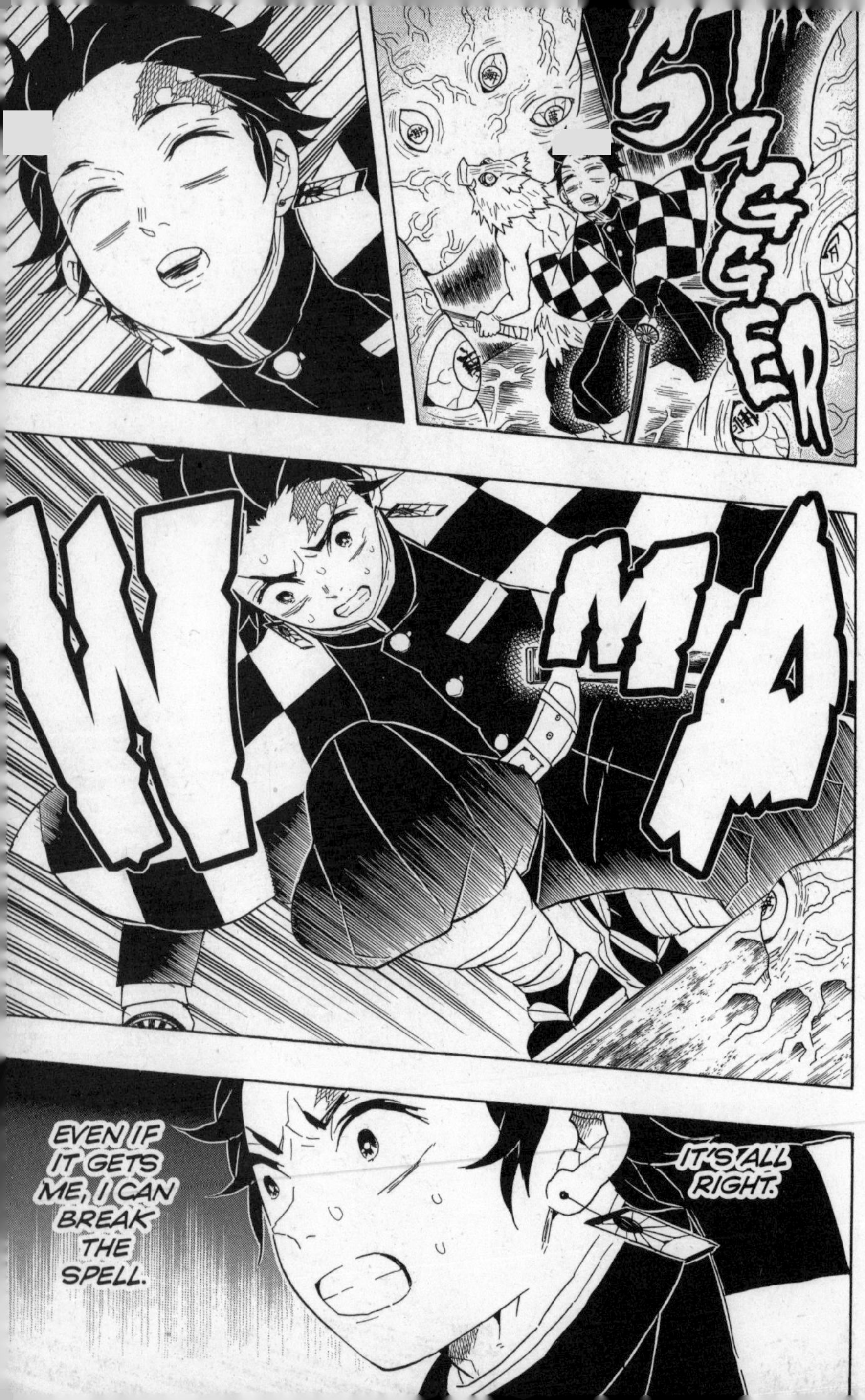
STAGGER
IT'S ALL RIGHT.
EVEN IF IT GETS ME, I CAN BREAK THE SPELL.

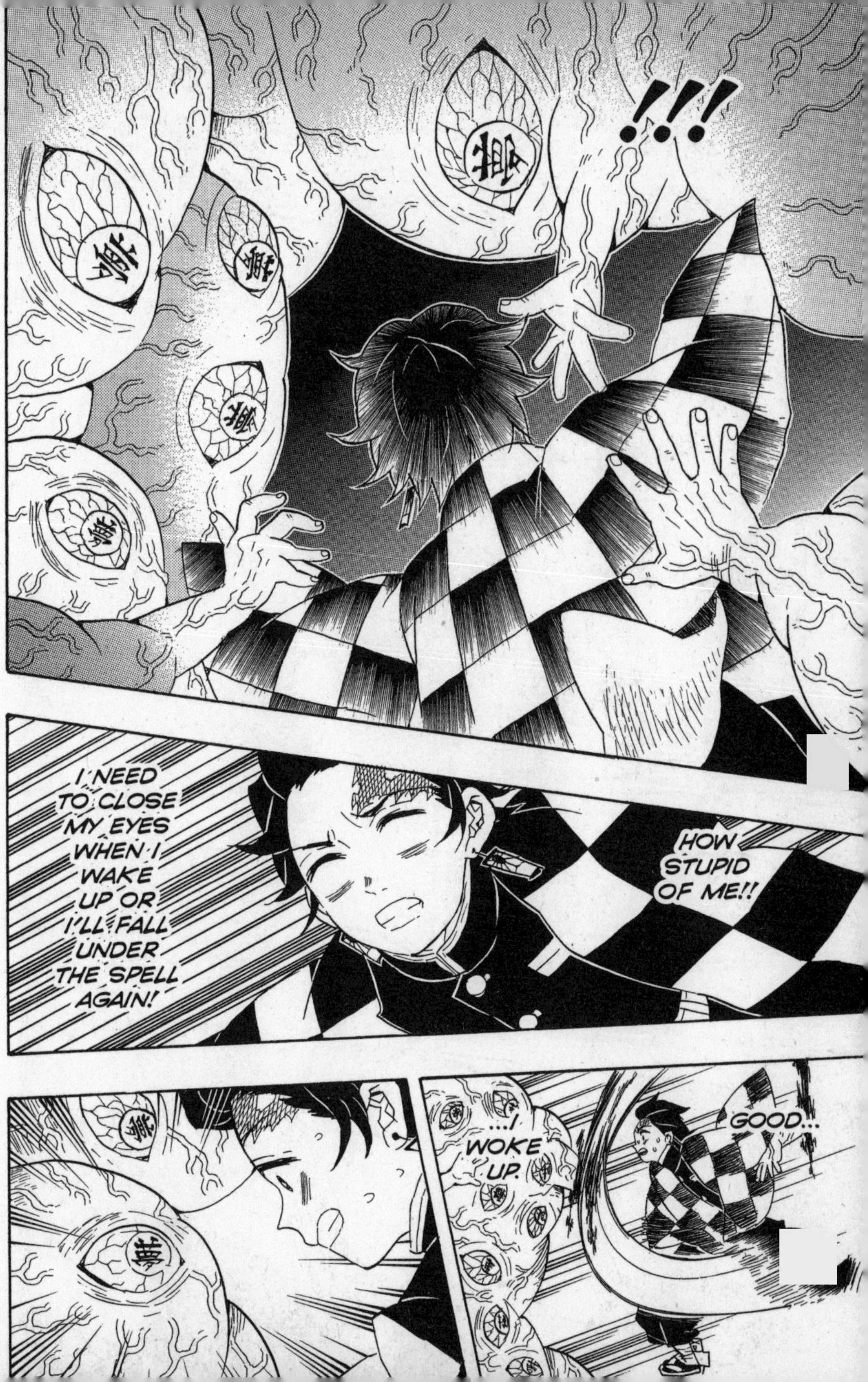
!!!
HOW STUPID OF ME!!
I NEED TO CLOSE MY EYES WHEN I WAKE UP OR I'LL FALL UNDER THE SPELL AGAIN!
GOOD...
...I WOKE UP.

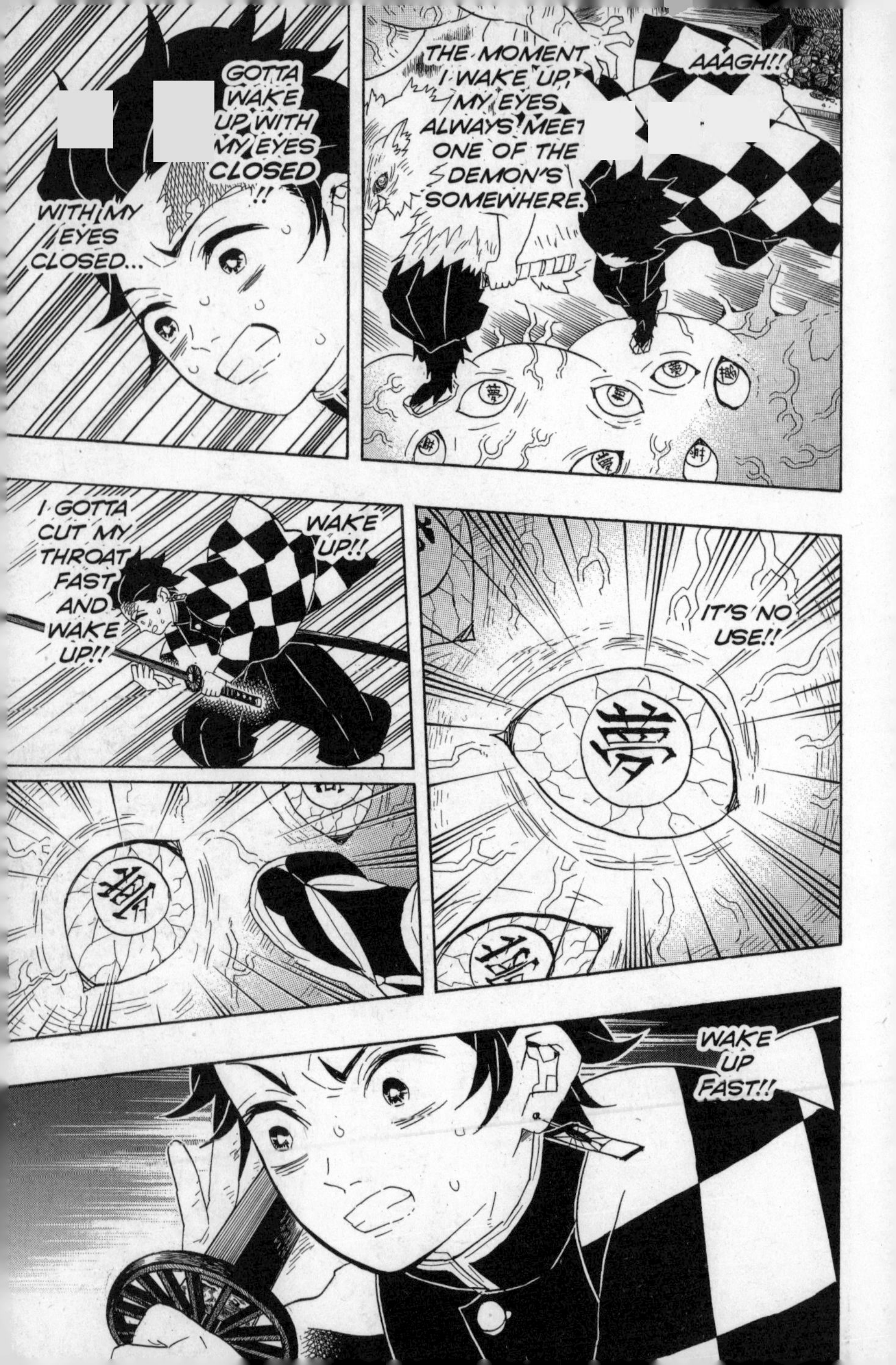
AAAGH!!
THE MOMENT I WAKE UP, MY EYES ALWAYS MEET ONE OF THE DEMON'S SOMEWHERE.
GOTTA WAKE UP WITH MY EYES CLOSED!!
WITH MY EYES CLOSED...
IT'S NO USE!!
WAKE UP!!
I GOTTA CUT MY THROAT FAST AND WAKE UP!!
WAKE UP FAST!!

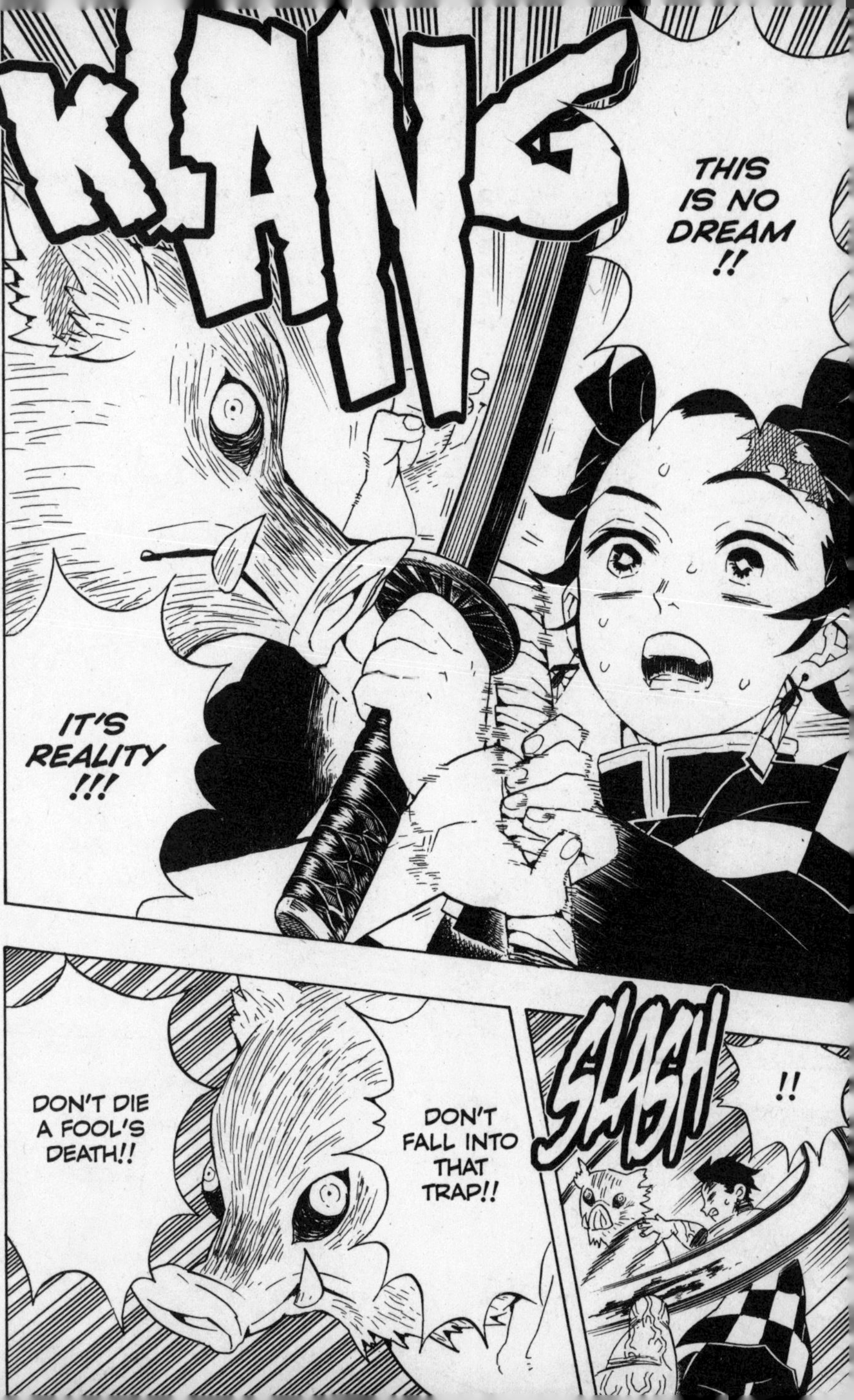
KANG
THIS IS NO DREAM!!
IT'S REALITY!!!
SLASH
!!
DON'T FALL INTO THAT TRAP!!
DON'T DIE A FOOL'S DEATH!!

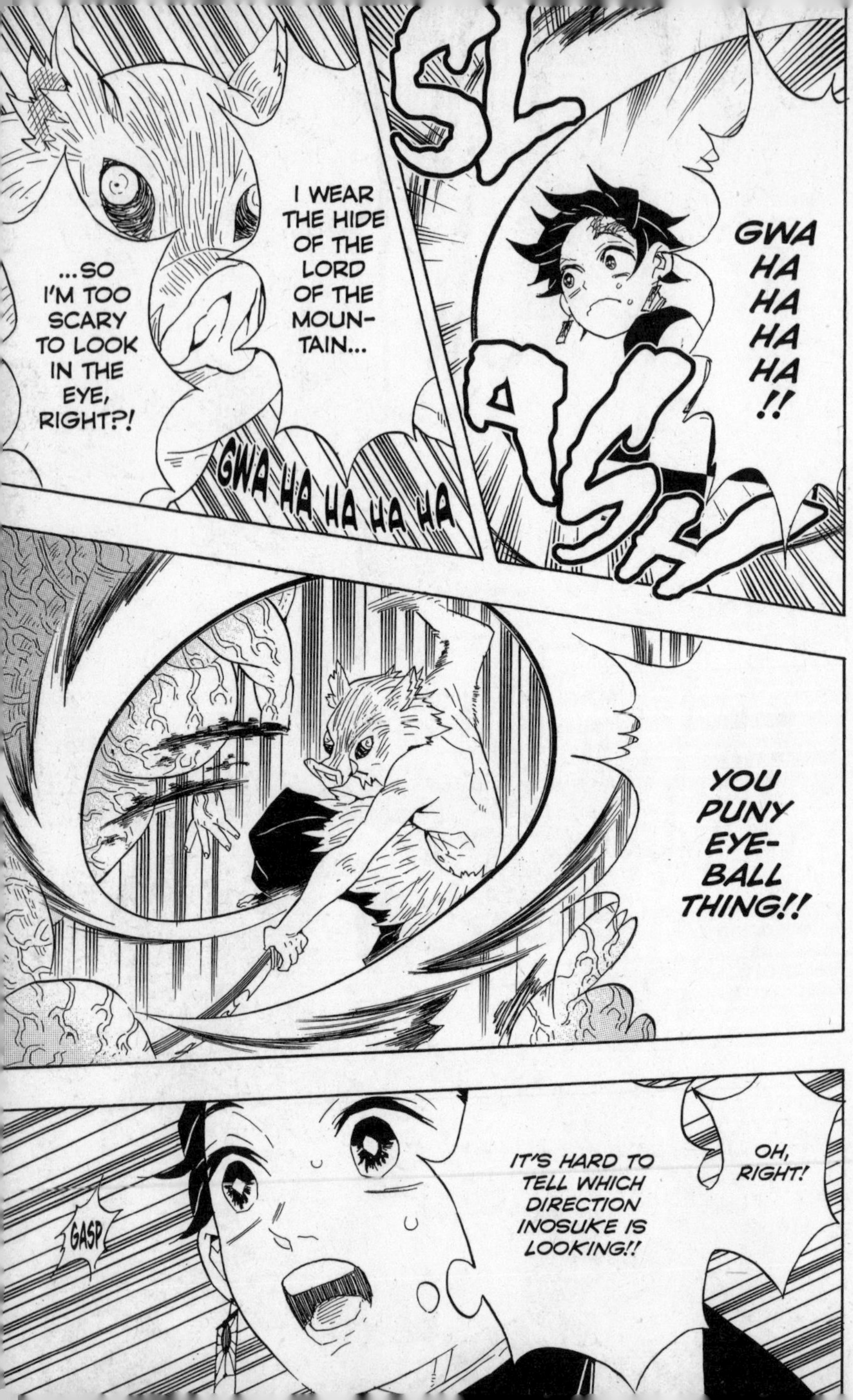
SLASH
GWA HA HA HA HA!!
I WEAR THE HIDE OF THE LORD OF THE MOUNTAIN...
...SO I'M TOO SCARY TO LOOK IN THE EYE, RIGHT?!
GWA HA HA HA HA HA
YOU PUNY EYEBALL THING!!
OH, RIGHT!
IT'S HARD TO TELL WHICH DIRECTION INOSUKE IS LOOKING!!
GASP

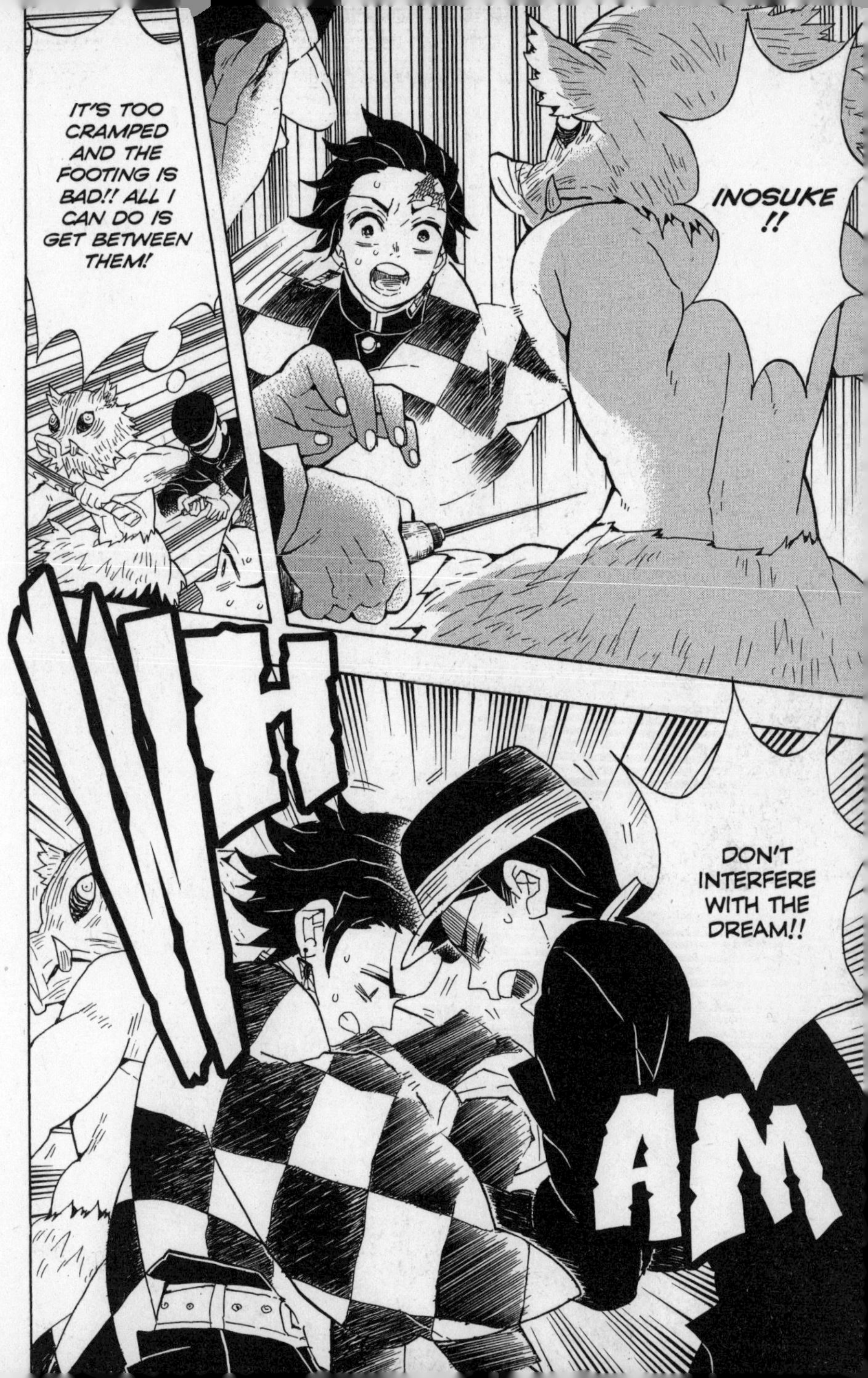
INOSUKE!!
IT'S TOO CRAMPED AND THE FOOTING IS BAD!! ALL I CAN DO IS GET BETWEEN THEM!
DON'T INTERFERE WITH THE DREAM!!
WHAM

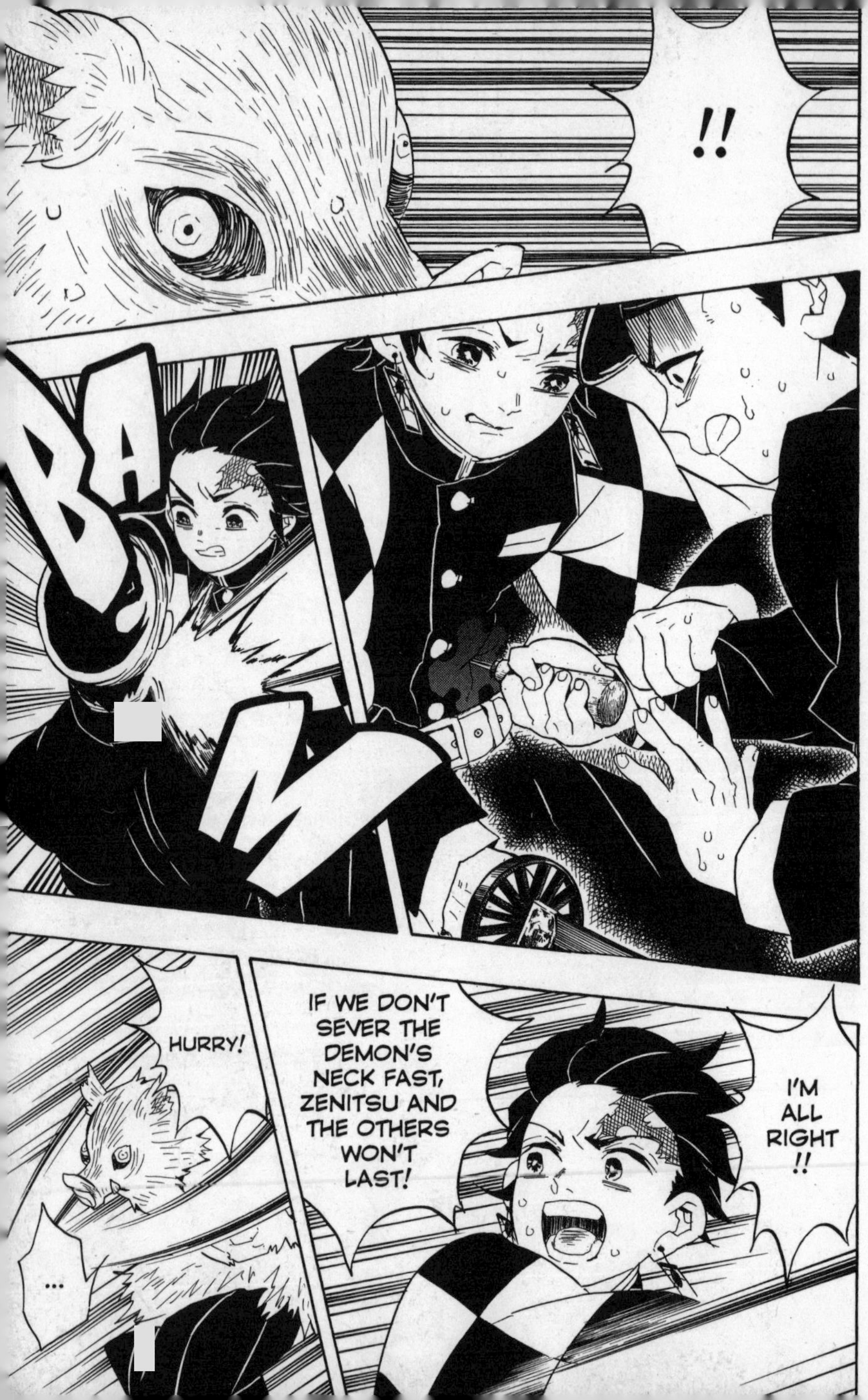
!!
BAM
I'M ALL RIGHT !!
IF WE DON'T SEVER THE DEMON'S NECK FAST, ZENITSU AND THE OTHERS WON'T LAST!
HURRY!
...

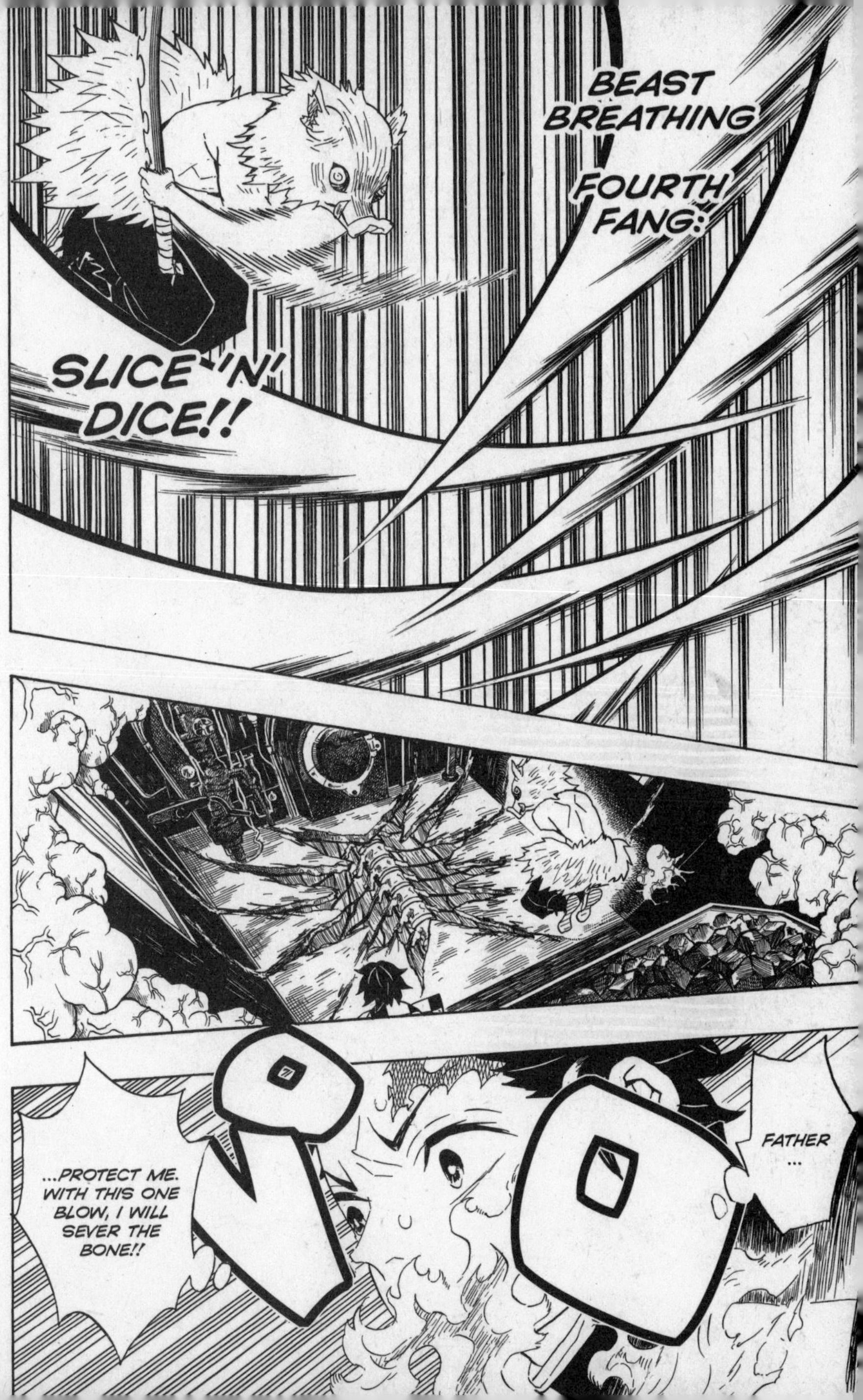
BEAST BREATHING
FOURTH FANG:
SLICE 'N' DICE!!
FATHER ...
...PROTECT ME. WITH THIS ONE BLOW, I WILL SEVER THE BONE!!

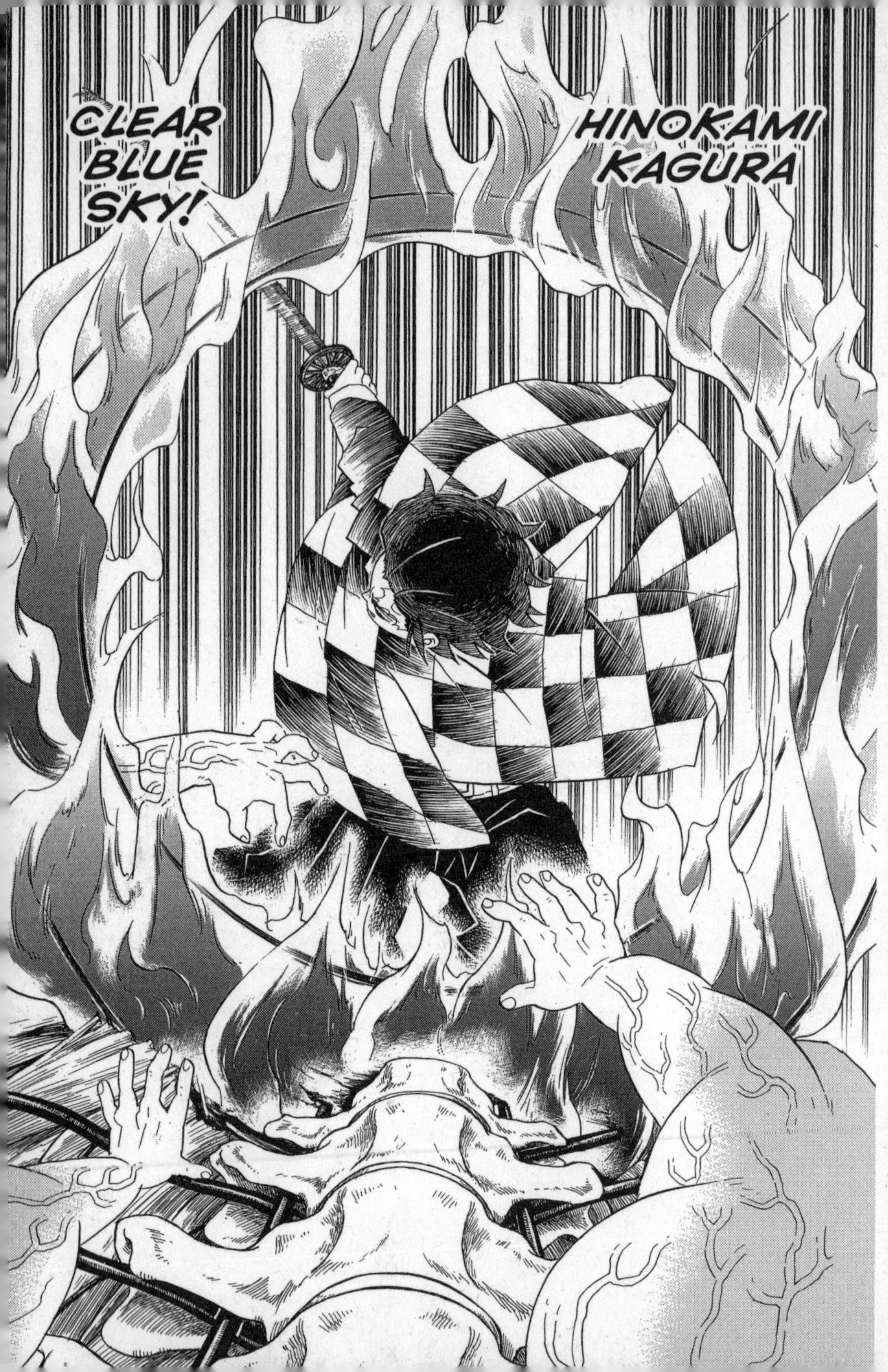
HINOKAMI KAGURA
CLEAR BLUE SKY!

Taisho Whispers

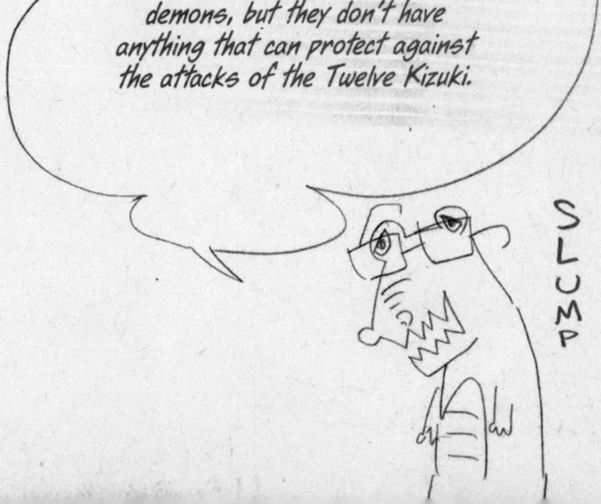
The corps uniforms can basically protect against heat, cold and the fangs and claws of midlevel demons, but they don't have anything that can protect against the attacks of the Twelve Kizuki.
SLUMP

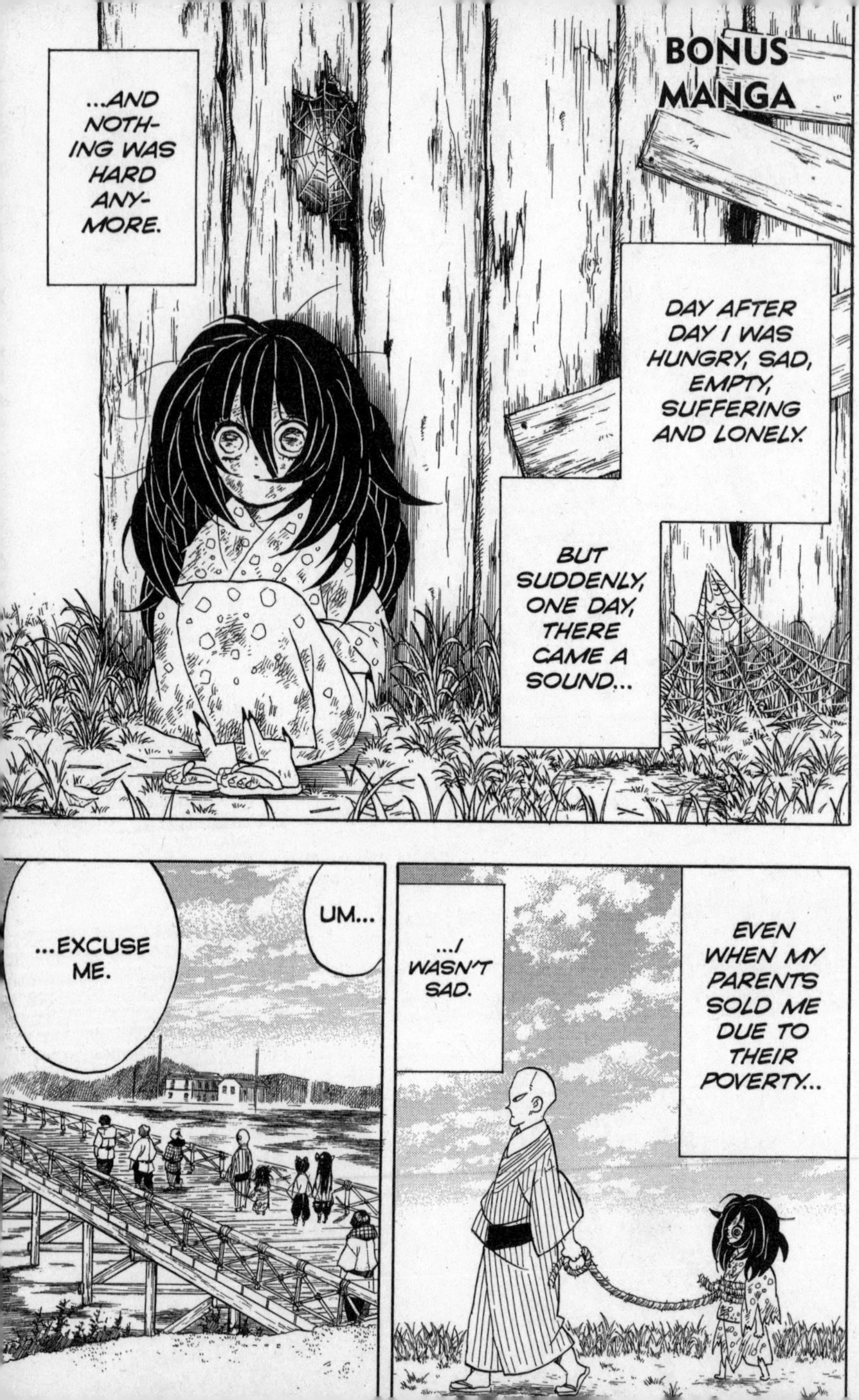
BONUS MANGA
DAY AFTER DAY I WAS HUNGRY, SAD, EMPTY, SUFFERING AND LONELY.
...AND NOTHING WAS HARD ANYMORE.
BUT SUDDENLY, ONE DAY, THERE CAME A SOUND...
EVEN WHEN MY PARENTS SOLD ME DUE TO THEIR POVERTY...
...I WASN'T SAD.
UM...
...EXCUSE ME.

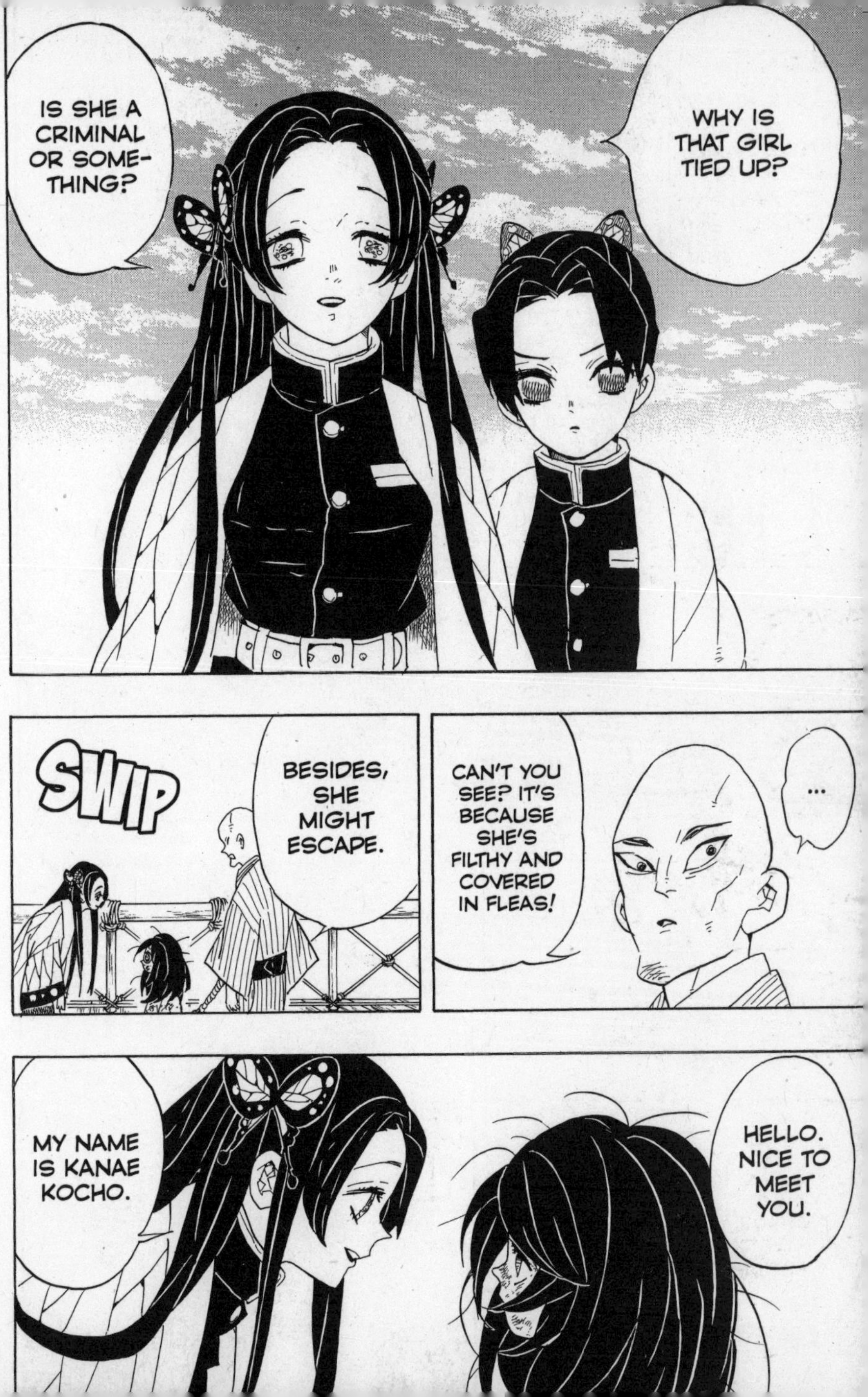
WHY IS THAT GIRL TIED UP?
IS SHE A CRIMINAL OR SOME-THING?
...
CAN'T YOU SEE? IT'S BECAUSE SHE'S FILTHY AND COVERED IN FLEAS!
BESIDES, SHE MIGHT ESCAPE.
SWIP
HELLO. NICE TO MEET YOU.
MY NAME IS KANAE KOCHO.

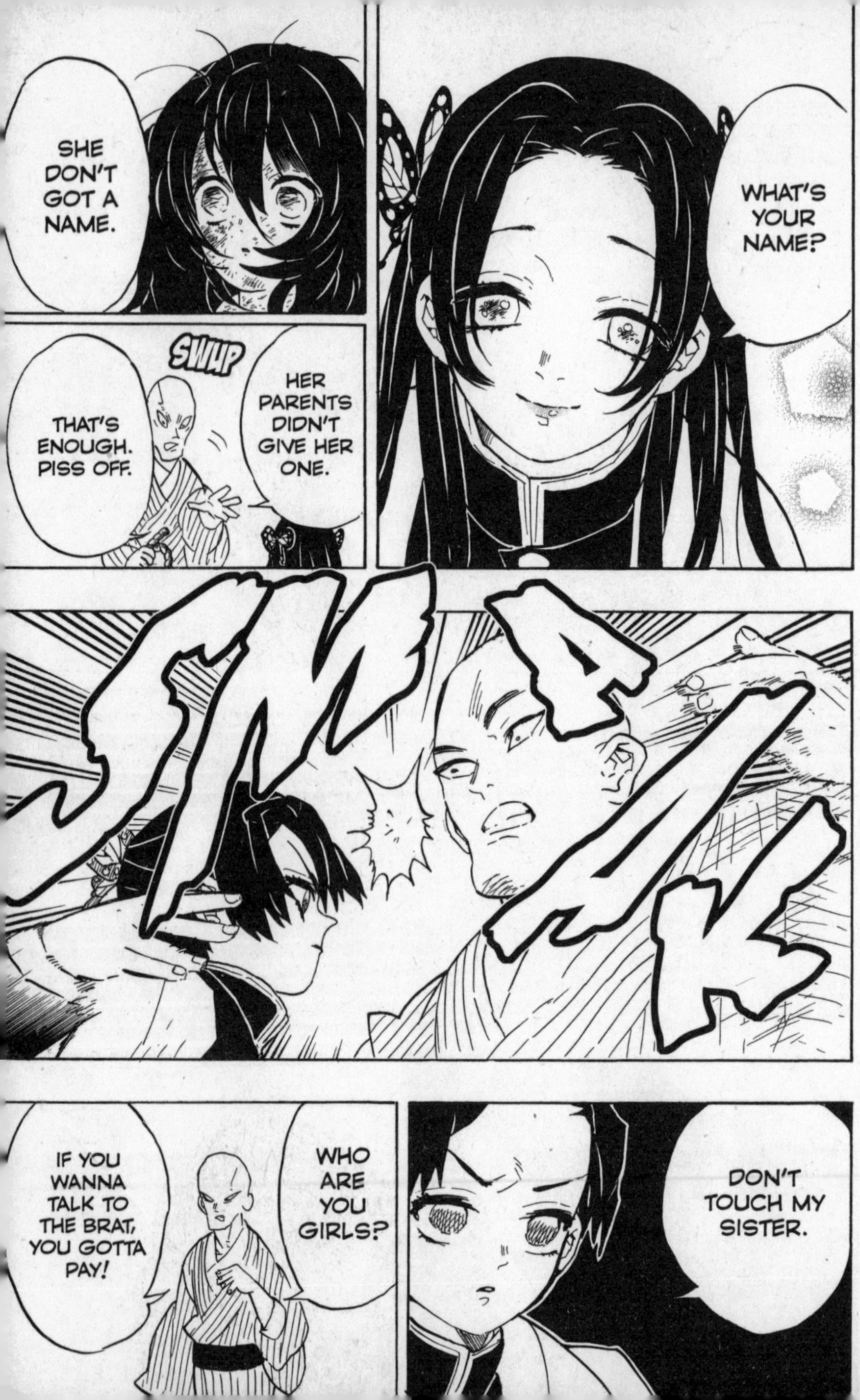
WHAT'S YOUR NAME?
SHE DON'T GOT A NAME.
SWUP
HER PARENTS DIDN'T GIVE HER ONE.
THAT'S ENOUGH. PISS OFF.
SMACK
DON'T TOUCH MY SISTER.
WHO ARE YOU GIRLS?
IF YOU WANNA TALK TO THE BRAT, YOU GOTTA PAY!

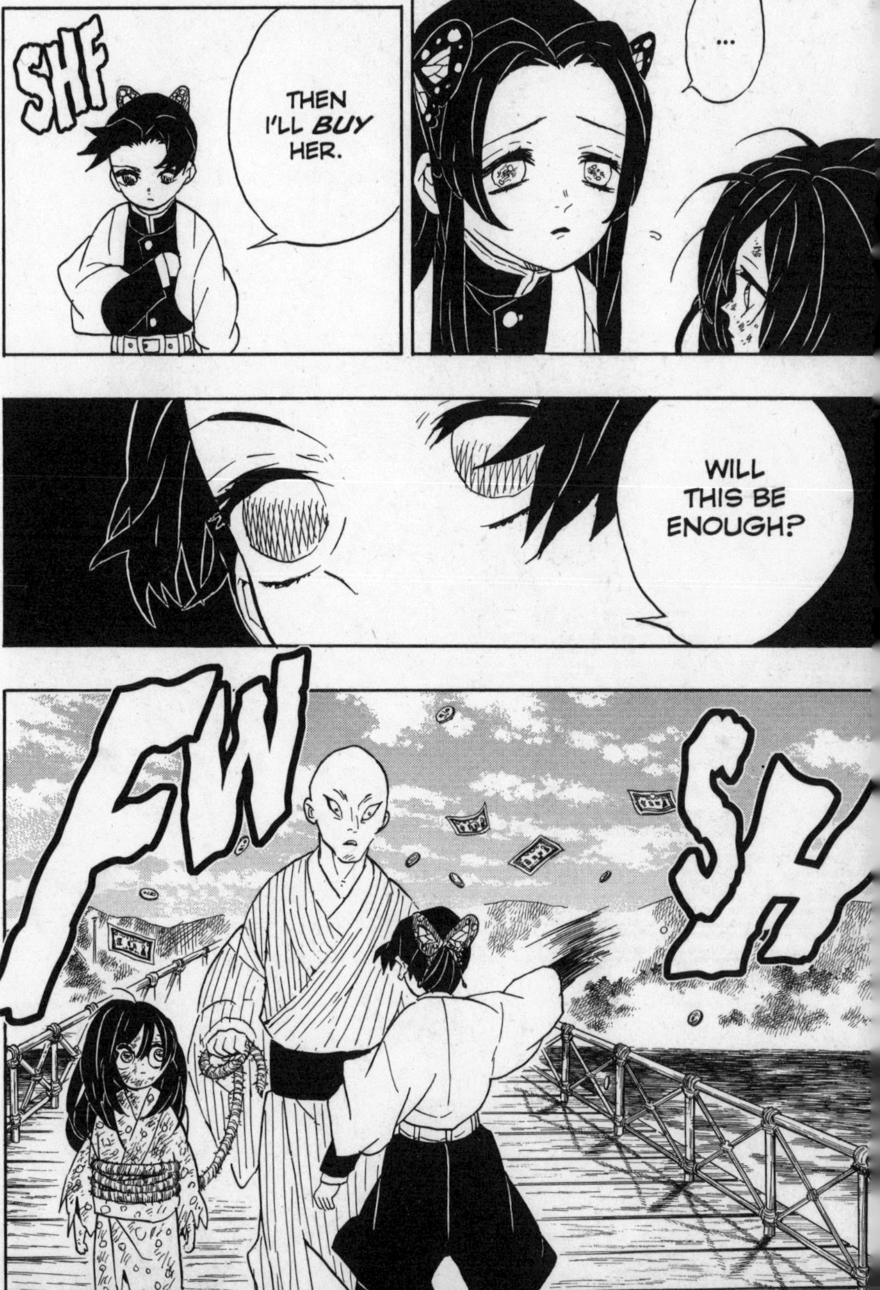
...
SHF
THEN I'LL *BUY* HER.
WILL THIS BE ENOUGH?
SH
FW

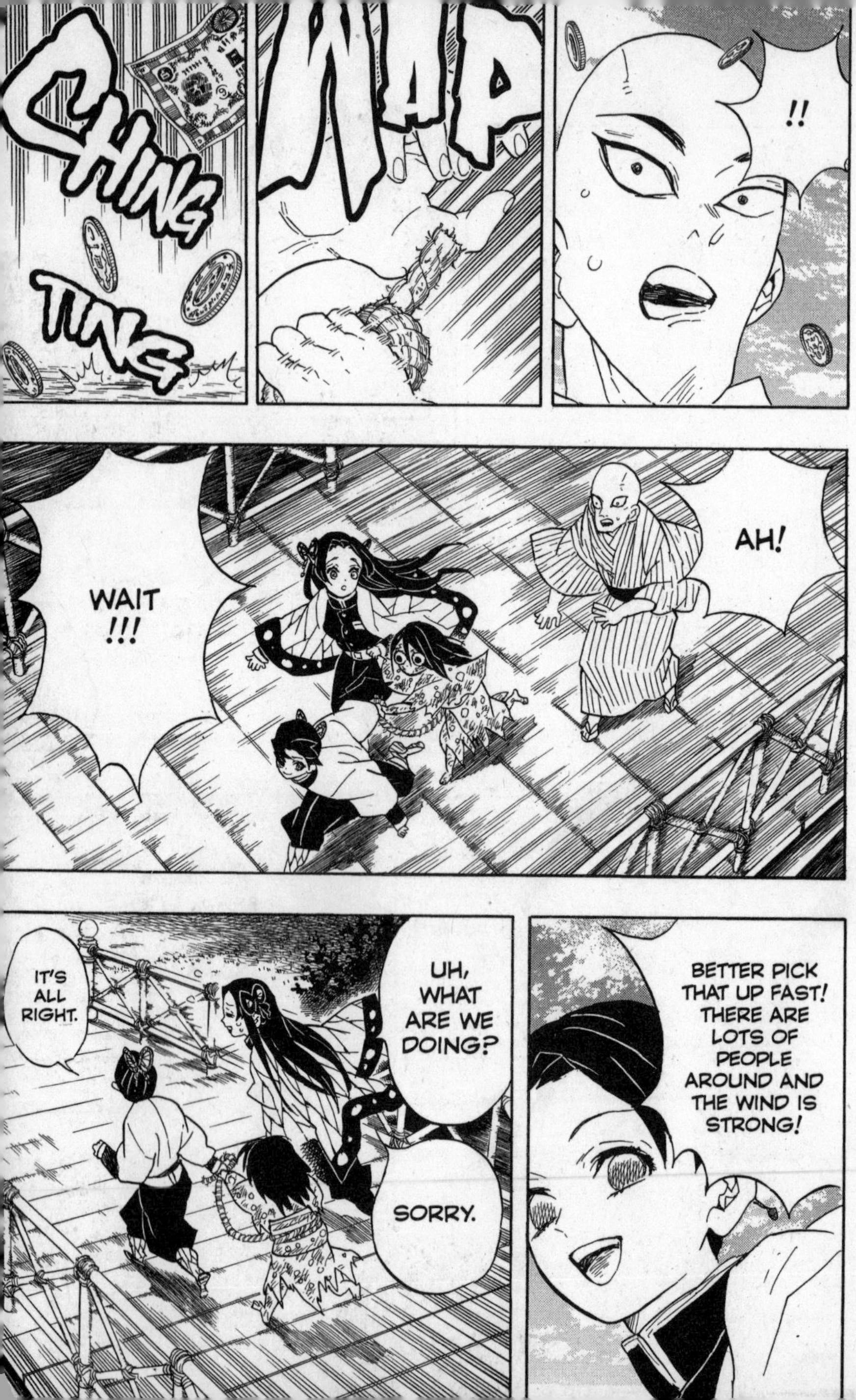
!!
WAP
CHING
TING
AH!
WAIT !!!
BETTER PICK THAT UP FAST! THERE ARE LOTS OF PEOPLE AROUND AND THE WIND IS STRONG!
UH, WHAT ARE WE DOING?
SORRY.
IT'S ALL RIGHT.

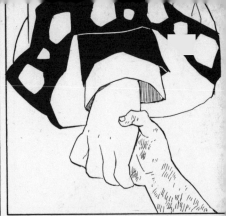

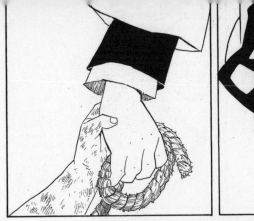

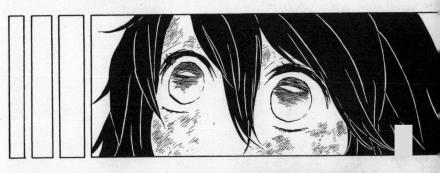

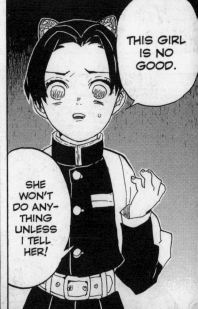

THIS GIRL IS NO GOOD.
SHE WON'T DO ANYTHING UNLESS I TELL HER!
EVEN MEALS. UNLESS I TELL HER TO, SHE'LL NEVER EAT.
HER STOMACH KEEPS GROWLING.
THERE, THERE... DON'T SAY THAT.
I LIKE TO SEE YOUR SMILING FACE, SHINOBU!
BUT...

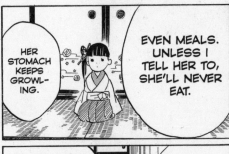

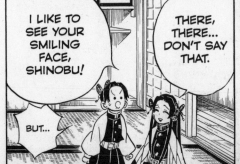

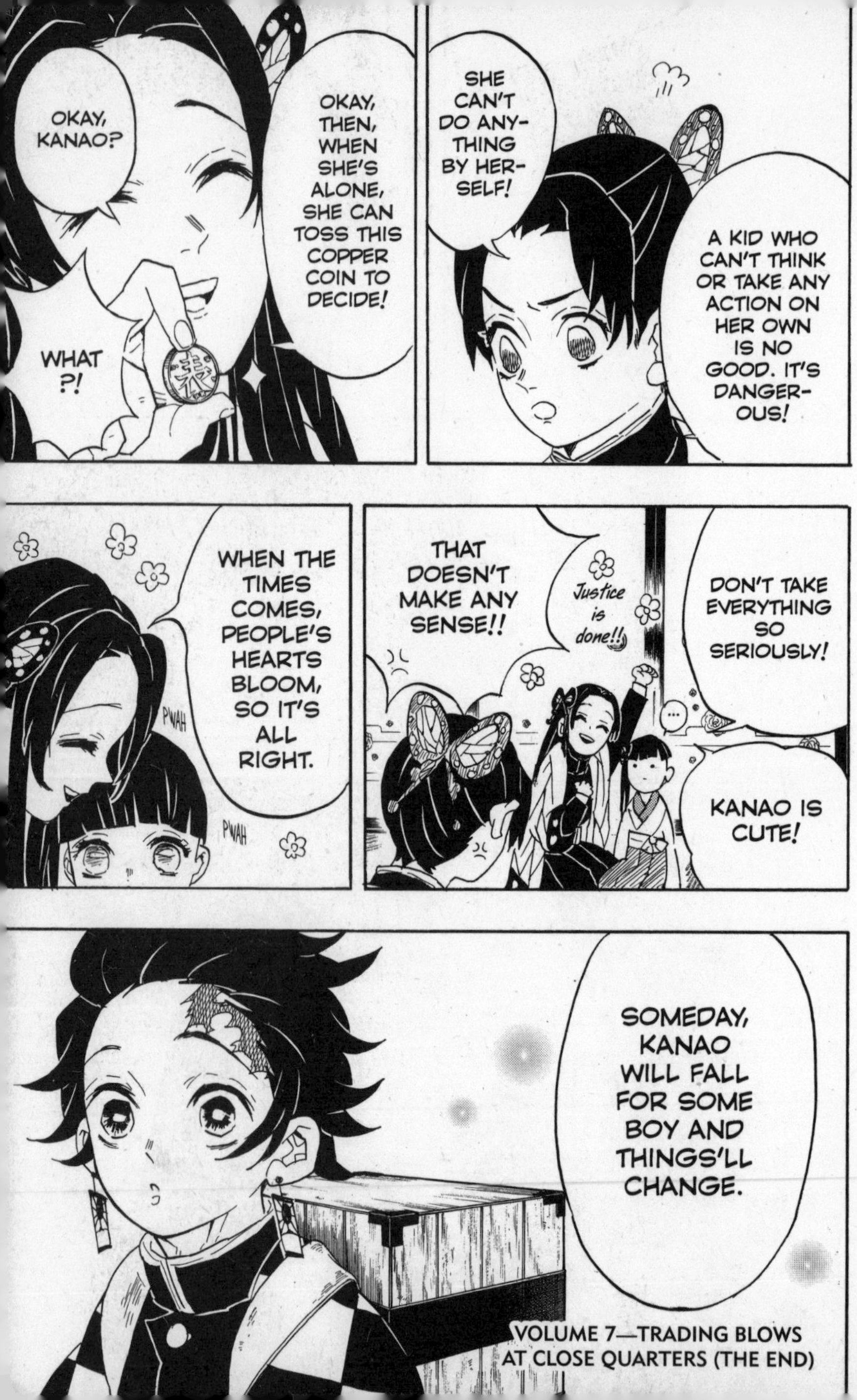
A KID WHO CAN'T THINK OR TAKE ANY ACTION ON HER OWN IS NO GOOD. IT'S DANGER-OUS!
SHE CAN'T DO ANY-THING BY HER-SELF!
OKAY, THEN, WHEN SHE'S ALONE, SHE CAN TOSS THIS COPPER COIN TO DECIDE!
OKAY, KANAO?
WHAT ?!
DON'T TAKE EVERYTHING SO SERIOUSLY!
KANAO IS CUTE!
Justice is done!!
THAT DOESN'T MAKE ANY SENSE!!
...
WHEN THE TIMES COMES, PEOPLE'S HEARTS BLOOM, SO IT'S ALL RIGHT.
PWAH
PWAH
SOMEDAY, KANAO WILL FALL FOR SOME BOY AND THINGS'LL CHANGE.
VOLUME 7—TRADING BLOWS AT CLOSE QUARTERS (THE END)

From *Weekly Shonen Jump*, combined issue No. 21-22, 2017

From *Shonen Jump* GIGA, Vol. 2, 2017

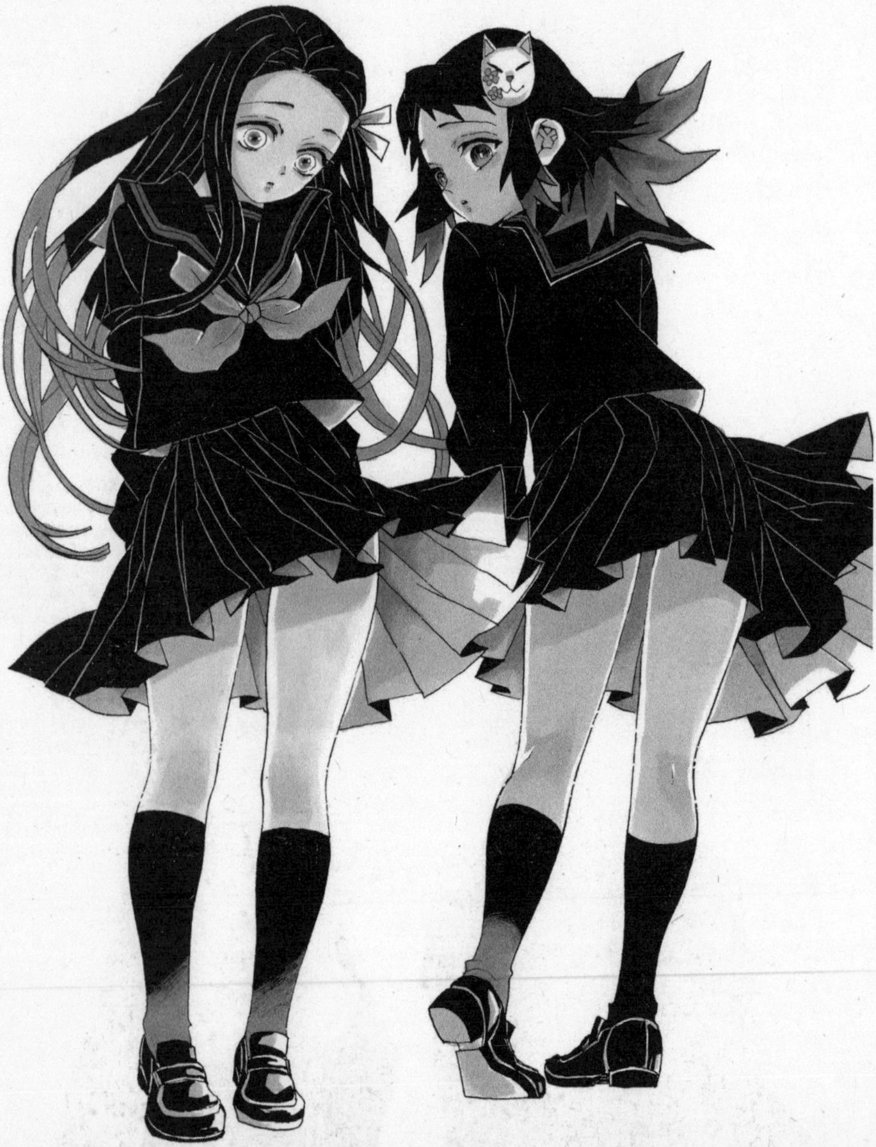

Junior High and High School ☆ Kimetsu Academy Story

Kyojuro Rengoku • history teacher

He's enthusiastic about education and has a strong love of history, so he sometimes throws students around during class and stages mock cavalry battles and so forth. He's popular among the students and no one at this school has poor grades in history.

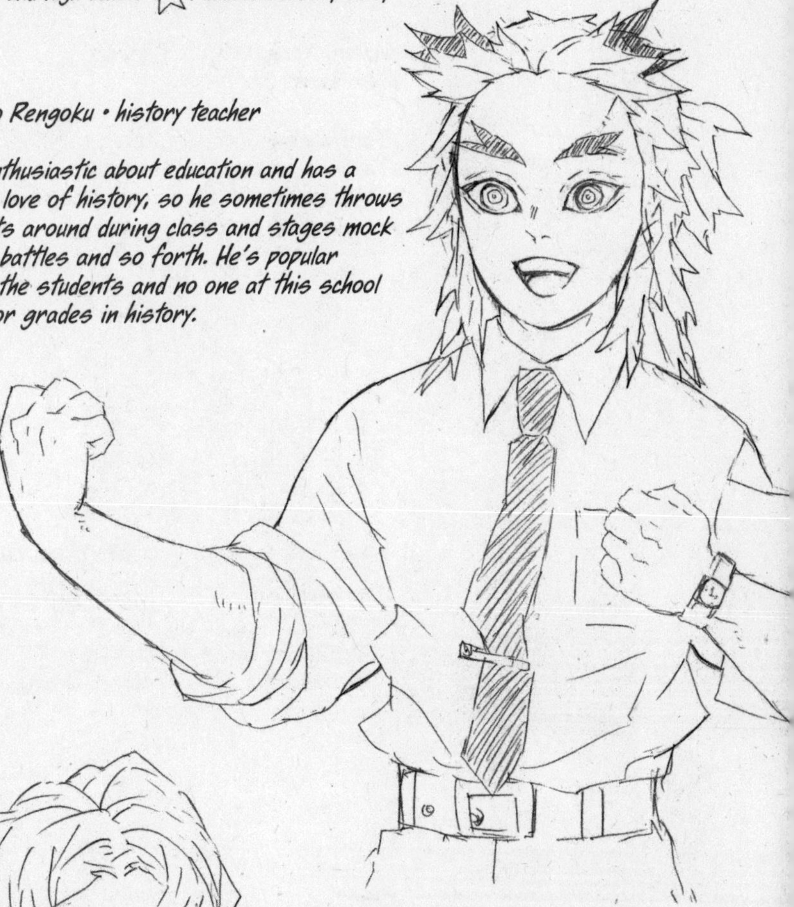

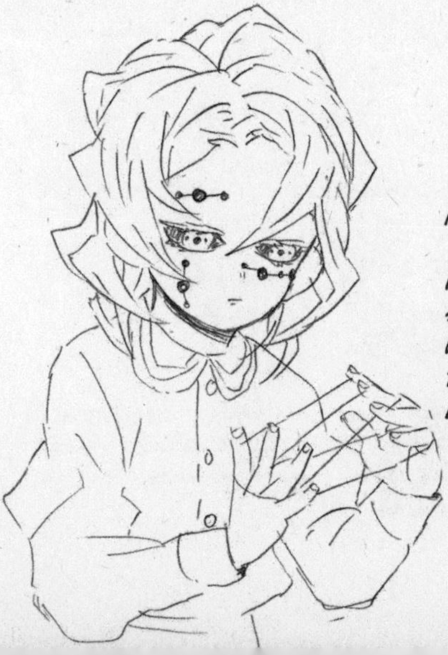

Rui Ayaki

He won the cat's cradle tournament and suddenly became the man of the hour. There was even a special feature in the Kimetsu town newspaper, and his cute, distinctive moles became a hot topic online.

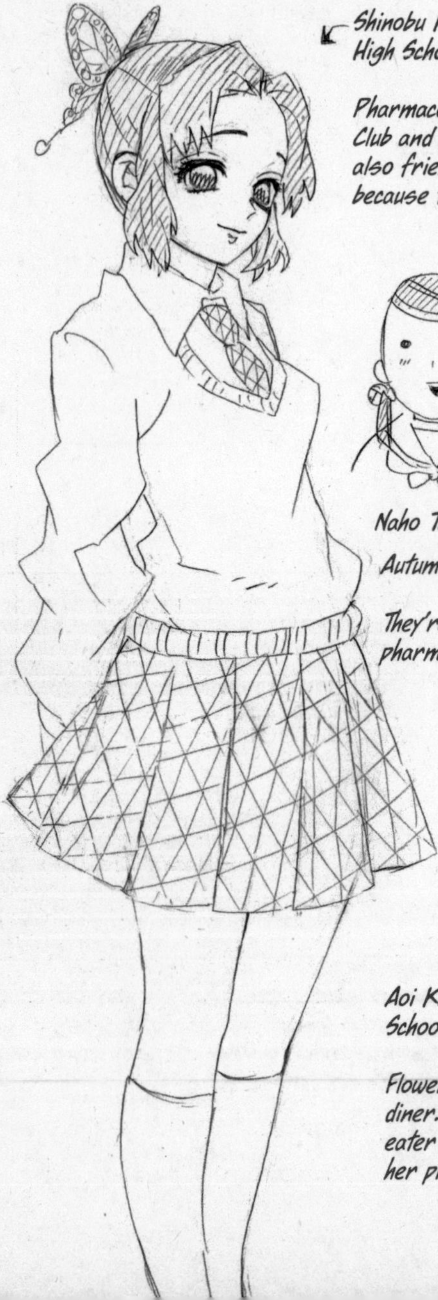

Shinobu Kocho • Class Mugwort, High School, 3rd Year

Pharmacology Club. Also belongs to the Fencing Club and has even won the championship. She's also friendly with the Flower Arrangement Club because their clubroom is close.

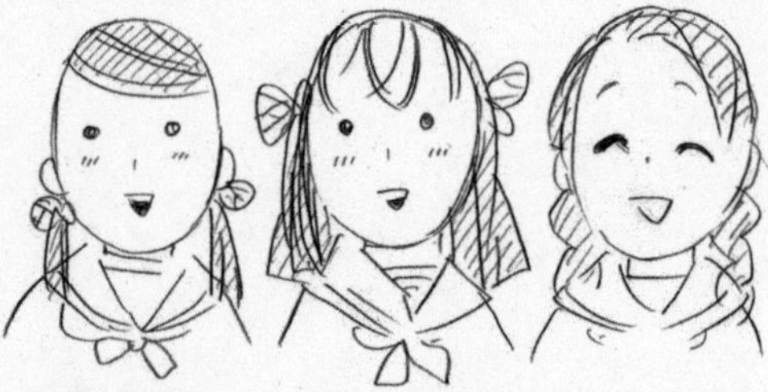

Naho Takada Kiyo Terauchi Sumi Nakahara

Autumn Leaves Class, Junior High, 1st Year

They're working hard to start a pharmacology club in junior high too.

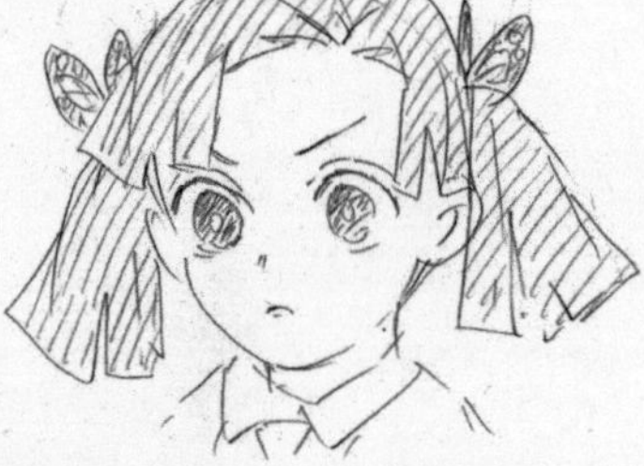

Aoi Kanzaki • Persimmon Class, High School, 2nd Year

Flower Arrangement Club. Her family runs a diner. She helps out a lot. A girl who's a big eater has been coming recently and causing her problems.

When studious Nariyuki tutors supergeniuses who are total dunces in their favorite subjects, he'll get a crash course in love!

[x] We + Never + × Learn

STORY + ART
Taishi Tsutsui

Nariyuki Yuiga comes from an impoverished family, so he's eager to secure a full scholarship to college before he graduates high school. His principal agrees, with one stipulation— he must tutor the most talented girls at school and make sure they get into their target colleges!

RATED T+ OLDER TEEN

VIZ

YOU'RE
WRO

DEMON SLAYER: KIMETSU NO YAIBA
reads from right to left, starting in the
upper-right corner. Japanese is read from
right to left, meaning that action, sound
effects and word-balloon order are completely reversed from English order.

DEMON SLAYER

KIMETSU NO YAIBA

In Taisho-era Japan, kindhearted Tanjiro Kamado makes a living selling charcoal. But his peaceful life is shattered when a demon slaughters his entire family. His little sister Nezuko is the only survivor, but she has been transformed into a demon herself! Tanjiro sets out on a dangerous journey to find a way to return his sister to normal and destroy the demon who ruined his life.

While under the care of the Demon Slayer Corps leaders, Shinobu, Tanjiro, Zenitsu, Inosuke and Nezuko have recovered. They have even learned a new and powerful technique—Total Concentration! They'll need this new power and all their skill on their next demon-hunting mission aboard the mysterious Infinity Train as it takes them into the dreams of demons!

Slayer 9.99 USA $12.99 CAN   £6.99 UK

viz.com   shonenjump.com

ISBN: 978-1-9747-0441-5

50999